AF352638

# TRANSFINITE LIFE

NEW JEWISH PHILOSOPHY AND THOUGHT

*Zachary J. Braiterman*

# TRANSFINITE LIFE

*Oskar Goldberg and*

*the Vitalist Imagination*

Bruce Rosenstock

Indiana University Press

This book is a publication of

Indiana University Press
Office of Scholarly Publishing
Herman B Wells Library 350
1320 East 10th Street
Bloomington, Indiana 47405 USA

iupress.indiana.edu

© 2017 by Bruce Rosenstock



The paper used in this publication meets the minimum
requirements of the American National Standard for Information
Sciences—Permanence of Paper for Printed Library Materials,
ANSI Z39.48-1992.

Manufactured in the United States of America

Cataloging information is available from the Library of Congress.

ISBN 978-0-253-02970-6 (cloth)
ISBN 978-0-253-03016-0 (ebook)

1 2 3 4 5   22 21 20 19 18 17

*For Harriet*

# Contents

# Acknowledgments

My first debt of thanks goes to Professor Manfred Voigts. Not only has his work on Oskar Goldberg, including his scholarly editions of Goldberg's books, essays, and related materials, been an indispensable resource without which this volume would hardly have been possible, but Professor Voigts has also been a generous interlocutor throughout the past several years. He has never stinted in his encouragement of my project, and he has shared valuable insights with me. There is barely a page that in some way does not reflect his influence.

I want to thank the Deutsches Literaturarchiv in Marbach for making available to me the Oskar Goldberg Nachlass. The generosity and patience of the librarians in the Manuscript Reading Room help to make this incredible archive one of the world's premier research institutions.

Above all, I want to thank my wife, Harriet Murav. She has accompanied the writing of this book with far more than patience. She has shared every stage of its development and has helped me rethink and reframe my work in important ways. Her yearlong stint at the Stanford Humanities Center in 2012–2013 made it possible for me to spend a very refreshing spring sabbatical semester working in Green Library on the history of German vitalism. I dedicate this book to her.

## Note on the Cover Art

The cover's painting by Sigmar Polke, "Untitled (2003)," is based on an advertisement for an exhibition of "Phantasmagoria" held at London's Lyceum Theater in the early 1800s, staged by the German inventor Paul de Philipsthal. The advertisement illustrated the effect known as the "Red Woman of Berlin."

# List of Abbreviations

| | |
|---|---|
| Goldberg-*Aufsätze* | Oskar Goldberg, *Zahlengebäude, Ontologie, Maimonides, und Aufsätze 1933 bis 1947* (Berlin: Königshausen & Neumann, 2013). |
| *Oskar Goldberg* | Manfred Voigts, *Oskar Goldberg, der mythische Experimentalwissenschaftler: Ein verdrängtes Kaptiel jüdischer Geschichte* (Berlin: Agora, 1992). |
| *Phil.* | Franz Josef Molitor, *Philosophie der Geschichte, oder Über die Tradition*, part 1 (Frankfurt am Main: Hermannschen Buchhandlung, 1827); part 1, 2nd ed. (Münster: Teissing'sche Buchhandlung, 1857); part 2 (Münster: Theissing'sche Buchhandlung, 1834); part 3 (Münster: Theissing'sche Buchhandlung, 1839); part 4, vol. 1 (Münster: Theissing'sche Buchhandlung, 1853). |
| *Reality of the Hebrews* | Oskar Goldberg, *Die Wirklichkeit der Hebräer*, Wissenschaftliche Neuausgabe, ed. Manfred Voigts (Wiesbaden: Harrassowitz, 2005). |
| *Theory of Reality* | Hans Driesch, *Wirklichkeitslehre: Ein metaphysischer Versuch* (Leipzig: Emmanuel Reinike, 2nd ed. 1922; 1st ed. 1917). |

# Introduction

THE "TALK OF the Town" section in the *New Yorker* of July 17, 1943, included a piece titled "Ghost Photographer" about a certain Dr. Oskar Goldberg. "He's a German scientist of undoubted repute," the writer explains. "Two years ago, when he arrived in this country as an émigré, he was sponsored by Thomas Mann, Albert Einstein, and other Germans of equal standing." Four months earlier (March 7, 1943), Goldberg had published on the first page of the *New York Spiritualist Leader*, a widely distributed newspaper at that time, a request for information about ghost and poltergeist sightings in the New York area.[1] This request, with his contact information included, had the heading, "Haunted Houses: Wanted for Tests." It was this advertisement that had caught the attention of the *New Yorker* writer. When he was interviewed, Goldberg explained that he was planning to undertake a scientific expedition to assemble photographic evidence of ghosts. "It's his notion that a picture of a ghost could be obtained with a camera using film sensitive to ultra-violet and infra-red rays," the writer notes. Goldberg said that he had learned how to actually see ghosts with the naked eye during his training under a yogi in India. In addition to his quest for scientific proof of ghosts and of life after death, Goldberg explained what his deeper motive was: "The only reason for psychic research is to release earthbound ghosts, all of whom are unhappy." In "Rules for Research in Hauntings," a piece Goldberg published in the *New York Spiritualist Leader* later that same summer, we learn that the reporting of "spontaneous" apparitions is a "religious duty" and that "anyone who conceals hauntings is acting unethically by preventing research in proofs of immortality."[2] The fact that a "German scientist of undoubted repute" was hunting for ghosts in New York in the middle of the Second World War could not help but arouse the interest of the *New Yorker* writer. Here was a "round, bald, kindly-looking man of fifty-seven" harmlessly and somewhat comically trying to find proof of life after death and, moreover, trying to redeem the unhappy dead.

Oskar Goldberg (1885–1952), as the *New Yorker* article attests, was never shy of publicity. In Weimar Berlin, Goldberg achieved a reputation among many young Jewish intellectuals as a brilliant Kabbalist with supernormal abilities to penetrate the secrets of the Hebrew Bible. Among those who were particularly drawn to Goldberg's ideas were the philosopher Erich Unger (1887–1950), a fellow student one year behind Goldberg at the Friedrich-Gymnasium; the legal and economic historian Adolf Caspary (1898–1953); and the artist, poet, and later photojournalist Simon Guttmann (1891–1990).[3] Outside of his circle of devoted followers, Goldberg's ideas received a wide and generally positive reception. Two noted historians of religion of the Weimar period, Robert Eisler and Franz Dornseiff, acknowledged the importance of Goldberg's first publication on the "numerical structure" of the Pentateuch, although they disputed his claim that it was beyond the power of human intelligence to fabricate.[4] Thomas Mann relied on Goldberg's 1925 magnum opus, *Die Wirklichkeit der Hebräer* (*The Reality of the Hebrews*), for his Joseph novels. In her autobiographical memoir, Margarete Susman, one of the most notable Jewish thinkers of the Weimar period, ranked Goldberg's book alongside Heidegger's *Sein und Zeit* (*Being and Time*) as the "two great metaphysical expositions of the world and human existence published in the German language in the interwar period."[5]

Alluding to the ancient historian Josephus's description of the "three sects" of the Jewish world of his day (Pharisees, Sadducees, and Essenes), the modern Jewish historian Gershom Scholem identified three Jewish "sects" in Weimar Germany: the one associated with art historian Aby Warburg's research library in Hamburg, the group of political philosophers and social scientists at the Institute of Social Research in Frankfurt, and the circle around Oskar Goldberg in Berlin.[6] Scholem, despite being a severe critic of Goldberg, thus testified to the historical significance of Goldberg's appeal for a certain group of young German Jews in Weimar. What drew this group to Goldberg was a profound desire to reconnect to what Goldberg called "Urjudaism," a form of militant communal existence that flourished when, according to the account in the book of Exodus, the people as a whole seemed to be gathered within the protective presence of their God, with the ark of the covenant in their midst and a column of fire leading them forward toward the promised land. This yearning for some restoration of a communal intensity of Jewish life took many forms at the time, including, of course, Zionism in all of its varieties. Goldberg's ideas offered a number of young Jews a path to a vitality of experience that, unlike Zionism, seemed unsullied by the pragmatic exigencies of world politics.[7] After the bloodletting of the First World War there arose among many young people, not just Jews, a thoroughgoing repudiation of anything less than a revolutionary, world-transformative form of politics. In 1921, Erich Unger, deeply influenced by Goldberg's ideas, published a book titled *Politik und Metaphysik* (*Politics and Metaphysics*) that argued for the possibility of a politics based on a people's latent biophysical power through which it might tap into transcendental sources of energy. Walter Benjamin was so taken with this book that in a letter to Gershom Scholem he called it "the most meaningful work on politics of our time."[8]

The sense that the very sources of life's *élan vital* could be directly tapped into, that the power of intuition or the imagination could transform the world, was certainly not limited to Goldberg and his circle. Such ideas, generally connected with the vitalist philosophy of Henri Bergson, were widely shared at the time. I hope to demonstrate that Goldberg's particular brand of Kabbalistic vitalism, indebted to the biologist and philosopher Hans Driesch rather than Bergson, offers a fascinating case study in what I call "the vitalist imagination." Whether embraced by reactionary or left-wing revolutionary thinkers, the vitalist imagination seemed to offer an alternative means of changing the world after humanity's faith in the Machine and technology had led to an unprecedented global catastrophe. Goldberg's participation in the attempt to harness the vitalist imagination in order to recreate a world out of joint has so far not been told. *Transfinite Life* seeks to fill the gap in this larger history.

Goldberg's Kabbalistic vitalism was based on a far-flung theory of what he called "the transcendental organism," the site not only of ideal forms of animal species but also of what the ancient world called "gods." Describing the God of the Hebrew Bible as the "prebiological" principle behind the transcendental organism, Goldberg constructed a metaphysical defense of the Jewish people as the bearers of a mission to free all of human life from the "organic lawfulness" that ruled all other animal existence. Goldberg sharply distinguished ancient Israel from its neighboring states. Only ancient Israel had transcended the worship of gods tied to the life cycle of birth, reproduction, and death. Arguing that the Five Books of Moses can be read as the narrative of God's "metaphysical war" with the "biocentric gods" that had once "colonized" the earth, Goldberg's book proposed to his contemporary Jews an anti-Zionist, anticolonial "transcendental politics" in opposition to Germany's intensifying biopolitical and geopolitical fantasies of the interwar years.

Goldberg's ideas about the transcendental realm of "biocentric gods" and their relation to the "metaphysical peoples" of antiquity, however, certainly lent themselves to misunderstanding. In 1954, Jacob Taubes published an essay about Goldberg in the *Partisan Review* titled "From Cult to Culture."[9] (The young Taubes had met Goldberg in 1938 when Taubes's father, Zurich's Chief Rabbi, offered him shelter after he left Germany and was traveling from San Remo to Paris.) Taubes took the essay's title from *Doktor Faustus*, Thomas Mann's masterwork about the sources of fascism in the heady mix of German Romanticism and the "twilight of the gods" mythology of death-embracing heroism. To round out his cast of characters, Mann offers a Jewish proto-fascist by the name of Dr. Chaim Breisacher. Breisacher believes that only a return to myth and cult can redeem humanity from its enslavement to the sterility of technological rationality. As Taubes points out, Breisacher is based on the figure of Oskar Goldberg. Taubes's essay attempts to defend Goldberg against Mann's unflattering caricature of Goldberg as a Jewish fascist, but he does acknowledge that Goldberg's theory about how the gods of mythology once bestowed on their worshippers a special biological prowess might seem to resemble the racist glorification of the pre-Christian vitality of the Teutonic "Volk."[10] Goldberg sought to counter such a misunderstanding, insisting that, except perhaps in the remotest regions of Tibet, "metaphysical peoples" were a thing of the past. I will argue in this book that one of Goldberg's most important aims in *The Reality of the Hebrews* was to offer a critique of the use of mythology to support state-based racism. But because Goldberg took seriously the power of myth to shape ethnic identity in antiquity, he opened himself up to the kind of misreading that Thomas Mann puts on display in *Doktor Faustus*.

Thomas Mann's caricature of Goldberg as a proto-fascist stands in sharp contrast to H. G. Adler's reception of Goldberg's ideas. Adler (1910–1988), the Holocaust novelist and sociologist best known today for his monumental study of the "model" concentration camp Theresienstadt where he was interned from 1942 to 1944, became acquainted with Goldberg and Unger in Berlin in 1932 when he attended the weekly sessions of the "Philosophische Gruppe" that were held in Unger's Berlin apartment.[11] Adler appropriates their concept of "reality" (*Wirklichkeit*), claiming that it can be transformed through the active power of human imagination. He argues that reality is not what it is claimed to be in a "superficial philosophy" that takes it to be "throughout all history an unchangeable and given quantity." Rather, reality is both mutable and malleable, sometimes in ways that can cause a certain group of humans (like the prisoners in the camp) to become less and less real, "improbable and ghostly" (*unwahrscheinlich, gespenstisch*).[12] Adler's Holocaust novels track his own descent into unreality and his sense of himself as lacking any concrete existence in the world.

Adler attempted to explain how the power of consciousness could transform reality into more benign forms in a work of philosophy that he began in 1932 under the influence of Unger's interpretation of Goldberg's ideas. This work, *Vorschule für eine Experimentaltheologie* (*Preparatory Lessons for an Experimental Theology*), was only completed in the year before his death in 1988.[13] In his book, Adler makes extensive use of Goldberg's *Reality of the Hebrews*. He argues, for example, that "the individual who held sway [within a folk group] in the age of myth possessed powers that have long since been lost: he knew himself to be in real and effective contact with beings of a higher order, beings that frequently revealed themselves to the folk group as well."[14] Adler goes on to explain how the "mythic-magical age" was succeeded by our modern "age of Ratio" and how a new age, an age of "intuition" that allows for a new relationship with the higher reality, is about to be inaugurated. This new age of intuition will consummate the "wish dreams" of humanity for a world of justice and peace.

It is quite remarkable that one and the same book, Goldberg's *Reality of the Hebrews*, could be read by Thomas Mann as a Jewish version of fascist myth-making and by H. G. Adler as a blueprint for creating a utopian social order through the power of "intuition," the same power that was revealed in the ancient world's mythic imagination. Goldberg was clearly a figure who elicited extreme reactions from those who read him or knew him personally. It would certainly be an exaggeration to say that his work served as a "Rorschach test" for his generation. However, it offers us a fascinating window on the powerful forces that can be unleashed—both destructive and creative—when the "givenness" of reality is called into question in the name of a radically transfigured future.

*Transfinite Life* is the first full-length study of Oskar Goldberg in English, and except for Jacob Taubes's 1954 essay "From Cult to Culture," there is practically nothing written in English on Goldberg.[15] Manfred Voigts published an intellectual biography of Goldberg in 1992 and has since written a considerable number of special studies of Goldberg's relationship to his contemporaries, most notably Thomas Mann, Gershom Scholem, Walter Benjamin, and H. G. Adler. Voigts has also reissued scholarly editions of Goldberg's several monographs and major essays.[16] Voigts's 1992 book and articles, while offering an indispensable treatment of what we know about Goldberg's life and relations with his contemporaries, do not attempt to provide a complete picture of the philosophical context of Goldberg's intellectual output. As a scholar of twentieth-century German literature, Voigts chooses to place Goldberg within the frame of early German Expressionism. My focus, as I have explained, is Goldberg's Kabbalistic vitalism. The Kabbalistic elements in his thinking will emerge in my presentation of his earliest work, *Die Fünf Bücher Mosis: ein Zahlengebäude* (*The Five Books of Moses: A Numerical System*, 1908) and his magnum opus, *Die Wirklichkeit der Hebräer* (*The Reality of the Hebrews*).

I precede my account of these books with an overview of the two sources besides the Kabbalah that nurtured Goldberg's vitalist imagination: first, the work of Hans Driesch, and, second, the mathematics of infinity introduced by Georg Cantor. Goldberg described himself as "close to the philosophy of nature circles [*naturphilosophische Kreisen*]" of the period,[17] in which Driesch and Cantor were key figures. The "philosophy of nature" (Naturphilosophie) had its origin in the early nineteenth century. Naturphilosophie sought to explain the phenomenal realm of light, magnetism, chemical bonding, and animal morphogenesis as the outward manifestation of fundamental dynamic tensions in the realm of *Geist*, Spirit. Naturphilosophie hoped to offer a window on the hidden interrelationship of all inanimate and animate existence, providing a unified account of all of nature as a system where living systems emerged from but were not reducible to physico-chemical systems. In the later nineteenth century, in large part as a reaction against the importing of positivist explanatory models from the physical sciences into accounts of embryological development by a new generation of biologists, Hans Driesch sought to place Naturphilosophie on a more secure footing by demonstrating the non-mechanical nature of cellular differentiation during the development of the sea-urchin embryo. Driesch published the results of his groundbreaking experiments in 1891.[18] Less than ten years earlier, Georg

Cantor claimed to find a secure footing for Naturphilosophie with his theory of the actual existence of infinite ("transfinite") numbers that he represented with the first letter of the Hebrew alphabet, aleph.[19] Each aleph, Cantor claimed, could be viewed as a rigorous mathematical model of what Leibniz, one of the most important sources of Romantic Naturphilosophie, called a "monad." The system of transfinite numbers, each containing the whole of its predecessor while also stepping beyond it to the next highest level of infinity, modeled the unity of existence glimpsed in Leibniz's monadology.

Driesch and Cantor exercised a wide influence on many German scientists, mathematicians, philosophers, and writers in the early decades of the twentieth century. It is possible to see many of these figures as engaged in different but related ways in the revival of the aspirations of Romantic Naturphilosophie toward a unified theory of space, time, matter, and life. I gather this broad intellectual enterprise under the single name "neo-Naturphilosophie," although I do not thereby wish to assert that it represents a movement as coherent as early nineteenth-century Naturphilosophie.[20] Neo-Naturphilosophie forms an essential background to Goldberg's Kabbalistic vitalism.

Despite being an important intellectual current in Weimar Germany, neo-Naturphilosophie remains understudied. I therefore spend the first chapter and some of the second chapter of *Transfinite Life* tracing its development. My aim is both to contextualize Goldberg's Kabbalistic vitalism and to provide an account of neo-Naturphilosophie's unique place in the wider history of the resurgence of vitalism in Weimar Germany. It is this strand of vitalism that many contemporary thinkers like Graham Harman, Isabelle Stengers, and Iain Hamilton Grant have appropriated in order to think beyond current forms of reductionist materialism.[21] The neo-Naturphilosophie current within twentieth-century vitalism differed in significant ways from the better-known *Lebensphilosophie* of the Weimar period. Neo-Naturphilosophie vitalism drew more from Aristotle than it did from Nietzsche. It tended to base itself on the observation of the apparent goal-directedness of embryonic development, rather than on the evolution of new species through random morphological changes and natural selection. And, in applying their biological theories to human society, neo-Naturphilosophie thinkers tended to be suspicious of claims that the state displays its vitality as an organism in risking its life in a geopolitical *Kampf ums Dasein* ("struggle for existence"). Rather, with their more holistic understanding, they tended to view history as the unfolding of a globally unified humanity.

Foregrounding Goldberg's relationship to neo-Naturphilosophie vitalism, *Transfinite Life* seeks to contribute to the growing body of work on the pivotal role of vitalism in twentieth-century culture and politics. These studies include Mark Antliff's examination of the anarchist artistic appropriation of Bergsonian vitalism in *Inventing Bergson: Cultural Politics and Parisian Avant-Garde*; Donna V. Jones's recent book on Francophone anticolonialist literature and vitalism, *The Racial Discourses of Life Philosophy: Négritude, Vitalism, and Modernity*; and Pheng Cheah's study of the place of the German idealist philosophy of *Bildung* or culture (a close cousin of Romantic Naturphilosophie) in *Spectral Nationality: Passages of Freedom from Kant to Postcolonial Literatures of Liberation*. All these books seek to identify the revolutionary and liberatory potential within vitalist thought. My study of Oskar Goldberg will also emphasize how his reception of vitalism grounds his revolutionary philosophy of history and of the role of the Jewish people in it.[22]

Oskar Goldberg was born in Berlin in 1885 and died in Nice in 1952. Although not averse to publicity, he was not one to bare his soul in public. We have precious little that allows us to form a picture of his personal life or demeanor. He was raised in an Orthodox household by his mother and paternal grandfather. Oskar's father, a Gymnasium teacher of the classics, died when Oskar was three years old. Taking him under his wing, Oskar's grandfather gave the boy a solid footing in Bible and Talmud. But it seems that Goldberg, probably influenced by his grandfather's acquaintances, soon departed from a traditional approach to Jewish learning and took up the esoteric teaching of the Kabbalah. In an unusually candid (for Goldberg) account of his early years, Goldberg relates how he first became a student of the Kabbalah. The account opens an unpublished composition written during the war while he was living in New York.[23] Goldberg writes about himself using the abbreviation "G." The piece begins, "Dr. G., when a boy of five years, was seeking the company of very old people. He happened to come into contact with old men who made kabbalistic experiments. The youngest among them was seventy-six years old and G. was initiated in their circle as youngest [*sic*] member." Goldberg relates that his seventy-six-year-old Kabbalist mentor suggested to him that he no longer occupy himself with Kabbalah once he reached the age of seventeen "because the Cabbala in Europe will enter into a stage of decay." Instead of continuing his "cabbalistic experiments," Goldberg should "rather go his own path and develop his own philosophical system." Goldberg adds, "G. followed this suggestion later on which proved to be good." Goldberg seems to have been very proficient in biblical studies even during his Gymnasium years. It took him only two years after graduating in 1906 (when he was twenty-one) to finish his book on the number system of the Pentateuch, a book that managed to draw the attention of some of the most respected scholars in Germany. Goldberg also says that his *Reality of the Hebrews* was already basically finished by that time. It seems likely, therefore, that Goldberg was indeed offered special training in Bible and Kabbalah from a very early age.

During his years in the Gymnasium, Goldberg gathered around himself a slightly younger group of three Jewish friends, all of whom were raised in assimilated bourgeois households and who remained loyal to Goldberg for most of their lives (I will say more about this group in chapter 2). Goldberg taught them his mathematico-Kabbalistic "number system of the Pentateuch." After graduating, Goldberg remained in Berlin for several years to continue his studies at two of the city's Orthodox rabbinical seminaries. During these early Berlin years, Goldberg and his friends were also active in the proto-Expressionist group, the Neuer Club, one of Germany's earliest venues for Expressionist poetry, drama, and philosophy. Just before the outbreak of the First World War, Goldberg studied what we would today call medical anthropology at the University of Munich (Ludwig-Maximillians Universität). While in Munich Goldberg also received training in naturopathic medicine, possibly at the Krankenhaus für Naturheilweisen, an institution founded in 1888 that remains active to this day.[24] During the early years of the war, Goldberg managed to do research in his special field of interest, ethno-psychophysiology, in Nepal where he also claimed to have learned how to see ghosts (I tell the story in the conclusion). In 1921, Goldberg married Dora Hiller, the cousin of one of the members of the Neuer Club, the social activist (pro–gay rights) Kurt Hiller. He had met Dora Hiller in 1917 at the Oriental Institute in Berlin where she was working on a translation of the Hindu theological writings of Swami Vivekananda (1863–1902). Although Dora Hiller was an active participant in the literary and cultural life of Weimar Berlin, we have no real knowledge of the married life of the couple.[25] From about 1927 until 1932, Goldberg was an important presence in the weekly meetings of the Philosophische Gruppe ("Philosophical Group") in Berlin. The meetings were organized by his student and closest friend, Erich Unger, in whose Charlottenburg apartment they were held. They were attended by many of Berlin's leading intellectuals, including Walter Benjamin, Alfred Döblin, Bertold Brecht, and Erich Engel, the director of the original production of Brecht's *Dreigroschenopfer* (*Three-Penny Opera*). Frequently, fifty or sixty were in attendance. Erich Engel took notes at many of these meetings.[26] After leaving Germany in 1932, Goldberg stayed (for reasons of health) in San Remo, Italy, until 1938. On his way to France where he hoped to settle in safety from Fascist and Nazi persecution, he spent some time in Zurich. There he was the guest of Rabbi Zvi Taubes (Jacob Taubes's father), who invited him to deliver some lectures to the Zurich Jewish community.[27] Goldberg left Switzerland and arrived at Montpellier in early September 1939. On September 21, after the outbreak of the war, Goldberg was ordered to report to an internment camp for German nationals. Later, he moved through a number of camps that the Vichy government had set up (St. Cyprien and Gurs among them). Through the efforts of the American Rescue Committee, Goldberg managed to get a special "protected person" visa to come to the United States in March 1941.[28] In the United States he renewed his connection to naturopathic medicine and helped create a medical school based on its principles. In 1943 he was interviewed for the "Talk of the Town" story in the *New Yorker* titled "Ghost Photographer," mentioned at the beginning of the introduction. Goldberg returned to France in 1948 soon after the death of his wife. In 1949 he served as the representative of American naturopathic physicians at the World Health Organization in Geneva. Goldberg died in Nice in 1952 where he had traveled seeking medical attention for a heart problem. He is buried in the Jewish section of a cemetery in Monaco.[29]

## Outline of the Book

Chapter 1 is devoted to exploring the revival of Naturphilosophie in the early twentieth century in Germany, focusing on the work of Hans Driesch, Germany's premier exponent of vitalism. As I mentioned earlier, there has recently been renewed interest in the intersection of vitalist philosophy, modernism, and radical politics in early twentieth-century Europe. Donna V. Jones's *The Racial Discourses of Life Philosophy* was particularly helpful to me in formulating my interpretation of Goldberg as a Jewish anticolonial vitalist. Jones shows how anticolonialist writers appropriated Bergsonian vitalism in order to turn the tables on its use by the right in discourses of race-based imperialism. I argue that Oskar Goldberg's appropriation of German vitalism performs a similar maneuver. In the case of Goldberg, however, the exponent of vitalism to whom he turned was not Henri Bergson, but rather Hans Driesch. Driesch is far less known today than Bergson, but at the time his reputation as a scientist and philosopher equaled that of Bergson.[30] Unlike Bergson, Driesch aligned himself with the phenomenological school descending from Franz Brentano and his most well-known student, Edmund Husserl. Brentano's renewal of Aristotelianism inspired Driesch's conception of the entelechy as the guiding principle in embryological development. I argue that Franz Brentano is, in fact, the thinker most responsible for the resurgence of Naturphilosophie in the early decades of the twentieth century. The phenomenological vitalism of Hans Driesch is the most significant influence on Goldberg's biological reinterpretation of the Kabbalah. But quite apart from his influence on Goldberg, Driesch and the wider group of neo-Naturphilosophie thinkers who drew inspiration from his critique of reductionism in the biological sciences play an important role in much of today's new thinking about biological systems. Although my focus in this book is on Goldberg's Kabbalistic vitalism, it is important to recognize that he is part of a much larger intellectual movement. Indeed, it is one of my goals in the book to offer an account of the nature of the vitalist imagination more generally and its particular efflorescence in the period around the First World War. To that end, I devote more time to Hans Driesch and neo-Naturphilosophie than might seem necessary simply to understand Goldberg's ideas. However, attending to the wider context of Goldberg's thinking will not only enrich our appreciation of Goldberg but also provide insight into one of the most important moments in the history of the vitalist imagination.

Chapter 2 turns to Goldberg, but also completes the account of neo-Naturphilosophie begun in chapter 1. In 1908 Goldberg published his first monograph, *Die Fünf Bücher Mosis: Ein Zahlengebäude*.[31] The monograph reflects what must have been the subject of Goldberg's presentations to his group of three Gymnasium friends, a group he dubbed the "Weltwurzel Club" (World-Root Club). As I explain in this chapter, the name of the club itself is significant for a number of reasons. "Root" is not only a mathematical term but is also the name of the consonantal clusters at the base of the Hebrew lexical system. The "world-root" is the name of God, the *tetragrammaton*, represented in the Hebrew Bible with the four letters *yod-hey-vav-hey*. Goldberg transcribes this name as IHWH, but it is more typically rendered YHWH (the rendering I use throughout this book). Goldberg claims that the numerological value of this name (its *gematria* value of twenty-six, as I explain in chapter 2) can be traced throughout the Pentateuch and, indeed, the world as a whole. The belief in a divine mathematical formula underlying all of creation is central not only to the Kabbalah but also to the Naturphilosophie tradition. In chapter 2 I explain how the mathematics of the infinite in the nineteenth century from Bernard Bolzano through Bernhard Riemann and Richard Dedekind to Georg Cantor was deeply intertwined with Naturphilosophie. The vitalism of neo-Naturphilosophie was also connected to mathematics, and a whole branch of "mathematical biology" begins at around this time. Goldberg, I argue, believes that the Pentateuch is both the product of and the gateway to the bio-mathematical source of all reality. Georg Cantor's theory of transfinite numbers serves Goldberg as a model of how to understand the bio-mathematics behind the transition from the infinity of the "prebiological" YHWH to the finite organisms that inhabit this world. The connection between Cantorian mathematics and Goldberg's "biological Kabbalah" (Scholem's phrase) has inspired the title of this book, *Transfinite Life*.

Chapter 3 turns to an unpublished work of Goldberg's from the same period as his *Five Books of Moses*. He titled it *Ontologie: Die Idee der Logik* (*Ontology: The Idea of Logic*). Goldberg's *Ontology* attempts to deduce the structures of the bio-mathematical realm (the transfinite or "transcendental" organisms that serve as structural models for the finite organisms of this world) from the "Uniqueness" that stands beyond all multiplicity. The most difficult section of *Ontology* deals with a theory of the "productive imagination." From Kant's theory of mathematics forward, the formal structure of the imagination was thought to be the source of the *a priori* truths of geometry. In the hands of the neo-Kantian philosopher Hermann Cohen and his student Ernst Cassirer, the productive power of the imagination came to figure as the source not only of geometric truths but also of all truths that could be expressed in mathematical form, including the truths of the physical sciences. Goldberg shares the neo-Kantian faith in the productive imagination, but for him, it is (as it was also for Salomon Maimon, Kant's first major critic) the gateway from the finitude of human cognition to the infinite source of all reality. As I have said, Goldberg's theory of the productive imagination is only sketchily developed in *Ontology*, but it forms the basis of Erich Unger's philosophical system. Unger's early work *Politik und Metaphysik*, highly praised by Walter Benjamin as "the most meaningful work on politics of our time" (*die bedeutendste Schrift über Politik aus dieser Zeit*),[32] offers a more complete version of Goldberg's theory of the productive imagination and its possible place in the construction of a new "metaphysical politics." I devote the final pages of chapter 3 to an explication of Goldberg and Unger's theory of the productive imagination and its power to bring about a "breakthrough act" that allows the infinite bio-mathematical realm to shatter the "givenness" of empirical reality.

At the center of my book is Oskar Goldberg's magnum opus, *The Reality of the Hebrews*, the subject of chapter 4. Couching his biblical interpretation of the Pentateuch in the terminology of the latest mathematics (especially the Cantorian mathematics of the infinite) and science (especially Driesch's vitalist biology), Goldberg argues that the first five books of the Hebrew Bible were a divinely inspired account of how the God of Israel had entered into a covenant with Israel to wage what Goldberg called a "metaphysical war" against the pagan gods surrounding Israel. Israel's metaphysical war involved the sort of forces that, for example, the Bible says were present in the pillars of fire and smoke that guarded the Israelites in their exodus from Egypt. Goldberg, taking such phenomena seriously as evidence of the metaphysical power of Israel's God to enter into this world as a living *corporeal* presence, argues that other gods also possessed such metaphysical powers. These other gods (the "elohim" referred to in the Bible) had used the different peoples of the earth in what Goldberg describes as their effort to "colonize" the planet. Goldberg explains how Israel's God could not create this empirical world without opening the world to these foreign transcendental forces. Israel's God begins a campaign against these powers from out of the desert wastes of the Sinai, the last area remaining to him from which to launch his effort at freeing humanity from the other elohim, the colonial oppressors of the earth's population. Israel's God enters the world through the sacrificial rituals performed at the tabernacle, using Israel's encampment sites as beachheads and staging grounds for the outworking of his metaphysical struggle against the imperialistic goals of the other gods. "The tent," Goldberg writes, "represents a dynamic system whose goal is to make God present. It contains for this purpose a motor that works day and night, namely, the sacrifices with their fire, smoke, and offerings, uniting physics and biology, cosmology and anthropology."[33]

Goldberg's "experimental ethnology," as he called it in *The Reality of the Hebrews*, argues that the people of Israel lend their collective biological energy to maintaining the link between the transcendental realm of God and the empirical world. Just like Israel's God, the other gods have their beachheads in the world, and their peoples to assist them in gaining an even wider foothold in the world. All this "transcendental politics" came to an end when ancient peoples, relegating their myths to the realm of mere poetic fantasy, lost touch with the transcendental world. Goldberg therefore believed that the age of the pagan gods and their battle for control of the earth had long since passed; however, he also believed that the God of Israel had not yet fulfilled his metaphysical struggle to free the earth of the principle at work in the pagan gods' colonialist power struggle. The God of Israel has not yet made the world a home for his full metaphysical power. What the Bible described as "the wars of the Lord" still remain to be fought. Chapter 4 concludes with Goldberg's reflections in *The Reality of the Hebrews* about the necessity for a new revelation, a new Torah, to help humanity restore God's presence in the world.

Goldberg, despite (or perhaps because of) his Orthodox background, had a profoundly ambivalent relation to the rabbinic tradition and the Jewish people in general. Goldberg's philosophy of Jewish history is the subject of chapter 5. The first part is devoted to the critique of Goldberg's philosophy launched by Gershom Scholem immediately after the publication of *The Reality of the Hebrews* in 1925. Throughout the rest of his life, in fact, Gershom Scholem remained an outspoken critic of Oskar Goldberg.[34] Gershom Scholem, deeply suspicious of Goldberg and very critical of his ideas, said in 1921 when he was invited by Dora Hiller to meet Goldberg at her home, "I am inclined to regard him as a representative of the devil in our generation."[35] Much later in his life, Scholem wrote that Goldberg's appropriation of Kabbalah represented "the exact counterpoint to what I was doing in taking up the study of Kabbalism" and that his own lifelong interest in Goldberg was "a kind of negative fascination."[36] I do not want to contest Scholem's negative assessment of the scholarly value of Goldberg's interpretation of the Kabbalah. Despite his impressive learning, Goldberg was not a trained historian of religion.[37] Scholem's lifelong opposition to Goldberg, however, goes far beyond the worth of his historical scholarship. First of all, his animosity to Goldberg had much to do with Scholem's relationship with Walter Benjamin, whose thinking revealed the influence of the Goldberg circle and of Erich Unger in particular. Scholem did his best to separate Benjamin from his ties to Unger. But the battle Scholem fought against Goldberg goes deeper than his personal fears that Benjamin might be drawn too close into Goldberg's orbit. At stake in the conflict between Scholem and Goldberg, I argue in chapter 5, is the revolutionary potential of the Hebrew Bible and the possibility of reconstituting a revolutionary Jewish peoplehood in relation to it.

Goldberg himself never spoke about Scholem's critique of his work, at least not in so many words. But he did present his own full-fledged philosophy of Jewish history in his 1935 book, published as part of the celebration of the eight hundredth anniversary of the birth of Moses Maimonides, *Maimonides: Kritik der jüdischen*

*Glaubenslehre* (*Maimonides: A Critique of Jewish Doctrine*).[38] The second half of chapter 5 is devoted to this work. In a letter to Ernst Jünger in occupied Paris from 1945, Carl Schmitt recommended this book, together with Bruno Bauer's *Die Judenfrage*, as essential reading for anyone interested in understanding the Jews.[39] Schmitt, who must have met Goldberg when he attended some of the meetings of the Philosophische Gruppe in Berlin, thought that "the Jewish philosopher Oskar Goldberg" had correctly pinpointed and described the nature of the Jewish problem, only he phrased it in terms opposite to the truth of the matter. Goldberg claimed that the Jews, with their latent "ritual-capable" metaphysical powers, were able to stand at the vanguard of an apocalyptic struggle against the powers of mechanistic technology. Schmitt told Jünger that Goldberg was correct about the nature of the apocalyptic struggle that faced the modern world, but was completely mistaken about which side the Jews were fighting on. Despite his anti-Jewish take on Goldberg's *Maimonides*, Schmitt understood quite well what Goldberg's book represented: a call for a revolutionary battle against the death-dealing forces of technology. In *Maimonides*, Goldberg explains that YHWH's metaphysical struggle still requires the help of the Jewish people as it did in the past, but now, just as at the time of the exodus from Egypt, YHWH is open to having others join the struggle, so long as they possess the same "ritual-capable" psychophysiology that will permit them to join their biological energies to the energies that remain latent within (at least some of) the Jewish people. Goldberg sees the new "metaphysical war" that YHWH is about to wage as one that would be directed against a different array of enemies from the colonizing gods of antiquity. Today's metaphysical war would be directed against the imperialistic, colonizing nation-states that, in 1914, had brought the horror of world war to the earth in their struggle for geopolitical dominance. The imperialistic nation-states no longer draw on ancient mythic *rituals* that once "realized" the ancient gods in the corporate body of the worshipping people. Instead, modern nation-states rely on *technologies* designed to make themselves gods on earth. Schmitt told Jünger that the problem of the modern world was, indeed, the triumph of technology over the vital forces of a unified people, but that the reversal of this triumph does not depend on Goldberg's "Hebrew metaphysics" but rather on the overcoming of what Schmitt considered to be the Jews' penchant for techno-rational abstract thinking. Schmitt simply could not accept Goldberg's characterization of the Jews as the potential vanguard of a new, anti-technological human inhabitation of the earth. Where Schmitt believed he saw the face of his "enemy" in Goldberg, many young Jews instead felt that Goldberg offered them a path away from the domination of the technological Machine and back to a lost, almost magical past predating the rise of "ethical monotheism," the faith of their liberal bourgeois fathers. Gershom Scholem understood very well the attractions of this path, and his own turn to Zionism was in part defined as a way to counter it, both for himself and for other young Jews.

As I have just noted, one of Goldberg's major themes is the triumph of materialistic technology over metaphysical ritual, especially in the European West. In making this point Goldberg was deliberately aligning himself with some of the most radical trends in European thought of the time. But Goldberg sought to distance his own critique of Western technoscience and his defense of myth from that of others, both on the left (George Sorel) and the right (Arthur Rosenberg). Goldberg argued that the Western imperial powers, in addition to replacing ritual with technology, had also created for themselves artificial myths in order to, as he put it in 1938, "lift up the thyrsos staff of Dionysus and fill themselves with the intoxicating thrill [*Rausch*] of its tragic grandeur." This ersatz mythic fervor, Goldberg goes on to say, is not the "old and true myth, but the myth of Sorel, the *myth of the twentieth century* [the title of Arthur Rosenberg's book], that can achieve no other success than to drive the masses into a pseudobaccantic frenzy."[40] Goldberg knew that he had to distance his own appropriation of myth from that of Sorel and Rosenberg. He wanted to appropriate the Pentateuch for a modern anti-technological revolution growing out of a renewal of the vital forces of the Jewish people, but in a way that did not valorize either irrational emotionality or racial atavism. The path he took to create a theory of this revolutionary Jewish peoplehood "out of the sources of Judaism" (to adopt Hermann Cohen's phrase in the title of his own very different book, *Religion of Reason Out of the Sources of Judaism*, also about the revolutionary potential of the Jewish people) is the subject of *Transfinite Life*.

In the conclusion I return to the wider context of vitalism in the early twentieth century that was the focus of chapter 1's discussion of Hans Driesch and neo-Naturphilosophie. I also return to Goldberg's interest in ghost photography. In attempting to contextualize both the resurgence of vitalism and the interest in ghosts during the early decades of the twentieth century, I present the broad outline of a theory of what I call "the vitalist imagination." The point of departure for my theory of the vitalist imagination is the brief "sketches and notes" section that concludes Adorno and Horkheimer's *Dialectic of Enlightenment*, in particular the pieces called "Interest in the Body" and "The Theory of Ghosts." Both of these pieces can be read together as offering a framework for understanding the modern resurgence of a belief in ghosts (and also of vitalism) as a response to the commodification of the human body in capitalism. Modern capitalist culture, Adorno and Horkheimer write, "treats the body as a thing that can be owned . . . distinguished from mind, the quintessence of power and command, as the object, the dead thing, the corpus."[41] The attack on the human body in modern capitalist culture elicits the response, one might even say the "immune" response, of the "vitalist imagination." Disagreeing with Horkheimer and Adorno's negative assessment of vitalism as a form of bourgeois false consciousness, I argue that the vitalist imagination should better be viewed as an essential resource of humanity in overcoming the threat posed by the mechanization and commodification of the human person. I link the vitalist imagination to the "productive imagination" that was so important for both neo-Kantian philosophy and for Goldberg. The productive imagination played an important role, too, in the phenomenological psychology of Franz Brentano and many of his students. Brentano's phenomenology, as I have mentioned, is one of the major sources of the "holistic" turn that inspired the resurgence of Naturphilosophie at the turn of the twentieth century and into its first decades.

My positive assessment of the vitalist imagination is based on the phenomenology of the imagination more generally. In explicating a phenomenology of the imagination that can ground a more positive evaluation of vitalism than Horkheimer and Adorno's, I turn in the conclusion of the book to one of the most important theoreticians of biological holism in the early decades of the twentieth century, Kurt Goldstein (1878–1965). In his major work, *Die Aufbau des Organismus* (*The Structure of the Organism*, 1935), Goldstein argues that the imagination makes it possible for the human being to relate to the environment so as to shape it in conformity with the fundamental needs of her existential condition. Goldstein, trained as a psychologist and neurophysiologist but also deeply grounded in philosophy, worked after the First World War with brain-injured soldiers. He noted their reduced linguistic and cognitive capacities, a result, he believed, of their attempt to avoid "anxiety" (*Angst*), a condition of "contentless consciousness," that is, the complete loss of their relationship to the world. The veterans would reduce their attention to the immediate objects in their surrounding and would deal with them in concrete categories. They could pick out something that had "the color of an apple," but they could not find something "red." Goldstein understood these symptoms as a direct result not so much of their brain injuries, but of the constriction of their whole being into the safety of the "given." To understand the behavior of these wounded veterans, Goldstein developed a broader holistic theory of the organism as seeking self-actualization through the reshaping of its environment by selecting out those aspects that were "adequate" to its flourishing as a "whole." Goldstein argued that all biological knowledge, if it is to be "adequate" to its object, must relate to the organism it studies in just the same way that the organism relates to its environment—that is, holistically.

Goldstein's epistemology of biological knowledge as itself an expression of the way that the human organism relates to its environment plays a significant role in George Canguilhem's vitalist epistemology in *Knowledge of Life*.[42] Canguilhem (1904–1995) argued, not unlike Horkheimer and Adorno but with a much more positive evaluation of vitalist thought, that vitalism is the expression of a "biological crisis" in the human species and an attempt to realign the relationship between technology and life, to recognize that the machine represents a limitation of organic freedom, rather than the model on which the organism should be understood. Goldstein and Canguilhem place vitalism and the imagination at the heart of humanity's response to the existential threat posed by machines that have ceased to expand the human organism's potential for shaping their world, but have, instead, constrained it and, one might even say, *unmade* it. To complete my sketch of a phenomenology of the vitalist imagination, I draw from the work of Elaine Scarry. Although I do not believe that she ever read Kurt Goldstein (but she may have known about his ideas through Canguilhem),[43] Elaine Scarry's phenomenology of the imagination in her path-breaking book, *The Body in Pain: The Making and Unmaking of the World*, has many points in common with Goldstein's approach. Like Goldstein, Scarry begins with a study of trauma victims who have been driven into a "contentless consciousness" she calls "aversiveness." Like Goldstein, she conceives of the imagination as the mediator of the human organism and the world, the shaper of the world into conformity with the existential needs of the whole being. Scarry, to the best of my knowledge, does not describe herself as a vitalist, but one of her key categories is "vivacity," and it is not at all inappropriate to place her work in the vitalist tradition of Goldstein and Canguilhem.

Scarry not only provides a capstone to my sketch of a phenomenology of the world-making imagination as the source of vitalism, she also offers a way to appreciate Goldberg's Hebrew metaphysics of the Pentateuch without all of its metaphysical baggage. Scarry's discussion of the Hebrew Bible in *The Body in Pain* is probably the least known and least read part of her work. In the final pages of the conclusion, I draw together the threads of vitalism, the imagination, and the Hebrew Bible's portrait of the God of Israel as the embodiment of humanity's belief in its own world-making power. I also return, finally, to Goldberg's interest in spirit photography, suggesting that it, too, is an expression of the same vitalist imagination that produced his Hebrew metaphysics. Spirit photography and Hebrew metaphysics both seek to redeem the suffering sentience of an "earthbound" humanity, a humanity trapped, or "engulfed" as Scarry would say, within the unfulfilled aspirations of transcendence engendered by its embodiment.

I devote Appendix I to Goldberg's relationship with Thomas Mann. Goldberg's *Reality of the Hebrews* was a significant source for Mann's investigation of the mythical dimension of the Hebrew Bible, especially the Joseph story.[44] Mann repaid the debt by using some of Goldberg's writings verbatim in his postwar novel, *Doktor Faustus*, where Goldberg is reworked into the figure of Chaim Breisacher, a strange and charismatic Jewish biblical scholar who seems to argue for a Jewish version of racist imperialism. Mann pictures Breisacher as a *reactionary* revolutionary who wants to tear down the decaying forms of bourgeois culture and replace them with the mythical reality of the sacrificial cult that once served as the center of every "authentic" people's national life. Mann's characterization of Breisacher as a prophet of cult replacing culture provided Jacob Taubes with the title of his 1954 essay on Goldberg, "From Cult to Culture." The caricature of Goldberg in Mann's *Doktor Faustus*, together with Scholem's dismissive characterization of him as no better than a charlatan, basically put the nail in the coffin of all further interest in Goldberg for about forty years, until Manfred Voigts took up his cause in the 1990s. But it would be wrong to say that Thomas Mann himself would have wanted to consign the historical Goldberg to oblivion or that he believed that Chaim Breisacher accurately mirrored the reality of Oskar Goldberg. The fact is that in 1936 Thomas Mann invited Goldberg to publish in his journal, *Mass und Wert*, the major German-language forum for anti-Nazi literary and philosophical writing, published in Zurich. And Mann gladly complied with Goldberg's request for a letter of reference when Goldberg emigrated to the United States in 1941.[45] Perhaps we should say that Thomas Mann found Goldberg to be a rather troubling figure to pin down.

Finally, Appendix II is devoted to the relationship between the appropriation of the Kabbalah in the work of the nineteenth-century Naturphilosoph Franz Joseph Molitor and the Kabbalistic interpretation of Oskar Goldberg. The question of Goldberg's debt to Molitor can only fairly be assessed after a detailed examination of Goldberg's synthesis of Kabbalah and neo-Naturphilosophie. It is certain that Goldberg was familiar with Molitor, but it is also quite clear that Goldberg diverges from Molitor in significant ways. Molitor deserves far more attention from scholars than he has so far received. While I cannot possibly do justice to Molitor in these few pages, I do suggest why Goldberg found his synthesis of Kabbalah and Naturphilosophie to be an important moment in the history of the reception of the Kabbalah.

## Notes

1. I want to thank the librarian, Dr. Celestina Savionius-Wroth (University of Illinois at Urbana–Champaign), for providing me with information about the newspaper. Circulation figures were not available, but Dr. Savonius-Wroth assures me that it was quoted (both positively and negatively) by other publications across the country.

2. The piece appeared in the Sunday, August 22, 1943, edition of the paper on pages 2 and 6.

3. Erich Unger will be the subject of further discussion in subsequent chapters. He is mostly noted today for the interest that Walter Benjamin showed in his work, especially *Politik und Metaphysik* (Berlin: David, 1921) and *Gegen die Dichtung: Eine Begründung des Konstruktionsprinzips in der Erkenntnis* (Leipzig: F. Meiner, 1925). Adolf Caspary was a prolific author with a wide range of interests. His book on the economic factors affecting military strategy continues to be cited in the secondary literature on the subject: *Wirtschafts-Strategie und Kriegsführung, wirtschaftliche Vorbereitung, Führung und Auswirkung des Krieges in geschichtlichem Aufriss* (Berlin: E. S. Mittler, 1932). Guttmann developed one of the most important photographic agencies in Europe, known as Report, after the Second World War, For a biography of Guttmann, see Nicholas Jacobs and Diethart Kerbs, "Wilhelm Simon Guttmann, 1891–1990: A Documentary Portrait," *German Life and Letters* 62, no. 4 (October 2009): 401–414.

4. The Viennese historian of religion Robert Eisler described Goldberg as a "learned and patient researcher" (*gelehrte und geduldige Forscher*). Robert Eisler, *Weltenmantel und Himmelszelt: Religionsgeschichtliche Untersuchungen zur Urgeschichte des antiken Weltbildes*, 2 vols. (Munich: C. B. Beck, 1910), 2:355. Franz Dornseiff also credits Goldberg for making an important contribution to the study of the numerological structures found in the Pentateuch. He calls Goldberg's book *seltsam* ("singular") (104) and distinguishes it from most other such books that simply indulge in *Psephisomanie* ("Ciphermania"). Franz Dornseiff, *Das Alphabet in Mystik und Magie* (Leipzig: B. G. Teubner, 1922), 110.

5. Margarete Susman, *Ich habe viele Leben gelebt: Erinnerungen* (Stuttgart: Deutsche Verlags-Anstalt, 1964), 333.

6. Gershom Scholem, *From Berlin to Jerusalem: Memories of My Youth*, trans. Harry Zohn (New York: Schocken Books, 1980), 147.

7. Another figure, Hans Joachim Schoeps, drew from Karl Barth and Kierkegaardian theology to argue for what Scholem criticized as a "Jewish pietism." On Schoeps as a Jewish theologian and historian of religion, see the essays in the recent volume of *Nexus: Essays in German Jewish Studies* dedicated to him (2014, vol. 2).

8. Gershom Scholem and Theodor W. Adorno, eds., *The Correspondence of Walter Benjamin*, trans. Manfred R. Jacobson and Evelyn Jacobson (Chicago: University of Chicago Press, 1994), 172. The letter is dated January 1921.

9. Jacob Taubes, "From Cult to Culture," in Jacob Taubes, *From Cult to Culture: Fragments towards a Critique of Historical Reason*, ed. Charlotte Fonrobert and Amir Engel (Stanford, CA: Stanford University Press, 2010), 235–247.

10. For a fuller assessment of Taubes's relation to Goldberg, see Manfred Voigts, "Jacob Taubes und Oskar Goldberg: Eine problematische Beziehung, dargestellt ahnend der erhaltenen Briefen," in *Abendländische Eschatologie: Ad Jacob Taubes*, ed. Richard Faber, Eveline Goodman-Thau, and Thomas Macho (Würzburg: Königshausen & Neumann, 2001), 447–464.

11. Adler discusses this time in his life in H. G. Adler, "Erinnerungen an den Philosophen Erich Unger," *Eckart* 3 (1960): 182–185, reprinted in *Erich Unger: Politik und Metaphysik*, ed. Manfred Voigts (Würzburg: Königshausen & Neumann, 1989), 65–69. For a brief biography of Adler, see Jeremy Adler, "February 8, 1942: H. G. Adler Is Deported to Theresienstadt and Begins His Life Work of Writing a Scholarly Testimony to His Experience," in *Yale Companion to Jewish Writing and Thought in German Culture 1096–1996*, ed. Sander L. Gilman and Jack Zipes (New Haven, CT: Yale University Press, 1997), 600–605. See also Julia Creet, Sara R. Horowitz, and Amira Bojadzija-Dant, eds., *H. G. Adler: Life, Literature, Legacy* (Evanston, IL: Northwestern University Press, 2016). The meetings of the Philosophische Gruppe began in 1927 and ended in the spring of 1933 when many of the Jewish regulars left Germany. Unger himself took his family to Prague, then Paris, and finally settled in London where, after the war, he renewed his friendship with H. G. Adler. At the sessions of the Philosophische Gruppe, Erich Unger would lecture on various topics of contemporary philosophic interest. Oskar Goldberg was always present and would sometimes contribute to the discussion. Manfred Voigts reproduces a personal letter of Esther Ehrman, Erich Unger's daughter, in which she lists the names of those who at one time or another attended her father's lectures. They include Alfred Döblin, Hans Reichenbach, and Carl Schmitt. See Manfred Voigts, "Ergänzungen und Korrekturen zum Goldberg-Buch," August 1995, included in later print runs of Manfred Voigts's *Oskar Goldberg*. See also Adler, "Erinnerungen an Erich Unger," esp. p. 68.

12. H. G. Adler, *Theresienstadt, 1941–1945: Das Antlitz einer Zwangsgemeinschaft*, 2nd ed. (Tübingen: J. C. B. Mohr, 1960), 666.

13. H. G. Adler, *Vorschule für eine Experimentaltheologie* (Stuttgart: Franz Steiner, 1987). For a discussion of Unger's influence on Adler, see Manfred Voigts, "H. G. Adler und Erich Unger: Versuch eines Zugangs zur 'Vorschule für eine Experimentaltheologie,'" in Manfred Voigts, *Jüdische Geistesarbeit und andere Aufsätze über Jakob Frank bis H. G. Adler* (Würzburg: Königshausen & Neumann, 2016), 381–402.

14. Adler, *Vorschule*, 92.

15. One should add to this short list an unpublished essay of Erich Unger about Goldberg that was translated into English by Unger's daughter, Esther Ehrman: Esther Ehrman, "Erich Unger's 'The Natural Order of Miracles': I. The Pentateuch and the Vitalist Myth," *Journal of Jewish Thought and Philosophy* 11, no. 2 (2002): 135–152, and "Erich Unger's 'The Natural Order of Miracles': II. The World of Nature and Miracles in the Pentateuch," *Journal of Jewish Thought and Philosophy* 11, no. 2 (2002): 153–189. Unger's basic point is that Goldberg attempts to render mythic thought in the terms of a coherent biological theory that Unger dubs "extreme vitalism." There is a brief treatment of Goldberg in Judith Friedlander, "Religious Metaphysics and the Nation-State: The Case of Oskar Goldberg," *Social Research* 59, no. 1 (1992): 151–168.

16. Manfred Voigts, *Oskar Goldberg, der mythische Experimentalwissenschaftler: Ein verdrängtes Kaptiel jüdischer Geschichte* (Berlin: Agora, 1992) (hereafter *Oskar Goldberg*). Voigts also republished Goldberg's major work: Oskar Goldberg, *Die Wirklichkeit der Hebräer*, Wissenschaftliche Neuausgabe, ed. Manfred Voigts (Wiesbaden: Harrassowitz, 2005) (hereafter *Reality of the Hebrews*). Voigts has also edited a collection of Goldberg's other writings: Oskar Goldberg, *Zahlengebäude, Ontologie, Maimonides, und Aufsätze 1933 bis 1947* (Berlin: Königshausen & Neumann, 2013) (hereafter Goldberg-*Aufsätze*).

17. He writes this in 1921 in a letter to Felix von Luschan, professor of anthropology at the University of Berlin. I discuss the letter in more detail in the beginning of chapter 1. The letter is in the Luschan Nachlass at the Humboldt-Universität in Berlin. Manfred Voigts brought it to my attention and shared a photocopy with me.

18. Hans Driesch, "Entwicklungsmechanische Studien: I. Der Werthe der beiden ersten Furchungszellen in der Echinodermenentwicklung. Experimentelle Erzeugung von Theil- und Doppelbildungen. II. Über die Beziehungen des Lichtes zur ersten Etappe der thierischen Formbildung," *Zeitschrift für wissenschaftliche Zoologie* 53 (1891): 160–184, translated as "The Potency of the First Two Cleavage Cells in Echinoderm Development. Experimental Production of Partial and Double Formations," in *Foundations of Experimental Embryology*, ed. Benjamin H. Willier and Jane M. Oppenheimer (New York: Hafner Press, 1964), 38–50.

19. Georg Cantor, *Grundlagen einer allgemeiner Mannigfaltigkeitslehre: Ein matemathisch-philosophischer Versuch in der Lehre des Unendlichen* (Leipzig: Teubner, 1883).

20. The best synthetic history of this movement is found in Anne Harrington, *Reenchanted Science: Holism in German Culture from Wilhelm II to Hitler* (Princeton, NJ: Princeton University Press, 1996). Harrington does not discuss the development of the Cantorian mathematics of infinity in relation to German "holism."

21. For a good introduction to this new appropriation of Naturphilosophie vitalism, see Levi Bryant, Nick Srnicek, and Graham Harman, eds., *The Speculative Turn: Continental Materialism and Realism* (Melbourne: re.press, 2011).

22. Mark Antliff, *Inventing Bergson: Cultural Politics and Parisian Avant-Garde* (Princeton, NJ: Princeton University Press, 1993); Donna V. Jones, *The Racial Discourses of Life Philosophy:*

*Négritude, Vitalism, and Modernity* (New York: Columbia University Press, 2010); Pheng Cheah, *Spectral Nationality: Passages of Freedom from Kant to Postcolonial Literatures of Liberation* (New York: Columbia University Press, 2003). I should also mention the important anthology *Understanding Bergson, Understanding Modernism*, ed. Paul Ardoin, S. E. Gontarski, and Laci Mattison (London: Bloomsbury, 2013).

23. The typescript is titled "Something of Human Interest." It is found in the Deutsches Literaturarchiv Marbach (DLM) Goldberg Nachlass, Kasten (box) 8. It does not seem to have ever been published, although it probably was intended for the *New York Spiritualist Leader*. Although it opens with a description of Goldberg's early Kabbalistic training, the main focus of the three-page essay is to explain why the work he is conducting on ghost photography is important for establishing proper relations between the "Occident" and the "Orient" (Goldberg specifically refers to Mongolia and Tibet): "The whole East has ancestry-cult, worship of the spirits of their ancestors. The cooperation with the Far East, especially Mongolia and Tibet, on the field of hauntings, is the political medium to establish a cultural friendship with the nations of the Far East."

24. After Goldberg came to the United States in 1941, he became active in the founding of the naturopathic National Medical University, based in San Francisco, as the president of its Educational Foundation and the developer of its three-year curriculum. In the Nachlass Goldberg in DLM, there is a lengthy typescript with the curriculum, demonstrating Goldberg's considerable knowledge of naturopathic medicine and its foundations in anatomy, endocrinology, and pharmacology. Goldberg seems never to have been a licensed practitioner of naturopathy, however.

25. Dora Hiller died in 1948 in the United States where she and Oskar had been living since 1941.

26. Voigts, *Oskar Goldberg*, 163.

27. Manfred Voigts, ed., *Jacob Taubes und Oskar Goldberg: Aufsätze, Briefe, Dokumente* (Würzburg: Königshausen & Naumann, 2011), 7.

28. When Goldberg and his wife arrived in the United States through the efforts of the American Rescue Committee, he went to the Institute for Social Research in New York and made certain that his close friend Adolf Caspary would also be able to leave the camp in southern France where he had been interned with Goldberg. See Manfred Voigts, "Oskar Goldberg und Thomas Mann: Die Revision eines Fehlurteils," in *Conditio Judaica: Judentum, Antisemitismus und deutschsprachige Literatur*, ed. Hans Otto Horch and Horst Denckler (Tübingen: Max Niemeyer, 1993), 366. Goldberg and Caspary were invited to France soon before the outbreak of the First World War by the anthropologist Marcel Mauss. See Marcel Fournier, *Marcel Mauss: A Biography*, trans. Jane Marie Todd (Princeton, NJ: Princeton University Press, 2006), 355.

29. For a full biography, see Voigts, *Oskar Goldberg*.

30. The only monograph devoted to Driesch in English is Horst Freyhofer, *The Vitalism of Hans Driesch: The Success and Decline of a Scientific Theory* (Frankfurt am Main: Peter Lang, 1982). For the best brief introduction to Hans Driesch in English, see Harrington, *Reenchanted Science*, 52–74 (in relation to Jakob von Uexküll) and 188–193 (for his opposition to Nazism). More recently, Jane Bennett has offered a nuanced appreciation of the significance of Driesch's vitalism as a precursor of the "new materialism." See Jane Bennett, *Vital Matter: A Political Ecology of Things* (Durham, NC: Duke University Press, 2010), 69–76. The most philosophically sophisticated exposition of Driesch can be found in Maurice Merleau-Ponty, *Nature: Course Notes from the Collège de France 1956–1960*, trans. Robert Vallier (Evanston, IL: Northwestern University Press, 2003), 230–243.

31. Oskar Goldberg, *Die Fünf Bücher Mosis: Ein Zahlengebäude. Die Feststellung einer einheitlich durchgeführten Zahlenschrift* (Berlin: 1908). Reprinted in Goldberg-*Aufsätze*, 21–68.

32. Walter Benjamin, letter to Gerhard Scholem, January 1921, in *Briefe: Band I, 1914–1947,* ed. Gershom Scholem and Theodor Adorno (Frankfurt am Main: C. H. Beck, 1994), 252 (translation mine). In the same letter, Benjamin says that he "has a very lively interest" in Unger's ideas, especially insofar as they "come surprisingly close" to his own reflections about the "psycho-physical problem" (253). (The full English translation of the letter is found in Scholem and Adorno, *The Correspondence of Walter Benjamin*, 172–175.)

33. Goldberg, *Reality of the Hebrews*, 176.

34. In a personal correspondence (email, March 3, 2012), the Jewish Studies scholar (Arizona State University) Hava Tirosh-Samuelson recalls her teacher's attitude to Scholem toward the end of his career: "As a student of Gershom Scholem, I remember the deep disdain and even hatred he had toward Oscar Goldberg."

35. Scholem, *From Berlin to Jerusalem*, 147.

36. Scholem, letter 145 to Lionel Kochan (in English), in *Briefe: Band III, 1971–1982*, ed. Itta Schedletzky (Munich: C. H. Beck, 1999), 161.

37. But we cannot merely dismiss Goldberg, as Scholem does, as a "confidence man" (*Hochstapler*). I previously mentioned that the Viennese historian of religion Robert Eisler, a close friend of the Assyrologist Fritz Hommel who was Scholem's Doktorvater (dissertation supervisor), described Goldberg as a "learned and patient researcher" (*gelehrte und geduldige Forscher*). Eisler himself was deeply interested in mystical numerology and refers to Goldberg's research as "according to those in a position to judge, successful." However, he did not agree with Goldberg's conclusion, namely, that no human intelligence could have constructed the numerical structures. Scholem met Eisler and had a more respectful though equally suspicious attitude toward Eisler's scholarship as he had toward Goldberg's. Eisler edited the first two publications of Scholem for his series *Sources and Studies in the History of Jewish Mysticism*, the only two works that appeared in the series. For Scholem's account of his meeting with Eisler, see Gershom Scholem, *From Berlin to Jerusalem*, 126–130. Scholem visited Eisler because Fritz Hommel had mentioned that he and Eisler had founded a group devoted to the study of the Kabbalah (the University of Munich possessed an exceptional collection of Kabbalist texts). Interestingly, Goldberg reports (in an unpublished manuscript titled "Something of Personal Interest" in the Goldberg Nachlass in the Literaturarchiv Marbach) that during his time at the University of Munich he and Fritz Hommel had founded a group devoted to the study of number mysticism in the ancient Near East. It would be rather ironic if Scholem's earliest publications were published under the auspices of a group that Goldberg had a hand in creating.

38. Oskar Goldberg, *Maimonides: Kritik der jüdischen Glaubenslehre* (Vienna: Verlag Dr. Heinrich Glanz, 1935).

39. Ernst Jünger, Carl Schmitt, and Helmuth Kiesel, *Briefe 1930–1983* (Stuttgart: Klett-Cotta, 1999), 84.

40. Oskar Goldberg, "Die griechische Tragoedie," *Mass und Wert: Zweimonatschrift fuer Freie Deutsche Kultur* 1, no. 5 (1938): 728–752; quote on 751–752; emphasis Goldberg's. Reprinted in Goldberg-*Aufsätze*, 227–248.

41. Max Horkheimer and Theodore Adorno, *Dialectic of Enlightenment: Philosophical Fragments*, trans. Edmund Jephcott (Stanford, CA: Stanford University Press, 2002), 193.

42. Georges Canguilhem, *Knowledge of Life*, trans. Todd Meyers (New York: Fordham University Press, 2008), 73; originally published in 1952 as *La connaissance de la vie* (Paris: Hachette).

43. Given her interest in the relationship between artifact and organism, I would expect that Scarry was familiar with Canguilhem's important treatment of the history and theory of the artifact in works he published well before her 1985 *Body in Pain*.

44. For a discussion of Mann's debt to Goldberg, see Voigts, *Oskar Goldberg*, 235–270. See also, for a view that differs from Voigts's of Mann's ultimate verdict that Goldberg was "a typical Jewish fascist" (if such a person could be "typical"), Christian Hühlhörster, *Ein "jüdische Diener der faschistischen Epoche"? Oskar Goldberg und Thomas Mann* (Paris: Didier, 2004).

45. Manfred Voigts, *Oskar Goldberg: Ein Dossier* (Munich: Carl Hanser, 1989), 54.

# TRANSFINITE LIFE

# 1 Hans Driesch and the Revival of Naturphilosophie

WE MAY BEGIN this chapter with Oskar Goldberg's own brief piece, "The Development of Biology." Goldberg wrote this essay for the English-language publication *Science and Culture* when he was living in the United States. At the opening of the essay Goldberg writes, "Since the times of the ancient Greeks there are two trends in biology, the science of life: mechanism and vitalism."[1] Goldberg claims that in his day "vitalism has conquered by the weight of the fact."[2] He briefly characterizes the transition from Aristotle's vitalism to Cartesian mechanism and the return to vitalism with the work of the biologist Hans Driesch. Driesch's vitalism rests on his discovery, which I describe in more detail below, that after the first mitosis of the fertilized sea-urchin egg, the cells remain "pluripotent," that is, they can each become a full organism if separated properly from one another. This discovery led Driesch to postulate a non-mechanical principle present within the cells that he called the "entelechy." This is a term that Driesch takes from Aristotle, so it would seem that biology had come round to its origins. But Goldberg asks at the end of the essay, "Is it actually true that we came back again to Aristotle?" He answers: "No, it is not. We have gone much, much further back. We have gone back many thousands of years to the primeval thought of the Kabbalah. . . . The experiments of Driesch are an excellent proof of the ancient Kabbalistic thought. It seems to be that the Kabbalistic sentence to which we refer is completely unknown.[3] Therefore we want to quote it here: 'The whole is not the sum of its parts. There is not the sum alone and the part alone. Truly, that is so: *the whole is contained in any of its parts.*'"[4]

The principle that the whole is not the sum of its parts is, I argue in what follows, the essential axiom of Naturphilosophie. Hans Driesch, as Goldberg points out, led the way in making this holistic axiom the guiding principle of a new era in the science of biology. Driesch himself probably did not know of the connection between his holistic biology and "ancient Kabbalistic thought," but he was definitely aware that he was returning to biology's roots in early nineteenth-century Naturphilosophie. The resurgence of Naturphilosophie that Driesch led in the last decade of the nineteenth century and the early decades of the twentieth has received less attention from historians of science than it deserves.[5] Without understanding this renewed interest in Naturphilosophie we cannot appreciate

Oskar Goldberg's rather audacious attempt to fuse Kabbalah with Driesch's vitalist biology. In this chapter I thus trace the rebirth of Naturphilosophie in Germany.

A letter of Oskar Goldberg written in 1922 offers further evidence not only of Goldberg's own interest in Naturphilosophie but also of its growing importance at that time.[6] Goldberg wrote the letter to the University of Berlin anthropologist Felix von Luschan in 1922 asking him to be his faculty sponsor on a dissertation. Goldberg hypothesized that individuals with exceptional psychic and physiological powers ("holy men") were at the center of the formation of the ethnic groups making up the archaic world of humanity.[7] Goldberg explains that he had gathered data on the exceptional physiological control shown by a certain yogic practitioner he had met in Geneva before the outbreak of the First World War and by other such religious adepts during a military-diplomatic trip to Indian Tibet at the beginning of the war. Von Luschan declined to be Goldberg's dissertation sponsor, suggesting that Goldberg's work, since it seemed more concerned with religious sectarianism than anthropology proper, might fit better within the Philosophy faculty, perhaps with Ernst Troeltsch as sponsor.

Goldberg's letter in response to von Luschan's rejection is quite interesting. In reply to von Luschan's point that environmental and climatic conditions are more important than religious factors in the formation of ethnicities, Goldberg writes that the question about the relative importance of environment and physiology in ethnicity formation is related to the "philosophical dispute between mechanism and vitalism." He then adds, "In the natural-philosophical circles with which my position is closely associated [*In naturphilosophischen Kreisen, denen ich nahestehe*], the present view is that when it comes to the processes that maintain life the mechanistic factor lies much more at its basis than does the vitalistic factor, but that when it comes to the origin of life the prospects of mechanistic explanation grow dimmer as we acquire deeper insights into the unities of cellular structure." Goldberg goes on to explain that he personally believes that the chasm separating the organic from the inorganic is not as great as the vitalists believe, because even molecular interactions cannot be explained entirely on mechanistic principles as "the effects of a part on the surrounding elements." He asks, "Why is it, for example, that the atomic complex 12, carbon, has the inherent capacity to form an interlocking chain in the special way it does?" Goldberg then claims, "This capacity cannot be produced by the atomic environment; it arises far more from the inwardness of the carbon atom itself [*aus dem Innern des Kohlenstoffatoms selbst*]." Goldberg concludes, "There is an autonomy not only in organic nature but also in inorganic nature, an inner specificity of lawfulness [*eine innere Eigengesetzlichkeit*], and it seems to me that the question concerning the cause of atomic properties is in principle no different than the question concerning the number 30, why it possesses the number theoretical properties that it does, properties that no prior nor later number possesses." Since even the properties of inorganic objects cannot be explained on mechanistic principles, all the more must "organisms possess inner form-building capacities, and this is the significance of the physiological factor" in the construction of ethnicities. Although Goldberg hopes to persuade von Luschan that his dissertation does in fact lie within the discipline of anthropology and that Troeltsch would not be an appropriate dissertation advisor, he concludes his response with a possible "solution" (*Ausweg*) that perhaps von Luschan would help him with: "In this connection [doing the dissertation in Philosophy], I would like to mention that a solution does present itself, but it still would require your good offices if it were to have a hope of success. The disciple of Professor Stumpf, the psychologist Professor Köhler, is currently lecturing on Naturphilosophie and is holding natural philosophical seminars. It is perhaps not entirely out of the question that he might consider my work even in its present form as a piece of natural philosophy." Carl Stumpf, a student of Franz Brentano, was not only Wolfgang Köhler's teacher; he was also the supervising director of Edmund Husserl's dissertation. In fact, Husserl dedicated his 1900 *Logische Untersuchungen* (*Logical Investigations*) to Carl Stumpf. The intersection of phenomenological psychology and vitalist Naturphilosophie in the early decades of the century had become by 1922, when Goldberg is writing to Luschan, one of the most productive areas of work in German philosophy and psychology, especially at the University of Berlin. Husserl himself began to be centrally concerned with the phenomenology of animal life.

Erich Unger, Goldberg's slightly younger friend and closest philosophical ally, was also committed to the renewal of Naturphilosophie. In an undated letter quoted in a biographical note appended to his posthumously published *Das Lebendige und das Goettliche* (*The Living and the Divine*), Unger explicitly states that he hopes to carry forward the goal of the Naturphilosophie of the early "romantic" thinkers like Schelling and Goethe, only in a more methodologically exacting and scientifically informed manner.[8] Unger's book, although it was published posthumously in 1966, was written around 1940. It shows the unmistakable traces of Unger's deep engagement with Driesch and the phenomenological vitalism of the 1920s. Unger's description of the unity of life nicely captures one of the basic themes of what I call "neo-Naturphilosophie." It also shows clearly how far removed neo-Naturphilosophie was from Nietzschean *Lebensphilosophie*.

> The living in the world is an actual unitary object throughout all *biological* formations. It is reproduced in the living wave of the generations. This unity encompasses all the species and forms of living things, and thus the living in the world is a total-object (*Gesamtgegenstand*). It is not a concept that is displayed in each species, the concept of life "in general," that constitutes this real unity in the sense of a total-object. It is not some postulated real Platonic universal or hypostasis, an idea or an immaterial image or immobile paradigm

beyond space. The unity is the actual tidal wave of life that is formed from the numberless generations of species. It courses throughout the ages of the world. It is a total-object because it has arisen from something unitary in reality (*etwas Einheitliches in der Wirklichkeit*), the primary and proper referent of the term "the living." It may be that this something has released one species after another or it may be that it provides the starting point for all species out of a common, self-differentiating originary organism. It the task of logic to describe the image of this total-object in all its details and to distinguish it from mere concepts or universals in the platonic sense with which it is often confused.[9]

What Unger here is describing as "the common, self-differentiating originary organism" is what the embryologist and philosopher Hans Driesch, as I explain in what follows, calls the "entelechy of entelechies." For Naturphilosophie and neo-Naturphilosophie alike, evolution, properly understood, is the unfolding of a single unitary life principle, a super-entelechy, throughout all the branches of life's phylogenetic tree. The philosopher F. W. J. Schelling (1775–1854) is generally credited with providing the theoretical foundations of Naturphilosophie in a number of works written from 1798 to 1810. Alexander von Humboldt, perhaps the greatest German scientist of that era, endorsed Schelling's Naturphilosophie and provided a succinct formulation of its guiding principle: "to arrive at a higher point of view, from which all formations and forces reveal themselves as one, living, internally active whole of nature. Nature is not a dead aggregate. She is 'for the enthusiastic researcher,' as Schelling expressed it in his wonderful essay on the plastic arts, 'the holy, eternally creative, primary force of the world, who actively generates and produces all things out of her self.'"[10]

The biologist Lorenz Oken (1779–1851) took Schelling's Naturphilosophie further than any other scientist of the day. Oken provided a detailed vision of what a philosophically grounded science of life would look like, with his extraordinary attempt, following the Aristotelian principle of taxonomy adumbrated in *De anima*, to organize all living forms in accordance with variations in the relative strengths and weaknesses of the organism's sensorium—from touch (the lowest sensory modality) through vision (the highest). Following Schelling's lead, Oken formulated his taxonomic system within the framework of an idealist metaphysics based on the polarity of a positive, centrifugal principle (identified with light in the natural world) and a negative, centripetal principle (gravity). This polarity arises from out of an undifferentiated condition (pure Identity) in which the polarity is only a latent potentiality. As the polarity emerges into actuality, there evolves a proliferation of ever more complexly balanced configurations of the positive and negative forces, from the mineral world (where crystalline shapes reflect the positive-negative balance) up through plants and animals. Not unlike the Leibnizian world of monads within monads, Oken's universe is a harmoniously balanced system in which each part refracts the whole at various levels of perfection.

Oken published a concise version of his system in his 1802 *Foundations of the Philosophy of Nature.*[11] In 1810 he completed the first edition of his massive *Handbook of the Philosophy of Nature*, a collection of 3,652 numbered paragraphs beginning with the derivation of all numbers from zero (with *plus one* and *minus one* representing the latent polarity in zero) and concluding with a description of how "man expresses the ultimate goal or purpose of Nature's design."[12] In the preface to the third edition of 1843, Oken summarizes his systematic classification of living things into five fundamental orders of advancing complexity, each representing one of the five senses:

> The first principles of the present work I laid down in my small pamphlet entitled *Grundriss der Naturphilosophie*. . . . I still abide by the position there taken, namely, that the Animal Classes are virtually nothing else than a representation of the sense-organs, and that they must be arranged in accordance with them. Thus, strictly speaking, there are only 5 Animal Classes: Dermatozoa [*Haupthiere*], or the Invertebrata; Glossozoa [*Zungenthiere*], or the Fishes, as being those animals in whom a true tongue makes for the first time its appearance; Rhinozoa [*Nasenthiere*], or the Reptiles, wherein the nose opens for the first time into the mouth and inhales air; Otozoa [*Ohrenthiere*], or the Birds, in which the ear for the first time opens externally; Ophthalmozoa [*Augenthiere*], or the Thricozoa [*Haarthiere*], in whom all the organs of sense are present and complete, the eyes being moveable and covered with two palpebrae or lids.[13]

At the pinnacle of the fifth and highest order (*Augenthiere*) stands the human being. The human being is the microcosm of the entire system of living things, "the universal portion of nature."[14] Falling short of human perfection, all other animals are "irregular men."[15] Since Oken believed that the embryonic development of each organism went through the stages of all "lower" orders, the human not only is the microcosm in which one can view the universal system of all living things but also human ontogenesis recapitulates the unfolding of the system from Dermatazoa to Ophthalmazoa.

Throughout his decades-long career at the University of Jena, Lorenz Oken remained a towering figure within German biological science. Stephen Jay Gould has described him as "one of the best comparative anatomists and embryologists of his day; his embryology of the pig and the dog (1806) are classics."[16] By the late nineteenth century, however, the case for orthodox Darwinism had triumphed over Oken's philosophical taxonomy based on the model of the human sensorium. The Darwinian Ernst Haeckel became the reigning scientific figure at the University of Jena (and, indeed, Germany as a whole). Oken's idealist Naturphilosophie and its sensorial taxonomy of living forms were dismissed as nothing more than fanciful speculation. They were dismissed, that is, until Hans Driesch returned to Oken's work and once again sought to provide an idealist foundation for the science of biology.

It is generally believed that Naturphilosophie met its demise in the middle of the nineteenth century with the rise of the positivist model of explanation in the physical and chemical sciences and with the emergence of Darwin's explanation of evolution on the basis of random phenotypical change and the survival of the fittest. But Naturphilosophie did not entirely succumb to these forces: it underwent a significant revival in the late nineteenth century that continued well into the early decades of the twentieth century. This revival included many of the most respected scientists of the period, Hans Driesch most notably. The philosopher Theodore Ziehen in 1922 wrote a monograph titled *Grundlagen der Naturphilosophie* (*Foundations of the Philosophy of Nature*) with the aim of explaining and supporting the "revitalization of the investigations of Naturphilosophie" [*Wiederbelebung der naturphilosophischen Untersuchungen*].[17] The Nobel laureate in chemistry for 1909, Wilhelm Ostwald (1853–1932), founded the journal *Annalen der Naturphilosophie* in 1902. The journal continued for ten years, publishing articles written by many of the major scientists and philosophers of the period, including Ernst Mach, Friedrich Ratzel, Victor Goldschmidt, Max Planck, Hans Driesch, and Wilhelm Fliess.

The willingness of the leading scientific minds of the day to engage in wide-ranging philosophical speculations about metaphysical questions, such as the origin of life and the nature of consciousness, testifies to the renewed significance of Naturphilosophie. Ostwald himself wrote a systematic presentation of the new Naturphilosophie in *Grundriss der Naturphilosophie* (*Outline of Naturphilosophie*) in 1908 in which he expressed his hope that "all the countless specialized fields of science would be brought together under a single, common guiding perspective so that their individual achievements could be brought into connection with the collective striving of all humankind."[18] What Ostwald appreciated about early nineteenth-century Naturphilosophie and what he sought to revive was its commitment to the unification of the natural and human sciences. The revival of Naturphilosophie in the life sciences was an attempt to overturn the apparent triumph of mechanistic models of explanation that left no room for the holistic and purpose-oriented expressions of a creative and living cosmos. But the revival of Naturphilosophie as reflected in Ostwald's *Annalen der Naturphilosophie* extended also into all areas of science, and it reflected the wider dissatisfaction (expressed particularly by Ostwald in chemistry and Ernst Mach in physics) with mechanistic models (of a rigid atom, for example) that seemed unable to accommodate the fluid properties of thermodynamic energy transformations.[19]

The revival of Naturphilosophie in the early twentieth century made its impact even on the leading school of philosophy at the time, neo-Kantianism. Ernst

Cassirer, Hermann Cohen's most brilliant student, published a major study of Leibniz in 1902 in which he argued that Leibniz's postulation of an infinitely reticulated universe of immortal monads is the inspiration lying behind modern mathematics and science:[20]

> Immortality had until Leibniz meant the transcending of the natural conditions of life, lifting human existence into a realm disconnected from birth and death. But Leibniz's introduction of the concept of immortality into the entire realm of the living meant that the boundary separating mortal life and immortality collapsed. Human existence was subject to the same laws as applied throughout nature. So the concept of immortality, which had been most intimately bound up with theology, became in Leibniz's philosophy the starting point of modern scientific rationality. . . . In the new direction given to the study of nature by the idea of immortality, the same causality and the same forces are thought to be at work in nature and in the history of humanity.[21]

As Cassirer claims, Leibniz's idea that the universe is a single, all-embracing, and continuously ramifying *living* reality is nothing less than a revolutionary break with theology and the inauguration of science's ambition to bring all phenomena within a unified set of laws. The living organism, for Leibniz, is the model of the whole universe's dynamic system of causes and forces. For Cassirer, there is no reason for modern science to disavow its origins in Leibniz. Cassirer's summation of Leibniz's view of the whole of nature as a dynamic, living system is one that Cassirer himself endorses, and it is one that perfectly encapsulates one of the central tenets of Naturphilosophie in general—the irreducibility of the organism to a machine: "The organism preserves traces of the infinity and continuity of being within itself. We are never able to delimit and specify its operation within any given number of fixed conditions and parameters the way we can with a machine. Its dynamic operation calls into question every such specification."[22] Cassirer's book on Leibniz is a masterful exposition of the German philosopher's work, but it is also a declaration of Cassirer's allegiance to the revival of vitalist Naturphilosophie in his own day. Cassirer believes that a scientifically informed Naturphilosophie cannot accept the existence of a special "life force," but that nonetheless it is possible to build a secure scientific edifice on Leibniz's anti-Cartesian insight that organisms are not mere machines—that they are, on the contrary, a hierarchic structure of unities within more encompassing unities and that at every level there is a need to appeal to a totalizing form to explain the observable phenomena of life.

Why was there a return to Romantic Naturphilosophie at the end of the nineteenth century? In this book's conclusion, I return to this question and formulate an answer that places the resurgence of Naturphilosophie in relation to the emergence in the late industrial period of technology and the machine as the paradigm for how to understand the nature of living organisms. I argue that neo-Naturphilosophie and vitalism more generally respond not only to the overemphasis upon machinal models of explanation but also to the capitalist culture of commodified and depersonalized objects. In this chapter I will limit myself to tracing the intellectual roots of the revival of Naturphilosophie. In what follows I hope to show that the revival of Naturphilosophie is due in large part to the new interest in Aristotle among philosophers and psychologists in the middle decades of the nineteenth century. Perhaps the most significant figure in this new interest in Aristotle is Franz Brentano (1838–1917), who studied philosophy under the leading Aristotelian scholar of the day, Friedrich Adolf Trendelenburg (1802–1872). Trendelenburg's critical importance in the history of philosophy has until quite recently been largely unexplored.[23] Trendelenburg's influence on Brentano is well known, but he also left his mark on Hermann Cohen, who studied with him as well. My focus in this chapter is on Brentano's Aristotelian phenomenology as a philosophical grounding for vitalist holism. Brentano, as I explain, attempted to harmonize Aristotle's theory of perception with the latest developments in empirical psychology ("psychophysics") in the study of the smallest perceptible changes in a varying stimulus. Hermann Cohen's early work on the infinitesmal calculus and its connection with Kant's principle (the "anticipations of perception") that every sensation of what is real, regardless of its phenomenal content, is characterized by a certain intensive magnitude (a degree representing the integration of infinitesmal elements) can be viewed as paralleling Brentano's Aristotelian framework for understanding the new psychophysics. Both Brentano and Cohen believed that the sensory manifold was organized by a unifying psychic power. Brentano returned to Aristotle, and Cohen to Kant, to explain the nature of this cognitive power. Although limitations of space prevent me from doing proper justice to Hermann Cohen's place in the history of the revival of Naturphilosophie, I will discuss his student Ernst Cassirer in chapter 2.[24] Let us now turn to Brentano.

After publishing a major study on Aristotle's psychology and his theory of the *nous poietikos* (active intellect), Brentano turned his attention to the current field of experimental psychology. He found that Aristotle's ideas could be of significant value in understanding the nature of perception and the "psychophysical problem" more generally. "Psychophysics" was the name that Gustav Fechner (1801–1887) gave to his studies of the relationship between measurable intensities of external stimuli and response thresholds reported by experimental subjects.[25] Brentano connected the Aristotelian insight that the mind (*nous*) unified the parts of the sensory field to the psychophysical study of consciousness.[26] We will note later that neo-Naturphilosophie thinkers drew heavily from Brentano's work on the logic of the part–whole relationship. As I previously mentioned, one could aptly describe the fundamental axiom of Naturphilosophie throughout its history as the view that the whole of a living organism is greater than the sum of its parts. The positivist model of explanation in the physical sciences in the middle decades of the nineteenth century had no room for the axiom of Naturphilosophie. It was only when philosophically trained psychologists, following the lead of Brentano, began to do work on the phenomenology of perception that it gained renewed traction in science, most especially in the biological sciences. Brentano's renewal of Aristotelianism challenged the dominant paradigm of positivist reductionism in the psychological sciences of the day and helped pave the way for the renewal of Naturphilosophie around the turn of the twentieth century. Hans Driesch acknowledged the influence of Brentano in a number of his works. Before turning to Driesch, therefore, it is useful to briefly examine Franz Brentano's phenomenological psychology.

## Wholes and Parts: The Phenomenology of Franz Brentano

Franz Brentano is perhaps today best known today because of the illustrious group of students he taught. During his career at the University of Vienna, Brentano taught not only Edmund Husserl (1859–1938), but also Sigmund Freud (1856–1939), Alexius Meinong (1853–1920), and Christian von Ehrenfels (1859–1932).[27] Brentano's first doctoral student was Carl Stumpf (1848–1936), a psychologist and philosopher who carried forward Brentano's phenomenological project at the University of Berlin during Oskar Goldberg's (and Erich Unger's) student years in Berlin. Hans Driesch, although not a student of Brentano, turned to the work of the Brentano school in the field of mereology (the logic of part–whole relationships) to find an explanatory framework within which to understand how a part of an organism (the fertilized egg) could become a whole organism and also how the stages of evolution might constitute parts of a larger whole—planetary and even cosmic life—with its own laws of development.

Brentano himself was deeply interested in what might be called the logic of organic change. His work in mereology was built on his early study of Aristotelian logic, biology, and psychology.[28] Brentano participated in a renaissance of Aristotelianism in the middle decades of the nineteenth century (in addition to Friedrich Adolf Trendelenburg, Brentano's teacher, one can also mention Félix Ravaisson, Henri Bergson's teacher). We can best understand Brentano's Aristotelianism as a challenge to the regnant positivism of the era and, in the field of biology, to the anti-teleological model of evolution that Darwin had advanced. Aristotle held that the living organism was a substantial whole comprised of two parts, form and matter, neither of which was separable from the other (except for the *nous*, or intellect, of the human being). Brentano adopted Aristotle's concept of organic substance as the basis for a general logic based on separable and inseparable part–whole relations. Brentano's return to an Aristotelian theory of organic substance as a whole comprised of inseparable parts pointed the way for Driesch's concept of organic wholeness [*Ganzheit*] that, Driesch thought, would better fit the facts of embryological development than the model of preformation with its postulation of molecular-level separable parts as "determinants" of cellular differentiation.

Brentano's influence extended quite far in turn-of-the-century German philosophy and psychology, including, as I have mentioned, to Edmund Husserl and Sigmund Freud. Brentano's heirs attempted to escape from the reductionism of positivist science and positivist psychology in particular by stressing the irreducibility of the wholeness of the object that is given in consciousness: the "inner presentation," as Brentano called it, is not merely a mechanical assemblage or additive sum of independent parts.[29] The heirs of Brentano wanted philosophy to do more than offer an account of the conditions of possibility of scientific knowledge, the task that most neo-Kantians claimed as their philosophical burden.[30] Brentano and his heirs hoped that philosophy could make an important contribution to our understanding of *lived* experience in its qualitative irreducibility to physico-chemical processes.[31] The science of acoustics, for example, might be able to explain how sound was propagated through air, but philosophy might hope to explain what it was like to *hear* a sound. In Brentano's appropriation of Aristotle's theory of perception, the way an object is presented to consciousness involves the reception of what Aristotle called "sensible forms." For example, one perceives Socrates sitting, that is, the *whole* consisting of a substance (man) and an accident (sitting) inhering in the substance as a part. One can say that for Brentano one *perceives* the content of the predicative judgment, "Socrates is sitting," as a whole. Brentano thus speaks of the *intentionality* of our perception of objects: perception is *directed toward a meaning* and is not reducible to sensible "simples" composed of, say, colors and shapes. In her recent book on Brentano, *Immanent Realism*, Lilliana Albertazzi explains that, in Brentano's theory of perception, "the act of presentation takes the form of a *whole* endowed with *parts* and *moments* of various kinds (objects, characteristic notes, aspects, modes of presentation and modes of recognition, formal and material connections among the parts, etc.) whose totality, however, amounts to something more than, and different from their arithmetic sum. Inner presentation is not *an extensional whole* where it is the parts that determine the whole according to some principle of composition; it is, in fact, the reverse."[32] Albertazzi underscores the different ontological relationships that obtain in "extensional" totalities where "parts determine the whole" and in those in which "the existence of the whole precedes the existence of the parts, which are *such* only in relation to the whole to which they pertain."[33] The latter kind of wholes, what Brentano calls "integral" wholes, includes not only the content of "intentional" presentations of such objects as "Socrates sitting" but also "intensive" magnitudes like color, since the color red, for example, is not perceived to be redder simply by enlarging the color field. We will see later that Driesch's vitalism draws inspiration from Brentano's theory of the ontological difference between part-determined (extensive) totalities and whole-determined totalities (both intentional and "intensive").

Brentano and his heirs pursue the phenomenological method to demonstrate the ontological irreducibility of integral totalities to their parts. Using the empirical data provided by phenomenological introspection, they seek to find an alternative to the reductionism of positivist science in which all wholes are explained entirely in terms of the nature of their component parts. Yet the positivist goal of reducing wholes to their component parts was contested not only in phenomenological psychology but also in biology, especially in the subfield of embryology. Hans Driesch's experimental successes in his battle against positivist reductionism in the field of embryology legitimated a return to the "axiom of Naturphilosophie" on the part of many biological researchers. The story of the emergence and success of Driesch's neo-Naturphilosophie will occupy us in the next sections of the chapter, but a few more words about Brentano's phenomenology are in order here, in particular his application of phenomenology to the question of the relationship between mind and body, the so-called psychophysical problem. This problem and Brentano's proposed solution to it were of central importance to the young Oskar Goldberg and Erich Unger, as I show in chapter 3.

I mentioned earlier that Brentano's Aristotelian phenomenology sought to provide an account of consciousness that could resolve the problem about how mind (*Geist*) and body (*Körper*) interact. Throughout his career, Brentano returned again and again to Aristotle's concept of substance as the whole of form and matter in order to understand the ontological basis for the mind-body relation as an aspect of the substantial unity of the human person.[34] Brentano's first formulation of the mind–body relationship in his early but very influential work, *Die Psychologie des Aristoteles* (1867), sets the basic framework for his later thinking.[35] The organic body functions in its material self-maintenance and self-regeneration as a single whole. The way that the parts are integrated into the whole is defined by a formal principle that is inseparable from its material base. In a plant, nutrition and growth are the primary organic functions, and the "vegetative soul" of the plant is indistinguishable from activities that bind the parts of the plant together into a whole. In the animal, sensations provide the organism with a connection to the external world in which the animal moves, primarily in search of nutrition but also to satisfy its other desires (pursuit of a mate, shelter, and so on). With the emergence of the simplest sense organs, the animal body remains a whole, albeit a more complex one. Sensations or *phantasmata* are not separable from the material base of the sense organs. In much the same way that greenness is part of a green leaf, greenness is part of the sense organ. For Aristotle, in fact, the two greennesses are one and the same thing realized in two different material substances.

In humans, *phantasmata* can be the material of further elaboration, so that not only is the human mind (*nous*) able to recognize that greenness is a species of the genus *color* and the higher genus *quality* but also the human mind is self-reflexive and able to perceive the seeing of color as an activity in its own right. Other animals are incapable of such abstract and self-reflexive cognitive acts. The human mind has both a receptive aspect (through which it can be affected by the *phantasmata* of the sense organs) and an active aspect (through which it raises the *phantasmata* into objects of abstract intellection, manipulation, and systematic organization into the scientific knowledge of nature). The receptive and active aspects of the mind are parts of the holistic functioning of the living human being, but the active mind (*nous poietikos*) poses the most vexing problem when it comes to the mind-body relationship. All the other aspects of the soul are shared with plants (nutrition, growth) and the other animals (perception, desires for food, mate, shelter). There is no real difficulty about understanding how the whole animal is involved in all these activities. But the active mind is where it seems that unextended, abstract qualities (greenness apart from any material substance) seem to come into existence as a different ontological entity from the *phantasmata* of the sense organs. The active mind, also, seems to be a different ontological entity, something that possibly could exist apart from the body of the human person.

What is the relationship between the active mind (*nous poietikos*) and the body? This question takes us to the heart of the psychophysical problem. In answering this question, Brentano develops Aristotle's theory of the soul in a controversial direction that later Aristotelian scholars have disputed. I am not interested in pursuing this dispute, but Brentano's solution of the psychophysical problem through his innovative interpretation of the *nous poietikos* is critical for understanding the development of Driesch's vitalism, as well as Goldberg's ontological theories, discussed in chapter 3.[36] Brentano argues that Aristotle believes that a human being's active mind *is a part of the whole of God's mind*. The active mind lifts *phantasmata* existing in the sense organs at the ontological threshold between matter and mind and raises them into the domain of thinking. The *phantasmata* have within themselves the potential for such treatment; greenness already contains within itself the higher genera of color and quality. The active mind transforms sensible qualities into abstract ones not by the process of comparison and generalization *but by a process of actualizing or illuminating their abstractness*. The human's *nous poietikos* grasps *phantasmata* as the divine mind does, and in doing so, the active mind realizes the power of the divine mind. Thus the active mind is the interface between nature and God. The mind-body problem is solved, both for Aristotle and for Brentano (who remained committed to an Aristotelian-Thomistic theology throughout his life), only by invoking a divine power that infuses the world in all its parts with a holistic force that draws matter into, first, the vegetative existence of the plant world, then the movement-capable animals with sense organs and *phantasmata*, and finally humans with minds that can abstract from the particularity of the *phantasmata* to reach both conscious self-awareness and ultimately the cognition of all of nature and of God himself. In Brentano's theologically tinged phenomenology we see the return of early nineteenth-century Naturphilosophie, but this time based on a more experimentally justified introspective psychology.

In a remarkable passage, Brentano explains how the active mind of God is responsible for transforming in an instant the potential human in the form of a fetus into a full human being in whom the active mind is present:

> The intellective part [another way of referring to the *nous poietikos*] of the human being must enter the fetus from the divine [*von der Gottheit*], and herewith, through its development, the fetus will reach its completeness as a human body. For just as the human soul cannot exist without the intellective part, so the human body is what it is only through the human soul, and therefore it is in the very same instant when the psychic part from the divinity [*der geistige Teil von der Gottheit*] is united with the body into a substance that the human body first becomes a human body and a new actual human being comes into being.[37]

Brentano explains that the moment of transformation when the fetus becomes human does not occur at conception. Instead, the fetus goes through a vegetative stage and then an animal phase until it is prepared to achieve its human form: "Only after it has passed through and shared in a vegetative and then a sensitive life, does the fetus arrive at the disposition by means of which, after the entrance of the psychic part, the production of a unified, psychic-bodily [*geistig-leiblich*] substance is possible."[38]

Brentano's discussion of Aristotle's psychology characterizes the psychophysical problem as the intersection of two themes: the consciousness of *phantasmata* as wholes with both sensory-concrete and abstract-ideal aspects (this is the process that Husserl, for example, later focuses on) and the morphogenesis of the human body from conception to birth (this will be Driesch's focus). For Brentano, both themes are interconnected. Transforming sensory data into abstract scientific structures and transforming the animal fetus into a distinctly human one are both accomplished through a noetic power that operates to bring order and form to the material world. We could say that the solution to the psychophysical problem required attention to the part–whole relationship as it is constituted in consciousness and as it directs the emergence of consciousness. For Brentano, the ultimate part–whole relationship was that between nature and God's mind. Brentano's theological concerns took a backseat in most of his later work (although they do resurface in his last writings on Aristotle), as did the question of the emergence of consciousness in embryological morphogenesis. Most of Brentano's students also distanced themselves from his theology and embryology, or the *theology of embryology*. But Hans Driesch, beginning with embryology, found his way to phenomenology and ultimately to theology, in large part inspired by Brentano (although he was not his student). Like Brentano, Driesch turned to Aristotle to find an answer to the particular problem that was puzzling him. In Brentano's case, the problem was the psychophysical relationship. In Driesch's case, the problem was how a single-celled fertilized egg can morph into a complex, multi-cellular organism. Brentano found help in answering his question in Aristotle's *nous poietikos*; Driesch found his answer in Aristotle's entelechy.

Before turning to Driesch in the next section, I want to connect what we have so far discussed with Oskar Goldberg. We will see in subsequent chapters that Goldberg and his friend and disciple Erich Unger, like many others of their generation, saw the psychophysical problem as the essential problem of philosophy. Unlike almost everyone else, however, they believed that the problem could never be satisfactorily addressed on only one level. They insisted that the resolution of the problem required the resources of biology (embryology and phylogeny), phenomenology (the study of the intentional objects of consciousness, especially of the imagination or fantasy), and also theology. It would not be going too far to say that Goldberg and Unger were among the most faithful heirs to Brentano's early attempt to offer a synthetic and *organic* vision of the vital interrelations among God, humanity, and nature. It should therefore not come as any surprise to learn that Walter Benjamin, who shared some of their interest in solving the psychophysical problem through phenomenology (it seems he was mostly influenced by Husserl), saw in Erich Unger someone who was working essentially on identical problems and coming to very similar conclusions.[39] I return to Benjamin's relationship with the Goldberg circle in chapter 5, but for the moment it is important to note how deeply immersed all these thinkers were in what I described as the resurgence of Naturphilosophie. Hans Driesch, as I now explain in more detail, provides the model of how neo-Naturphilosophie strives to recreate an Aristotelian system on the foundations of modern biology, psychology, and metaphysics.

## Hans Driesch's Experiments with Sea Urchins

Any account of Driesch's vitalism must begin with his disagreement with August Weismann. Among the defenders of orthodox, "mechanistic," Darwinism, none was more outspoken than Weismann. Weismann believed that random alteration in what he called the "determinants" of the germ cell was the underlying cause at work in evolution. And the functioning of the determinants within the organism was, Weismann also thought, purely mechanical: separated determinant elements were like invisible machines churning out differentiated somatic cells from the chemical building blocks of the organism.

Weismann and other "developmental mechanists" hypothesized that embryonic morphogenesis was based on the gradual disaggregation of a complex molecular structure whose various parts would become the kernels of all the distinct cellular types found in the mature organism. This theory was called "preformationism." Driesch argued against Weismann for what was then called "epigenesis."[40] According to the epigenetic account of embryonic development, the multicellular complexity of a mature organism arises from a unicellular stage that is characterized by its "omnipotentiality," that is, its potentiality to develop into all of the different cell types. In the unicellular stage, there is no invisibly small "preformed" model of the complex adult directing the manufacturing of different cell types. Rather, there is a sort of generic possibility for differentiating into *any* of the cells, and this generic possibility grows into the specific structures and tissues of the organism in the development of the embryo. This movement from generic potentiality to specific actuality was, in the eighteenth century, called "evolution" ("rolling out") and later called "epigenesis." Where the preformationists imagined a tiny machine inside the fertilized egg that got divided up into different cell types (one part for an eye cell, another part for a muscle cell, for example) as the embryo matured, the epigeneticists imagined a vital power that shaped the embryo's development from omnipotential generic beginning to complexly differentiated end.

Driesch's training was in embryology, and he is recognized as one of the most important researchers of his day. His embryological studies in the 1880s tested the validity of the preformationist theory that Weismann, together with Wilhelm Roux (1850–1924), had recently advanced to explain the process of embryological development. After performing what are still considered to be groundbreaking experiments with sea urchin embryos in the hopes of confirming the Weismann-Roux theory, Driesch instead found himself forced by the results to reject preformationism. Driesch spent the remainder of his career working out a new model not only for embryological development (ontogenesis) but also for evolution as a whole (phylogenesis).

It would be hard to exaggerate the importance of the debate between the preformationists and the epigeneticists for the future history of evolutionary biology. We are today seeing a renewal of the debate, despite the fact that molecular biology seemed for some time to have settled the question in favor of the preformationist model (distinct gene sequences are responsible for cell type differentiation). Epigenetics, now understood as the "plasticity" of genes for variable kinds of expression or what Driesch called the "prospective potentiality" of the germ plasm, is acknowledged today to play a significant role not only in the ontogenesis of the organism but also in the evolution of new species. The debate today is certainly informed by a vastly increased understanding of the mechanisms at work at the cellular level, but the fundamental issue remains nearly the same.[41] The issue, as Wilhelm Roux phrased it in 1885, is this: "Is embryonic development . . . a new formation [*Neubildung*] of a manifold [*Mannigfaltigkeit*] or is it the coming-into-visibility [*Sichtbarwerden*] of a manifold that we had previously been unable to see?"[42] Roux chooses the second alternative as the only one compatible with a mechanistic understanding of how change occurs in the natural world. Given the conditions within which the fertilized ovum develops, the emergence of complexity, Roux believed, could only be explained if it already exists at the outset, albeit in a form that only models in miniature its final stage. Driesch opted for the plasticity of the germ cell, and his choice, despite being on the losing side for many decades, is now making a significant return in current biological theorizations of embryological development. I have more to say about this in what follows.

In 1888 Roux published results of experiments performed on the frog embryo that seemed to bear out his and Weismann's preformationist theories. Roux killed one of the two daughter cells after the first division of the fertilized frog egg and observed that a half-embryo developed; "it was as much half as if a fully formed embryo of a certain stage had been cut in two by a razor," as Driesch explains in one of his fullest accounts of his own theory of embryonic development, *The Science and Philosophy of the Organism*, a two-volume work written in English containing his Gifford Lectures delivered at the University of Aberdeen in 1906 and 1907.[43] Driesch undertook to confirm Roux's experiment, this time using sea urchin embryos rather than frog eggs, but his results were entirely the opposite of Roux's. Rather than killing one of the two cells of the embryo after its first division, Driesch shook the sea urchin embryo so that the cells separated. He discovered that each cell developed into a complete, although somewhat smaller, sea urchin. Driesch had shown that either of the two daughter cells of a fertilized sea urchin egg could become a full sea urchin. Normal embryonic development could be overridden by a indivisible *something* that survives the splitting of the embryo and that can create a living whole out of each of the embryo's halves. Driesch called this something a "prospective potency." At different stages of ontogenesis, this prospective potency narrows from an "omnipotential" (interestingly, we today call stem cells "pluripotent") stage where each cell can become the complete organism to a final stage where the differentiated cell can only generate another cell identical to itself. Driesch did take note of the fact that certain cells of the mature organism retain a prospective potency that is activated when, for example, a limb is severed and then regenerated (a phenomenon he observed in certain lizards). Although he considered regeneration to be another demonstration of the existence of a prospective potency that guides the development of the organism, his attention was focused on the more impressive morphogenesis involved in embryonic development from fertilized egg to complete organism.

Driesch's experiments with sea urchin embryos persuaded him that Weismann had to be wrong about the way that somatic cells develop from the fertilized egg. According to Weismann, each of the two daughter cells only contained half of the determinants, one receiving the frontal set and the other the dorsal set: a cell with only a set of frontal determinants could not produce a complete sea urchin. But this theory could not explain the results of Driesch's experiment. In contrast, Driesch argued that normally each of the two daughter cells would be responsible for the two major poles of the mature sea urchin, frontal and dorsal. If the omnipotential power of the fertilized egg could be reactivated in the separated daughter cells of the embryo after its first cell division, then invisible "determinants" could not be responsible for cell differentiation.

Rejecting Weismann's mechanistic account of ontogenesis, Driesch turned to vitalism. For him, vitalism's essential meaning was that life was "autonomous," a term Driesch used to capture the idea that life was indeed subject to laws, but that these laws were "peculiar to the phenomena in question." The view that the laws governing biological phenomena are not reducible to the laws that govern inorganic phenomena does not commit one to positing the existence of some immaterial entity that is responsible for this autonomy, such as a "soul" or a "life force." Driesch knew that previous vitalist theories had parted company with science's commitment to the regularity of law when they had hypothesized the existence of such entities. Driesch therefore returned to Aristotle's vitalism with its emphasis on the inseparability of form and matter in the organism. He adopted from Aristotle the term "entelechy" to name the informing and organizing principle at work in ontogenesis. As Driesch explained, the Greek term, coined by Aristotle, means "something that bears the end [*telos*] in itself." Since the end is the whole organism, Driesch's entelechy is a principle that is not itself a spatially separable part of the organism, but is present from the first stage of ontogenesis to the end and throughout the organism's life. It is revealed in the omnipotentiality of the early cells and also in the fully realized, harmoniously functioning organism. Driesch denies that it works the way efficient or mechanical causes do, by direct action. Rather, its only means of functioning is by inhibiting or not inhibiting certain processes in the organism. The entelechy conducts the organic symphony, as it were, but does not actually play any of the instruments of the organic orchestra.

Driesch's appeal to the notion of entelechy results from his struggle to account for the phenomena of epigenesis that he observed in his embryological studies: the reality of "newly built" complexity emerging over time. Biologists today no longer talk about "prospective potencies" or "omnipotentiality" or "entelechy," but they do invoke the concepts of epigenesis, plasticity, and the emergent properties of complex systems whose operation is not reducible to the laws governing the separate component elements of the system. Driesch did not know how a complex genome composed of DNA could be "something that bears the end in itself," but he would not be surprised to learn that this genetic "entelechy" was much more than an accumulation of parts, each possessing a one-to-one correspondence to a different cellular structure or function. The recent turn to epigenetics in biology, while it cannot be described as any kind of "vitalism," shares more with Driesch's epigeneticist account of ontogenesis than just the name. For example, the late biologist Robert Rosen describes the genome as a "network of interacting multistate elements whose characteristic features involve temporal patterns of expression."[44] Rosen, like Driesch, sharply distinguishes such a complex network from typical physical systems that he describes as purely "reactive": "It is hard to imagine an analog of this kind of encoding [in a complex network] for, say, a gas obeying the van der Waals equation."[45]

The field of what is today called "systems biology" studies the dynamic relations among the various systems of the organism, especially those at the cellular level, including gene regulation networks and protein interaction networks. These interacting networks can be mapped as a multidimensional "space of states" of complexly co-varying variables. A "space of states" is not the "real" space in which the cell is located, but a space of possible relations among the cell's changing systems. When graphed, it can resemble a topographic map whose rising and falling terrain plots the probable course of the system's dynamic transformations over time. Driesch, as we see later, speaks about the entelechy as "a relation of order and nothing else" and also as an "intensive manifold." These admittedly vague definitions of entelechy, I submit, point in the direction of what systems biology means by "space of states." One of Driesch's students, Ludwig von Bertalanffy, is credited by systems biologists with having established a major piece of the theoretical basis of systems biology, the "general theory of systems."[46] In a later section of this chapter I discuss some of von Bertalanffy's contemporaries who, in the 1920s, formed a group interested in "theoretical biology."

I emphasize the continuing significance of Driesch's anti-reductionism because many scientists are today rather dismissive of the vitalist tradition in biology, which may seem to lend support to the description one sometimes reads of Goldberg's biological theories—that they are "pseudoscientific"—when I associate him with early twentieth-century neo-Naturphilosophie. My point, however, is that Driesch's vitalism certainly cannot be dismissed as "pseudoscience" and that his anti-reductionist arguments for the "autonomy of life" remain relevant to this day. In the next section of the chapter I discuss Driesch's attempt to revive two of early nineteenth-century Naturphilosophie's most ambitious goals: to provide a complete taxonomy of all living forms and to demonstrate that the goal of all life is ultimately *the transcendence of death*. When Goldberg claimed that Driesch's holistic vitalism returned to the Kabbalah in his essay, "The Development of Biology," he was perhaps not entirely mistaken. In the second volume of *Philosophy and Science of the Organism* Driesch offers, tentatively to be sure, a theory of God's self-unfolding "reality" whose concluding expression would be nothing less than the redemption of all life from the vicissitudes of mortality. Driesch's most ambitious philosophical work is his *Wirklichkeitslehre (Theory of Reality)*,[47] a work that has much in common with Goldberg's *Reality of the Hebrews*. In the following section I sketch Driesch's metaphysical speculations about God's self-unfolding as he develops them in *Philosophy and Science of the Organism* and also *Theory of Reality*.

## Driesch's Metaphysics and the "Enigma Philosophicum" of Death

The first volume of Driesch's *Philosophy and Science of the Organism* concludes with a negative assessment of both Darwinian and Lamarckian theories of the evolution of the species. Driesch in fact refuses to describe them as theories of "evolution" properly understood, since the term "evolution" in biology, deriving as it does from the term "evolutio" that was used in the eighteenth century as a synonym for "epigenesis," should only be used to refer to change that is not accidental in nature but is rather entelechial (directed toward a final state). Even the most committed mechanist would never dream of describing the development of the embryo as a series of random changes in the embryo as it adapts to various alterations in its amniotic environment. Embryonic morphogenesis is unarguably shaped by an informing principle, whether we call it a nonspatial entelechy or the genome. Therefore Driesch chooses to describe Darwinian or Lamarckian theories as theories of "descent" or "transformism," rather than as theories of "evolution." His point is that each theory describes the necessary conditions for the emergence of a new species (changes in individuals that offer them an adaptive advantage), but it does not explain why these conditions operate in the first place. Why do new species emerge among some populations and not others? Is there an organizing principle that could explain why the evolutionary tree looks the way it does? Driesch argues that a proper theory of evolution would take the form of an "organic systematics" that would explain not just the mechanisms underlying the emergence of the species but also the ordering principle that accounts for when and where and in what temporal sequence these mechanisms are activated. Organic systematics would explain *the overarching entelechy behind evolution*. Just as Driesch believed that an entelechy is manifested in the process of embryonic ontogeny, he thought that it might also be found in the phylogenetic evolution of the species.

Driesch insists that it is important for biologists to at least ask "whether there could be found any principle of another type in the realm of synthetic a priori judgments which could allow an inherent sort of evolution of latent diversities."[48] He explains that in geometry, for example, it can be demonstrated (i.e., shown to be a synthetic a priori judgment) that the genus "regular bodies" or, more precisely, "equilateral and equiangular polyhedra," can have only five species (those with 4, 6, 8, 12, and 20 sides). Would it be possible, Driesch asks, to find an organic systematics corresponding to the spatial systematics of geometry?[49] At the present moment, he explains, "We do not understand the *raison d'être* of the system of organisms; we are not at all able to say that there must be these classes or orders and families and no others, and that they must be such as they are."[50] To make Driesch's "organic systematics" perfectly clear, we could say that the hypothesis at its heart is this: the evolution of the species (phylogeny) is (or is built upon) the ontogenesis of a single evolving animal, each of whose organs is a different species. Goldberg will call this overarching entelechy the "transcendental organism" and connect it to the Kabbalistic idea of the Primal Man, Adam Kadmon. But I am getting ahead of myself.

Driesch did not claim to be able to discern with any clarity the overarching entelechy that evolved through time as one species emerges after another. But if there was a real "organic systematicity" to the classificatory system of orders, classes, genera, families, and species, it would allow him to round out his empirical work in embryology with a grand systematic edifice, a modern version of the Aristotelian "chain of being" that would account for the place and function of each specific entelechy. When Driesch held out the possibility of an "organic systematicity," he was fully aware that he was returning to Lorenz Oken and the fundamental project of Naturphilosophie, the rational taxonomy of all living beings: "There *can* be a philosophy of nature [*Naturphilosophie*] resting on the foundations of criticism, and evolving a real system of nature from reason without the use of uncontrolled imagination; and there *will* be such a system some day, there *will* be a *system* that really deserves to be called philosophy of nature in the old sense of this term."[51] Much of the second volume of *Science and Philosophy of the Organism* is devoted to explaining how a new Naturphilosophie *can* be constructed on the "foundations of criticism" (Driesch means by this an analysis of the transcendental conditions of possibility of the experience of purposiveness) and why a new Naturphilosophie *must be* constructed if biological science is ever to be "rational," that is, capable of explaining organic phenomena in terms of laws that take into account the irreducible end-directedness of living organisms.

Driesch's argument that biology would never be placed on a rational foundation until it could account for the multiplicity of living organisms and their evolutionary development as a systematic structure was taken quite seriously by one of the foremost biologists of the era, Jakob von Uexküll. Von Uexküll's concept of the "structural plan" (*Bauplan*) that is a sort of Platonic Idea of the anatomical structures and physiological processes associated with each species captures precisely Driesch's concept of the entelechy. In his *Umwelt und Innen-*

*welt der Tiere* (*Outer and Inner Environment of Animals*) (1909),[52] von Uexküll argues that the fullness of living beings on the earth constitutes a single harmonious whole in which each species creates a self-contained world within the whole. Von Uexküll thus attempts to create the rational biology that Driesch proposes as the ultimate desideratum of the science by meticulously analyzing the interlocking worlds that each species creates. Even though he acknowledges the facts of Darwinian evolution, von Uexküll refuses to consider evolution as driven by random change and the selection of the fittest. It is, rather, the unfolding of life-worlds, the differentiations of a general *Bauplan* of organic existence into species, each of which is a perfect world in its own right. This quasi-Leibnizian vision of a sort of pre-established harmony of species-worlds leads von Uexküll to an understanding of animal ecologies (the study of interlocking systems of behavior and environment) that was and remains in large part unrivaled. His vision of all life as the embodiment of a transcendental system of structural plans, a sort of Platonic realm of organic Ideas, was a further influence on Goldberg who, as I have said, believed that Driesch, unwittingly to be sure, had given a modern expression to the ancient Kabbalistic notion of Adam Kadmon, the Primal Man. For Goldberg, Adam Kadmon is what he calls the "Idea of Biology," the "preformation site" of all "transcendental organisms," the structural plans of all the species. Von Uexküll understood the life-world (*Umwelt*) of an animal as in perfect synch with its particular sensory physiology and its unique set of perceptual schemas or ways of apprehending the infinite qualitative possibilities in its environment (*Umgebung*). This approach laid the foundations of what could be called "ecological phenomenology."

Near the end of the second volume of *Science and Philosophy of the Organism*, Driesch turns from the possibility of a rational science of "organic systematicity" to more speculative, one may even say imaginative, thoughts about the way that entelechy might be realized in nature. Organic systematicity suggests the possibility that there is but one super-entelechy that comes into manifestation in the unfolding life of all organic beings throughout the history of life on earth. But Driesch goes further, suggesting that there is no reason to limit the spatial sphere of the entelechy to our planet. Perhaps there are forms of organized life elsewhere in the cosmos; indeed, Driesch speculates that entire star systems may manifest entelechial organization:

> Many cosmic constellations of masses, like the single planetary systems, for instance, are very typical in their specificity, as far as we know, and are not reducible to any sort of mere symmetry in space, as the chemical elements are on the theory of electrons. Now it certainly is by no means proved at present that categorical teleology is applicable to planetary or sidereal systems, that there is anything like individuality to be found in them. But, on the other hand, it must be granted that such a view may be possible and may be proved

some day, and we know that not only Fechner, in an almost poetical form, but also other philosophers, regarded planetary systems as real "organisms."[53]

In *Theory of Reality*, his metaphysical magnum opus, Driesch offers different reasons for believing in the possibility of forms of conscious life that include not only planets and stars but even postmortem existence beyond all bodily forms. He finds evidence of postmortem conscious life in abnormal psychic phenomena. The fact that a nonspatial component (the entelechy) unfolds in time suggests that the entelechy may also be independent of time, that is, it may arise from a timeless dimension and return to it. But is there any *singleness*—that is, *personhood*—possible for such a nonspatial, nontemporal being? "After death is the psychical-totalizing aspect of the experience-bearing single being [*der seelish-ganzheitliche Teil des erfahrungshaften Einzelwesens*] preserved in any form of singleness [*Einzel-wesenheit*] or not?" Driesch asks.[54] If it is spatiotemporal organic matter that individuates the entelechy as a single being, then after death an individualized identity is lost. After death, the individual would cease to remain a person. But Driesch points to evidence that the entelechy is not individuated by matter, but that it rather has its own internal form of individuation or "personhood." He points, first, to how in abnormal cases of embryological development a single fertilized egg can become more than one individual and, conversely, how the conjunction of fertilized eggs can in some cases produce a single, unusually large, individual. Matter by itself, therefore, does not determine the singleness of the individual. Furthermore, it is not the psychic element that determines the singleness of the person, since the study of abnormal psychology attests to the possibility of multiple identities sharing a single body. Finally, Driesch points to the way that the individual is the bearer of more encompassing identities, of ethnological "supraindividual" (*übereinzelne*) personhoods, as when the individual engages "in procreation, in being a part of larger system, in mutual interactions, and, psychically, in moral consciousness and moral relations."[55] All of this indicates that personhood is not limited to a single spatiotemporal embodiment. We know at least that personhood is not necessarily dependent on material embodiment and that therefore a postmortem personhood is not in principle impossible. "All that is organic," Driesch concludes, "is in some unknowable way the Reality-phase (*Wirklichkeitsphase*) of *one thing*; it enters into a Reality-phase in which it is many single things, and it knows itself as a single thing, and comes into appearance by virtue of making itself single. But the single being enters back again, upon its death, into that indescribable, superpersonal *one* Reality-phase that *perhaps* does not extinguish its singleness."[56] In his final comments about the "Reality-phase"—the realm that is the "before" and "after" the limited time of embodiment as an experiencing "I"—Driesch points to the promise of psychic research into telepathy and clairvoyance, phenomena that he believes have some evidential support, and to communication with the dead, something that Driesch thinks is not impossible:

> Without holding anything back, let me dare to say this: a single definitive case of the continued activity in this world of someone who has died would mean more for earthly humanity than everything that its so-called culture, including philosophy, has ever meant. Certainly philosophy as it exists today, in so far as it has overcome materialism and "critical" mechanistic scientism, shows that all that is earthly counts for little. It is this insight that allows us to hope that the terrible lusting after power that has dragged our generation into the moral abyss of wars, revolutions, and breaches of all forms of trust, will come to an end. But that one single case of a different kind of "fact" would speak to humanity with a far different kind of impressive force, declaring that humanity's true "empire" [*Reich*] is no sort of contingent political empire whose lust for power is insatiable, but is an empire *not of this world.*[57]

From this passage we may understand better why Driesch assumed the presidency of the International Society for Psychical Research from 1926 to 1928 and also why thinkers like Henri Bergson and William James also supported this institution.[58] Oskar Goldberg, as I described in the Introduction, also hoped to demonstrate conclusively the reality of postmortem existence. Death, as Driesch argues in *Theory of Reality*, may be the *enigma philosophicum*, but its salience for the generation who knew the horror of the First World War arose from much more than its theoretical interest. The end of warfare and the coming of a new world order demanded more than international congresses and treaties. It demanded a metaphysical revolution that would be the culmination of the scientific revolution of the seventeenth century.

Driesch brings his *Theory of Reality* to a close with reflections about the relationship between the divine Absolute and human history. Because Driesch insists that only entelechial totalities have a ground in Reality, the metaphysical meaning of human history, if there is one, would depend on the existence of some entelechy or constellation of entelechies coming into appearance in the course of history. Since every entelechy is *supra*-personal—that is, since it is a nonspatial whole that is expressed in this or that material particular, but is not identical to any particular living being—the question about the metaphysical meaning of history (as distinct from the meaning of an individual human life) can be put this way: Is there any evidence for a supra-personal entelechy, a self-unfolding Organism, coming into appearance in human history? Driesch considers the only possible evidence of such a supra-personal entelechy in history to be the way that humanity has progressed in knowing (*Wissen*). What Driesch means by this concept includes, but is hardly exhausted by the historical development of science (*Wissenschaft*). What Driesch also means by the progress of knowing goes well beyond the increase in the scientific understanding of nature and technical *know-how*. Rather, Driesch describes the progress of knowing as a development of "the glimpsing of new tasks and new solutions" (*Schau neuer Aufgaben und neuer Lösungen*).[59] Driesch offers a few examples: the intuition of how an arch can be built, the intuition of what torture on the rack or slavery "means."[60] Advances in mechanics and ethics, Driesch argues, *might* be advances in the way that knowing in Reality unfolds itself in time, with each advance marking a new "intuition" of the ultimate human task, namely, to achieve the most manifoldly reticulated and all-embracing totality of knowing or, in other words, to completely participate in knowing as it is in Reality.[61] This is a sort of Aristotelian "salvation history," but it does not exhaust what Driesch has to say about the possibility that the unfolding of life as a whole (and not merely history) is moving in the direction of a universal *redemption from suffering*. The coming to appearance of the Absolute as the progress of knowing has as its goal the triumph of purpose over accident, of life over death.

Despite certain points of similarity, Driesch's theory of the Absolute as Knowing is very far from that of Hegel. Hegel's self-professed "theodicy" saw history to be a slaughter-bench in the service of the actualization of *Geist* as self-consciousness. Driesch, who also considers his philosophy to offer a theodicy, rejects the idea that any single death is final or that suffering is in service of a higher good. Suffering is the result of the Absolute's coming to appearance in space and time, and Driesch near the end of his *Theory of Reality* declares that it is beyond our ability to comprehend *why* the Absolute involves itself at all with finite, material reality. Perhaps this is simply how the Absolute comes into being, by evolving through time; or perhaps the Absolute *chooses* to assume the burden of suffering so that the multifarious world of living beings might know a measure of self-standing individuality. Where Driesch reveals his humility before these ultimate questions, Oskar Goldberg will turn to the Kabbalah for guidance. But despite his profession of ignorance concerning the mysteries of the Absolute, Driesch shares with Goldberg the conviction that the yearning for redemption from the vicissitudes of suffering and death is the deepest impulse of living things.

## Theoretical Biology

Before turning to Goldberg in chapter 2, I want to conclude this chapter with an all-too-brief discussion of the work of a group of biologists who formed the core of the new scientific discipline of "theoretical biology" that arose in the early decades of the twentieth century. These biologists were looking to reinterpret Driesch's entelechy as an intensive manifold in terms that could be given mathematically precise form and thereby become experimentally verifiable. Some of the ideas of these theoretical biologists later play a major role in the exposition of Goldberg's fusion of Kabbalah and biology.

In 1901 the botanist Johannes Reinke published a book titled *Einleitung in die theoretische Biologie (Introduction to Theoretical Biology)*.[62] The preface sets the agenda of a new discipline: "One has heard hardly anything today about a theoretical biology, and even less about it as a coherent discipline. Scattered across the many specialized works in biology one finds mentions of theory, and even titles that refer to the theory of this or that individual branch of the discipline. [Reinke here footnotes an 1894 work of Hans Driesch, *Analytische Theorie der organischen Entwicklung (Analytic Theory of Organic Development)*.] Also one finds in the writings of philosophers from Greek antiquity to the present a number of different investigations of questions touching on theoretical biology. But despite all of this, we still await a worked-out theory of life."[63]

The next six hundred pages of Reinke's book provide only an "introduction" to theoretical biology. In the following decades, many other biologists will tackle the same subject. These biologists fully accepted the "axiom of Naturphilosophie"— that the organic whole is greater than the sum of its parts. Reinke devoted the first chapter of his book to the question of how theoretical biology was distinct from Naturphilosophie. He concluded that Naturphilosophie simply took a too speculative approach to biological phenomena, but that in its rejection of the positivist and materialist-mechanistic models of explanation as having the same exclusive legitimacy in living systems as in nonliving ones, Naturphilosophie and theoretical biology were united. But Reinke insists that theoretical biology must resist the temptation to engage in discussions of some "cosmic intelligence" at work in the phenomena of life. He wants theoretical biology to remain firmly rooted in empirical data.

The theoretical biologists who followed Reinke's lead sought to develop experimental models of the structuring principle of the organism that would allow them to offer *experimental* evidence of how Driesch's entelechy actually managed to play a role in the morphogenesis of the organism. They turned to mathematics for this purpose, developing Driesch's suggestive description of the entelechy as an "intensive manifold." As I mentioned above, Driesch's theory of the intensive manifold as the shaping force behind embryological development has been updated in recent years by systems biologists who have shown that embryological morphogenesis, with its growing density of "invaginating" cellular surfaces, is best characterized as a self-regulating sequence of "state spaces."[64] Systems biologists most frequently trace their approach not to Driesch but to the group of those younger theoretical biologists—most notably, Alexander Gurwitsch, Hans Spemann, Ludwig von Bertalannfy, and Paul Weiss—each of whom sought to give a more precise and experimentally verifiable interpretation of Driesch's concept of entelechy. We must also mention in this context the ecological biologist Jakob von Uexküll, whom I discussed earlier. While it is true that he and Driesch had a falling out during the First World War over von Uexküll's claim that the nation-state was an organism requiring war for its rejuvenation, nonetheless von Uexküll must be considered, even after the war, a major figure in the Driesch-inspired theoretical biology movement. Indeed, one of his major texts is titled simply *Theoretische Biologie*.[65] Most of these theoretical biologists, in addition to doing pathbreaking work in experimental biology (Spemann won the Nobel Prize in 1935), published theoretical overviews of their discoveries as monographs in the series, *Abhandlungen zur theoretischen Biologie* (*Monographs in Theoretical Biology*). Their theoretical work is an important though largely unknown chapter in the history of vitalism. Although I only offer a cursory discussion of theoretical biology in what follows, I return to some of its basic themes in later chapters. The basic ideas of the theoretical biologists will help us understand Goldberg's key notion of the "transcendental organism" and Unger's concept of the organism as "system of forces" (*Kräftesystem*) operating through an "all-at-once causality" (*einmalige Kausalität*).

In 1923 Alexander Gurwitsch (1874–1954), a leading Soviet biologist, published *Versuch einer synthetischen Biologie* (*Essay in Synthetic Biology*) in the *Monographs in Theoretical Biology* series.[66] In place of Driesch's entelechy, Gurwitsch introduced the concept of "field." The "parameters" of the field are the "species constants" that govern the development and physiology of the organism. He argues that the field operates as a "purely dynamic surface that, without any material substrate, is preformed; what I am introducing is the concept of a dynamically preformed *morphe*."[67] The field is a "definitely configured and localized spatial region," which is distinguished from Driesch's entelechy by being *spatial* where Driesch's concept is *nonspatial*. Gurwitsch is indeed close to what today is called a "state space," a configuration of space that defines the contours along which energy has a tendency to flow (the example is sometimes offered of how a whirlpool-shaped movement forms in a stream in front of a boulder). Gurwitsch insists that his "field" is not reducible to the parts that compose it: "Organic events and organic impulses do not play out *inside* of cells, but in the space *between* them."[68] Gurwitsch calls his field theory of the organism "practical vitalism."[69] In an article published in English in 1915 titled "On Practical Vitalism," Gurwitsch acknowledges that the theoretical foundations of "practical vitalism" lie in "Naturphilosophie."[70]

Another, younger member of the theoretical biology group in the 1920s was Paul Weiss (1898–1989). Paul Weiss developed Driesch's concept of entelechy into what he, following Gurwitsch, also called a "field theory" of morphogenesis. Weiss's first publication on the field theory of organic development comes in 1923 in a discussion of experiments he performed dealing with the regeneration of an amputated salamander limb.[71] He published a monograph titled *Morphodynamik* in 1926 in which he expands on his work with salamanders and describes the field structure of the sea urchin.[72] Summarizing his morphodynamic theory in a later work written after he emigrated to the United States and became a professor of biology at the University of Chicago, Weiss explains that the sea urchin egg has two poles, one where the yolk cells are most concentrated (the "vegetative pole") and the other where the organism proper is growing (the "animal pole"). Weiss states that the animal pole should not be thought of as a "prominent particle from which special actions emanate in all directions" but rather as "an imaginary center in which we visualize as concentrated the organizing activities which in reality span the whole animal district. The point itself has no more material reality and distinctiveness than have the center of gravity of a physical body or the population center of a country."[73]

Yet, just as the animal pole includes "organizing activities" that "span the "whole animal district" from an "imaginary center," so does the vegetative pole. As the organizing activities develop and the "material substrata" of the vegetative and animal poles shift into new structures, one must imagine that there is a "displacement of their focal points." The "organizing factors" that enter into dynamic relations as they shift focal points are what Weiss calls "fields." He defines them as follows: "Briefly, once more, they are the factors which *cause the originally indefinite course of the individual parts of a germ to become definite and specific*, and, furthermore, cause this to occur *in compliance with a typical pattern*."[74] The "typical pattern" is unique to each species, that is, it and all the subsystems it defines are "specific." Of course, there are physico-chemical "triggers" associated with the unfolding field pattern, but the development of the embryo cannot be explained merely as the effect of these causally enchained triggers. The "typical pattern" lends this development its spatiotemporal shape. Weiss goes on to describe the "typical pattern" in terms that can best be described as a manifold or, as it today would be called, a "state space":

> A *field* is the condition to which a living system owes its typical organization and its *specific* activities. These activities are specific in that they determine the *character* of the formations to which they give rise. In this they differ essentially from what we have called trigger reactions. Since it is inconceivable that order could emerge from an irregular, chaotic play of forces, and inasmuch as the action of fields does produce spatial order, it becomes a postulate that the *field factors* themselves possess definite order. The *three-dimensional heterogeneity of developing systems*, that is, the fact that these systems have different properties in the three dimensions of space, must be referred to a *three-dimensional organization and heteropolarity of the organizing fields*. In this respect the organization of a field bears some remote resemblance to that of a crystal whose electrical and optical properties also differ distinctly in different directions.[75]

The field theory of the organism is one of the most productive developments of neo-Naturphilosophie's postulate that the whole is greater than the sum of its parts. It has had considerable influence within "normal" biological science. It was also important for Oskar Goldberg. Goldberg in *The Reality of the Hebrews* makes considerable use of the concept of an organic energy field that is a species-wide "pattern." We can see evidence of Goldberg's awareness of the new field theory when he says, for example, that a folk group can serve as "the whole 'multiplicity' [*die ganze 'Vielheit'*]" for the "operational basis or 'energy field' [*Operationsbasis bzw. 'Kräftefeld'*]" of the transcendental organism (or god) that "'develops,' that is, separates out" in the folk group.[76] Elsewhere Goldberg explains that insofar as a folk group is the "energy field" of a god, it "provides the god its body."[77] Goldberg's disciple, Erich Unger, explicitly refers to Weiss's field theory in *The Living and the Divine*, the book I quoted from at the top of this chapter.[78] Unger devotes a full chapter of his book to "The Field as a Concept." Unger explains that the structural field is "both first and last in the entire course of the phases of development; first, in terms of a simple tension potential; last, in terms of the matter-filled form. The potential must not be thought of as a kind of fixed pastry-cutter, shaping something from outside, but rather as a central impulse, an inner form driving outwards from the centre; intensities of varying ranges link up together into an intensity whole, which is that inner form."[79] Unger credits Goldberg with having articulated a similar theory to his own "field" theory in *The Reality of the Hebrews*.

I want to conclude this overview of theoretical biology with one figure who is certainly at the margins of this group, but who is the only one to have explicitly engaged with the work of Oskar Goldberg. I am referring to the "euvitalist" Karl Camillo Schneider (1867–1943?).[80] Schneider wrote a very favorable review of Goldberg's *Reality of the Hebrews*, describing it as very close to his own theories.[81] He was not wrong to believe that he and Goldberg shared much in common. Schneider's "euvitalist biology" is one of the most imaginative versions of theoretical biology to be produced in the early decades of the twentieth century. It was given as a series of lectures in the department of botany at the University of Vienna, and it was certainly intended to be a work within the then-accepted field of theoretical biology. But because of its speculative nature it may be better characterized as a work of neo-Naturphilosophie. It reveals the rather thin line between "normal" science and philosophy in the German academy at that time.

Schneider's euvitalism enters into the rather speculative realm of *fourth-dimensional* life. Schneider observed a considerable increase in the interest in the fourth dimension not only in Einsteinian physics but also throughout contemporary culture.[82] He correlated the rise in significance of the concept of fourth-dimensionality to the "striking manner in which mysticism and occultism are afoot in our time." He believed those phenomena "operate entirely in the fourth dimension."[83] Schneider, as we see, believed that a proper understanding of the fourth dimension would enable science finally to come to grips with the reality of paranormal phenomena, such as clairvoyance, telekinesis, telepathy, and ghosts. Schneider's theories provide an interesting parallel to those of Goldberg and will in some measure help us to understand Goldberg better. He is a fitting figure with which to conclude this chapter's discussion of the revival of Naturphilosophie in the early twentieth century.

Building explicitly on the Einstein-Minkowski theory of four-dimensional space-time, Schneider, agreeing with Einstein, argued that space-time is a single energy field with distinct topological configurations. The gravitational force of the sun is, in the Einstein-Minkowski theory, simply the way objects move in the warped contours of space-time caused by the mass of the sun. "According to Einstein, space is four-dimensional, that is, it is curved because of the masses that are found in it, and in virtue of this curving it is the bearer of gravitational effects or, in other words, it is the sum of gravitational fields." The fourth dimension of this curved space is time, which likewise is warped by the masses of the objects. That is, the greater the gravitational field, the greater will be the curvature of space and also the slower will time flow (relative to an observer farther from the deforming effects of the gravitational field).[84]

Einstein and Minkowski did not believe that four-dimensional space-time was a distinct dimension that was separate from the space and time of the world we normally inhabit. In contrast, Schneider imagined that the fourth dimension was a "space of a higher order" than the space-time that Einstein considered to be four-dimensional.[85] Schneider considered the fourth dimension to be an entirely different dimension from Einstein-Minkowski's space-time. Within Schneider's higher-order fourth dimension, consciousness has an entirely different experience of objects than it does within the space-time world of our normal environment.

Schneider begins his account of way that consciousness works in the fourth dimension by invoking a short, imaginative work titled *Vier Paradoxa* (*Four Paradoxes*). Gustav Fechner (1801–1887), who founded experimental psychology in the middle decades of the nineteenth century (and also one of the greatest representatives of Naturphilosophie in Germany at the time, although his speculations about living planets and spiritual plants were too extreme to be developed by people like Driesch and the cohort of theoretical biologists who followed him), composed *Vier Paradoxa* under the pseudonym "Dr. Mises," a narrator with a satirical and moralizing bent.[86] One of the chapters of this little book is titled "Space Has Four Dimensions." In this chapter Fechner imagines that three-dimensional objects in their movement through time constitute a four-dimensional, nonmoving "beam" (*Balken*): a human would display a metamorphosing beam from childhood to old age, each slice of which is a moment in one life. The consciousness of this "beam" would grasp the whole of the individual's life with all of its separate moments as a single field of objects. The fourth-dimensional experience according to Fechner is, in Schneider's words, "the all-in-one experience [*Ganzheitserlebnis*] of the objects whose phenomenological presentation in their temporal succession makes up the content of our world."[87] Schneider takes Fechner's imaginative rendering of a four-dimensional, conscious "beam" beyond even this all-in-one experience. He argues that within the fourth dimension it would make no sense to speak of distinct subjectivities separated by spatial boundaries. Just as consciousness would not be limited to experiencing time as a series of distinct "now" moments, it would also not be limited to experiencing space from distinct "here" positions. "With time joined to space," Schneider writes, "the boundaries of consciousness that had previously separated us with razor sharpness from the experience of the other person are now dissolved. Objects no long face us from a particular perspective corresponding to the viewer's position, but they exist in a general view [*in allgemeiner Schau*], as free bodily forms, around whose entire structure we are, as it were, able to see with a single glance."[88] The experience we have in the fourth dimension is that of a "sensory subject" freed from all bodily limitations. The sensory subject is, therefore, a "general subject."

Schneider claims that the form of experience that a four-dimensional consciousness possesses is not entirely foreign to us. We know of such "supertemporal" consciousness in certain exceptional cases of clairvoyance [*Hellsehen*] where we are able to experience a spatially and temporally distant event with hallucinatory presentness. Such hallucinatory clairvoyance is rare in advanced societies, but it characterizes the "mentality of uncivilized humans [*Wilden*], humans in their natural state [*Naturmenschen*]."[89] The experience of clairvoyance offers us a direct vision of the meaningful interconnection among apparently disparate objects and events: a clairvoyant medium, for example, can "see" the relationship between a particular object and the persons who once owned it. The clairvoyant, as Schneider describes her, has an ability to perceive what Benjamin would call the "aura" surrounding an object. In clairvoyant vision, objects are viewed as the concretion-points of meaningful intentionalities. The experience of the fourth-dimensional consciousness is a pure experience of the meaningfulness of things. There is nothing contingent in the experience of the world of objects given to fourth-dimensional consciousness. "Meaning [*der Sinn*] is the teleological relationship of all objects for a general subject who experiences all objects as a sensory subject in accordance with their general and lawful interconnection, whereas in [consciousness-independent] nature there is only a relationship of contingency, a relationship of probability, which exists entirely independently of any subject as an independent relationship of one object to another."[90] The consciousness of humans and even many nonhuman animals is able to view natural objects as instruments or tools (Schneider refers to the work of Wolfgang Köhler with great apes in Tenerife), and in this way consciousness imbues three-dimensional nature with a measure of intentionality. What consciousness that operates within the fourth dimension experiences is thoroughly imbued with intentionality because consciousness no longer separated from its objects at all: the "sensorial subject" is itself "one part of a metaphenomenal totality."[91]

Schneider acknowledges that his conception of the fourth dimension differs significantly from that of Einstein. Einstein does not conceive of space as imbued with consciousness. But Schneider argues that without a conscious subject it is inappropriate to say that space has any dimension at all. That is, it makes no sense to speak of a "here and now" as a space-time point without reference to an observing "eye." In the absence of a percipient subject, there is only a "force structure" [*Kraftstruktur*] that can be mathematically described, but that does not have spatial or temporal properties. Schneider, claiming to base his interpretation on the work of the mathematician Hermann Weyl, conceives of the force structure in the absence of consciousness to be a purely mathematical continuum that, on the entry of consciousness, comes to expression as the experienced world of space and time. The emergence of consciousness in the world depends on the prior unfolding of the mathematical continuum of the force structure into curved space-time with its electromagnetic fields, light, and matter. The transition from mathematical force structure to curved space-time is what Schneider calls "cosmogenesis."

Schneider explains that the force structure underlying four-dimensional space-time is energy in a state of pure potentiality; it is pure extensivity without actual dimensionality; its temporality is that of an eternal "now." The force structure, Schneider contends, is what scientists at the time referred to as "aether." From out of the force structure of the aether emerges both curved space with its gravitational and electromagnetic fields and also the space and time and matter of our normal experience. The emergence of consciousness is not, according to Schneider, a mere contingency. The mathematical structure of the aether undergirds the physical laws governing electromagnetism and gravity and the movement of matter in space and time. The transition from aether's mathematical structure to electromagnetism, gravity, and matter is goal-directed: it is the emergence of consciousness. After the transformation of the atemporal and nonspatial mathematical structure of aether into the force fields studied by physics, the next stage in cosmogenesis required for the emergence of consciousness is the evolution of life. With the coming of the more complex vertebrates, the stage is set for the final emergence of what Schneider has called the "sensorial subject" whose consciousness is able to rise beyond its limited space-time perspective and become a "general consciousness" that can intuit the eternal mathematical structure of aether and the teleological meaning that it makes possible. The final goal of the evolution of conscious life is to view cosmogenesis *sub specie aeternitate.*

The vision of cosmogenesis as an eternal now would, in effect, render all events as happening simultaneously, which means that the "eye" of consciousness would become infinitely large, just the way that a traveler at the speed of light would acquire infinite mass. The aether structure of pure energy potential would become the completely actualized light-filled universe. The consciousness of the sensorial Subject holds both moments together in virtue of the mathematical nature of the two conditions: aether is the infinitely complex structure of possible points within a four-dimensional continuum; light-filled space (time has stopped moving at the speed of light) is the completed infinity that is held in potentiality within the aether. Number [*Zahl*] is the binding fabric holding cosmogenesis together. For the general sensorial Subject, number expresses itself as a single all-embracing "Idea." Each Idea, Schneider says, corresponds to one of Cantor's transfinite numbers (which I explain in chapter 2).

The general sensorial Subject who intuits all of cosmogenesis as an Idea with one complex mathematical structure extending from the force potentiality of aether to the energy actuality of light is God. Insofar as cosmogenesis involves the evolution of life and the emergence of space and time as they are consciously experienced by living beings, God himself evolves and enters into space and time. In the earliest stage of human evolution, God begins to recognize himself within the natural world of space and time as an all-pervasive life force. The "primitive" peoples experience divine intuition within the mythic ideas that concretize the general Idea within an infinitely rich sensorial embodiment that appears to them within their tribal collectivity as powerful hallucinations. In their hallucinatory experience of the world, Schneider explains,

> The excitatory condition within the nervous system is sidestepped; the world is frozen round about in an overwhelming experience, and the inner energy structure [of the living person] is frozen and returns to its aether-state, the supporting foundation of supersensory experience. Just as normal sensory experience depends upon the state of an excitatory impulse and the responses of the motor functions of the body, so supersensory experience depends upon the state of the aether which is characteristic of the sensory Subject. . . . The central moment [in hallucination] is when motor subjectivity is overcome and objects are transformed into subjects. . . . Only on the basis of hallucinatory consciousness is it possible to explain the kind of expressions that are typical of primitive humans, such as that a certain corpse is alive or that a pathway is moving like a snake or that a stone speaks and lives.[92]

Schneider believed that the hallucinatory group consciousness of primitive humanity is simply an early stage in the evolution of an entirely new form of collective consciousness in which the divine general Subject would be fully and self-reflexively actualized within humanity: "We civilized humans still lack the complete experience of the Subject insofar as we remain in the first place individual persons and our experience is not that of the evolving general Subject (the World-Subject) [*werdendes Allgemeinsubjekt (Weltsubjekt)*]. When we can experience this, a new culture will arise."[93] The goal of this new culture, says Schneider, is "the enlivenment of the world, the subjectification of objects, the divinization of nature."[94] Adopting Schelling's notion that gender equality (the balance of the two opposing forces in nature) is the mark of a mature species, Schneider argues that the female will occupy a far more important place in the new world culture than she presently does. Schneider "euvitalism" captures all the fundamental goals of Romantic Naturphilosophie.

Schneider's "euvitalistic biology" is a bold attempt to incorporate Naturphilosophie within the framework of Einsteinian relativity theory. His claim that the mathematics of the aether's force structure might eventually provide a basis for explaining psychic phenomena like clairvoyance and even telekinesis, however audacious, is not so terribly removed from the speculations of Hermann Weyl. A major contributor to the refinement of relativity theory in relation to quantum physics, Weyl believed that matter "appears as an agent that by virtue of its essence, lies beyond space and time." Weyl goes on to add, "This agent may just as well be creative life and will as matter."[95] Schneider ventured into the uncharted territory of the realm "beyond space and time" that Weyl believed was inaccessible to scientific study. As Schneider himself recognized, his bold speculations about the evolution of God within the framework of space and time bears close similarities to those of Goldberg at about the same time. Both men were developing their ideas independently of each other, and the convergences of their thought are due to their common source in the deepest currents of Naturphilosophie, both in its Romantic and more modern forms: the faith in the natural cosmos as the unfolding of a divine drama whose denouement was the coming into being of a new collective consciousness through which the world might be enlivened and divinized.

Schneider, in his review of Goldberg's book, recognizes the fundamental similarity of their views. His one disagreement is that he believes, as he says, that the task of leading humanity into the new culture of the future will fall to the "Aryan superman," rather than, as Goldberg believes, to the Jewish people. (One can only imagine what Goldberg thought when he read the review, which we know he did because he refers to it in later curricula vitae, and its concluding its laudatory account of his work with this anti-Semitic twist.) In fact, Schneider's racial bias blinded him to Goldberg's true position, that *no biologically related people exists any longer* and that, even if one did exist, it could not *in principle* be the vehicle of the transformation of human history. Israel's God precisely works *through* biology in order to *transcend* it.

Let us turn now to Oskar Goldberg.

## Notes

1. Oskar Goldberg, "The Development of Biology," *Science and Culture* (February 1944): 2–6. The publication was designed for an educated but nonspecialist audience. This article was not selected by Manfred Voigts to be included in Goldberg-*Aufsätze*. I found it among the books and pamphlets collected in the Deutsches Literaturarchiv Marbach (DLM) in the library holdings, in Kasten (box) 2.

2. Ibid., 2.

3. Goldberg must have had the German word "Satz" in mind, because he wrote "sentence." A better translation of "Satz" in this context is "axiom" or perhaps "proposition."

4. Goldberg, "The Development of Biology," 6; emphasis Goldberg's.

5. For some of the difficulties in separating out the various strands of vitalist thought in the period, see Oliver A. I. Botar, "Defining Biocentrism," in *Biocentrism and Modernism*, ed. Oliver A. I. Botar and Isabel Wünsche (Surrey, UK: Ashgate, 2011), 15–46. In a recent study of scientifically marginalized discourses of the last two centuries, the historian of religion Kocku von Stuckrad writes that "in Germany between 1900 and 1930, there emerged a whole movement of scientists, philosophers, and lay authors who speculated about the spiritual dimensions of nature." Von Stuckrad himself only touches briefly on this movement, but he concedes that "contributions like these have only rarely been looked at by historians, although they had decisive influence on how Germans of the Weimar Republic and later periods conceptualized nature, science, and culture." Kocku von Stuckrad, *The Scientification of Religion: An Historical Study of Discursive Change, 1800–2000* (Boston: Walter de Gruyter, 2014), 85–86. He goes on to add that even the Green movement has roots in the writings of this period. I am unable to offer a full treatment of Naturphilosophe from the Romantics to the Green movement, but in this chapter I do offer a detailed examination of one of the most prominent of the writers of this group, Hans Driesch, and an overview of a number of others who followed him and took his ideas in different directions.

6. The letter is found in the Felix von Luschan Nachlass at the Humboldt-Universität in Berlin. Manfred Voigts kindly shared a photocopy with me.

7. Felix von Luschan's predecessor in the chair of anthropology, Adolf Bastian (1826–1905), had very likely influenced Goldberg in his thinking about the role of holy men in the formation of ethnic groups. Bastian had argued that "in the demon-ridden, frightful dream world of the state of nature there were individuals with certain nervous predispositions who come to dominate over others through that which they can see in ecstatic visions. The great majority of the group tremble in fear when these visions are related to them, but they do believe in them. . . . They take upon themselves the shamans and 'paye' folk group as their 'dux ex virtute' [leader chosen for his virtue] under variously agreed upon terms such as are revealed in the disparate ethnic forms of priestly kingships that offer themselves to our study." Adolf Bastian, *Zur Lehre vom Menschen in ethnisher Anthropologie* (Berlin: D. Reimer, Hoefer & Vohnsen, 1895), viii. We know that Goldberg was quite familiar with Bastian's work because he named a collection of notebooks (preserved as a Konvolut in the Goldberg Nachlass) "From Plato to Bastian." (For a list of other notebook Konvolut titles, see Manfred Voigts, *Oskar Goldberg*, 340.) Felix von Luschan was far more positivist in his proclivities than Bastian. Bastian would almost certainly have welcomed Goldberg's dissertation proposal.

8. Erich Unger, *Das Lebendige und das Goettliche* (Jerusalem: Hatehiya, 1966), 183–184. The translation of Unger's book is available at www.torah-study-for-women.org/unger/index.htm. Translations throughout are mine unless otherwise noted.

9. Ibid., 60–61; emphasis Unger's.

10. Alexander von Humbolt, *Kosmos, Entwurf einer physischen Weltbeschreibung*, 5 vols. (Stuttgart: Cott'sche, 1845–1858), 1:39. The passage is quoted and translated in Robert J. Richards, *The Romantic Conception of Life: Science and Philosophy in the Age of Goethe* (Chicago: University of Chicago Press, 2002), 144 n43. Richards's book is the best introduction to Romantic Naturphilosophie available in English.

11. Lorenz Oken, *Grundriß der Naturphilosophie, der Theorie der Sinne und der darauf gegründeten Classification der Tiere* (Franfurt: Eichenberg, 1802).

12. Lorenz Oken, *Lehrbuch der Naturphilosophie*, 3rd ed. (Zürich: Friedrich Schulteß, 1843), 521, par. 3631. Translation in Lorenz Oken, *Elements of Physiophilosophy*, trans. Alfred Tulk (London: Ray Society, 1847). Quotation at 663 from the English translation.

13. Oken, *Lehrbuch*, ix; Oken, *Elements*, xi.

14. Oken, *Lehrbuch*, 521, par. 3631; Oken, *Elements*, 663.

15. Oken, *Lehrbuch*, 307, par. 2115; Oken, *Elements*, 373.

16. Stephen Jay Gould, *Ontogeny and Phylogeny* (Cambridge, MA: Harvard University Press, 1977), 39, available at www.sjgarchive.org/library/ontogeny.html.

17. Theodore Ziehen, *Grundlagen der Naturphilosophie* (Leipzig: Quelle & Meyer, 1922), 18.

18. Wilhelm Ostwald, *Grundriss der Naturphilosophie* (Leipzig: Philipp Reclam, 1908), 5.

19. On the conflict between mechanists and "energeticists," see John T. Blackmore, *Ernst Mach: His Life, Work, and Influence* (Berkeley: University of California Press, 1972), 204–231. On Ostwald, see Britta Görs, Nikos Psarros, and Paul Ziche, eds., *Wilhelm Ostwald at the Crossroads between Chemistry, Philosophy, and Media Culture* (Leipzig: Leipziger Universitätsverlag, 2005). I wish to thank an anonymous reviewer for drawing my attention to the wider context of neo-Naturphilosophie in the debate between mechanist and energeticist models of explanation in the physico-chemical sciences.

20. Ernst Cassirer, *Leibniz' System in seinen wissenschaftlichen Grundlagen* (Marburg: N. G. Elwert'sche Verlagsbuchhandlung, 1902). Ernst Cassirer has recently received two major treatments that have reassessed his position in the history of twentieth-century philosophy, largely in a positive and sympathetic fashion. Peter Eli Gordon, *Continental Divide: Heidegger, Cassirer, Davos* (Cambridge, MA: Harvard University Press, 2010), situates Cassirer at the center of the philosophical debates of the Weimar period; Christian Möckel, *Das Urphänomen des Lebens: Ernst Cassirer's Lebensbegriff* (Hamburg: Felix Meiner, 2005), argues persuasively for Cassirer's important contribution to the "life philosophy" that preoccupied so many thinkers in the first decades of the twentieth century.

21. Cassirer, *Leibniz' System*, 417–418.

22. Ibid., 404.

23. See now Frederick C. Beiser, *Late German Idealism: Trendelenburg and Lotze* (Oxford: Oxford University Press, 2013). For an earlier treatment of Trendelenburg that argued for his influence on John Dewey's pragmatist philosophy of nature, see Gershon George Rosenstock, *F. A. Trendelenburg: Forerunner to John Dewey* (Carbondale: Southern Illinois University Press, 1964).

24. For a fascinating and deeply informed study of Hermann Cohen's early work on infinitesmal calculus and its influence on later developments in neo-Kantian philosophy, see Marco Giovanelli, "Hermann Cohen's *Das Prinzip der Infinitesmal-Methode*: The History of an Unsuccessful Book," *Studies in History and Philosophy of Science* 58, Part A (2016): 9–23.

25. The basic study of Fechner's psychophysics and his more speculative interests is Michael Heidelberger, *Nature from Within: Gustav Theodor Fechner and His Psychophysical Worldview* (Pittsburgh: University of Pittsburgh Press, 2004).

26. I will discuss at greater length Brentano's analysis of the Aristotelian theory of *nous*. For a discussion of Brentano's dependence on Aristotelian psychology, see the excellent study of Lilliana Albertazzi, *Immanent Realism: An Introduction to Brentano* (Dordrecht: Springer, 2006): 43–82.

27. Meinong and Ehrenfels are not familiar names today. For an excellent discussion of the place of Meinong in the Brentano school and his relation to the larger anti-positivist currents of fin-de-siècle Europe, see David Lindenfeld, *The Transformation of Positivism: Alexius Meinong and European Thought, 1880–1920* (Berkeley: University of California Press, 1980). For an excellent introduction to Christian von Ehrenfels and his foundational work in Gestalt psychology, see Barry Smith, "Gestalt Theory: An Essay in Philosophy," in *Foundations of Gestalt Theory*, ed. Barry Smith (Munich: Philosophia, 1988), 11–81. Ehrenfels is known mostly today for his theoretical work on "Gestalt qualities," but he also made a significant contribution to neo-Naturphilosophe with his *Kosmogonie* (Jena: Eugen Diederichs, 1916). In this book, Ehrenfels argues for a duality of "henogenic" (unity producing) and "chaotogenic" (disorder producing) forces operative throughout nature. Ehrenfals postulates the pure contingency of any given order in the world, but also the existence of an ordering principle that continuously operates to create new levels of order, from inorganic matter in three-dimensional space to living forms and finally consciousness. The ordering principle is God, but Ehrenfels's God is not the God of rationalist metaphysics but the God of a probabalistic universe where opportunities for new levels of order arise only because of the groundless contingency of the chaotogenic principle. Ehrenfels argues in *Kosmogonie* that "our human experience of knowledge, will, and intuition is part of a divine super-consciousness that has finally entered into an awareness of its own purposive intentions. We therefore can hope that we not only understand the goal and the direction of this divine consciousness, but that we become active participants in realizing its intentions" (*Kosmogonie*, 203). It is astonishing that this optimistic vision of the "metaphysics of human history" could have been published in the middle of the First World War.

28. For a brief introduction to Brentano's mereology, see Barry Smith and Kevin Mulligan, "Pieces of a Theory," in *Parts and Moments: Studies in Logic and Formal Ontology*, ed. Barry Smith (Munich: Philosophia, 1981), 13–109. For fuller treatments of Brentano and his immediate students, see Barry Smith, *Austrian Philosophy: The Legacy of Franz Brentano* (Chicago: Open Court, 1994), and Albertazzi, *Immanent Realism*.

29. Smith and Mulligan ("Pieces of a Theory," 481) provide a very helpful "genealogical tree" that lays out the relationship between Franz Brentano and his various students through four "generations." Driesch was not a student of Brentano, but he does refer to him in his writings on logic.

30. Heinrich Rickert, a leading exponent of neo-Kantianism, offers a clear statement of the "task" of philosophy in relation to science:

> Theoretical philosophy understands the concept of the totality of reality as a task for knowledge. Philosophy engages this task insofar as it is itself a science dealing with the values [*Werte*] that each specific science deals with in its own distinct spheres of reality. Philosophy thus avoids ever coming into conflict with these sciences. The knowledge of reality in all of its separate parts must be left to the specific sciences, and philosophy acquires its universality by seeking to explicate the knowledge of reality [of the specific sciences] in its most overarching goals as a single unity. Philosophy understands in this way how in the theoretical life of human beings the knowledge of reality reveals itself to be an always-striven-for and never-achieved totality, and in this way philosophy grasps the totality of reality itself, to the extent that all the sciences together are able to grasp it. (Heinrich Rickert, *Die Philosophie des Lebens: Darstellung und Kritik der philosophischen Modeströmungen unserer Zeit* [Tübingen: J. C. B. Mohr, 1920], 191–192.)

31. The emphasis on the irreducibility of lived experience to any mechanistic explanation is most often associated with the work of Wilhelm Dilthey (1833–1911). However, as Lindenfeld, *The Transformation of Positivism*, 172, points out, Dilthey developed his notion of historical understanding further after studying the phenomenology of Edmund Husserl.

32. Albertazzi, *Immanent Realism*, 129; emphasis Albertazzi's.

33. Ibid., 130.

34. For a number of excellent treatments of Brentano's ontology of substances as whole–part structures, see the essays in Dale Jacquette, ed., *The Cambridge Companion to Brentano* (Cambridge: Cambridge University Press, 2004). See esp. Arkadiusz Chrudzimski and Barry Smith, "Brentano's Ontology: From Conceptualism to Reism," 197–219.

35. Franz Brentano, *Die Psychologie des Aristoteles, insbesondere seine Lehre vom Nous Poietikos* (Mainz: Franz Kirchheim, 1867).

36. In the conclusion I will discuss the work of the psychologist and neurophysiologist Kurt Goldstein whose clinical studies of brain-injured veterans of the First World War persuaded him that they had lost their capacity for "abstract" categories and were reduced to the "concrete" ones. Goldstein appeals to Husserlian phenomenology and Gestalt psychology to explain the meaning of these terms, but they seem clearly to ultimately derive from Brentano's conception of the active mind (*nous poietikos*) and its ability to transform the concrete *phantasmata* of the sense organs into abstractions.

37. Brentano, *Die Psychologie des Aristoteles*, 199.

38. Ibid., 202.

39. See, for example, Benjamin's remarks to Gerhard [Gershom] Scholem in his letter of January 1921 when he writes that he has had "an extremely lively interest" in Unger's ideas, especially in relation to the "psychophysical problem" where Unger's theories "have some points in common with my own." Gershom Scholem and Theodor W. Adorno, eds., *The Correspondence of Walter Benjamin*, trans. Manfred R. Jacobson and Evelyn M. Jacobson (Chicago: University of Chicago Press, 1994), 173. Benjamin's own work on the psychophysical problem and his debt to phenomenology have been extensively treated in Peter Fenves, *The Messianic Reduction: Walter Benjamin and the Shape of Time* (Stanford, CA: Stanford University Press, 2011).

40. For an excellent overview of the preformationism-epigenesis debate and its historical background, see Paul S. Agutter and Dennis N. Wheatley, *Thinking about Life: The History and Philosophy of Biology and Other Sciences* (Dordrecht: Springer, 2009), 129–145.

41. One of the most sophisticated discussions of the issues raised by Driesch's criticisms of reductionism in embryology is found in Robert Rosen, *Anticipatory Systems: Philosophical, Mathematical, and Methodological Foundations* (New York: Springer, 2012), 172–181. Although Rosen does not believe that Driesch's notion of the autonomy of life (the irreducibility of the laws of organic phenomena, especially development, to the laws of inorganic phenomena) can be sustained (because these laws are themselves more complicated than Driesch allowed), he insists that life is an "anticipatory system," that is, "a system containing a predictive model of itself and/or of its environment, which allows it to change state at an instant in accordance with the model's predictions pertaining to a later instant" (313). Although Rosen is not a vitalist, his notion of the "anticipatory system" captures the properties of life that Driesch correctly argued could not be explained on the basis of the models of explanation in physics at that time.

42. Wilhelm Roux, "Zur Orientierung über einige Probleme der embryonalen Entwicklung," *Zeitschrift für Biologie* 21 (1885).

43. Hans Driesch, *The Science and Philosophy of the Organism*, 2 vols. (London: Adam and Charles Black, 1908–1909); quotation is found in vol. 1, p. 59. While this book provides a full

account of Driesch's ideas, it does not add significantly to what Driesch had written in some of his earlier texts, which seem to have been what Goldberg was reading in the early 1900s when he was formulating the basic contours of his metaphysical vitalism and his interpretation of the Pentateuch. Among Driesch's earlier works, three stand out as most important: *Die Biologie als selbstständige Grundwissenschaft* (Leipzig: Wilhelm Engelmann, 1893); *Analytische Theorie der organischen Entwicklung* (Leipzig: Wilhelm Englelmann, 1894); and *Die "Seele" als elementarer Naturfaktor: Studien über die Bewegungen der Oganismen* (Leipzig: Wilhelm Engelmann, 1903).

44. Rosen, *Anticipatory Systems*, 183.

45. Ibid.

46. For a discussion of the cell's "distributed, self-regulatory systems" as a "continuously variable space of states," see Benjamin de Bivort, "Cellular Level Gene Regulatory Networks: Their Derivation and Properties," in *Systems Biology for Signaling Networks*, ed. Sangdun Choi (New York: Springer, 2010), 429–446. For a succinct account of systems biology, see Hiroaki Kitano, "Scientific Challenges in Systems Biology," in Choi, *Systems Biology*, 3–13. For von Bertalanffy's debt to Driesch, see Ludwig von Bertalanffy, *General Systems Theory: Foundations, Development, Applications* (New York: George Brazillier, 1968), 40–41.

47. Hans Driesch, *Wirklichkeitslehre: Ein metaphysischer Versuch*, 2nd ed. (Leipzig: Emmanuel Reinike, 2nd ed. 1922; 1st ed. 1917) (hereafter *Theory of Reality*).

48. Driesch, *Science and Philosophy of the Organism*, 1:247.

49. When we come to examine Driesch's metaphysics in what follows we will find that it is plausible that he had read and was influenced by Franz Brentano's two books on Aristotle published in 1911, *Aristoteles und seine Weltanschauung* (*Aristotle and His Worldview*) (Leipzig: Quelle & Meyer) and *Aristoteles Lehre vom Ursprung des menschlichen Geistes* (*Aristotle's Doctrine concerning the Origin of the Human Mind*) (Leipzig: Veit & Comp.). It seems that Brentano may also have read Driesch. Brentano uses the example of the five possible regular solids to explain how it might be the case that each star, for Aristotle a living being with an intelligence, was a different "species" (*Spezies*) and that the number of such single-instance species "might be as limited as the number of stereometric figures" (Brentano, *Aristoteles Lehre*, 122).

50. Driesch, *Science and Philosophy of the Organism*, 1:247.

51. Ibid., 2:126; emphasis Driesch's.

52. Jakob von Uexküll, *Umwelt und Innenwelt der Tiere* (Berlin: Julius Springer, 1909).

53. Driesch, *Science and Philosophy of the Organism*, 2:351.

54. Driesch, *Theory of Reality*, 330.

55. Ibid., 333.

56. Ibid., 334.

57. Ibid., 339; emphasis Driesch's.

58. On Driesch's long and serious engagement with parapsychology, see Freyhofer, *The Vitalism of Hans Driesch*, 151–156.

59. Driesch, *Theory of Reality*, 218.

60. Ibid., 349. To fully unpack Driesch's concept of "task," I would need to bring it into relation to what he says about it in *Die Logik als Aufgabe: Eine Studie über die Beziehung zwischen Phänomenologie und Logik. Zugleich eine Einleitung in die Ordnugslehre* (Tübingen: Mohr, 1913), 70–77. Briefly, a task emerges from the consciousness accompanying one's perception of an object as a "not yet fulfilled finality" (*noch nicht erledigte Endgültigkeit*) (*Logik als Aufgabe*, 70). What this means is that the object seems to be part of a meaningful whole or order that is not yet fully given in experience but that is indicated by the signs of order in the present consciousness.

61. Brentano claims that Aristotle believes that the human being is capable of and has the goal of development of an "intuitive knowledge of God" (*anschauliche Erkenntnis Gottes*). "In the light of this goal, every deformity [*Mißbildung*] on the path towards it in the world of plants and animals and every deformity that arises in human life as well (suffering, error, crime, the passing away of the individual and of whole peoples and civilizations), all of this would belong to a sort of embryonic preparatory period [*eine Art embryonaler Vorbereitung*] from which all opprobrium would fall away" (Brentano, *Aristoteles und seine Weltanschauung*, 143). It seems that Brentano is here indebted to Driesch's 1908 *Science and Philosophy of the Organism* for his reference to the history of life as a sort of embryonic development of the full actuality of the "intuitive knowledge of God"; it is also likely that Driesch is in turn indebted to Brentano for his conception of Knowing, *Wissen*, as the highest fulfillment not only of the individual human but also of humanity as a whole.

62. Johannes Reinke, *Einleitung in die theoretische Biologie* (Berlin: Gebrüder Paetel, 1901).

63. Ibid., iii.

64. For a clear and case-based discussion of the way that genes define state spaces in the morphogenesis of an organism, see Luis Mendoza, Denis Thieffry, and Elena R. Alvarez-Buylla, "Genetic Control of Flower Morphogenesis in *Arabidopsis Thalliana*: A Logical Analysis," *Bioinformatics* 15, nos. 7/8 (1999): 593–606.

65. Jakob von Uexküll, *Theoretische Biologie* (Berlin: Gebrüder Paetel, 1920).

66. Alexander Gurwitsch, *Versuch einer synthetischer Biologie*, Abhandlungen zur theoretischen Biologie 17 (Berlin: Gebrüder Borntraeger, 1923). For the life and work of Gurwitsch, see Lev Beloussov, John M. Opitz, and Scott F. Gilberg, "Life of Alexander G. Gurwitsch (1874–1954) and His Relevant Contribution to the Theory of Morphogenetic Fields," *International Journal of Developmental Biology* 41 (1997): 771–779. Gurwitsch published several articles in Wilhelm Roux's *Archiv für Entwicklungsmechanik*, one of the foremost journals in the field of embryology. (After the First World War, Roux invited Gurwitsch to hold a professorship in Berlin, but Gurwitsch declined, preferring to stay in the Soviet Union.) Gurwitch is only recently being reread. See, for example, the Tufts University biologist Michael Levin's work on morphogenetic fields in "Morphogenetic Fields in Embryogenesis, Regeneration, and Cancer: Non-local Control of Complex Patterning," *Biosystems* 109, no. 3 (2012): 243–261. Since 1994 there have been three "Alexander Gurwitsch Conferences" organized by Russian and German biophysics researchers, most recently in 2004. Gurwitsch is also credited with having discovered the phenomenon called "biophotonic" radiation, a form of ultraviolet radiation associated with cell division.

67. Gurwitsch, *Versuch einer synthetischer Biologie*, 34.

68. Ibid., 72; emphasis Gurwitsch's.

69. Ibid., 35.

70. Alexander Gurwitsch, "On Practical Vitalism," *American Naturalist* 49, no. 588 (1915): 763–770. The reference to "Naturphilosophie" is on page 770.

71. Paul Weiss, "Die Regeneration der Urodelenextremität als Selbstdifferenzierung des Organrestes," *Naturwissenschaft* 11, no. 31 (1923): 669–677.

72. Paul A. Weiss, *Morphodynamik: Ein Einblick in die Gesetzung der organischen Gestaltung an Hand von experimentellen Ergebnissen*, Abhandlungen zur theoretischen Biologie 23 (Berlin: Gebrüder Borntraeger, 1926). See also Paul A. Weiss, "Morphodynamische Feldtheorie und Genetik," *Zeitschrift für Induktive Abstammungs- und Vererbungslehre*, Supp. 2 (1928): 1567–1574. The most accessible account of the field theory of morphogenesis is found in Paul Weiss, *Principles of Development: A Text in Experimental Embryology* (Chicago: University of Chicago Press, 1939). After leaving Germany in 1931 to teach at Yale, Weiss went on to a

distinguished career in embryology and neurobiology at the University of Chicago (1933–1954) and the newly created Rockefeller University (1954–1969). He was elected to the National Academy of Arts and Sciences in 1954 and was awarded the National Medal of Science by President Jimmy Carter in 1979. For an overview of his life and work, see Jane Overton, *Biographical Memoir for Paul Alfred Weiss 1898–1989* (Washington, DC: National Academies Press, 1997), available at www.nasonline.org/publications/biographical-memoirs/memoir-pdfs/weiss-paul.pdf.

As I have mentioned, Ludwig von Bertalanffy was another important "theoretical biologist." Today he is known as one of the founders of systems theory. For Weiss's relation to von Bertalanffy, see Manfred Drack, Wilifried Apfalter, and David Pouveau, "On the Making of a System Theory of Life: Paul A. Weiss and Ludwig von Bertalanffy's Conceptual Connection," *Quarterly Review of Biology* 4, no. 82 (2007): 349–373. Recently, Weiss's theoretical approach to developmental biology has been reassessed as providing an important new paradigm for biological research. See Bernd Rosslenbroich, "Outline of a Concept for Organismic Systems Biology," *Seminars in Cancer Biology* 3, no. 21 (2011): 156–164. Weiss's post-1950 papers are collected in Paul Weiss, *Dynamics of Development: Experiments and Inferences* (New York: Academic Press, 1968).

73. Weiss, *Principles of Development*, 290.

74. Ibid., 290; emphasis Weiss's. In a footnote to this definition of "field," Weiss explains that the biologist Hans Speman (1869–1941), Nobel Prize recipient for his work on embryonic "organizer centers," had pioneered the field concept in work that first appeared in 1921 and that independently, but at nearly the same time, Alexander Gurwitsch had published results of embryological experiments that led him to a similar field concept. For Speman's organizer concept, see Hans Spemann, "The Organizer-Effect in Embryonic Development," Nobel Lecture, December 12, 1935, Nobelprize.org, http://www.nobelprize.org/nobel_prizes/medicine/laureates/1935/spemann-lecture.html.

75. Weiss, *Principles of Development*, 291; emphasis Weiss's.

76. Goldberg, *Reality of the Hebrews*, 156.

77. Ibid., 158.

78. Erich Unger, *Lebendige und Goettliche*, 113–135.

79. Unger, *Lebendige und Goettliche*, 152–153.

80. Karl Camillo Schneider was a professor of zoology at the University of Vienna from 1911 until 1931. Schneider's career ended in 1932 when he made an attempt on the life of a rather hard-nosed dean of his university who refused to fund one of his experiments in telepathy and questioned Schneider's choice of course topics. Schneider was judged to be mentally disturbed at his trial, and he was allowed to live in retirement on his brother's estate. For a brief biographical note with bibliography, see Markus Flatscher and Richard Hörmann, eds., *Ferdinand Ebner: Tagebuch 1918* (Vienna: LIT, 2014), 341.

81. Karl Camillo Schneider, "*Die Wirklichkeit der Hebräer* von Oskar Goldberg," *Zeitschrift für Parapsychologie* 2 (1928): 113–117; quotation on p. 114.

82. Schneider's observation is amply confirmed by the magisterial study of Linda Dalrymple Henderson, *The Fourth Dimension and Non-Euclidean Geometry in Modern Art* (Princeton, NJ: Princeton University Press, 1983).

83. Karl Camillo Schneider, *Euvitalistische Biologie: Zur Grundlegung der Kultur* (Munich: J. F. Bergmann, 1926), 168.

84. "Summarizing, one can conclude: every occurrence in a physical system is dilated [*verlangsamt*] when this system is subjected to a translation of its movement. This dilation however takes place only from the standpoint of a different coordinate system (of an observer)."

See Albert Einstein, "Die Relativitätstheorie," in *Die Kultur der Gegenwart: Ihre Entwicklung und ihre Ziele* [*The Culture of the Present: Its Development and Its Goals*] 3rd Abt., vol. 1, ed. Paul Hinneberg (Leipzig: B. G. Teubner, 1915), 703–713; quotation on p. 712.

85. Schneider, *Euvitalistische Biologie*, 180.

86. Gustav Fechner (Dr. Mises), *Vier Paradoxa* (Leipzig: Leopold Voss, 1846).

87. Schneider, *Euvitalistische Biologie*, 170.

88. Ibid., 172.

89. Ibid., 173.

90. Ibid., 177.

91. Ibid., 177.

92. Ibid., 195.

93. Ibid., 214–215.

94. Ibid., 208.

95. Hermann Weyl, "Two Letters by Einstein and Weyl on a Metaphysical Question," in Hermann Weyl, *Mind and Nature: Selected Writings on Philosophy, Mathematics, and Physics*, ed. Peter Pesic (Princeton, NJ: Princeton University Press, 2009), 25–28. For Hermann Weyl's own positive evaluation of Naturphilosophie, see Erhard Scholz, "Weyls Infinitesmalgeometrie (1917–1925)," in *Hermann Weyl's Raum–Zeit–Materie and a General Introduction to His Scientific Work* ed. Erhard Scholz (Basel: Birkhäuser, 2001), 48–104, esp. 83–84.

# 2  Georg Cantor and the Mathematics of God

OSKAR GOLDBERG'S VITALIST philosophy draws its inspiration from both the early nineteenth-century Naturphilosophie of F. W. J. Schelling and Lorenz Oken and the neo-Naturphilosophie of Hans Driesch and other biologists and phenomenological psychologists of the early decades of the twentieth century. One of the features of Naturphilosophie throughout its history was its reliance on mathematics to provide a foundation for its dynamic conception of nature. At the conclusion of chapter 1, I discussed the University of Vienna zoologist Karl Camillo Schneider's concept of "number" to supply a foundation for his theory of the mathematical structure of the infinite aether in which God is present as a force structure in pure potentiality. Schneider was by far the most speculative of the life scientists who were seeking a more holistic explanatory model for organic phenomena. Theoretical biologists like Ludwig von Bertalannfy, Alexander Gurwitsch, and Paul Weiss offered far less speculative explanatory models that made use of mathematics, especially topology, to account for cellular differentiation during embryological development. To their names, let me add that of another University of Vienna life scientist, Hans Przibram (1874–1944), who argued for a new "mathematical biology." Przibram notes that "in the history of the biological sciences the Romantics, who seem more appealing to us, were much more prepared to travel mathematical paths than our contemporaries."[1] Goldberg's neo-Naturphilosophie vitalism, we will find, is very much like its Romantic precursor in its turn to mathematics. The mathematical basis of Goldberg's Kabbalistic Naturphilosophie is the subject of this chapter.

Goldberg's first publication, *Die fünf Bücher Mosis: Ein Zahlengebäudge* (*The Five Books of Moses: A Numerical Structure*), is an exercise in mathematical Kabbalah: it offers an account of the numerical structure of the Pentateuch, the Five Books of Moses, based on the traditional method of numerological hermeneutics called *gematria*.[2] I explain the method of *gematria* later in the chapter, but first let me present Goldberg's other source for his mathematical interpretation of the Pentateuch: the theory of infinity developed in the work of nineteenth-century mathematician Georg Cantor. In the Goldberg Nachlass at the German Literature Archive in Marbach there are dozens of notebooks from the time of writing of his first book on the number system of the Pentateuch. One of these notebooks is titled "Philosophie der Mathematik" (Philosophy of Mathematics) and another "Probleme der Naturphilosophie" (Problems of Naturphilosophie), demonstrating the close relationship between these two fields in Goldberg's mind. In these notebooks, Goldberg writes at considerable length about the process that may have taken place in the infinite mind of God that led to the generation of the "number system" underlying both the empirical world as a whole and the Pentateuch more specifically. In what sounds like a reworking of Schelling's speculations about the ground of God's decision to create the world in his *Weltalter* (*Ages of the World*),[3] Goldberg writes in one notebook of God's will being divided between a choice to "build a series [of numbers]" or not to build such a series. The production of a number series after an "arbitrary action" (*Willkürakt*) leads to the creation of the "continuum." The continuum is then divided into discrete numerical structures through "negation," that is, the finitization (limiting through negation) of the infinite continuum.[4] Thankfully, Goldberg's early book on the number system of the Pentateuch avoids any mention of such speculative ventures into the infinite mind of God. But it is important to note that for Goldberg the number system of Pentateuch was simply one particular finitization of the divine infinite.

One early notebook in the Goldberg archive is titled "Theoretische Physik." (Theoretical Physics). Its opening words capture the basic principle of Goldberg's mathematical Naturphilosophie: "The number series corresponds to the continuum. If one passes beyond the number series to infinity there arises a formal system. A formal system is the 'pure form' of the number series."[5] Goldberg's reference to the continuum and his view of the number series as a "pure formal" system derives from Georg Cantor's revolutionary publications in the mathematics of infinity from the 1880s. Goldberg's reliance on Cantor for his mathematico-Kabbalistic Naturphilosophie comes out most clearly in a passage from another (untitled) notebook in his archive:

> The number system displays intentional structures [*Absichten*] without itself being intentional. There is a structure-building force. The Pentateuch wrote itself.[6] That *yod* [the Hebrew letter representing 10 in the system of *gematria*] and *kof* [the letter representing 100] both can be seen as equivalent to 1 [if we discount the zeros] is the idea of a theory of sets [*Idee der Mengenlehre*] in the ancient world. There are higher unities, higher Alufs [the first letter of the Hebrew alphabet, more typically rendered *aleph*] as Kantor [*sic*] calls them, that however are equivalent to One. *This is the source of gematria.* (Emphasis Goldberg's.)

For our purposes, it is not essential that we understand at this point exactly what Goldberg is saying in this note. In the next section I explain what Goldberg takes from Cantor's theory of the infinite, namely, a concept of the actual or completed infinite as a "pure form of the number series." Cantor offered Goldberg a rigorous proof that infinity was not sheer endlessness, but rather a complete unity or "transfinite number," as Cantor described the number he designated with the Hebrew letter aleph. What is more, Cantor showed that there is an infinity of transfinite alephs. Goldberg believed that Cantor's theory of transfinite numbers provided access to the interior of God's infinite mind. Indeed, Cantor believed this too.

Cantor's mathematics of transfinite numbers comes at the conclusion of a history of speculation about the nature of infinity and the continuum beginning with Leibniz. Because this speculation looked for a way to understand the infinite as a single whole structure, it had close ties with Naturphilosophie's attempt to describe the infinite universe as a single unified whole. After tracing the development of Cantor's theory and its relation to Naturphilosophie in the next section, I then turn to Goldberg's earliest efforts to read the Pentateuch through the lens of a Cantorian-Kabbalistic Naturphilosophie.

## The Mathematics of Infinity: An Overview

It is sometimes wrongly claimed that Romantic Naturphilosophie represents a turn away from the quantitative abstractions of mathematics toward a purely qualitative understanding of natural phenomena. The contemporary philosopher Alain Badiou has gone so far as to describe the "disentanglement of philosophy and mathematics" in the early nineteenth century as "the Romantic speculative gesture par excellence."[7] Perhaps this holds true for Hegel, the philosopher whose disparagement of "bad infinity" comes in for particular criticism by Badiou, but not for many of the other thinkers associated with early Naturphilosophie. Lorenz Oken, for example, wrote, "Organic objects are self-activating whole numbers."[8] The Romantic poet Novalis (Georg Philipp Friedrich Freiherr von Herdenberg, 1772–1801) devoted considerable effort to creating a mathematical version of Naturphilosophie, although he never managed to synthesize his fragmentary aphorisms into systematic form. One of his aphorisms, for example, reads, "The highest life is mathematics."[9] Bernard Bolzano (1771–1848), a leading mathematician and pioneer in the mathematics of infinity, demonstrates his allegiance to Naturphilosophie when he places on the title page of his *Paradoxes of the Infinite* a quotation from Leibniz: "I stand for actual infinity so much that instead of admitting that Nature abhors it, as it is commonly said, I hold that [Nature] assumes it everywhere, in order to signal better the perfections of its Author."[10]

Probably the most philosophically astute historian of the speculative tradition conjoining the mathematics of infinity with Romantic Naturphilosophie was the neo-Kantian Ernst Cassirer (1874–1945), whose work on Leibniz I briefly discussed in the opening of chapter 1. Cassirer, influenced by his teacher Hermann Cohen, considered the mathematics of infinity (the continuum) to hold the key to a new rapprochement between Kantian idealism and modern science. Cassirer therefore returns to Leibniz, together with Newton considered as the "inventor" of infinitesimal calculus, in order to explore the origin of the modern scientific consciousness. The historian of science Marco Giovanelli claims that "Cassirer's book on Leibniz, for all its limitations, can be considered as one of the classics of the so-called Leibniz-Renaissance at the turn of the century, together with the books of Bertrand Russell and Louis Couturat."[11] Unlike his teacher Hermann Cohen, Cassirer believed that the rapprochement between Kantian idealism and science would bring physics and biology into much closer connection, with biology taking pride of place: Newton's infinitesimal calculus based on atoms and discontinuity, for Cassirer, must take a backseat to Leibniz's calculus based on "fluxions" and the unbroken continuity of nature.[12] Cassirer considered the mathematical principle of continuity that lies at the basis of Leibniz's version of the infinitesimal calculus to be most perfectly expressed in the unfolding growth of an organism.[13] In *Leibniz's System and Its Scientific Foundations*, Cassirer traces the connection between organic becoming (*Werden*) and infinitesimal calculus back to Leibniz's foundational "principle of continuity"—the principle that nature unfolds in a continuous and unbroken progression of forms in accordance with a transcendental, generative lawfulness.[14] Cassirer considers Leibniz to have been the first to have applied a mathematically rigorous understanding of continuity to both physics and biology, thus offering "the first application [of mathematics] to concrete, living reality." Cassirer concludes, "It is therefore not only indefensible as a matter of actual fact, it is also historically mistaken, to think that mathematical rationalism is necessarily in conflict with a developmental-historical worldview. This alleged opposition . . . fails when it comes to the mathematics of the infinite, the mathematics of becoming."[15]

Cassirer's magisterial treatment of the new "mathematics of the infinite" is found in his 1910 *Form and Function*.[16] His description of how the new mathematics moved away from Euclidean geometry's emphasis on the description of geometric figures to the new analytic geometry of figures as *functional relations of order* is worth quoting in full:

> In the analysis of the infinite in geometry, . . . the curve is here . . . conceived as a certain order of points; but this order, which as it is immediately given is a highly involved serial form, is conceptually analyzed as a manifold of simpler laws of serial order, that mutually determine each other. The concrete form is analyzed into a concrete form of *virtual* grounds of determination, which are assumed to be different from point to point. The geometrical form, which from the standpoint of direct intuition and elementary synthetic geometry, seems to something absolutely known and immediately comprehensible, appears here as a mediated result. The form is as if resolved into manifold

strata of relations, which are superimposed upon each other and which, by the definite type of dependence among them, finally determine a single whole.

Herewith is determined a problem of comprehensive significance. The construction of curves out of the totality of their tangents, as shown in infinitesimal geometry, is only an example of a procedure of more general applicability. All mathematical conceptual construction sets itself a double task, in fact the task of the analysis of a certain relational complex into elementary types of relation and the synthesis of these simpler types and laws of construction into relations of higher orders. The analysis of the infinite is logically a first and complete expression of this intellectual tendency. For even here mathematical investigation advances beyond the mere consideration of magnitudes and turns to a general theory of functions. The "elements" here joined into new unities are themselves not extensive magnitudes which are combined as "parts" of a whole, but are forms of function which reciprocally determine each other and unite into a system of dependencies.[17]

According to Cassirer, Kant was wrong to think that the immediate intuition of spatial forms is the basis of geometry. Rather, the comprehension of the spatial form rises to its true mathematical precision when the form is seen as the "mediated result" of "manifold strata of relations" that are not "extensive magnitudes" but rather "forms of function." The key point is that *even infinity must yield to the form-generating power of the mind.* Although Cassirer is typically identified as a neo-Kantian, he goes far beyond Kant when he credits the mind with the power to discover the creative "laws of construction" by which spatial order is generated. Cassirer goes beyond Kant when he argues that the creative power of the imagination can generate multidimensional spatialities.[18] The phenomenal realm of space and time is governed not only by mechanical laws but also by laws that produce "new unities" that are greater than the sum of their parts. *The phenomenal realm is the extensive unfolding in space of a complex manifold of law-defining functions.* This is the core of Cassirer's transformation of the Kantian notion of the ideality of space and time: the productive imagination is not enchained to the everyday world of experience. We see later in this chapter how important this idea is for Goldberg and Unger as well.

The modern mathematics of unfolding forms that is rooted in the creative imagination is, according to Cassirer, adumbrated in Goethe's "organic concept of form," the so-called Urphenomena underlying the multiplicity of natural beings. Cassirer explains that for Goethe the authentic imaginative power (*echte Einbildungskraft*) of the natural scientist provides an "originary-genetic intuition [*ursprünglich-genetische Anschauung*] that seeks to construct and grasp any existing entity [*das Seiende*] in its ideality, whether on the basis of the general law or the individual form of becoming [*sei es aus dem allgemeinen Gesetz, sei es aus der individuellen Form des Werdens*]."[19] For Cassirer, the static picture in Kant's model of the "schemata of the imagination" needs to be replaced by a dynamic and "living" conception of the power of the imagination to synthesize "relations of higher orders," even to the point of *giving a number to infinity.* While it was the development of infinitesimal calculus by Newton and Leibniz and later advances in analytic geometry that set the foundations crucial for the "mathematics of becoming," Cassirer acknowledges that it was first Georg Cantor who successfully demonstrated that the mind, *pace* Kant, could in fact overcome the gulf separating finitude and infinity. *Infinity is not the unknowable "beyond" of the series of finite numbers; it is the construction of a "logical function" capable of totalizing the series as it is given by its generative law.* In the remainder of this section I briefly discuss the way in which Georg Cantor imagined his revolutionary theory of transfinite numbers to offer, at last, a way to show how God's Infinity manifested itself within the living reality of the material world.

We may most appropriately begin our account of Cantor's new theory of transfinite numbers with Bernhard Riemann (1826–1866) whose non-Euclidean geometry of the manifold (*Mannigfaltigkeit*) provides the essential background to Cantor's theory. Riemann believed that his work on the mathematics of the manifold placed Naturphilosophie on a new mathematical foundation. As Cassirer helps us to understand, the early Naturphilosophers sought above all else to understand organic phenomena as concrete manifestations of the Leibnizian infinitesimal calculus, that is, as "fluxions" synthesizing an infinite number of separated elements into a higher integral unity. What Riemann provided was a way to understand space itself as a medium in which *organic* integral unities could be fully at home. In place of Newton's empty and homogeneous space, Riemann offered a space that was alive with force fields. The way that physical force fields appeared to operate at a distance (gravitational attraction, for example) seemed to Riemann to be inexplicable if one assumed that space was only the empty location in which discrete objects were positioned. He wondered: What if the three spatial dimensions were *created* by the variations of some underlying force?[20] Riemann looked for a different way to understand geometry that would allow him to redefine the dimensions of space as the creation of varying and interrelated intensities of a force. This led Riemann to his notion of multiple-dimensioned manifolds.

For Riemann, the manifold is not a single magnitude, but is a complex *relationship* among covarying properties. As Cassirer would put it, spatial *forms* are a product of mathematical *functions.* The historian of mathematics José Ferreirós describes Riemann's manifold as "the totality of all possible outcomes of a measuring experiment in which the values of two, or perhaps *n*, physical magnitudes are determined for a given physical system."[21] When we think today about Riemann's manifolds we often connect them, correctly, with non-Euclidean geometry. The geometry of a torus (one of whose geometric forms is the donut, another being a coffee cup) is non-Euclidean because the shortest distance between any two given points (what Riemann called the "geodesic") is *not* a straight line, but a curve on its surface. In non-Euclidean geometry, two manifolds are identical, despite the very different actual shape they may have, if all its geodesics have the same length (there is no stretching the geodesics, just twisting). Because a manifold is created by forces acting together that are also in tension with one another, Riemann thought of space not as an empty and homogeneous receptacle but as the creation of what he called "binding forces that act upon space" (*auf den Raum wirkende bindende Kräfte*).[22] (It is not a far step from space-forming fields of energy to the concept of *biological* force fields that were postulated by vitalist life scientists like Hans Driesch and his younger followers whom I discussed in chapter 1.)

Riemann imagined that we live on a surface of a very slightly curving space. "If we prolong all the geodesics [lines] starting in a given surface element," Riemann speculated, "we should obtain an unbounded surface of constant curvature, i.e., a surface which in a flat manifoldness of three dimensions would take the form of a sphere and consequently be finite."[23] The antinomy that Kant posed in the *Critique of Pure Reason*—either the universe is infinite or it is finite, but arguments for each alternative lead to contradictions—is settled by showing that it is *both* infinite (unbounded) and finite. We are today familiar with the idea that space is curved, but this was something quite radical when Riemann first broached it 1854. The idea that infinity and finitude could be reconciled through a theory of space as a dynamically organized manifold of points played an important role in Cantor's transfinite number theory.

Before turning to Cantor, a few more words about Riemann are in order. Riemann believed that his mathematics of manifolds could be used to fulfill the dream of Naturphilosophie: a synthetic portrait of the *living universe*. Riemann claimed that his theory of manifolds offered a rigorous interpretation of Gustav Fechner's concept of the world soul, the living infinite totality of the cosmos. Fechner (1801–1887), as I mentioned in chapter 1, was one of the founders of experimental psychology, but his interests extended far beyond "psychophysics" and measuring the thresholds of perceptibility of different sensory stimuli—the important and groundbreaking work on which his reputation today largely rests. In 1854, Fechner published a three-volume work, *Zend-Avesta, or Concerning the Things of Heaven and the Beyond*, dealing with the levels of consciousness that subtend our everyday threshold of experience, levels that widen out to include all living things in a single, embracing planetary consciousness.[24] *Zend-Avesta* is a testament to Fechner's capacious and imaginative vision of the planet as a single, immortal, living organism. Riemann wrote that *Zend-Avesta* was a "life-giving word, creating new life for both our science and our faith."[25] Among Riemann's posthumously published essays one can find extended attempts at formulating a revised Leibnizian metaphysics based on the elementary "psychic quantum"

(*Geistesmasse*) with "inner manifoldness" (*innere Mannigfaltigkeit*) that comes into expression at various discrete zones (*Orte*) and that organizes space into dynamic force fields. Each psychic quantum seeks to reproduce itself by conjoining with others of similar quality and producing an enlarged, new "psychic quantum": "the most general and simplest expression of the effective power of earlier psychic quanta is reproduction, which consists in the striving of one psychic mass to generate another one similar to itself."[26] Fechner introduced the idea that the earth is one large, living ecosystem, and Riemann saw that Fechner's living earth-system could be modeled as a very complex, multidimensional manifold of self-reproducing points of varying psychic intensities.[27]

Georg Cantor (1854–1918) was no less interested than Riemann in finding the mathematical foundations of a unified theory of the universe, although Cantor did not share Riemann's Fechnerian pantheistic tendencies. Rather, Cantor believed that he had uncovered the deep structure of God's transcendental and infinite mind. In his 1883 essay titled *Foundations of a General Theory of Manifolds*,[28] Georg Cantor revolutionizes number theory by proposing the existence of numbers situated between absolute infinity and finite integers. He claims that there is a series of "transfinite" numbers lying between all the finite numbers and the "true infinite or Absolute, which is in God."[29] "What I assert . . . is that there is after the finite a *transfinite* (which one can also call *superfinite*), that is, an unlimited hierarchy [*Stufenleiter*] of definite number classes that in their nature are not finite but rather infinite, although, exactly like the finite, they can be determined through certain well-defined numbers each of which is different from the other."[30] It is important to note that Cantor explicitly describes his theory of transfinite numbers as a theory of actually existing numbers, each an *infinite number*, leading up to the "true infinity" in God.[31] Cantor claims that his theory offers a fulfillment of the metaphysical aspirations of Leibniz and Spinoza to bridge the gap separating the infinite God from the finite world. In particular, he claims that his theory at last gives rigorous expression to Spinoza's doctrine that God is the infinite substance of which there are both *infinite modes* (the transfinite numbers) and *finite modes* (the finite numbers).[32]

Cantor's "manifold" (*Mannigfaltigkeit*) is a term that in his work refers to what mathematicians today call a "set" containing members whose relationship to one another is defined by some "generative principle" (*Erzeugungsprinzip*) or law. For example, the set of all finite integers (1, 2, 3, and so on) is a set of numbers defined by what Cantor calls the "first generative principle"—"the addition of a unity to an already present number" (*die Hinzufügung einer Einheit zu einer vorhandenen gebildeten Zahl*).[33] Cantor's *Foundations* introduces the concept of *transfinite* numbers with what Cassirer calls "a new perspective" (*ein neuer Gesichtspunkt*) on the infinite series of numbers produced one after another by Cantor's first generative principle.[34] Instead of looking at the series as an endless, continuous succession of numbers in the process of unfolding, Cantor asks us to see it as *having produced* an "entire assemblage" (*ganze Inbegriff*) of numbers:

> The formation of the finite real integers . . . rests upon the principle of adding a unity to an already present number; I call this method of generation, which, as we shall soon see, plays an essential role in the building up of the higher integers, the *first principle* of generation. The number of numbers . . . is infinite and there is no greatest among them. *However contradictory it might be to speak of a greatest number . . . there is nothing offensive in thinking of a new number . . . which will be the expression of the idea that the entire assemblage [of integers] is given in its natural, orderly succession.*[35]

The new perspective on the infinite series of numbers involves what Cantor calls a "logical function" that totalizes their infinite succession and then creates a new number that is "the next greater number to all of them."[36] Cantor calls this logical function the "second principle of generation." (Goldberg speaks of it as the "pure form of the number series.") Although Cantor suggests that the logical function is connected to the power of the mind to form abstract concepts (*Begriffe*), he denies that the totalized infinity—he calls it the "authentic infinity" (*eigentliche Unendlichkeit*)—is merely a subjective mental phenomenon. The first number ("ordinal") generated by the logical function is what Cantor designates with the Greek letter omega ($\omega$), whose "cardinality" is represented by the Hebrew aleph.[37] The letter $\omega$ has what Cantor calls an "intrasubjective" or "immanent" mental reality because it can be given a defined meaning within the conceptual framework of number theory. But $\omega$ and all the other transfinite numbers also have a "transsubjective" or "transiente" reality in the world of "corporeal and spiritual" nature:[38]

> We can speak of the reality or the existence of the integers, whether finite or infinite, in two senses: . . . Firstly, integers may be considered real in so far as they occupy an entirely definite place in our understanding on the basis of definitions . . . . I propose to call this kind of reality of our numbers their *intrasubjective* or *immanent* reality. Secondly, reality can be ascribed to numbers in so far as they must be taken as an expression or image of the events and relationships of that outer world which is exterior to the intellect, as, for example, the various number classes (I) (II) (III) etc. are representatives of powers which are actually found in corporeal and spiritual nature. This second species of reality I call the *transubjective* or *transiente* reality of the integers.[39]

When Cantor speaks about "number classes (I) (II) (III) etc." he is referring to the fact that the first and second generative principles can also be applied to $\omega$ itself to yield a whole new infinite series. This new infinite series cannot be matched in a one-to-one correspondence to the infinite series of finite numbers and therefore constitutes a new "number class" or "cardinality." Each number class of transfinite numbers follows the previous class in an endless series of classes that makes the endless series of *finite* numbers (1, 2, 3, and so on) seem like a "completely evaporating nothingness" (*ganz verschwindendenes Nichts*) in comparison.[40] This series of transfinite classes, Cantor claims in *Foundations*, ends in the "Absolute," the "true infinity in God." Not only does Cantor assert that ω has a transubjective reality in virtue of being logically consistent and compatible with other mathematical concepts but all the other ordinals in every number class also exist, or have their instantiation, within "corporeal and spiritual nature." This sort of reality Cantor calls "transiente," and he says it is the business of metaphysics to clarify how a logically consistent concept like "transfinite number" actually is instantiated in the world. That it is so instantiated, Cantor is certain. The connection between mathematics and reality, Cantor states, "has its real grounding in the *unity of the all, to which we ourselves belong.*"[41]

Cantor explains the objective reality of all transfinite numbers in a note where he identifies his position with that of Plato. Cantor quotes the historian of philosophy Eduard Zeller's description of Plato's theory of the relation of mind and reality: "The extent to which our representations [*Vorstellungen*] coincide with the truth—and this assumption Plato shares with others (Parmenides)—is the extent to which their object must possess reality, and vice versa." When Cantor, therefore, offers a theory of transfinite numbers, he is offering a theory of numbers that have "objective reality" (*gegenständige Realität*), despite the fact that we do not yet know where in the world to find them instantiated.[42] The future will disclose the nature of their existence: "I know of nothing that stands in the way of forming new numbers as soon as the progress of science suggests or even demands the introduction of one from among these new, countless number classes." The future use of the transfinite numbers will make possible, Cantor declares, "an organic explanation of nature."[43]

What justifies Cantor's confidence that his transfinite numbers are not merely figments of his imagination? Cantor's proof that there is an actual number greater than any finite number involves the theorem, named after him, that the number of subsets of any set is greater than the number of the members of the set. The number of subsets of any set is called its "power set." If Cantor's theorem applies to the set of all integers, then there must be a number corresponding to the power set of the set of all integers, and that number is necessarily greater than any number in the set. The proof of Cantor's theorem for the infinite set of finite integers is quite ingenious and not terribly difficult to grasp, but for our purposes it is enough to know that Cantor had demonstrated to his satisfaction (and to all mathematicians after him) that there indeed does exist a number greater than any finite number.[44] More important for us is Cantor's argument that the existence of this transfinite number (and the infinite number of such transfinite numbers whose existence he also proves) *depends on the creative power of the divine intellect.*

To understand the theological foundation of Cantor's mathematics of the infinite, we need to recall that he describes the first transfinite number ω as the product of a "logical function." This "logical function" involves shifting one's intellectual perspective on the infinite series of finite integers so that one sees them not "from the inside" as an infinitely "growing" series, but rather one considers them "from the outside" in "the defined form of the completed infinite" (*in der bestimmten Form des Vollendetunendlichen*).[45] The mathematician David Hilbert explains Cantor's point this way: "When we have counted 1, 2, 3 . . . , we can regard the objects thus enumerated as an infinite set existing all at once *in a particular order*."[46] It is essential to note that the possibility of totalizing all the finite numbers depends, first of all, on the existence of a "particular order" of succession that governs *all* of them. Thus, for Cantor "well-orderedness" is a necessary feature of every ordinal, finite as well as infinite. The intellect can perform the "logical function" of unifying an infinite set by seeing its well-orderedness in one glimpse. If the human intellect can do this, then the divine intellect can unify the infinity of all transfinite numbers. In this way, Cantor believed that humans share in the infinite nature of the Absolute: "The words 'finite understanding' which one hears so often in no way hit the mark; however limited in truth human nature may be, it still partakes greatly of the infinite and I declare that if in many respects it were not itself infinite, the firm conviction and certainty as to the existence of the Absolute, to which we all agree, would be inexplicable."[47] Cantor's *Foundations* thus takes mathematics to the limits of theology; indeed, it can be said to be founded on theology.[48]

The historian of mathematics Michael Hallett points out in his study of Cantor's mathematics of infinity how essential theology is to Cantor's project. Hallett explains that Cantor went much further than mathematical theory requires: "as far as mathematics is concerned establishing possibility and abstract existence (via coherence and inner consistency) is all that matters. . . . Cantor went further and claimed that much of this abstract transfinite world is represented in the concrete physical world of God's creation."[49] For Cantor, numbers are not the products of human psychological capacity, for then there could not be infinite numbers (or, for that matter, very large numbers that we cannot at once see as a single whole). It is, in the final analysis, *God himself* who guarantees the existence of well-orderedness, and it is God who makes this well-orderedness a reality in both the realm of number and the realm of created things. And as we have noted, well-orderedness is basic to Cantor's definition of number.

In the final pages of his 1885 essay in the journal *Acta Mathematica*, "On Various Theorems from the Theory of Point Sets," Cantor explains that his theory of "point sets" (*Punktmengen*) was never meant to be purely speculative. Rather, "it was undertaken with a view to its application in the field of mathematical physics and other scientific disciplines."[50] Cantor goes on to explain that he believes that "the final or truly *simple* elements of matter must be assumed to be *an actually infinite number* [*actuel unendlicher Zahl*] and that the spatial [*das Räumliche*] must be viewed in a *completely extensionless and purely punctual way*."[51] (It is possible that Karl Camillo Schneider's discussion of number as binding together the potential state of the aether and the fully actualized state of light-filled space is indebted to Cantor.) Cantor then draws on Leibniz to describe the spatial number-point-set as a monad, but he distinguishes between two different classes of number-point-set monads: one that would make up "bodily matter" (*Körpermaterie*) and another that would make up "aetherial matter" (*Äthermaterie*). The first, he says, would correspond to the finite number class (the numbers 1, 2, 3, and so on), and the second would correspond to the transfinite numbers. He suggests that the interaction of finite and transfinite spatial number-point-sets could account for the five fundamental forms in which matter appears or has effective force: "as conditions of aggregated matter, as chemically distinct kinds of matter, as light and warmth, as electricity, and as magnetism." Although Cantor never went further with his suggestion about how transfinite number theory could be used to explain the various kinetic and electromagnetic phenomena of matter, we can certainly see how clearly indebted this suggestion was to early speculations among the Naturphilosophers about the underlying dynamic properties of matter.

The relationship between Naturphilosophie and mathematics can be said to reach a peak in the work of Georg Cantor. Cantor's conception of the transfinite number, a number that totalizes the infinity of all finite numbers, offers the basis for an "organic" conception of number, a number that is greater than the sum of its parts. We see in the next section how important Cantor's number theory was for the development of Goldberg's version of mathematico-Kabbalistic vitalism.

## The World-Root Club and Goldberg's *Five Books of Moses*

At the opening of chapter 1 I discussed a letter that Goldberg wrote in 1922 to the anthropologist Felix von Luschan, in which he outlined his dissertation proposal concerning the role of holy men in the formation of ethnic groups in antiquity. I noted that Goldberg positions himself in the letter as "close to Naturphilosophie circles." The letter also makes it clear that Goldberg considered mathematics to be deeply connected to the vitalist principle underlying Naturphilosophie. It explains that there is no sharp break between inorganic and organic phenomena: in both, the whole is greater than the sum of its parts. Goldberg goes so far as to claim that numbers also are more than aggregates of identical units. Goldberg offers the number 30 as an example of a number with unique characteristics that differentiate it from all other numbers (perhaps he is thinking about how its prime roots—2, 3, and 5—are the first three primes in the number series).

Goldberg's definition of life in *The Reality of the Hebrews*, published in 1925, is essentially mathematical, relying on the notion of well-orderedness as the defining mark of the organism. He offers his definition as the conclusion of a mathematical interpretation of what he calls "the transcendental organism" in which the "Idea of biology" is realized. I devote more attention to the notion of the transcendental organism in chapter 4, but for now it suffices to say that Goldberg claims that the "biology-productive principle" that creates the transcendental organism is one that overcomes the contradiction between infinity and finitude. He speaks of the transcendental organism as the "actualization of the contradiction, the finitization of the infinite."[52] Defining the organism as the "finitization of the infinite" not only reveals Goldberg's mathematically tinged vitalism but also indicates one of the inspirations behind Goldberg's conception, namely, Georg Cantor. Michael Hallett aptly describes Cantor's essential insight as that, between the finite numbers and the humanly ungraspable "Absolute Infinity in God," there exists an intermediary "realm of infinities which can be rationally subjugated, which are mathematically determinable, . . . what Cantor calls the transfinite."[53] What Cantor's theory of transfinite numbers achieves is the *finitization of the infinite*. That is, Cantor is able to bring finite and transfinite numbers within a single mathematical theory that makes infinity *calculable*. This is so important for Cantor that he offers in Latin his fundamental principle: "Omnia seu finita seu infinita *definita* sunt et excepto Deo ab intellectu determinari possunt" (All forms whether finite or infinite are *definite* and, with the exception of God, are capable of being intellectually [mathematically] determined).[54] Cantor, as we saw in the previous section, claims that the finitization of the infinite provides the foundation for an "organic explanation of nature," but he never goes into much detail about how one might use transfinite numbers to explain organic phenomena. That task is the very essence of Goldberg's project.[55]

For Goldberg, the intermediary realm between God's Absolute Infinity and the finite world is the realm of the "biology-productive principle," a principle of *organic well-ordering* that he calls the "transcendental organism." Although in chapter 4 I discuss Goldberg's "biology-productive principle" in much more detail, it is useful to quote an important passage about this principle from *The Reality of the Hebrews* in full here, despite its length. It provides us an idea of the way that Goldberg links the Cantorian mathematics of infinity with biology:

> Since the biology-productive principle is situated between the infinite and the finite actuality, it can be conceived properly neither as the one nor as the other. It must therefore bring to expression the conceptual categories of *both* regions in a *new synthetic* unity. The biology-productive principle is, grasped categorially, the intermediate conceptual region between "unity" [*Einheit*] and "multiplicity" [*Vielheit*]. It is "multiplicity" in so far as it appears as a "unity." It is the "multiplicity-unity" [*Vielheitseinheit*]. Since a *real* classification proce-

dure [*Zuordnungsmethode*] corresponds to this formal one, it follows that for the character of the biology-productive reality the two greatest oppositions in existence, infinity and finitude, are not only unified but also actualized: it is therefore the actualization of the contradiction, the finitization of the infinite.

The three related categorial concepts of "unity," "multiplicity-unity," and "multiplicity" have a certain determinate relationship to the principle of uniqueness [*Einmaligkeitsprinzip*]. While the authentic unity certainly corresponds to that which is unique (what can appear only once), in the realm of pure multipleness [*Vielmaligkeit*], every multiplicity [*Vielheit*] can appear frequently, any number of times that one may choose. The conceptual intermediary region of the "multiplicity-unity"—which has a middle position—has as its formal meaning the "multiplicity" of "uniquenesses," in that it appears in the form of a region where, on the one hand, every "multiplicity" (and every member of the natural number series is one such) is coordinated with [*geordnet zu*] a "unity," whereas on the other hand each such summative unity (in contradistinction to the realm of pure multipleness) can appear only once. This *structure* of a conceptual intermediate region between "unity" and "multiplicity," that is composed of a "multiplicity" of "uniquenesses," from which it appears as a "multiplicity-unity," leads to another kind of space-principle than the ordinary one.

Empirical space, the "ordinary" space-principle, Goldberg goes on to explain, is homogeneous, and all its parts (or building blocks) are similar in kind. For this reason each position in ordinary space can be exchanged for any other one that one likes without thereby causing a change. But there is a *transcendental* space-principle that is of a *heterogeneous* nature. This is the space composed of a "multiplicity" of "uniquenesses." This multiplicity constitutes the "transcendental organism." It is made up of elements that (as "uniquenesses") are indivisible (*unteilbar*) and different in kind (*ungleichartig*). Since no position in this space is exchangeable with another because each one is endowed with a special value in its own manner, if there is a change of position, there is also necessarily a change in value. From this it follows that, in heterogeneous space, the *principle of positional value* holds sway. It therefore resembles a finite, living organism whose parts cannot be interchanged without the destruction of the wholeness of the organism. The organism shapes space into a well-ordered system of positional values. This is true of the infinite transcendental organism and also of the finite organism.

Goldberg's concept of the transcendental organism is the biologization of the mathematical "space composed of 'multiplicities' of 'uniquenesses.'" In effect it *biologizes Cantor's transfinite numbers*. In the quotation from one of Goldberg's untitled notebooks that I presented at the beginning of this chapter, Goldberg writes of the transfinite numbers as "higher unities" that lie behind the mathematico-textual productions studied by *gematria*. But there are also *biological* productions that are also mathematically structured: these are the unique unities located within the heterogeneous space of the "transcendental organism." Goldberg has in effect brought together the Kabbalistic understanding of God as the Infinite (Eyn Sof) from which emanates a series of mathematically structured "worlds" (reflecting in different ways the ten "Sephirot," a term that has a root meaning of "count") with Cantor's theory of transfinite numbers. Goldberg then combines the Kabbalistic understanding of these transcendental worlds as having a single living form (that of Adam Kadmon, the primordial human) with Driesch's conception of the organism as an "intensive manifold."[56] The details of Goldberg's mathematico-biological reinterpretation of Kabbalah (thankfully, far less complex than the Kabbalah itself) are the subject of chapter 4. For now I want to trace the development of his theory in his earliest work on *gematria* in the Pentateuch, *The Five Books of Moses*.

Goldberg first expounded the discoveries he claimed to have made concerning the "numerical structure" of the Pentateuch in a club he founded during his Gymnasium years, and he published *The Five Books of Moses* soon after graduation. He called the club the "World-Root" (*Weltwurzel*) Club. Goldberg formed it with three of his closest friends at the Friedrich-Gymnasium (later Friedrich-Wilhelms Gymnasium) in Berlin: Erich Unger (1887–1950), Erwin Loewenson (1888–1963), and Edgar Zacharias (1888–1922). Each of the four friends was given a mathematical "name" using the radical sign for the fourth root, beneath which was a fraction with a denominator of 63 and a unique numerator for each friend.[57] The four friends continued to hold "Wurzel-Sitzungen" (root-sessions) after their graduation in 1907 until the outbreak of the First World War. Loewenson and Unger (whom I introduced briefly in chapter 1), together with the essayist and social activist (pacifism and gay rights) Kurt Hiller, formed their own club at that time, the Neuer Club (New Club). The Neuer Club was a group of poets and writers, almost all of them Jewish, who shared a common rejection of what they considered to be a lifeless and "decadent" bourgeois culture. Seeking new sources of artistic inspiration in the unconscious as well as in the "primitive," the Neuer Club embraced a Nietzschean affirmation of the Will to Power. Their "Neo-pathetic Cabarets" became widely known for showcasing the latest productions of Georg Heym, the most talented poet of the group, and the philosophical ruminations of Loewenson and Unger, as well as presentations and discussions of new work by Hugo von Hoffmanstahl, Franz Wedekind, and others. The Neuer Club is recognized today as a major contributor to the emerging Expressionist movement in Germany at the turn of the twentieth century.[58] Although Goldberg largely held himself aloof from active participation in the Neuer Club, his World-Root Club can be thought of as constituting a sort of inner circle within it. Unger, Loewenson, and Zacharias can be seen as "initiates" in Goldberg's unique version of an anti-decadent renewal of Jewish vitality through a reading of the Pentateuch as the revelation of a divinity "beyond good and evil."

In addition to helping to organize the activities of the Neuer Club, Loewenson and Unger after their graduation from Gymnasium in 1907 were working toward doctorates in philosophy at the University of Berlin, where the Brentano school of psychological phenomenology held sway under Brentano's student (and later rector of the university), Carl Stumpf. The other member of the World-Root Club, Edgar Zacharias, was studying medicine. Goldberg himself, in addition to pursuing studies in medicine and ethnology, was engaged in advanced research in the Hebrew Bible, rabbinic literature, and Kabbalah at two of Berlin's Orthodox rabbinic training schools.[59]

Loewenson's correspondence with Unger from 1908 to the outbreak of the First World War provides us with a glimpse into the activities of the World-Root Club.[60] The activities mostly consisted of Goldberg's exposition of the numerical structures of the Pentateuch and the Kabbalistic-mathematical principles at their origin. Arguing that the metaphysical structure of reality was mathematical in nature, Goldberg hoped to show his friends how the unfolding of the divine Infinite into the finite forms of the created world was mirrored in the numerical patterns that could be discerned in the Pentateuch. What is more, he sought to persuade them that this unfolding was a living process. Finite organic forms, for Goldberg, were complexly structured manifolds unified by a certain formula or numerical arrangement. We have seen that Hans Driesch's vitalism was similarly based on the idea that an "entelechy" or "intensive manifold" guides the ontogenesis of the organism. We will see that Goldberg understood the God of Israel to be a sort of *living number*, the "Weltwurzel" itself. An individual, possessed of the proper insight into God's mathematical nature, could actually intervene in the causal nexus of nature to bring into being something entirely new and unforeseen. The goal of the World-Root Club, as Goldberg put it in his *Ontology*, an unpublished document dating from these years, was not merely to understand the world, but to *transform it*. In the "root-sessions," Goldberg was working out a theory of what could be called the *revolutionary power of the divine Number*.

In a letter written to Unger in the summer of 1909, Loewenson describes his attempt at explaining Goldberg's "number system" (*Zahlensystem*) of the Pentateuch to their mutual friend Kurt Hiller. Hiller "lay exhausted on the sofa" after Loewenson's disquisition. Loewenson reports Hiller's response: "There are only three possibilities in regard to Goldberg. First, he is a fraud who must, on account of his blasphemies, be arrested and put in prison. Second, he is pathological and has added things up incorrectly for so long that they have finally come out right. Or, third, he is *the* genius, *the* genius, *the* genius, for whom the world has waited for the five thousand years of its existence." Loewenson replied that Goldberg can actually *see* the numbers behind the letters of the Hebrew Bible intuitively and that there is something "prophetic" (*prophetenhaft*) in this ability. Loewenson, indicating his inclination to opt for Hiller's third option as the likeliest truth about Goldberg, declares that Goldberg's intuitive prophecy is in fact the highest form of genius. Hiller retorted that the business about "seeing" numbers only demonstrates that Goldberg is a fraud. Anyway, he continued, a genius of this magnitude would radiate brilliant light, like Jesus. Loewenson says that this is correct, but that light emanation only happens when the genius "feels completely well and powerful," an infrequent occurrence. We are left with the impression from the letter that Loewenson considered Goldberg to be someone with unheralded abilities to penetrate the mysteries of the Pentateuch, and he believed that Goldberg's discoveries would have wide-ranging implications, at least for the future of biblical studies, and perhaps even for humanity as a whole. Loewenson certainly did not agree with Hiller that Goldberg might turn out to be a fraud, nor that he might be a pathological personality.

Loewenson's conception of Goldberg's stature as a thinker is perhaps best captured by a remark he made in a letter to Unger comparing him to Novalis. Loewenson called Novalis the "holy child of Romanticism" and the discoverer of "the highest concept of philosophy."[61] After the publication in 1908 of the "Mathematical Fragments" and "Natural Philosophical Fragments" of the Romantic poet, Loewenson sent a letter to Unger in which he quoted long passages from these works.[62] The passages he chose express the same fundamental conception of the deeper nature of reality as both mathematical and life-infused that Goldberg had been developing in his studies of the Pentateuch. Novalis's aphorism, "the life of the gods is mathematics," is a sentiment that, as we see, informs Goldberg's entire reading of the Pentateuch. Loewenson writes to Unger about Novalis that "I see from all that I am reading a *great* [*große*] system. One will perhaps understand it after one will have understood Oskar."[63] Despite his nearly adulatory respect for Goldberg, Loewenson did not feel compelled to serve as an explicator of Goldberg's thought. Erich Unger, however, did feel so compelled. Unger's entire philosophical output reverts again and again to Goldberg, especially to his *Ontology*, an unpublished text that dates from the same period as the "World-Root" sessions. (I devote chapter 3 to Goldberg's *Ontology*.)

There is one more letter from Loewenson to Unger that sheds light on the World-Root Club. It is a remarkably personal confession about its importance in the lives of its members. After telling Unger that he is nearly finished with a tongue-in-cheek send-up of Schopenhauer, a "metaphysics of sympathy" (*Mitleidsmetaphysik*), Loewenson goes on to explain how the four members of the World-Root Club exemplify this metaphysics. The passage is not meant to be taken completely seriously, but the feeling it reveals is surely not feigned:

> In the activities of sympathy, (of justice, of love for one's fellow human,) of erotic love, of magic, there lies an unconscious-intuitive cognition of the mystery of the *principium individuationis* (which is the fact that *the Will is whole and undivided in me*, but also *whole and undivided* in *you, whole and undivided* in Oscar, and whole and undivided in Zacha). That, despite this, the four members of the World-Root all *exist* [*bestehen*]: but they are only in appearance (phenomenally) divided, whereas considered as thing in itself (noumenally) the Will is only one and identical with itself.[64]

To point to the World-Root Club as a signal example of the undivided Will is, despite the playful and exaggerated tone, a remarkable testimony to the emotional bond that seems to have held the club together.

This is all the evidence about the World-Root Club that we can glean from Loewenson's correspondence with Unger. We are able to conclude that the number mysticism of the Pentateuch was its central focus. The members also seem to have believed that Goldberg was working out with them a biblical "system" no less significant than that revealed in the mathematical and philosophical fragments of the Romantic poet Novalis. The name that Goldberg chose to give his club, "World-Root," reveals his own lofty conception of what he was trying to teach his friends about the nature of the Pentateuch and the Hebrew language more generally. An unpacking of the significance of the name "World-Root" can take us directly into the heart of Goldberg's number mysticism, the theme of *gematria* in the Pentateuch.

The word "root" (*Wurzel*) is not only a reflection of the club's numerological studies ("root" as in "square root") but it is also connected with one of the first things one learns in studying Biblical Hebrew. The relatively small vocabulary of Biblical Hebrew is built out of an even smaller number of "roots" of one, two, or (typically) three consonant "radicals." The roots (*shoreshim*) function like elemental building blocks, creating a system of semantically interconnected words that sometimes may seem quite distinct in their surface meaning. The word for "bread" (and sometimes more generally "food") for example, shares the same root as the word for "war" (*lamed-chet-mem*). The shared root does not reflect an accident of homophony as it might in an Indo-European language like English (where "bread" and "broad" have the same consonants but no shared semantic valence). In Hebrew, as in all Semitic languages, a root that is found in different words, in this case *lamed-chet-mem*, almost always reveals a semantic connection among the words: "food" and "war" are apparently part of one semantic field because the land that produces food is frequently the object of military contestation (or food shortages often lead to war).

In addition to its system of roots, there is another possible type of connection one can make among the words of the Hebrew language. The Hebrew alphabet can be used as a number system: the first ten letters represent the numbers one through ten; the next nine letters represent the numbers twenty, thirty, and so on until one hundred; and the last three letters represent two hundred, three hundred, and four hundred, respectively.[65] The search for hidden relations among the words of the Hebrew Bible based on their number values (the sum of the values of the letters of the word) is called *gematria* (by the rabbis of the talmudic era). Goldberg devotes his first book, *The Five Books of Moses: A Numerical Structure*, to demonstrating the importance of the *gematria* value of the name of God, YHWH, in the Pentateuch. I first describe Goldberg's evidence for this claim based on a discovery he made about a certain passage in the book of Genesis, and then I offer a brief assessment of its plausibility.

The name of God as it is rendered in the four consonants YHWH—*yod* (10), *hey* (6), *vav* (5), *hey* (6)—adds up to the number 26 according to *gematria*. In what is a tour-de-force of numerological analysis in *The Five Books of Moses*, Goldberg shows that in the twelve verses containing the genealogy of Noah's son Shem (Genesis 10:21–32), the number 26 reappears quite frequently. There are 26 descendants of Shem mentioned (his five sons; four grandsons through his son Aram; and his seventeen grand-, great-grand, and great-great-grandchildren through his son Arpachshad); there are 104 words in all twelve verses ($4 \times 26$); there are 390 letters in all these words ($15 \times 26$); and finally if one adds up the numerological value of the names of the sons one gets a multiple of 26 ($244 \times 26$). In fact, if one divides the descendants into two groups of thirteen (Shem's last-mentioned great-great-grandson Yoktan has thirteen sons) and adds up the numerological value of each group of names, the resulting sum in both lists of thirteen sons is also divisible by 26 (3,588 and 2,756, respectively).

Goldberg's discoveries about the importance of the number 26 in the genealogy of Shem seemed to him to provide evidence for the divine inspiration of the Pentateuch. Before I explain his theory of divine inspiration in more detail, let me first share what recent scholarship has to say about the case of *gematria* he presents. The first securely attested case of using Hebrew letters as numbers comes from the year 78 BCE (on coins of the Hasmonean king Alexander Jannaeus using the Hebrew letters *kaf* and *hey* to represent the number 25, the year of the reign of Alexander Jannaeus in which the coins were minted, with *kaf* representing the number 20 and *hey* representing 5). The late date for the use of the Hebrew alphabet as a number system is somewhat surprising because the Greek alphabet, which was adopted from the northwest Semitic Phoenician alphabet and was therefore a close "cousin" of the Hebrew alphabet, was used as a numbering system as early as the fifth century BCE. The late Hellenistic date for the appearance of the Hebrew alphabet-number system makes Goldberg's claim to have discovered *gematria* based on the four letters of God's name somewhat questionable. The book of Genesis in which the genealogy of Shem is found was certainly fixed in the form we currently have it much earlier than 78 BCE. Based on the absence of archeological evidence for the use of the alphabet as a numbering system before the late Hellenistic period, most biblical scholars today doubt that *gematria* has any basis in the actual text of the Hebrew Bible. Indeed, most rabbinic and Kabbalistic *gematria* does in fact seem rather far-fetched. This implies that what Goldberg claimed to have found in the genealogy of Shem—the repeated encoding of the number 26—could not really be present in the biblical text. If the use of Hebrew letters to represent numbers was a late Hellenistic innovation, then it would not have been known to the biblical scribes that the four letters of YHWH added up to the number 26. Based only on the archeological evidence we possess about the first secure date when *gematria* was used in ancient Israel, we must conclude that the fact that Shem has 26 descendants (and all the other ways that 26 is encoded in these verses) is a happy coincidence, only retrospectively significant once YHWH is discovered to have a *gematria* value of 26. Either all the *gematria* in these verses is simply a statistical fluke, or if it is intentional, it was deliberately inserted into the book of Genesis by the much later rabbinic tradents known as the Masoretes (sixth through tenth centuries CE). The latter possibility, however, seems unlikely given the extraordinary respect for the received text that the Masoretes otherwise displayed.

But there is another way to reconcile Goldberg's discovery of the encoding of the number 26, the *gematria* of YHWH, in the genealogy of Shem with the archeological record. It might neither be a statistical fluke nor a tampering with the received text on the part of much latter rabbis. Georges Ifrah, the author of a magisterial work on the history of numbering systems, believes that certain cases of biblical numerology (he mentions the 26 sons named in the genealogy of Shem, to which he also adds the fact that there are 26 generations from Adam to Moses) may in fact go back to the pre-exilic period.[66] The biblical scholar Jack Sasson has also advanced the possibility ("with due trepidation") that it may not be mere coincidence that the *gematria* value of YHWH (26) is also the number of generations from Adam to Moses.[67] More recently, Israel Knohl has argued that the number 26 can be found in Miriam's Song of the Sea (Exodus 15:1–18) and the Song of Moses (Deuteronomy 32).[68] Ifrah and Knohl speculate that pre-exilic Temple scribes could be responsible for inserting these cases of *gematria* into the Pentateuchal text (especially since they are associated with the four-letter name of God, YHWH).[69] About the late date of the archeological evidence for *gematria*, Knohl writes, "The fact that the representation of the numerical value of letters is not demonstrated in mundane use in ancient Israel before the Hellenistic period may point to the possibility that this method was a sacred secret knowledge that was kept in closed circles."[70] Similarly Ifrah, also acknowledging the absence of evidence of the alphabet being used as a number system before 78 BCE, suggests that the scribes' use of *gematria* was reserved for sacred purposes and was not disseminated outside the Temple. When Second Temple scribes became aware in the Hellenistic age that the Greeks were using their own alphabet as a numbering system, they allowed their numeration system to also be used for secular uses. It would be easy to imagine that Second Temple Sadducean priests under a Hasmonean king would be willing (or possibly compelled) to share their esoteric knowledge with a ruler who also served as High Priest. Based on Ifrah's and Knohl's hypothesis about a secret, pre-exilic scribal practice of *gematria*, we may admit the real possibility that the numerological code with the number 26 in the genealogy of Shem is neither a mere coincidence nor a late rabbinic tampering with the biblical text. Indeed, it is very hard to imagine another explanation for this phenomenon that does not rely on a highly improbable conjunction of coincidences.

Goldberg, like both Ifrah and Knohl, believed that the *gematria* of the name of God in the passages where he found it (the genealogy of Shem most particularly) was not a coincidence. Unlike Ifrah and Knohl, however, he did not attribute it to an esoteric tradition or "secret knowledge" possessed by the Temple scribes and priests. Rather, as we will see, Goldberg believed that this *gematria* reflected a sort of "automatic writing" dating to the very earliest transcription of the Pentateuch. But we do not have to agree with Goldberg's theory of the inspired origin of *gematria* to take seriously the possibility that the *gematria* based on the number 26 in the genealogy of Shem that forms the centerpiece of Goldberg's *Five Books of Moses* is not a mere figment of his overactive imagination. The still classic book on the subject of alphabets and number mysticism by Franz Dornseiff, *Die Alphabet in Mystik und Magie* (1922), referred to Goldberg's discovery positively and took his presentation of the *gematria* in the genealogy of Shem quite seriously.[71] Dornseiff, however, thought that Goldberg's *gematria* discovery was not a product of early scribal activity, but rather reflected Masoretic tampering with the text of the Hebrew Bible.[72] As I have just explained, we do not need to posit a late rabbinic tampering with the Hebrew Bible in order to explain certain convincing cases of *gematria* in the text. We may admit the possibility that *gematria* based on the name of God (YHWH) may have been placed in the Pentateuch by pre-exilic Temple scribes who had come to use the Hebrew alphabet as a number system sometime before the sixth century BCE. Even if we agree to date the origin of biblical *gematria* to pre-exilic Temple scribes, however, we certainly do not need to appeal, as Goldberg does, to a supernatural source for the presence of *gematria* in the Pentateuch. The *gematria* patterns in the genealogy of Shem, as a matter of fact, would not be too difficult to encode.[73] In attempting to explain the mathematico-biological structure of both the universe as a whole and the Pentateuch more particularly, Goldberg carried *gematria* far beyond what modern historical scholarship could ever endorse. Despite this fact, however, it is important for us to follow the development of Goldberg's thought into these more speculative realms.

Goldberg explains how the number structure of the Pentateuch came into being as "automatic writing" not in his early *Five Books of Moses* (which only offers the evidence, not the process) but in a section of his later book, *The Reality of the Hebrews*, in which he lays out what he calls the "metaphysics of language." Goldberg there describes the connection between the Hebrew language more generally and the mathematical structure of the transcendental realm. Although it was published much later than the World-Root Club's final sessions, *The Reality of the Hebrews*, as Goldberg explains in a preamble to the work, was unfolded as a private "presentation" (*Darstellung*) from 1903 to 1909, overlapping with at least some of the years that we know the club was meeting. In fact, we are on pretty secure ground in thinking that the World-Root Club was the site of many if not all of the private presentations of *The Reality of the Hebrews*. Therefore we may rely on *The Reality of the Hebrews* to help us understand Goldberg's early investigations into the Pentateuch's number system.

According to Goldberg's metaphysics of language in *The Reality of the Hebrews*, the numerological patterns of the Hebrew Bible derive from a God who both *creates with* and *reveals himself through* numbers.[74] Numbers mediate between a "personal" lawfulness of nonrepeatable living individuals and a "natural" lawfulness of mechanically repeating, interchangeable units. Numbers, Goldberg explains, have both kinds of lawfulness: although each whole number is a certain sum of identical 1's, they also possess unique individual features; for example, the number 63 is divisible by the sum of its digits (9). In his letter to Felix von Luschan, as I explained earlier, Goldberg offers the number 30 as an example of how each number has unique properties. One of the areas of number theory is the study of "special numbers"—those that display certain unique properties. Today, for example, numbers like 63 that are divisible by the sum of their digits are called "Harsad numbers." According to Goldberg, numbers can mediate between the transcendental and the empirical realms because having both a "metaphysical" aspect as "individuals" with unique properties (a "uniqueness" in a "multiplicity of uniquenesses," as we saw above in Goldberg's discussion of the transcendental organism) and also a merely mechanical aspect as the sums of the self-same repeating unit (counting mere aggregations found in "ordinary" homogeneous empirical space), they can mediate between the "personal" nature of spirit and the impersonality of matter.[75] Numbers are the "language" through which spirit forms matter into organized and meaningful patterns, whether those patterns are found in a living organism or in speech and writing. Biblical Hebrew is the *psychophysical* revelation of God's creative power of joining matter and spirit by means of numbers. In the following passage Goldberg first explains the nature of language in general as the bond between a folk group and its god, and then he elaborates the special case of Hebrew:

The language of a folk group [*Volk*] that possesses a bond to the transcendental reality plays an essential role both in establishing the bond and in the maintaining of the bond. Language in such a case has an aspect that is removed from merely subjective "arbitrariness" and expresses *objectively* the relationship between the folk group and its God. Language in this objective aspect is part and parcel of the psychophysical constitution of the folk group and, in actual fact, is identical with the relationship between the folk group and its God. This is especially the case when the language that serves as the site of expression for the formula [relating God and folk group] has an *immanent* mathematical significance, one that is unique to it in virtue of its very structure. And this is true of the Hebrew language. Its most obvious feature is the way it constitutes a treasury of words built up out of roots of 1, 2, or 3 elements that are non-vocalic (consonants). It is evident that Hebrew is a *combinatory language* and that the meaningful content of all its words depends upon the permutations and variations of—in every case—no more than three consonantal roots. Correspondingly, it is evident that incomparably more permutations in this "combinatory language" have a meaningful content, a "sense," than a consonant-vowel language does, most of whose arrangements are senseless and whose combinatorics [*Kombinatorik*] is nothing but idle play. The letters of the Hebrew alphabet do not merely have numbers associated with them; on the contrary, the letters *are* numbers. This is so because the Hebrew language arises—as does the language of every metaphysical folk group [i.e., a folk group with a relationship to a god]—from the fundamental relationship between spirit and matter that is constitutive of the human races and their languages. But the Hebrew language reaches all the way to the primordial points of contact [*Urbeziehungen*] between spirit and matter. One side of these contact points—and it must be made clear that there are several such—is the deeper (esoteric) numerical significance of the language. Only these primordial contacts allow us to understand that speaking and counting, or more precisely writing and counting (*safar*) are identical at their source.[76]

Although a full explication of this passage must await a more detailed examination of *The Reality of the Hebrews* in chapter 4, this much is clear: Goldberg postulates a profound connection between the "combinatorics" of the Hebrew consonantal root system and the mathematical "combinatorics" underlying the connection between spirit and matter, the primordial elements from which the world is made. The World-Root Club, then, was studying nothing less than the transcendental reality that comes to expression in the language of the Hebrew Bible.

There is, in fact, one word in particular whose consonantal root, according to Goldberg, uniquely reflects the connection between the Hebrew language and the transcendental reality. That word is *shem*. *Shem* means "name," but its two root consonants, *shin* and *mem*, are also found in the word *shamayim*, "heavens." Goldberg says that a better translation of *shamayim* than "heavens" is "world," that is, "the totality of all that there is."[77] In the phrase, "heavens [*shamayim*] and earth" in the very first verse of Genesis, Goldberg explains, *shamayim* refers to the "infinite actuality," whereas "earth" refers to the realm of finite actuality. The verb *shamam* also has the same root letters as *shem* (with the *mem* doubled, a typical verb-forming pattern in Hebrew), and its meaning, according to Goldberg, shows the basic connotation of the root: "to harden, to crystallize" (*erstarren, krystallisieren*). The crystal formation, Goldberg comments, is a "system." *Shem*, when understood through the semantics of the other words that share the same root consonants, refers to a *transcendental world system*.[78] "Name" is a noun whose connotation, according to Goldberg, includes "world." And what is a world? A world is a system of values, what Goldberg calls "a space of positional values" (*Raum des Stellenwertes*).[79] This ordered space is what "name" (*shem*) refers to.

The philosopher Alain Badiou, with whose assessment of the Romantic gesture against mathematics I disagreed at the beginning of the chapter, has developed a mathematical philosophy that in certain points resembles Goldberg's. We should not be surprised that Badiou, a philosopher who claims to unfold the ontological implications of Cantor's theory of transfinite numbers, would have points in common with Goldberg. One such point is Badiou's conception of the "transcendental organization of a world."[80] A world's transcendental organization (and for Badiou any whole composed of related parts, from an organism to a solar system, can be called a "world") gives value differences to an undifferentiated manifold. Badiou introduces his concept of the transcendental organization of a world as a way to explain how an infinitely large and disorganized realm of "unbounded" but countable beings could ever come to be bound together into structured infinite-finitudes, the "stability of worlds."[81] This is the same problem that Goldberg addresses with his concept of *shem* as a transcendental ordering system. In place of an undifferentiated dispersion of beings, Badiou describes the transcendental organization of a world as always something "local"—that is, it is a self-enclosed structure—and also as having an order based on differential values. "The transcendental must make possible the 'more' and the 'less.'"[82]

I invoke Badiou because, precisely like Goldberg, he develops his philosophy within the modern paradigm of mathematical thinking about the infinite. This modern paradigm is founded on the notion of a set (in German, *Mannigfaltigkeit* or *Menge*). For Badiou as for Goldberg, every "world" is a "finitization of the infinite" (*Verendlichung der Unendlichkeit*), or as Badiou puts it, "all worlds are indeed infinite, but denumerable."[83] Like Badiou, Goldberg employs Cantor's set-theoretical mathematics of the infinite to explain the coming into being of "transcendental world systems." I discuss the details of Goldberg's Cantorian exegesis of the Pentateuch in chapter 4. For now, let me simply summarize what I have so far said: a world system in the Pentateuch is called a *shem*, a "name," and it represents an ordered system in which an infinite multitude (e.g., the infinity of possible sound values that can be counted as elements of a meaningful combination of sounds, a word) can be given differential positional values. A world system exists as an ordered manifold within a heterogeneous space. According to Goldberg, every folk group's language is a phonic medium in which a transcendental world manifests itself. Every language reflects the world of its speakers because both language and world reflect a single transcendental *shem*.

However, among the many languages, Hebrew holds a privileged position. This is so because of the fact that *shem* is not only a common noun (meaning "name") but it is also a proper noun, the name of a particular individual, Shem, one of the sons of Noah. *Shem* is the name of the ancestor of all the peoples who speak Semitic languages, the languages in which consonantal root combinatorics most especially reveal the meaningful structure of a "world system." The Hebrew people will actually come to know the Name of God, Yahweh (YHWH), the creator of *all* transcendental world systems. In this Name, Goldberg will argue, the language of the Hebrew people finds its crystallization point. Recall that the meaning of the biliteral root is found in the "geminate" verb form *shamam*, to harden or crystallize. The Pentateuch is the crystallization of the Name within a single document. When it comes into being in time, it is produced as a written text through the automatic writing of a scribe whose consciousness is in contact with the "world root." This is a basic Kabbalistic doctrine. And this is why a club calling itself "World-Root" would focus all its energies on unpacking the numerical structure of the Pentateuch. At the heart of the World-Root's studies is the Name of names, Yahweh. It is, as we have seen, also at the heart of Goldberg's first publication, *The Five Books of Moses*. For Goldberg, it could hardly be coincidental that the *gematria* value of the name of God, 26, is also the number of Shem's ("Name's") sons. Nor could he consider it coincidental that the number of words in the verses of the genealogy is a multiple of 26, and that the number of letters is also a multiple of 26, and that the sum of the *gematria* of the first thirteen names of the sons is a multiple of 26, as also is the sum of the *gematria* of the second group of second names. When he added to this case additional evidence (most of it not nearly as persuasive as the genealogy of Shem's *gematria*) from other passages, Goldberg thought he had found proof that the entire Pentateuch was a "number structure" that had "crystallized" the divine *shem* in the Hebrew language.[84] Israel Knohl speculates that Temple scribes might have wished to honor the unrepresentable YHWH by concealing his name in the biblical text.[85] Goldberg depersonalizes the phenomenon of *gematria* and makes it a matter of crystallizing a transcendental "world" in the medium of the Hebrew language.

When Goldberg republished his discoveries about the genealogy of Shem in 1947 in a series of articles in *La Revue Juive de Genève*, his introductory remarks clearly reveal his pride in the achievement of his early years. Having shown to his satisfaction that "the same dynamic that had produced the extraordinary events about which the Pentateuch reports had also formed the structure of the Pentateuch itself," Goldberg believed that he had uncovered something like an eighth "wonder of the world":

> A "wonder from primordial time" [*Wunder der Urzeit*] had been dug up. Someone once compared the method I had used in my establishment of the number system with Schliemann's excavation of Troy. People had said that Troy must exist, but no one knew anything exact about where it was. Schliemann just went over there and started to dig. If the metaphysical Being [*Instanz*] behind the events of the Pentateuch and the Pentateuch itself were to speak today, it might say in paraphrase of the words of Deuteronomy 30:11: "The proofs for the metaphysical origin of the Pentateuch are not beyond your grasp nor are they far from you. You don't need to cross the sea to Palestine or to Babel to set up archeological digs in order to find recordings and inscriptions that demonstrate the veracity of the stories of the Pentateuch. The Pentateuch requires no proofs brought from outside. It carries the legitimation of its origin within itself."[86]

In Goldberg's eyes, the discoveries he made laid the foundation for a wide-ranging reevaluation of the philosophical foundations of biblical scholarship. But, more significantly, they led to nothing less than a new Kabbalistic-Cantorian theory of creation. Goldberg's new mathematical Kabbalah required a new ontology and a new logic to provide it with a solid philosophical foundation. This new ontology and logic are the topic of chapter 3.


## Notes

1. Hans Przibram, *Form und Formel in Tierreiche: Beiträge zu einer quantitativen Biologie I–XX* (Leipzig: Deuticke, 1922), x.

2. Oskar Goldberg, *Die fünf Bücher Mosis: Ein Zahlengebäude. Die Feststellung einer einheitlich durchgeführten Zahlenschrift* (Berlin: [Verlag David,] 1908). Reprinted in Goldberg-*Aufsätze*, 21–68.

3. Schelling's *Weltalter* was never published in his lifetime. However, Goldberg would have been able to read the so-called Erstes Buch of *Die Weltalter* in *Friedrich Wilhelm Joseph von Schellings Sämtliche Werke*, Division I, vol. 8 (Stuttgart: J. G. Cotta'scher, 1861), 195–344.

4. All of these notebooks in fact show the influence of the early work of F. W. J. Schelling. The idea that negation (Schelling speaks of "inhibition") brings about a finitization of infinity can be found, for example, in F. W. J. Schelling's 1799 work, *First Outline of a System of the Philosophy of Nature*, trans. Keith R. Peterson (Albany: State University of New York Press, 2004). Schelling writes: "But now, how must one represent an infinite series if it is only the external exhibition of an original infinity? Are we to believe that the infinite is produced in the series through aggregation, or rather ought we to represent any such series in continuity, as one function running to infinity?" (16). A little further along Schelling answers: "The succession in the series signifies only, as it were, the individual inhibitions which continually set bounds to the

expansion of that magnitude into an infinite series" (16). More important than detailing Schelling's influence is to note, as I have done in chapter 1, the intellectual context provided by the reemergence of a Schellingian Naturphilosophie in German biology in the late nineteenth and early twentieth centuries. I discuss Goldberg's possible debt to a contemporary of Schelling, Franz Joseph Molitor, in Appendix II.

5. DLM Goldberg Nachlass, Kasten (box) 7.

6. In Schelling's *Philosophie der Kunst* (*Philosophy of Art*) we find a similar point about how the mythological poetic productions of the ancient world "can be thought of neither as intentional nor as unintentional." He attributes the production of mythology, which he says has "absolute objectivity," to the expression not of any individual or even group of individuals but of "the whole working as a single individual." This is exactly the view that Goldberg and Unger will seek to explicate through a theory of the collective, psychophysical source of the imagination. F. W. J. Schelling, *Philosophie der Kunst*, in *Sämtliche Werke*, Division 1, vol. 5 (Stuttgart: J. G. Cotta'scher, 1859), 414. Manfred Voigts brought this passage to my attention. The influence of Schelling on Goldberg is unmistakable. A central thesis of Schelling in his philosophy of mythology is the simultaneous emergence of ethnicities and mythologies, for example, and this is also Goldberg's governing principle. See, for example, F. W. J. Schelling, *Historical-critical Introduction to the Philosophy of Mythology*, trans. Mason Richey and Markus Zisselsberger (Albany: State University of New York Press, 2007), 85–101. While a study of Schelling's influence on Goldberg is certainly warranted (and would require a close reading of the notebooks in the Nachlass), I am interested in the more proximate sources of Goldberg's mathematico-biological interpretation of the Kabbalah in Driesch and Cantor.

7. Alain Badiou, *Theoretical Writings*, ed. and trans. Ray Brassier and Alberto Toscano (London: Continuum, 2005), 22.

8. Lorenz Oken, *Grundriß der Naturphilosophie, der Theorie der Sinne und der darauf gegründeten Classification der Tiere* (Franfurt: Eichenberg, 1802), 145.

9. Georg Philipp Friedrich Freiherr von Herdenberg, *Novalis' Werke in Vier Teilen*, ed. Hermann Friedemann, part 4 (Berlin: Bong & Co., 1908). I am indebted to Manfred Voigts for drawing my attention to Novalis as a precursor of, and possible source of, Goldberg's mathematical Naturphilosophie (personal email communication).

10. Bernard Bolzano, *Parodoxien des Unendlichen* (Berlin: Mayer & Müller, 1889).

11. Marco Giovanelli, "Hermann Cohen's *Das Prinzip der Infinitesmal-Methode*: The History of an Unsuccessful Book," 23, available at http://philsci-archive.pitt.edu/id/eprint/11818.

12. For a detailed explanation of the way that Cassirer departs significantly from Cohen's understanding of Leibniz's infinitesmal calculus, see ibid., 23–26.

13. For a discussion of Cassirer's organicist theory of the "form-forming" nature of *Geist* as an offshoot of *Leben*, see Reto Luzius Fetz, "Forma formata—Forma formans: Zur historischen Stellung und systematischen Bedeutung von Cassirer's Metaphysik des Symbolischen," in *Lebendige Form: Zur Metaphysik des Symbolischen in Ernst Cassirer's "Nachgelassen Manuskripten und Texten,"* ed. Reto Luzius Fetz (Hamburg: Felix Meiner, 2008), 15–34.

14. Ernst Cassirer, *Leibniz' System in seinen wissenschaftlichen Grundlagen* (Marburg: N. G. Elwert'sche Verlagsbuchhandlung, 1902). Perhaps one ought to mention a long-forgotten philosopher who, following Cohen but independently of Cassirer, foregrounded the mathematical concept of function in his interpretation of Kant's theory of experience: Ferdinand Jakob Schmidt, *Grundzüge der konstitutiven Erfahrungsphilosophie als Theorie der immanenten Erfahrungsmonismus* (Berlin: B. Behr, 1901), 126–136. It is possible that Goldberg was personally familiar with Schmidt (1860–1939), who taught philosophy in various Berlin gymnasia before joining the philosophy faculty of the University of Berlin in 1913. There are various ter-

minological and thematic overlaps between Goldberg's *Ontology* and Schmidt's argument that the subject-object dichotomy can be overcome if one starts from the "totality of the given" that transcends also the individual consciousness and extends to the infinite (*Grundzüge*, 90–92).

15. Cassirer, *Leibniz' System*, 422.

16. Ernst Cassirer, *Substanzbegriff und Funktionsbegriff: Untersuchungen über die Grudfragen der Erkenntniskritik* (Berlin: Von Bruno Cassirer, 1910). English translation: *Form and Function & Einstein's Theory of Relativity*, trans. William Curtis Sawbey and Marie Collins Sawbey (Chicago: Open Court, 1923).

17. Cassirer, *Form and Function*, 75–76; emphasis Cassirer's.

18. The noted neo-Kantian philosopher Alois Riehl discusses Kant's early pre-Critical views about the nature of space in *Der philosophische Kritizismus: Geschichte und System*, 2nd ed., 2 vols. (Leipzig: Wilhelm Engelmann, 1908). He points out that Kant maintained a dynamic view of space grounded in the attractive force of underlying material substances. If these forces did not operate in proportion to the *square* of the distance between the substances, but in proportion to the third or fourth power of the distance, Kant speculates that the human mind might have a different intuition of space and a geometry of more than three dimensions corresponding to this intuition. After quoting a passage from an early work of Kant that speculates about "higher" geometries than that of three dimensions, Riehl concludes, "This theory seems to me to be a prophecy of non-Euclidean geometry" (1:329). Kant later rejected the idea that space could have multiple dimensionalities where Newtonian three-dimensional space would be but one "region" of much more complex spatialities. Riemann argued that Newtonian space is what defines a "neighborhood" in an *n*-dimensional manifold (so that living on the surface of a sphere would seem like living in the Newtonian universe). Cassirer broke through the limitations of the Kantian view to a recognition of the revolution brought about by Riemannian non-Euclidean spaces.

19. Ernst Cassirer, *Die Begriffsform in mythischen Denken* (Leipzig: B. G. Teubner, 1922), 38. Christian Möckel, *Das Urphänomen des Lebens: Ernst Cassirer's Lebensbegriff* (Hamburg: Felix Meiner, 2005) offers a persuasive reappraisal of Cassirer as an advocate for a Goethean view of the root identity of the creative imagination and the mathematico-organic becoming of natural phenomena.

20. In Bernhard Riemann, *Gesammelte mathematische Werke und wissenschaftlicher Nachlass* (Leipzig: B. G. Teubner, 1876), one can find unpublished speculations about the flow of a "space-filling stuff" (*raumerfüllende Stoff*) with varying intensities at different atomic points by which the phenomena of gravitation, light, heat, and electricity can be explained (see esp. 528–538).

21. José Ferreirós, *Labyrinth of Thought: A History of Set Theory and Its Role in Modern Mathematics* (Basel: Birkhäuser, 2007), 47.

22. Quoted in Detlef Laugwitz, *Bernhard Riemann 1826–1866: Turning Points in the Conceptions of Mathematics*, trans. Abe Shenitzer (Boston: Birkhäuser, 1999), 220.

23. Riemann's discussion of the possibility that we live on the surface of a finite, curved space is quoted in Jeremy Grey, *Worlds out of Nothing: A Course in the History of Geometry in the 19th Century* (London: Springer, 2007), 200.

24. Gustav Theodor Fechner, *Zend-Avesta oder über die Dinge des Himmels und des Jenseits*, 3 vols. (Leipzig: Leopold Voß, 1854).

25. Riemann, *Gesammelte mathematische Werke*, 482.

26. Ibid., 510.

27. Riemann's Leibnizian-Fechnerian world of interacting and self-reproducing psychic quanta may be looked at as a precursor to another great mathematician's organicist

philosophy, the process philosophy of Alfred North Whitehead. It can also be compared with Hermann Weyl's "agent theory" of matter that I referred to in chapter 1, note 95.

28. Georg Cantor, *Grundlagen einer allgemeiner Mannigfaltigkeitslehre: Ein matemathisch-philosophischer Versuch in der Lehre des Unendlichen* (Leipzig: G. B. Teubner, 1883). This is the separate publication of the fifth and final article in a series of articles titled "Ueber unendliche, lineare Punktmannichfaltigkeiten" published from 1879 until 1883. I will refer to Cantor's essay as *Foundations* in what follows, and I will give page numbers from the more easily accessible journal version in *Mathematische Annalen* 21 (1883): 545–591. I have adopted (with slight alterations) the English translation, available online in typescript facsimile but never published, by George A. Bingley for the "Classics of St. John College" (1941) titled *Transfinite Numbers*. A facsimile of the typescript is available at http://formandformalism.blogspot.com/2011/06/georg-cantors-1883-grundlagen-article.html.

29. Cantor, *Foundations*, 556.

30. Ibid., 557.

31. For a complete discussion of Cantor's theological and philosophical views, and a publication of the letters in which these views were developed, see Christian Tapp, *Kardinalität und Kardinäle: Wissenschaftshistorische Aufarbeitung zwischen Georg Cantor und katholischen Theologen seiner Zeit* (Stuttgart: Franz Steiner, 2005). See also Bruce H. Hedman, "Cantor's Concept of Infinity: Implications of Infinity for Contingence," *Perspectives on Science and Christian Faith* 46 (1993): 8–16, and, more recently, Rüdiger Thiele, "Gregor Cantor (1845–1918)," in *Mathematics and the Divine: A Historical Survey*, ed. Teun Keutsier and Luc Bergmans (Amsterdam: Elsevier, 2005), 523–548. For a general treatment of Georg Cantor's mathematics, see Joseph Warren Dauben, *Georg Cantor: His Mathematics and Philosophy of the Infinite* (Princeton, NJ: Princeton University Press, 1979), and also Michael Hallett, *Cantorian Set Theory and Limitation of Size* (Oxford: Clarendon, 1984).

32. Cantor, *Foundations*, 558.

33. Ibid., 576.

34. Cassirer, *Substance and Function*, 82.

35. Cantor, *Foundations*, 577; emphasis mine.

36. Ibid.

37. Cantor will later use the Hebrew letter aleph with a subscript zero, "aleph-null," to designate not the *ordinal* greater than all natural numbers, which has its identity dependent on the ordering of the natural numbers, but the *cardinal* representing the entire class of natural numbers, irrespective of their order. Consider, for example, how 4 can represent the *fourth* number in a certain sequence (1, 2, 3, 4), or it can represent any group of four things (any group of four numbers, as well). In the former sense, 4 is an ordinal number; in the latter sense, it is a cardinal number. $\omega$ is the first ordinal after all finite ordinals, but aleph-null is the cardinal number of any group that has as many members as the set of all finite ordinals.

38. $\omega+1$, $\omega+2$, and so on; $2\omega$, $2\omega+1$, and so on; $\omega^2$, $\omega^2+1$, and so on; the sequences go on to infinity, each sequence constituting a "number class" or cardinality called an "aleph." We may well ask whether there is an ordinal to represent *all* these number classes; in other words, a sort of *trans-transfinite* ordinal. This is the so called Burali-Forti paradox: if there is such an ordinal, it is itself a member of the class of all the ordinals, but then it would not be the ordinal greater than all ordinals, since it is not greater than itself. Cantor avoided this paradox by positing that what lies beyond all the ordinals is the Absolute Infinity or God. We talk more about this in what follows.

39. Cantor, *Foundations*, 562; English translation slightly altered from Bingley's *Transfinite Numbers*, 114. For the meaning of the "number classes," see note 38.

40. Cantor, *Foundations*, 588. For examples of the increasing sequences of ordinals, see note 38.

41. Ibid., 563.

42. In chapter 4 I return to Cantor's Platonism. We will see that the philosopher Gottlob Frege basically accused Cantor of creating numbers simply by fiat, as if he were God. Gershom Scholem, who studied with Frege, will call this "ontology by fiat" (*Konstatier-Ontologie*) and accuse Goldberg of doing it (and also Benjamin). Scholem was decidedly in Frege's camp: he believed that the Lurianic Kabbalah was also a form of "ontology by fiat" that generated infinitely numerous intermediary beings between the Infinite God and the finite world.

43. Cantor, *Foundations*, 581.

44. Cantor's proof depends on the idea that a subset might actually contain the number corresponding to the number of elements in the subset ([1, 2, 3, 4] is an example). Now imagine a subset defined as the set containing all the numbers *without* that property. How many numbers are in this subset? If the number of these numbers is itself a member of the set, then that number has the property that should exclude it from the subset. If, however, it is not found in the subset, then it has the property that should place it in the subset. Therefore, there can be no natural number corresponding to the subset. Put differently, this subset (the set of all natural numbers without the stipulated property) cannot possibly be the $n$th subset of the natural numbers. To count it, therefore, we require a number greater than any natural number. Voila, the first transfinite number, the number corresponding to the power set of all the integers. Cantor's defenders were compelled to respond to the problem of certain paradoxes to which his theory seemed exposed. Perhaps the most significant paradox has to do precisely with Cantor's power set theorem and is related to the Burali-Forti paradox mentioned earlier. If the power set theorem is true, then the set of all sets is therefore a member of itself (it is a set) and is also greater than itself (it includes all of its own subsets). Cantor believed that the Absolute Infinity (God) included all lesser infinities and was itself not included within any set (it was therefore not a member of itself). This theological solution was not satisfying to Cantor's defenders, and they offered other solutions (Bertrand Russell's theory of types is one such solution).

45. Ibid., 566.

46. David Hilbert, "On the Infinite," in *Philosophy of Mathematics: Selected Readings*, ed. Paul Benaceraf and Hilary Putnam, 2nd ed. (Cambridge: Cambridge University Press, 1983), 183–201; quotation on p. 189; emphasis mine. It is important to note that it is the fact that a single ordering principle holds throughout the infinite series that allows for the totalization of the series. An infinitely large, random collection of numbers could never be totalized. Hilbert's original essay, "Ueber das Unendliche," was delivered as a lecture in 1925 and published in *Mathematische Annalen* 95 (1926): 161–190.

47. Cantor, *Foundations*, 557.

48. Among contemporary philosophers, Alain Badiou has most seriously attempted to draw out the implications of Cantor's mathematics of the infinite for ontology and theology. See, for example, Alain Badiou, *Briefings on Existence: A Short Treatise on Transitory Ontology*, trans. Norman Madarasz (Albany: State University of New York Press, 2006). Badiou in this work says that the "aim of philosophy is . . . to restitute the infinity to the banality of manifold-being, as mathematics has invited us to do since Cantor" (30). Badiou builds his ontology on Cantor's theorem that the power set of any set (manifold) is always greater than the set itself (i.e., the number of subsets of a set is greater than can be enumerated by all the elements of the set, even if there are an infinite number of elements). For Badiou, this means that philosophy must break with the "metaphysics of the One," the idea that there is a totality or unity encompassing all beings. All totalities are shattered by the "event" of the transcendence of the set, the appearance of a new manifold beyond the sequence of the old one. There is some resemblance to Goldberg's idea of "Hebrew metaphysics" as based on a radical "discontinuity principle," as I explain in chapter 3. However, Goldberg did imagine that a certain unifying principle—the

YHWH-Force that generates all manifolds—could be discerned in reality. Goldberg, unlike Badiou, retains a place for Cantor's God, the Absolute Infinite.

49. Hallett, *Cantorian Set Theory*, 23.

50. Georg Cantor, "Über verschiedene Theoreme aus der Theorie der Punktmengen," *Acta Mathematica* 5 (1885): 105–125; quotation on p. 122.

51. Ibid., 123.

52. Goldberg, *Reality of the Hebrews*, 180.

53. Hallett, *Cantorian Set Theory*, 14.

54. Cantor, *Foundations*, 176. Quoted in Hallett, *Cantorian Set Theory*, 14. Translation is Hallett's.

55. I do not mean to say that Georg Cantor was the only inspiration for Goldberg's discussion of the transcendental organism as the finitization of the infinite. Cantor was himself immersed in the Naturphilosophie of the mid-nineteenth century, and his mathematics of infinity can be said to formalize some of the basic presuppositions of Naturphilosophie. In Appendix II I examine another source of Goldberg's mathematical conception of the transcendental organism, the Naturphilosoph and Kabbalah interpreter Franz Joseph Molitor. Goldberg could be said to update Molitor through Cantor.

56. One of the most accessible accounts of the Kabbalistic theory of emanation and Sefirot can be found in Gershom Scholem's treatment of these themes in the earliest known Kabbalistic treatise, the *Sefer ha-Bahir*, in Scholem, *Origins of the Kabbalah*, trans. Allan Arkush (New York: Jewish Publication Society, 1987), 123–151.

57. While a radical sign for the fourth root makes sense for a club with four members called "World-Root," the fractions assigned to each friend have no obvious meaning. However, 63 has certain unique properties that may have appealed to Goldberg: it is divisible by the sum of its digits (9), and it is divisible by 7, which for Goldberg was one of the Bible's most significant numbers.

58. The most detailed study of the Neuer Club, together with an extensive collection of some exemplary writings of its members, is found in Richard Sheppard, ed., *Die Schriften des Neuen Clubs, 1908–1914*, 2 vols. (Hildesheim: Gerstenberg, 1980). An excellent treatment of the Neuer Club in relation to both Expressionism and vitalism is Gunter Martens, *Vitalismus und Expressionismus: Ein Beitrag zur Genese und Deutung expressionistischer Stilstrukturen und Motive* (Stuttgart: W. Kohlhammer, 1971). Erich Unger's writings from this period are collected in Manfred Voigts, ed., *Von Expressionismus zum Mythos des Hebräertum: Schriften 1909 bis 1931* (Würzburg: Königshausen und Neumann, 1992). For Goldberg and Unger in relation to Expressionism, see Manfred Voigts, "Jüdisches Denken im Frühexpressionismus: Oskar Goldberg und Erich Unger im Zeichen Friedrich Nietzsches," in *Jüdischer Nietzscheanismus*, ed. Werner Stegmeier and Daniel Krochmalnik (Berlin: de Gruyter, 1997), 168–186.

59. Goldberg says that he studied higher biblical criticism with Dr. Joseph Wohlegemuth, the director of the Rabbiner-Seminar in Berlin, and also traditional rabbinic biblical exegesis with Rabbi Abraham Biberfeld at the Beit Hamidrash in Berlin (which he identifies as "in der Heidereutergasse"). See Oskar Goldberg, "Eine Geheimschrift in den fünf Büchern Moses: Das Zahlengebäude des Pentateuch," in Goldberg-*Aufsätze*, 355–387; see pp. 355–356.

60. The letters of Loewenson to Unger are published in the first volume of *Die Schriften des Neuen Clubs*. Letters with reference to the "Root-Sessions" are 28.VII.1909 and 29.IV.1910. In the former letter, Loewenson refers to someone who questions Goldberg's identity as a "world genius" on the basis that, were he one, he would not concern himself with "idle number mysticism and Hebrew verse quasi-aesthetics" (70). For brief descriptions of Unger, Loewenson, and Zacharias, see Sheppard's biographies in vol. 2, appendix II.

61. Sheppard, *Die Schriften des Neuen Clubs*, 2:325.

62. Ibid., 1:36–37. For the Novalis Fragments, see Herdenberg, *Novalis' Werke in Vier Teilen*. The Fragments are found in the section titled "Vierter Teil: Fragmente II—Tagebücher—Aufsätze." I am indebted to Manfred Voigts for drawing my attention to Novalis as a precursor of, and possible source for, Goldberg's mathematical Naturphilosophie (personal email communication).

63. Sheppard, *Schriften des Neuen Clubs*, 1:42. I am indebted to Manfred Voigts for drawing my attention to this statement, as well as to Loewenson's interest in Novalis (private email correspondence).

64. Letter of Loewenson to Unger, 29.IV.1910, in Sheppard, *Die Schriften des Neuen Clubs*, 1: 321.

65. For the development of the alphabetic numbering system in ancient Israel from the period of the monarchy through the Roman period, see Georges Ifrah, *The Universal History of Numbers: From Prehistory to the Invention of the Computer*, trans. David Bellos, E. F. Harding, Sophie Wood, and Ian Monk (New York: John Wiley & Sons, 2000), 233–239.

66. Ifrah, *The Universal History of Numbers*, 254.

67. Jack M. Sasson, "A Genealogical 'Convention' in Biblical Chronology?," *Zeitschrift für alttestamentische Wissenschaft* 90 (1978): 171–185. The reference to Moses's place in the genealogy is on p. 171n2. In a private email correspondence, Professor Sasson stated that this *gematria*, if it is not a mere coincidence, must go back to the pre-exilic period, around the sixth century BCE.

68. Israel Knohl, "Sacred Architecture: The Numerical Dimensions of Biblical Poems," *Vetus Testamentum* 62 (2012): 189–197.

69. Ifrah, *The Universal History of Numbers*, 239.

70. Knohl, "Sacred Architecture," 196.

71. Franz Dornseiff, *Das Alphabet in Mystik und Magie* (Leipzig: B. G. Teubner, 1922), 110.

72. One notable exception to the consensus view that *gematria* among the Jews is a late Greco-Roman invention and that all *gematria* in the Hebrew Bible reflects Masoretic tampering was the scholar Robert Eisler. Eisler devotes considerable time in his 1,000-page magnum opus *Weltenmantel und Himmelszelt* to showing that the Greeks learned how to encode *gematria* into their texts from their contact with the Near East. Eisler, a Jew, argued that the use of the alphabet as a numbering system does not begin with the Greeks but with the Semites of "eastern Arabia or Chaldea." (*Weltenmantel und Himmelszelt: Religionsgeschichtliche Untersuchungen zur Urgeschichte des antiken Weltbildes. 2 vols* [Munich: C. B. Beck, 1910], 2:356.)

73. The spelling of many words and names in these verses, as also throughout the entire Hebrew Bible, allows for the insertion of an additional *yod*, *hey*, or *vav* to represent the long vowels ee, ah, and either o (as in "toe") or oo. Given the ability to add or subtract these three letters with the values 10, 5, and 6 from words and names with these long vowels, it is not too difficult to get the *gematria* in a given set of verses to work out as one desires. The fact that these three letters (called *matres lectionis*, or reading helpers) are also found in the name of God and were in fact used to represent God's name in three rather than four letters (YHW) would mean that the scribes who used them to code the *gematria* value 26 might have imagined that they were simply weaving the name of God into the biblical text, somewhat like *sealing the text with its author's signature*. Perhaps they imagined that the Hebrew alphabet and the name of God were uniquely suited to one another. Admittedly, I am now venturing into speculation that carries us far away from Oskar Goldberg, but it is interesting to contemplate the possibility that Goldberg may offer us an insight into the theological worldview of these scribes, even if we do not share his conviction that this worldview reflects the divine "reality." Goldberg, of course, was aware of the possible use of *matres* to encode desired *gematria*, but he believed that, when all

the other mathematical phenomena in the Pentateuch are taken into consideration (he pointed to the multiple encodings of the number 7 in repeated phrases, for example), it becomes nearly impossible for a human mind to have constructed the whole mathematical edifice of the text. We do not need to find his claim to be plausible to take seriously the idea that the Temple scribes were deeply interested in the *gematria* of God's name.

74. For a recent discussion of the idea, widely shared throughout the ancient Near East, that number-letters are the building blocks of creation, see Tzahi Weiss, *Otiyot she-nivre'u ba-hen shamayim ya-arets: Ha-meḳorot yeha-mashma'uyot shel ha-'isuḳ be-otiyot ha-alefbet ke-yeḥidot 'atsma'iyot ba-sifrut ha-Yehudit ba-'et ha-'atiḳah ha-me'uḥeret* (Letters by which Heaven and the Earth were created: The origins and meanings of the perceptions of individual letters as alphabetic units in the Jewish literature of Late Antiquity) [Hebrew] (Jerusalem: Mosad Bialik, 2015).

75. In the final pages of chapter 3 I examine Unger's treatment of Pythagoreanism in his *Against Poetry*, published in the same year as *Reality of the Hebrews*. His conception of Pythagoreanism, which (in agreement with Robert Eisler's view) he claims has a Semitic origin, restates Goldberg's analysis of the transcendental significance of numbers.

76. Goldberg, *Reality of the Hebrews*, 30. Goldberg's metaphysics of language closely resembles Schelling's treatment of the relationship between language, religion, and ethnicity in his *Historical-critical Introduction to the Philosophy of Mythology* in Lecture Six (pp. 85–101).

77. Ibid., 7.

78. The crystalline structure is Wilhelm Worringer's signal example of the mathematical *abstraction drive* in art. In *Abstraktion und Einfühlung, ein Beitrag zur Stilpsychologie* (Neuwied: Heuser'sche Verlags-Druckerei, 1907), Worringer describes this drive as typical of the "Oriental" folk groups who seek to find a transcendental realm beyond the "arbitrariness" of the "infinitely changing play of Being" (*unendliche Wechselspiel des Seins*). Worringer was widely read by the young Jewish poets and writers like Erwin Loewenson, Kurt Hiller, and Erich Unger, who formed the core of the Neuer Club. The biologist Hans Przibram whom I mentioned in the opening of this chapter devoted his efforts to creating a mathematical model of the living organism and explored the idea that living beings first emerged as crystalline molecular structures. See Hans Przibram, "Kristall-Analogien zur Entwicklungsmechanik der Organismen," *Archiv für Entwicklungsmechanik der Organismen* 26, nos. 1–2 (1906): 207–287.

79. Goldberg, *Reality of the Hebrews*, 181.

80. Alain Badiou, *Logics of Worlds, Being and Event 2*, trans. Alberto Toscano (London: Continuum, 2009), 123.

81. Ibid., 101.

82. Ibid., 102.

83. Ibid., 335.

84. I mentioned in the introduction that the historian of religion Robert Eisler praised Goldberg's book on the number system of the Pentateuch. In note 72, I mentioned how Eisler's major thesis was that early Semitic number mysticism that was similar to what the later texts of the Kabbalah attest influenced Greek Pythagoreanism in the seventh century BCE, as well as much later Hellenistic number mysticism (the *Syballine Oracles*, for example). After having now discussed Goldberg's *Five Books of Moses* and assessed some of its claims, I would like to look more closely at what Eisler had to say about Goldberg's book. As I just explained, Eisler in *Weltenmantel und Himmelszelt* (*World Cloak and Heavenly Tent*) argued for an early Semitic origin (based on number mysticism) for the use of the alphabet as a numbering system. He put forth evidence of the use of *isopsephy* (the Greek term for "equal value of alphabet-number sums," in other words, Greek *gematria*), in the fragments of the pre-Socratic philosopher Pherecydes. (The evidence, if true, would date the Greek use of the alphabet as a number sys-

tem to the late sixth century BCE rather than to the fifth century BCE when we have secure archeological evidence for it, but unfortunately his evidence is not particularly persuasive.) After offering his evidence for numerology in Pherecydes's text, Eisler continues,

> After all of these clearly noteworthy connections [of the numerological values of words in Pherecydes's text], it seems to me to be less methodologically justified to describe it all as a play of pure chance that has by sheerest accident spread itself out through this entire text and now entraps gullible modern interpreters, rather than to accept the possibility that the Ionian Pherecydes and his whole Pythagorean-Orphic theological school has taken over this art [of numerology] from Asia Minor, where this kind of Kabbalistic activity will come to be widely attested . . . . The purpose behind this [numerological] practice cannot be better appreciated than by reference to the psychologically very interesting fact that in recent days the learned and patient researcher [Oskar Golberg is named in a footnote] hoped to demonstrate the presence of a similarly complex play of numbers in the Masoretic redaction of the Pentateuch, a remarkable case of abstruse artistry (according to those in a position to judge, he was successful). In his [Goldberg's] opinion, this goes far beyond the ability of the human mind to accomplish and he therefore believes that he has found a new proof for the divine origin of the holy scripture in each of its letters. If one considers that the Orphics, following the pseudepigraphic principle of the entire religious output of the Orient, presented their work as the inspiration of the "Titan Phoebus Helios," we may see their use of the art of numerology as a way to persuade a much more naïve public of the inspired character of their "pile of books." (Eisler, *Weltenmantel und Himmelszelt*, 2:355–356.)

Eisler found in Goldberg's book confirmation of his own theory that alphabet numerology derives from a very early Kabbalistic-Pythagorean-Orphic tradition arising in the Near East in the early first millenium BCE. He attributes alphabet numerology to the desire of the author to trick a naïve reader into believing in the divine origin of his text. It seems more likely, however, that the author or scribe shared this mind-set and was himself persuaded of the divine origin of his capacity to produce numerological patterns. (See note 73 for a further explanation of these numerological patterns.) It is perhaps not so much that Goldberg fell for a scribal trick, as Eisler suggests, as that he entered so completely into the scribe's worldview that he could not contemplate the possibility that the Pentateuch's *gematria* was the product of a purely human artifice.

85. Knohl, "Sacred Architecture," 196: "These literary and numerical means of making God present have special significance in a society that forbids representing God's image with a statue or picture."

86. Goldberg, "Eine Geheimnisschrift," in Goldberg-*Aufsätze*, 358.

# 3 Goldberg's *Ontology* and Unger's *Politics and Metaphysics*

WHAT MUST THE ontological structure of the world be like for it to be possible that a certain written document—the Pentateuch—could be a number system of the World-Root Name of God, YHWH (Yahweh)? This is the fundamental question addressed by Goldberg's unpublished *Ontology*, whose subtitle is *The Idea of Logic: An Introduction to Ontology*.[1] Manfred Voigts claims that Goldberg's *Ontology* was composed at around the same time as the writing of *The Five Books of Moses: A Number System*, therefore sometime between 1908 and 1911. Goldberg's friend and disciple Erich Unger makes significant use of the basic concepts of *Ontology* in one of his earliest publications from 1911, thus confirming Voigts's dating. Unger's short piece "Nachts" ("At Night") is a conversation between two friends, one of whom has been diagnosed with a psychiatric illness. Unger puts the following words in the mouth of the "insane" friend:

> Not only is the will as it exists in our upper consciousness an assumed mind-set [*Haltung*], so too is *seeing* and *reality*, the very things of the outer world— these apparently so constant, objective, and independent impressions of the senses, they are also a pose [*Pose*] . . . that one can *give up*. This constancy, this unchangeableness, this hardening of dead and lifeless things that for thousands of years have followed the same psychic laws, this boring lawfulness: . . . behind it all stands a horror of unnatural secrets, a fear of unmasterable new things, that is holding back the entrance of uncountable possibilities.[2]

This is not the tone of Goldberg's *Ontology*, but it does reflect quite well its underlying thesis: the constancy of the world is an illusion, and a different order of the world is possible. After the First World War, Unger continued to write philosophical treatises based on the ideas presented in Goldberg's *Ontology*. Unger's later work provides a useful restatement of some of the more elliptical formulations of *Ontology*. Goldberg claims, for example, that his *Ontology* offers a method for the production of an entirely new way to experience reality through the use of the imagination (*Phantasie*). His account of this "production method" (*Herstellungsmethod*) constitutes the most difficult part of this work. I therefore supplement Goldberg's obscure account with material from Unger's *Politik und Metaphysik* (*Politics and Metaphysics*, 1921) and *Gegen die Dichtung* (*Against Poetry*, 1925), despite the fact that these works postdate Goldberg's *Ontology* by more than a decade. In addition to providing a useful point of access to Goldberg's theory of the productive imagination, Unger's books are important works in their own right and deserve much more critical attention than they have so far received.[3]

Goldberg opens his *Ontology* by situating his work within the history of logic since Aristotle. Previous logical systems abstracted from the content of sentences in order to represent the formal structure of the sentences independently of any content. Goldberg claims that this rejection of all content in favor of formal structure has been the source of traditional logic's "sterility." The formal structure sets up laws for all possible true statements to follow, but it is indifferent about what those sentences actually mean. This raises the question of why the necessary laws of all truths would be indifferent to truth itself: "Why did the creator of logic bind himself with laws that are indeed unchangeable (unalterable) but are nonetheless completely indifferent?"[4] The contentless abstraction of logic seeks to provide the formal structure of the natural-language sentences of everyday use. But what if natural language itself were nothing but a pale imitation of a language system whose logic is not abstract but "concrete," that is, its logic is inseparable from the content of its sentences (as in the case of the Pentateuch as Goldberg understands it). Goldberg claims that traditional logic is nothing more than a grammar of everyday speech, whereas it ought to reveal the transcendental language of creation itself: "Language can have a dignity similar to that of logic itself. But, as I will show, this language is not language in its *empirical* form. The latter is just a linguistic fragment to which logic is commonly brought into connection. But it is nothing more than a grammar for everyday use."[5]

Goldberg thus is looking for a logic that would apply not to the "linguistic fragment" that is our everyday speech, but to a language totality where "the *logical elements themselves*, i.e., the concepts—and not merely the logical connections among these elements in sentences and conclusions, are related to one another in an unequivocal and specific relationship, much the way that the elements of the periodic table are structured in chemistry."[6] Goldberg seeks to explicate the possibility of a logical structure whose conceptual elements are meaningful in themselves, possessing a relationship to one another independently of any arbitrary arrangement that one might make of them in everyday language. Such a system of concepts, Goldberg claims, "would not be the accidental product of an individual subject in his relationship to the external world, to an object, or the thing-in-itself, or whatever one wants to call this other pole." Rather, "this system of concepts would be derived from a single ur-concept from which they can be deduced and with which all the sentences and conclusions in which they are expressed are related in a univocal and specific manner."[7] Goldberg, in effect, wants a logic that does not merely reflect the abstract structure of language, but reveals the very *source* of language itself. Since Goldberg compares the conceptual system he wants to develop to the periodic table of the chemical elements, we might call the "ur-concept" the "God-particle" out of which all the other concepts (i.e. elements) are built.

The ur-concept that Goldberg will select to ground his "completeness system of concepts" is "Uniqueness" or "Singleness" (*Einmaligkeit*). (I will stick with "Uniqueness" because it fits better with Goldberg's explication of the concept, as I will show.) Although Goldberg does not directly appeal to his numerical analysis of the Pentateuch to justify his choice of ur-concept, it is not too difficult to understand how "Uniqueness" figures as the conceptual underpinning of the Pentateuch. Goldberg's decision to begin his logic with the ur-concept "Uniqueness" demonstrates that his *Ontology* should be read as describing the conditions of possibility of the Pentateuch as the mathematical and linguistic articulation of the Name of God. Uniqueness is the concept whose singular instantiation is God himself. God's name, "YHWH," indicates God's incomparable identity. The name YHWH is revealed by God to Moses at the burning bush (Exodus 3:13–16). God also refuses then to identify himself in any way except to say, "I am (or, will be) who I am (will be)." His name, YHWH (*yod-hey-vav-hey*), resembles the four consonants of "I am" (*aleph-hey-yod-hey*). The name, it is being suggested, simply means "I am who I am." In effect, the Pentateuch is declaring that the proper name of God, although in itself untranslatable, connotes *a being who can only be said to be self-identical.* God is unique. YHWH is not an instance of a wider genus.

The uniqueness of God is also revealed in Moses's declaration in Deuteronomy that "YHWH is One [*echad*]" (Deuteronomy 6:4). In his restatement of his theory of the number system of the Pentateuch published in *La Revue Juive Genève* in 1947, Goldberg emphasizes the significance of the declaration "YHWH (is) Echad." He explains that the number value (*gematria*) of YHWH is 26 and that the number value of the word "Echad" is 13: "26 is the number-value of the Name of God YHWH and 13 is the number-value of the ordinal name Echad, i.e., one. Throughout the entire Pentateuch there runs in a number-script *a single sentence* which is again and again expressed in the equations of the number system and it states: 26 is 13, YHWH is One, God is One."[8] How does the ur-sentence "YHWH is One" help us to understand that the ur-concept of the Pentateuch is "Uniqueness"?

First, we need to unpack the significance of the meaning of "one" when used as a predicate of YHWH. The oneness of God is not due to the fact that he is one instance of a general concept, "god," of which there might be other such instances (but in fact there are not). Rather, God's oneness is his utter Uniqueness, his inability to be grasped by a general concept. This is something that Hermann Cohen puts clearly in the very first sentence of his posthumously published work, *Religion der Vernunft aus den Quellen des Judentums* (*Religion of Reason out of the Sources of Judaism*, 1919). Goldberg would not have known of Cohen's work at the time of the composition of his *Ontology*, but Goldberg would certainly have studied Cohen's earlier *Ethik des reinen Willens* (*Ethics of the Pure Will*, 1904) where the same point is made.[9] Cohen opens *Religion der Vernunft* this way: "Instead of the Oneness of God we assert that Uniqueness [*Einzigkeit*] is the content of monotheism. Oneness only indicates the opposite of the multiplicity of the gods."[10] For Goldberg, Uniqueness is the generative ur-concept for the Pentateuch's sentence, "YHWH (is) Echad," The task that Goldberg sets himself in his *Ontology*, then, is to explicate how from the ur-concept of Uniqueness all the other concepts can be derived.

Goldberg first explains that the ur-concept "Uniqueness" is the source of what he calls "the multiplicity of uniquenesses." This multiplicity is actually an infinity of distinct structures, each of which, according to Goldberg, is what the Pentateuch calls a "name" (*shem*). In chapter 2 I discussed Goldberg's notion of *shem* as a world-system that is embodied in the languages of the ancient ethnic groups spoken of in the Pentateuch. To each such group there corresponds a transcendental *shem*, a structure within the fullness of the "transcendental organism." As I will explain in more detail in chapter 4, Goldberg identifies the transcendental organism as the Primal Man, Adam Kadmon. The Many that arises from the unique One are many "names"—what could be called the primordial language of (constituting) Adam Kadmon. This language is not a particular *empirical* language, but the living expression of God's Name as a transcendental system of *organic elements of a larger whole.* These "names" or elementary structures of the "transcendental organism" are not conceived as having organic material form, but as being mathematically definable structures or fields of force. The *Ontology* offers the logic of the one and unique "name"—the Name of Names. This is not a formal logic without content, but rather the logic of the language of creation.

Before turning to a more detailed explication of Goldberg's *Ontology*, I want to draw attention to one of Goldberg's most interesting theoretical precursors in the search for the abstract logic underlying the language of creation, a thinker with whom Goldberg seems to have been quite familiar. Adolf Bastian (1826–1905) was the first German researcher to hold an academic post (at the University of Berlin, from 1866) in the newly emerging field of Anthropology.[11] Bastian was the director of the university's Museum für Völkerkunde (Ethnological Museum) beginning in 1869 and also of the independent Königliches Museum für Völkerkunde (Royal Ethnological Museum) from the time of its opening in 1886. It was Bastian who brought the anthropologist Felix von Luschan to Berlin. Von Luschan, as I discussed in chapter 1, was the professor under whom Goldberg hoped to write his doctoral dissertation on the relationship between "holy men" and the formation of ethnic groups. Von Luschan turned Goldberg down because his proposal did not fit with von Luschan's emphasis on geographic factors in ethnology. Had he been alive when Goldberg submitted his proposal, Bastian would have likely welcomed Goldberg's approach to ethnic formation through holy men. In fact, Bastian himself believed that individuals with unique psychophysical constitutions emerge as leaders in the group and start the process of ethnic formation.[12] We know that Goldberg was quite familiar with Bastian's work because he named one of his collections of notes in his Nachlass, "From Plato to Bastian."[13] It is quite likely that Bastian's ethnological theories exercised considerable influence on Goldberg. But Bastian's theory of "ethnic elementary thoughts" (*ethnische Elementargedanken*) seems also to have been important for Goldberg's *Ontology*.[14]

Bastian argued that, by gathering as much information as possible "through induction and the comparative-genetic method," the ethnological researcher can rediscover the primordial "ethnic thoughts" that form the basis of all cultural productions. Building up from these elementary thoughts to more advanced "socio-ideas," the researcher can come ever closer to an understanding of the "cosmic infinity" in which individual consciousness can ultimately find a harmonious union with the all-pervading spirit of God. Bastian compared the researcher's recovery of humanity's primordial ethnic thoughts from among the welter of cultural phenomena to the way that mathematicians use infinitesimal calculus (Bastian even mentions Georg Cantor[15]) to find the rational number that defines the limit toward which the irrational number, represented as an infinite series of ever-smaller fractions, approaches:

> Even from our earth-bound, planetary standpoint we can, through sufficient advances in inductive research, achieve an enlarged foundation for all the phenomena that we observe in the universe. We can grasp the world as the revelation of a Creator. Our vision can even reach into the cosmic infinities, among which are the irrationals whose limit point can never be found except through an asymptotically approaching sequence (of rationals) that is the result of a "probability calculus" by means of which the essential lawfulness [of the world] is able to be logically computed. Connected with this method of calculating [irrational numbers through a sequence of rational ones] we must introduce the comparative-genetic method in psychology. This method allows us to gain access to the foundation of our psychophysical nature through whose investigation we discover the common ethnic thoughts behind our socio-being [*Gesellschaftswesenheit*] in its various geographic-historical provinces.[16]

Bastian's method of "logical calculation" (*logische Rechnen*) in ethnology—the search for a rational crystallization point in the manifold of phenomena—is very close to what Goldberg proposes as the "absolute logic" whose explication is the foundation of his *Ontology*. Both Bastian and Goldberg propose a mathematical logic or "calculus" that is premised on the latent existence, within the infinite manifold of experience, of primordial "general ideas" at the psychophysical limit point of consciousness where individuality merges into collectivity. And for both

Bastian and Goldberg, these primordial ideas appear in the thought of the "dark intimations of the worshipper of the fetish" and also in "the ideas of metaphysics that have been as far as possible denuded of all linkages to the sensual and the corporeal."[17] Bastian's theory that primal ethno-ideas arise at the limit of our psychophysical nature is absolutely fundamental to Goldberg as well as to Unger, as we will see. Goldberg and Unger will take the somewhat elliptical formulations of Bastian and transform them into what might be called an "ethnological phenomenology."

## The Argument of the *Ontology*

Goldberg declares at the beginning of his *Ontology* that he wants to transcend the "sterility" of logic and of philosophy and make logic *productive*: "In contrast with the longstanding, sterile conception of philosophy as a theory of what is given in experience, one needs to conceive of philosophy as a theory of the *coming* experience [*das kommende Erfahrung*]. This means: it does not have as its guiding question, How does one explain what is given in experience?, but rather, How is an in principle new but previously occluded kind of experience possible? Philosophy thereby becomes the production [*Herstellung*] of another reality."[18] Philosophy, we could say, must provide the means for making the leap out of the endless chain of causes and effects in the givenness of the empirical world to a new level of existence, one commensurate with our ability to experience new worlds. If philosophy is to meet the demands of becoming a means for the "production of another reality," it must discover a new kind of logic, one that goes well beyond both empty formalism and the transcendental categories of Kant's system. The only appropriate logic for a truly productive philosophy is one that is *absolute*, that is, one not concerned with sterile relationships among empty concepts but rather with the *unconditioned power that generates relationships.*

Goldberg makes it clear that the goal of logic should not be to reduce all relationships (he mentions three in particular: subject-object, matter-spirit, immanent-transcendent) to one pole of the pair, but to discover the one domain from which all such relationships can be generated. The contradictions or oppositions between the related terms should not "sublated" (*aufgehoben*), but rather shown to originate in a "relation-producing principle": "One makes one's way beyond the concept of relation by deciding to allow the dualism to remain in place and to get outside of it not in a one-sided way, that is, from the side of one pole [of the dualism], but rather from the complexity [of both poles], the *fact of the relationship itself*, and in this way to move from the relationship to the relation-*producing* principle [*relation*erzeugende *Prinzip*]."[19]

Goldberg argues that the search for a relation-producing principle must take logic to a concept that is absolutely *unique* (*einmalig*), for otherwise it would itself be the product of a logically prior relation-producing principle. Every relation contains a multiplicity of terms, minimally two but perhaps many more, and even infinitely many more terms. The whole numbers, for example, are defined by a relationship of succession by adding one, and they constitute an infinitude of terms. The concept that "absolute logic" requires is one that *produces* relations among multiple terms, but that is itself not a member of any relationship or multiplicity. The concept, then, that Goldberg chooses as the first concept of his "absolute" logic is, as I have already explained, Uniqueness, *Einmaligkeit*.

Goldberg's choice of Uniqueness as his logic's ur-concept is, as I have argued, motivated by what he believes he accomplished in *The Five Books of Moses*, namely, the proof that the whole of the Pentateuch is the unfolding of the sentence, "YHWH (is) One." We also saw how Hermann Cohen privileges Uniqueness as a key concept in both his ethics and his philosophy of religion. We find a similar valorization of *Einmaligkeit* in Walter Benjamin's aesthetics. Benjamin uses the concept of *Einmaligkeit* to describe the auratic quality of a work of art, and he specifically opposes auratic *Einmaligkeit* to the mechanical reproduction of the artwork. Benjamin is working within a similar problematic to that of Goldberg: the concept of *Einmaligkeit* must underwrite the possibility of a whole realm of *Einmaligkeiten* (Uniquenesses). For Benjamin, a vital artistic tradition reaches back to a ritual or sacred context and carries forward the auratic quality associated with the sacred. It does so not through a mechanical copying of its historical model, but by an imaginative resurrection of the creative power of the work itself.[20] Goldberg and Benjamin want to distinguish a multiplicity that is simply an aggregation of indifferent, valueless, and atomized individuals from a multiplicity of heterogeneous and unique elements standing in differential relations to one another.[21] As we will see in chapter 5, Benjamin felt a deep affinity with the work of Goldberg's disciple, Erich Unger, although he seems to have been put off by what he called the "unclean aura" of Goldberg himself. At this point I merely want to draw attention to one important overlap between Goldberg (mediated by Unger) and Benjamin, an overlap that can help us appreciate a little better the broader significance of Goldberg's concept of Uniqueness.

Beginning with the concept of Uniqueness, Goldberg asks how one reaches multiplicity. This is the initial question of his ontology: How does the Many emerge from the Unique One? How can we logically generate multiplicities when the starting point is pure Uniqueness? Because YHWH is the Unique One, he is not a member of a multiplicity. Every set defined by a concept with more than one member (a multiplicity), for example, the set of all dogs, is not a set with only one unique instance. There cannot be many identical uniquenesses falling under a general concept.[22] Goldberg posits that there are only two possible ways for multiplicities to arise from Uniqueness: (1) Pure Uniqueness is taken to be a primary unity and then divided up without remainder into a multiplicity of equivalent unities, or (2) the "exclusiveness of Uniqueness as the sole concept is broken through [*durchbrochen*]."[23] Goldberg goes on to describe the "breakthrough" into a multiplicity of uniquenesses as an "interruption act" (*Unterbrechungsakt*). This is Goldberg's way of rendering the theological concept of *creatio ex nihilo*. Creation "breaks into" the self-sameness of the primal Uniqueness. With the first method of division, however, the unique oneness is dissolved and no longer exists as such; with the interruption act the unique oneness continues to exist in its own sphere apart from the multiplicity in which it is refracted. In the first case, where the unity is divided into equivalent elements, there cannot be any relationship between the Unique One and the multiple and equivalent onenesses since the original One is divided up and therefore no longer exists: the Many replaces the One. There is a complete loss of transcendence, and all that is left is "pure multiplicity" (*reine Vielheit*). There are two kinds of pure multiplicity formed by the division of oneness into equivalent units, Goldberg will later explain. One is the multiplicity of an endless series (such as that of all whole numbers). The other is the multiplicity of a set (*Menge*), of a "closed" group (a finite collection of numbers, for example). In neither kind of multiplicity is there any real unity. There is no organized wholeness in which the parts occupy "value-laden" or qualitatively distinct positions. Only through an "interruption act" that preserves Uniqueness in its transcendence can there be a "multiplicity of uniquenesses," each characterized by the fact that it is a unified whole composed of qualitatively distinct elements. No uniqueness is identical to another; no uniqueness is one instance among many of an overarching general concept. Goldberg calls each of the uniquenesses a "positional value system" (*Stellenwertsystem*).[24] Each and every uniqueness manifests an aspect of the originary Uniqueness.

If we want a concrete example of this abstract description, we may best think of how in the first chapter of Genesis the "image of God" is realized in the human pair, the male and female, each a unique being and together forming the image of God. Put simply, humans are from the start a multiplicity of uniquenesses. As many commentators have pointed out, the Bible describes all other animals as "kinds," but the human being is not created as a "kind" (*min*). Before the creation of empirical humans, according to Goldberg in *The Reality of the Hebrews*, there was the creation of Adam Kadmon, the primal human. Adam Kadmon was composed of a multiplicity of unique elements, each a unique part of the "transcendental organism." The first interruption act does not create empirical humans, but Adam Kadmon. The second interruption act corresponds to the emergence of empirical humanity. As we will see in chapter 4, this is where the unity of the transcendental organism as an organized multiplicity begins to unravel. The task that Goldberg sets for his "absolute logic" as it is concretized in *The Reality of the Hebrews* is the production of the unity of the transcendental organism in the empirical world. This involves what Goldberg calls "transcendental politics." But let us remain with Goldberg's *Ontology.*

Goldberg calls each uniqueness generated by the "interruption act" a "multiplicity-unity" (*Vielheitseinheit*). A multiplicity-unity is different from the two types of "pure" multiplicities formed by division, the multiplicities of the infinite series (*Reihe*) and the finite set (*Menge*). Goldberg calls each uniqueness a "multiplicity" because it is not the one pure uniqueness (it is not the Unique One), but it is nonetheless a one or "unity" (rather than a infinite series or a finite set) because it is a whole whose parts occupy value-laden places in a "positional value system." The relationship between Uniqueness and the "multiplicity-unities" is a relationship of "non-universal validity" (*Unallgemeingültigkeit*). The relationship of non-universal validity means that the multiplicity-unities (each a uniqueness of a different kind from the others) have achieved a sort of independence vis-à-vis pure Uniqueness. Non-universal validity reveals a "striving" on the part of the multiplicity of uniquenesses to break free of the rule of universal validity; in other words, "to delimit the validity of logic."[25] Goldberg says that the "striving" leads to *contradiction*. The multiplicity-unity is a contradiction because it is a single entity that is not, however, an instance of a general concept. Each multiplicity-unity limits itself *locally* as one among a unified grouping of multiplicity-unities, each distinct from the others but each defined by its relationship to the others. This is what Goldberg in *Ontology* calls "the localization of the contradiction."[26] In *The Reality of the Hebrews*, Goldberg also calls this the "finitization of the infinite." Each multiplicity-unity finitizes the infinite because it is a unity that is greater than all of its parts; therefore, no matter how many parts it may contain, there is a *more* that cannot be counted among them. This more, this unifying power, is greater than any finite group and is therefore *infinite*. Yet, it is not an *endless* infinity (like the series of ordinal numbers), but a *delimited* (*begrenzte*) infinity that is a unified whole. It is what the mathematician Georg Cantor called an "authentic infinity," the infinite *number* that is greater than any finite number, the transfinite number. I explained in chapter 2 the importance of Cantor's theory of transfinite numbers and the role that Cantor hoped it would play in the revival of Naturphilosophie. Goldberg identified the uniquenesses within the transcendental organism with these transfinite numbers, thereby making Adam Kadmon the embodiment of what I am calling "transfinite life."

Let us recall where we stand now in the unfolding of the "absolute logic" of the *Ontology.* Goldberg has set out the formal conditions of a multiplicity whose parts stand in a relationship of non-universal validity to pure Uniqueness. These parts are described as "multiplicity-unities," each is distinct from the others, and within each the elements are positioned in an ordered arrangement of differing values or intensities. Each part is found within a "positional value system"

(*Stellenwertsystem*). This is Goldberg's ontologization of Cantor's theory of transfinite numbers. Goldberg is now prepared to begin to expound how his "absolute logic" can be used in relationship with the actual content of experience. His logic, he says, has not been developed by abstracting from experience in order to discover the laws of thinking that would apply to any content whatsoever; instead his logic is designed to be filled with content. Each "multiplicity-unity" is a formal structure of a transcendental "world system." Recall what Goldberg said was the goal of his *Ontology*: to "produce a new reality." To produce a new reality we must bring a new world system (*shem*) into being. The world system that Goldberg wants to bring into being is not merely *one* of the worlds within the hierarchy of worlds: it is nothing less than *the world system as a totality*—Adam Kadmon, to use the language of *The Reality of the Hebrews*.

Goldberg undertakes the task of laying out the organon for the production of Adam Kadmon in the final two sections of *Ontology*. The production method (*Herstellungsmethod*) does not require new technologies for manipulating matter or energy. Rather it requires new methods for accessing the power of the "interruption act" (the creative act itself) that brings the multiplicity of uniquenesses into being. These methods require a new use of the imagination (*Phantasie*) to interrupt the apparently unbreakable cause-effect sequence governing the temporal unfolding of the empirical world. Logic and philosophy more generally must cultivate the power of the imagination to *experience what has never yet been experienced*, the "coming experience."

Before he provides his account of what this new use of the imagination implies, Goldberg explains that his approach is not the only one in contemporary philosophy that seeks to escape from the sterility and emptiness of earlier thought. Goldberg is aware that he is not the first to defy the Kantian stricture against any "metaphysical experience," that is, the experience of something not given in a finite spatiotemporal framework. The passage in which Goldberg explains his disagreement with these rival anti-Kantian philosophical groups who also bemoan the sterility of logic includes the clearest programmatic statement in all of his writing about his relationship to vitalism. It is therefore necessary to spend time with this passage before we turn to his organon of the reality-producing fantasy.

Goldberg acknowledges that there are thinkers who, like him, seek to bring philosophy into contact with "the things themselves." These thinkers offer "intuition" as the method to arrive at things "in their totality" (*Ganzheit*). In using intuition rather than abstract logic, they hope to arrive at concrete totalities rather than empty generalities. Their model of such concrete totalities, Goldberg explains, is taken from biology, and the goal-directed activities that seem to these thinkers to be signs that a totality—a "superindividual soul"—are present in the organism. This kind of biologistic logic, Goldberg says, is found in "the more recent Naturphilosophie that has led as a consequence to Lebensphilosophie."

Goldberg does not name names here, but his reference to "intuition" and biology makes it clear that he at least has Henri Bergson in mind. By invoking "Lebensphilosophie," he probably is targeting the broad swathe of thinkers, many of them members of the early Expressionist circle known as the Neuer Club (discussed in chapter 2), who joined Bergson's *élan vital* to Nietzsche's will to power. Goldberg's objection to intuitionist philosophical theories of living "wholeness" is that they are looking for wholeness in the wrong place. They are looking for wholeness as an *immanent* principle in the empirical realm, but intuition, because it positions itself immanently in the empirical world, will never discover the unity it is seeking.

To explain why intuitionist philosophies will never discover the wholeness they are looking for, Goldberg reiterates his distinction between multiplicities formed by division and those formed by the "interruption act." Since intuition seeks to find wholeness immanently in the empirical realm, the multiplicity in which it seeks wholeness has no relation to a transcendent multiplicity-unity. But without that relationship, the only kind of multiplicity one can experience is that of multiplicities formed through division, rather than through the interruption act. As I have already explained, Goldberg claims that this sort of division-produced multiplicity can be viewed in two ways: "(1) the multiplicity as an open series [*Reihe*]; (2) the multiplicity as a closed set [*Menge*]." When intuitionists seek unity from within an empirical multiplicity, they can only grasp "the eternal middle, the not-coming-to-an-end, the non-completeable, the endless regress."[27] This is the infinity that Cantor called "inauthentic," the infinity of the ever-increasing series of natural numbers, for example. In that series, going backward into the negative numbers and forward into the positive ones, every number is in the middle of the series. Considered as the infinite extent of time backwards and forwards, every moment is also the middle. The intuitionists plunged themselves into this ever-increasing flux of time in order to experience pure continuity or duration. Bergson, for example, believed that in experiencing this pure duration, intuition had reached a level below the abstract quantification of time into discrete segments. Perhaps Goldberg has in mind a statement like the following from Bergson: "What is duration within us? A qualitative multiplicity with no likeness to number; an organic evolution which is not yet an increasing quantity; a pure heterogeneity within which there are no distinct quantities."[28] But Goldberg objects to this way of understanding the immanent flux of time. For Goldberg, the only way to grasp a true heterogeneity is to grasp a wholeness of positionally distinct elements (*Stellenwertsystem*). This cannot be achieved by plunging into the flux of time, but by grasping the way that it reflects a transcendental pattern. This is how Goethe encouraged scientists to view the multiplicity of empirical phenomena: to seek the Urphenomenon that they all differently refract.

Goldberg sees a dangerous alliance between immanentist intuitionism and acquiescence in the givenness of the structures that are alleged to lift human life into a "higher" unity, but that instead only position the individual as a cog within the machinery of the state. In what is certainly the most pathos-laden passage in an otherwise very dry text, Goldberg in *Ontology* describes how the "deeper reason" for the appeal of immanentist intuitionism lies in an "immanent law of inertia" that leads one to always "work with what is *given*."[29] This inertia is revealed in both a general acquiescence to the givenness of reality and a general disdain for anything that smacks of "metaphysics": "Since the symptoms of this inertia are shown in the satisfaction with what is already in place and in the contentment with the givens of nature, it turns out that qualities which are by definition metaphysical and therefore exceed the limits of physics are reduced without exclusion to the usual and normal processes of the empirical world of things."[30] This is an "optics" that only serves as a "mirror for the thoroughly familiar objects of a mundane reality" (*sattsam bekannte Dinge einer alltäglichen Wirklichkeit*). The cure for this inertial tendency is "to find the courage to proceed constructively [*konstruktiv*], that is, to push on to the region *prior* to the realm of the given." Doing this, "one will notice that one has broken through sterility, since one will have thereby penetrated to the *productive principle* of the given."[31] Intuitionists, in contrast, end up only unifying "*everything* (i.e., the entirety of time) into a single unity without differences." And this leads to the greatest catastrophe that can befall thought: "The unity concept that should have brought forward the *new* where each unity must be different from every other, ends up making *everything* (i.e., any period of time) new. As a consequence, nothing else ever happens except that everything stays always 'the New' [*beim Neuem*]."[32]

Goldberg's critique of Bergsonian intuitionism and Lebensphilosophie finds a resonant echo in Alain Badiou's critique of the vitalism of thinkers like Henri Bergson and Gilles Deleuze. I do not want to enter into the debate about whether or not Badiou has fairly represented the targets of his critique, but I do want to note how similar his criticism is to that which Goldberg levels against intuitionist vitalism. First of all, the essential point for both critiques is that the intuitionist thinker has effaced the possibility of "the new" or of an "event" that disrupts the regime of repetitive, mechanical normality. Badiou writes that in the case of Deleuze, the "event"

is that which composes a life a little like a musical composition is organized by its theme. The event is not what happens to a life, but that which is in that which happens, or that which happens in that which happens. Hence there can only be one Event. Amid the disparate material of a life, the Event is the Eternal Return of the identical, the undifferentiated power of the Same: "powerful inorganic life." When it comes to any multiplicities whatever, it is of the essence of the Event to compose them as the One that they are, and to exhibit this unique composition in potentially infinite variations.[33]

Badiou concludes that, for Deleuze and other immanentist vitalists, the event is the "immanent mark of the One-result of all becomings." Again, I am not concerned here in defending Badiou's critique of Deleuze and other immanentists. Rather I want to highlight how both Badiou and Goldberg agree that from *within* a multiplicity there can only be discovered the sort of unity (the "One-result") that will never offer anything really new. What Badiou offers instead is "a pure cut in becoming" that "disjoins the previous state of an object (its site) from its subsequent state."[34] When he talks about the "pure cut" Badiou is alluding to the mathematical theory of the cut introduced by Richard Dedekind to define irrational and rational numbers in one and the same way (rather than leaving the irrationals in their own domain as the unactualizable limit of an infinite series). Valorizing indivisible and infinitely variable continuity (the Bergsonian duration) over the "cut," Deleuze and other immanentists actually deprive life of any possibility of a real event, a real break with the past. Strikingly, Goldberg, too, immediately after his criticism of Bergsonian intuitionism in *Ontology*, explains that the fundamental flaw with that theory is its failure to grasp Dedekind's reformulation of the nature of rational and irrational numbers on the basis of the cut. His argument is quite illuminating and deserves our close attention.

Goldberg says that intuitionists attribute a purely negative valence to rationality, that is, they believe that reason can never access the immediacy of an indivisible wholeness within experience. Intuitionists therefore embrace the irrational as the realm of the direct experience of wholeness. This is the space where "Naturphilosophie" turns into "Lebensphilosophie," where the attempt to offer a mathematically rigorous understanding of nature is replaced by the valorization of the irrational as the upsurge of the will to power. The intuitionists go astray because they imagine that the rational and the irrational stand in "mutually exclusive opposition" to one another.[35] But, Goldberg argues, the opposite is the case: "The irrational is that region which is produced through two rational factors." What Goldberg is referring to here is the famous definition of irrational numbers provided by Richard Dedekind's "cut."[36] Dedekind begins with a definition of a rational number as one that "cuts" the rational number line in two, creating a set of rational numbers greater than it and another set lesser than it. The rational number making the cut is either the greatest number of the one group or the smallest number of the other group. One can quickly see how the "cutting" number cannot be the end-point of *both* sets of numbers, so one set is therefore "open." Since there are an infinite number of rational numbers (fractions) between any two rational numbers, the "open" end cannot have an end point that is a rational number (otherwise it would be the *very next rational number after the cut with no intervening gap,* but between every two rational numbers there is an infinity of other rationals). The end point of the open side of the cut is therefore an *irrational* number. Every irrational number can be precisely defined as lying "between" two classes of rational numbers on either side of a cut. The irrational number is defined, as Goldberg says, by two "rational factors."

How does this definition help resolve the problem that the intuitionists grasp, but do not properly address, namely, how to create wholeness or unity out of a multiplicity. The intuitionists are like mathematicians before Dedekind: they want to grasp the unity of the whole number line, rational and irrational numbers together, by plunging into the "flowing and indivisible movement" as it generates without break the whole continuous line from one end to the other. They seek to experience, as Badiou puts it, "the becoming of becoming."[37] They do not want to analyze the number line (or time) into points ("cuts"), fearing the loss of the flowing wholeness as it dissolves into parts. Yet Dedekind shows that the wholeness of the continuous number line, comprising both rational and irrational numbers, can *only* be generated out of rational factors defining an infinitude of points on the line in terms of "greater than" and "less than." The bottom line is that, unlike the intuitionists, Goldberg does not prioritize irrational duration over mathematically rigorous rationality. Another way to say this is that Goldberg is not a mystic.

Having distinguished his own method for achieving wholeness in the midst of the empirical world from those of the immanent intuitionists, Goldberg turns to a detailed account of that method in the remaining two sections of *Ontology*. Although these two concluding sections are only two of eleven sections, they take up nearly half the essay (twenty-two of fifty-two pages). Goldberg describes what these sections expound as "the ontological method": "The final demand that yet must be met that we have placed upon our [absolute] logic is that it must lead us to *content*. When does logic have content? In contrast with the formation of propositions and syllogistic proofs in formal logic, this happens when the results of its logical operations do not take off by themselves to float in the air but rather acquire a *bearer* [*Träger*]. It is therefore an essential demand of logic that the system of concepts it produces is furnished out ontologically [*ontologisch gedeckt*]."[38]

To furnish the system of concepts (each of which is a Uniqueness, or multiplicity-unity) with ontological reality first requires finding the appropriate content for the concepts that are coordinated with the multiplicity of uniquenesses. Goldberg has argued that to each multiplicity-unity there corresponds a unique concept, since the whole of the multiplicity-unities is what he called a "completeness system of concepts." We know that each multiplicity-unity is a structured "positional value system," but we do not yet know what its content is. We have, we might say, *transfinite numbers*, but we have *nothing to count*. One can invent any number of possible candidates for the sort of object that would be countable by a transfinite number, that is, infinities of objects totalizable within a single unifying concept. Goldberg reminds us that Plato thought that the Ideas were truly existing uniquenesses, that is, they were unique multiplicity-unities.

The Idea of the Table somehow is a unique Table in which all empirical tables "participate." But Goldberg argues that Plato's method of relating countable objects to a transcendental Idea fails because it allows too many things to be countable, namely, everything named by a common noun. Goldberg would surely disagree with the contemporary philosophical position called "mereological universalism," according to which any group of things is legitimately described as a unique object. For Goldberg, authentic "multiplicity-unities" in the empirical realm must have corresponding transcendental structures, but how do we know how to distinguish between such authentic "multiplicity-unities" and mere aggregations of things? Why doesn't the tip of my nose and the Eiffel Tower constitute an authentic "multiplicity-unity"?

Goldberg attempts to answer the question of what empirical content to provide to the multiplicity-unities by examining the logic of the concept in general. A concept can either be identical to its object or distinct from it. A transcendental multiplicity-unity *is* a concept, a sort of Platonic Idea, marked by what Goldberg calls "pure Being," the coincidence of concept and object.[39] A transfinite number is definable within the system of all transfinite numbers by its position in the series of transfinite numbers. Its "concept" is its ordinality, and the number itself is nothing more than its ordinality. Concept and object are one. But in the empirical world, a concrete multiplicity-unity is an object that is not identical to its concept. A number of horses, for example, is not equivalent to the concept "horse." When a concept is not identical to its object, their relationship is a certain kind of contradiction (X is *not identical* to Y), but it is not a complete contradiction. We have, as Goldberg puts it, a move from pure Being to a "limitation" (*Einschränkung*) of Being. "And what does the limitation of Being mean?" Goldberg asks. "To answer this we need to understand what it means for pure Being to involve the identity of concept and object. It means that pure Being is *completed* Being. And therefore the case where concept and object are not identical is "still-*not*-completed Being, of just-*becoming*-completed Being." A transfinite number is a totalized, completed infinity; the infinity of finite numbers (1, 2, 3 and so on) is not completed, but the counting *has been completed* with the first transfinite number.

Up to this point, we are not too far removed from Plato's metaphysics of Ideas and concrete particulars. (Cantor also admitted that his transfinite numbers resemble Platonic Ideas.) We have a realm of pure Being composed of concepts identical to their objects (the Idea of a Table is itself a *complete* or *perfect* table) and a realm of Becoming composed of particulars that are in a state of flux. Goldberg continues to follow Plato when he asks what sort of thinking grasps concrete particulars. His answer: *representational thinking* (*Vorstellung*) or *thinking in images.* "image-thinking [*Vorstellung*] is that aspect of thinking that stands in *contradiction* with the object with which it is connected."[40] The way that image-thinking (or, more simply, *imagination*) contradicts its object is that the image can either include too much or too little of the object. Goldberg's pursuit of the content of his abstract multiplicity-unities (what are they concepts *of*) now switches over to a pursuit of the "proper object of imagination," the object that would be an example of "becoming-completed Being." Clearly, no already completed object, no object with "a constant magnitude and fixed outline," will be such an object.[41] At this point we may recall what the "insane" friend says in Unger's "At Night," namely, that the world of objects in everyday experience is simply the result of a "pose" that consciousness assumes to prevent the deeper secrets of the universe from emerging into the light of day. To access these secrets would be to reach the "proper object of imagination." It would allow "new things" to begin to come into being, to begin their process of transition from not-yet-completed Being to completed Being.

The "proper object of imagination" will be, at its inception, a "becoming-completed Being." An example of "becoming-completed Being" will only be found in the *variation* of an object through time. Here Goldberg seems to have finally parted company with Plato. For Plato, the whole realm of Becoming is in some sense illusory, in contradiction with the pure truth of the Idea. Goldberg believes, however, that it is precisely in the variability of an object that one might find a "proper object of the imagination" that would serve as an example of a transcendental multiplicity-unity. But what kind of variability could serve as an example of the pure Being of an abstract multiplicity-unity? The answer: a variability that *can be completed*. (Back to the tip of my nose and the Eiffel Tower: Goldberg would say that there is no change over time from one condition of this pair of things to another condition in which the second condition can be described as "more complete" than the first condition.) Such a variability would not be like the infinity of a series without any end that is created by the repeated addition of one element to another (like the infinite series of integers), nor would it be a mere aggregation of elements (like the things randomly assembled on top of a table). The variability that Goldberg is looking for would be captured in imagination not as a series of changes of a single already identifiable object (like the changes in position of a moving automobile, for example), but as an unfolding of a unity out of a multiplicity. But what object would serve to reveal such an unfolding unity or completedness? What single object offers access to the process in which a multiplicity-unity comes into being?

Goldberg replies that, if one examines the entire field of experience, no *single* object presents itself that could reveal the *inner process of change as a movement toward a completed form*. Therefore, imagination must reach beyond any singe object and encompass the *realm of experience as a complete whole*. The whole universe is, in other words, the unfolding evolution of manyness into unity. The problem for Goldberg is to explain how the imagination might grasp the totality of the universe as its object.[42] Kant had declared that such a complete grasp of experience as a whole was impossible for the imagination. But Kant had assumed that the totality of experience meant the totality of all objects in the universe past, present, and future. Goldberg will suggest that in fact there is another way to access the totality of experience, not as a single given object but as a single object in the process of becoming complete. Rather than attempting to encompass the *outward* limits of experience (the totality of all objects), Goldberg turns to the *inner* limits (the point where consciousness confronts the coming-into-being of experience as such).[43]

Goldberg, let us recall, wants to find an object within experience where variability without fixed identity—but not sheer, endless variability—can be discerned. He wants to find an object that displays the becoming-completed of a multiplicity-unity. And this object, this inner limit of experience, is nothing other than the imagination itself.[44] "We now have to do not with any random single object but with such an object that presents the whole realm of experience and that presents it as the realm of Becoming in itself. This object must be constantly changing itself because by virtue of its very definition it is 'in becoming,' that is, it finds itself in a condition of not-yet-completed Being. It changes itself in such a direction *as if* it wants to be released from this condition, that is, as if it wants to *become* complete."[45] What Goldberg is describing is a self-altering subjectivity whose alteration is directed toward a desired goal, a telos. Although any organism could be so described, the only one that provides an access point to the whole of experience is the conscious human subject. In becoming conscious of his own goal-oriented becoming, the human subject is aware also of the becoming of experience as a whole:

> And now imagination displays itself at last in its authentic function: it corresponds to Becoming. It is the imagination of Becoming itself, that is, it is by its nature a self-altering, processual something. And from this it follows that the imagination of the object that is the totality of experience corresponds to the imagination of a totality in change, that is, of a *sequential process* [*Ablauf*]. In this way, what we mean by change acquires a different meaning. Because the object of experience is a flowing one [*ein fliessender*], it must possess an immanent law governing its process if the "flux" [*Fluß*] is not going to be simply chaotic, that is, if it is not going to never even get a start in its movement. And since now the totality of what is given is grasped as a single object [i.e., the imagination itself], it turns out that there can only ever be a single course the process takes.[46]

Perhaps we ought not to be too surprised to find that Goldberg believes that self-consciousness, the power of the imagination itself, is the key to answering the question about the content of the concepts in the transcendental realm of multiplicity-unities. As I have said, these multiplicity-unities are revealed to be the constituent parts of a transcendental organism in *The Reality of the Hebrews*. They are themselves not alive, but they are the structural "positional value systems" that define as an abstract formal pattern the inner lawfulness of a particular organism's growth. The human organism is patterned after the *whole* of the realm of multiplicity-unities (the human is created "in the image" of the transcendental Adam), and therefore if a human is able to experience her own change toward a completed state as a single process, she would be in touch with the coming into being of the completedness of all experience. In other words, her own sense of wanting completion would reflect the world's tendency toward completion. (The human as the evolving microcosm refracting nature's evolving macrocosm, with the imagination as the site where both evolving processes dynamically intersect, is one of the principal themes of Romantic Naturphilosophie.) But, of course, what the individual's imagination must grasp is not the sheer chaotic flux of change, but the deeper lawfulness governing this change and the true unity toward which the multiplicity of the moments of life is directed. This unity is not a single organism's particular possession; it would only be completed in a multiplicity-unity that truly embodies the transcendental multiplicity-unity. The task of imagination, then, is to connect with this *collective* unity as it is coming into being in the individual. By connecting with this collective unity in the depth of the individual, imagination will be enabled to *produce the coming experience*, to create the next stage in the coming-to-be complete of *humanity as a whole*. We can see here the influence of Bastian and his theory of universal ethno-ideas that reflect a species-wide consciousness, but there are many other possible sources that Goldberg could have drawn from, including Schelling's Naturphilosophie and the emerging literature concerning the ideational and archetypal content of the unconscious mind in Freud and especially in Jung. Rather than concentrating on bringing the unconscious archetypes into relation with a single human consciousness in order to heal the individual's neuroses (as Jung does), Goldberg is only interested in connecting the individual to the collective power of the human imagination in order to heal society's fragmentation and atomism.

Goldberg's *Ontology*, when it turns to the method of allowing the becoming-completed stream of imagination to flow freely, is not easy to follow. It is hampered by the abstract and formal terms in which Goldberg has forced himself to speak. He does talk about imagination, fantasy, and experience, but he does not permit himself to talk about organisms as multiplicity-unities or biological processes as self-altering and goal directed. He does not provide concrete examples of what imagination will find when it seeks to experience the coming-into-being of the human as such within the welter of changing impressions within consciousness. What he does say is that consciousness would experience "universalia."[47] We do not get much help from *Ontology* in understanding what that term means more precisely. Fortunately, Erich Unger will employ this term when he uses Goldberg's *Ontology* for his own purposes, providing a much more fleshed-out account of how the imagination can access these universalia.

In the next section of this chapter I turn to Erich Unger's *Politics and Metaphysics* (1921) and a section from his *Against Poetry* (1925) to provide a fuller picture of Goldberg's ideas in *Ontology*. But let me offer an orientation for what follows. Recall what Franz Brentano said about the active mind (*nous poietikos*) in his early work, *Die Psychologie des Aristoteles* (discussed in chapter 1). I invoke Brentano again here because, in some respects, he is the formative thinker for the entire revival of Naturphilosophie in the second half of the nineteenth century. Whether or not Goldberg and Unger had read Brentano, in one way or another they are working within his sphere of influence. Brentano, as I explained in chapter 1, saw the active mind as the solution to the psychophysical problem of how human consciousness is related to the human body. He argued that Aristotle appealed to God's active mind as the agent that transforms the unformed fetus into a specifically human fetus by introducing the active mind in an instant. In that instant, a fetus that is only an animal fetus becomes a human fetus. The specificity of the human being as such is the capacity to actualize *phantasmata* (the sensory qualities generated by the sense organs) into ideal or abstract objects (from this particular greenness to greenness and color and quality in increasing orders of abstraction, each order a part of the particular awaiting the active mind to actualize it). Just as the active mind actualizes the sensible particulars within the sense organs, it actualizes the disposition of the animal fetus to become human. The transformation of a *phantasma* into an ideal abstraction and the transformation of the animal body into a human body both take place in an instant. There is, therefore, a potential correlation between both transformations. It would not be taking too much of a leap to say that, when the active mind actualizes ideal abstractions, it might be reaching a generic level correlated to the generic origin from which the human fetus emerged. That is, instead of saying that consciousness *rises* to form abstractions, it could be said that it *descends* beneath the surface level of sense *phantasmata* to the generic-animal reality from which the human fetus emerges. Perhaps *color* as the genus of greenness is not *less concrete* than greenness but is *more concrete*, that is, more related to the underlying organ as a color-receptive organ. Furthermore, it is perhaps the case that in forming abstractions one might be coming closer to the origination point of the human: the moment that the divine active mind intersects the empirical world and transforms an animal fetus into a human fetus.

We can perhaps understand Goldberg as seeking a way to use the imagination to reactivate Brentano's *nous poietikos*, the "productive intellect." Brentano himself believed that it was possible for a single human being to attain a form of personal disembodied immortality through the exercise of the *nous poietikos*.

Goldberg wants to produce not a disembodied state of immortality for the individual, but an embodied immortality within the collective social organism that is the telos of history. So this is how we ought to think about Goldberg's ontological method: as a method of returning consciousness to the point where animal becomes human through the eruption of the divine into the empirical world. It is a method based on imagination (*Phantasie*) and the dissolution of the fixed contents of consciousness into undifferentiated and more generic elements that are *not-yet-completed* and *not-yet-differentiated* forms or qualities. In a word, it is a method for regression to the divine source of human life. And if human life holds virtual possibilities of psychophysical activity that have not yet been actualized (or perhaps were only actualized in the mythic period of history), then regression to the divine source could conceivably activate those latent possibilities. Unfortunately, Goldberg never puts things this clearly (if this is clear). Erich Unger, however, does go a long way to making all this clear, as I explain next.[48]

## Erich Unger's *Politics and Metaphysics*

Goldberg's ontological method relies, as we have seen, on imagination (*Phantasie*) to open itself to a realm, on the other side of our empirical world, where the *yet-to-be-completed* is found in its latent, undifferentiated, virtual state. We noted that Goldberg argues that his ontological method does not merely seek to describe *how* the experience of a new reality was possible, but to actually *produce* it. Unger in *Politics and Metaphysics* shows how imagination can shatter the givenness of the political structures of the world and inaugurate an entirely new form of social reality. Goldberg's projected but never-written final section of *Ontology* was titled "Logik und Macht" ("Logic and Power"), and it was likely that it was intended to be a discussion of the way that authentic "multiplicity-unities" are constituted on the level of politics. This is exactly the topic of Unger's *Politics and Metaphysics.*

Unger's fundamental philosophical interest was in the "psychophysiological problem"; his doctoral thesis is titled "Das psychophysiologische Problem und sein Arbeitsgebiet" (The psychophysiological problem and its research field).[49] In the dissertation, Unger attempts to move beyond the way that the mind-body problem was studied in neo-Kantian and phenomenological circles at the time, namely as a theory of consciousness and its objects. Unger argues that the philosophical problems concerning consciousness and its objects can best be addressed through a close examination of the "fringe" phenomena reported in medicine and anthropology involving hypnosis, dissociated psychic states (the "double-ego"), trance, ecstasy, and so on. He claims that the mind-body problem parallels the problem of the relationship between the metaphysical and the physical and that it is in the abnormal and unusual states of human consciousness that this parallel formation is most able to be studied. In particular, Unger claims that the mind-body problem needs to be placed in the context of *collective* ritual-induced experiences, because it is only in these phenomena that one begins to recognize the truly heightened power of human psychophysiology and the full capacity of imagination to transform it. It is clear that Unger is influenced by Goldberg's understanding of the metaphysical reality behind the rituals of the ancient Hebrews, but is attempting to bring Goldberg's theories into conversation with current philosophical approaches to consciousness.

Unger's most extended treatment of the mind-body problem does not, in fact, come in his dissertation (which is largely a report on the current state of the question in philosophy, medicine, and anthropology), but in works he published from 1921 to 1930. In what follows I focus on his *Politics and Metaphysics*, published a year before he completed his dissertation.[50] I also introduce his 1925 work, *Against Poetry*. Both of these works made a deep impression on Walter Benjamin, who, like Unger, took the psychophysical problem to be the central one of philosophy and the key to a cultural critique of modern technological consciousness—the target of Goldberg's and Unger's work as well. Unger's *Politics and Metaphysics* bears the stamp not only of his immersion in the current neo-Kantian and phenomenological literature about the nature of consciousness and its objects but also of Goldberg's *Ontology*. *Politics and Metaphysics* will help us give flesh to Goldberg's abstract and abstruse discussion of the limit site between the totality of our normal experience of the "Dingwelt" and our imaginative access to a metaphysical reality as it enters the empirical domain as a not-yet-completed and unformed representation.

Unger opens *Politics and Metaphysics* by claiming that no "uncatastrophic" politics is possible unless politics becomes "metaphysical." Far from being impractical, Unger claims, metaphysical politics is the only one that can provide the means to achieve the fundamental goal of politics, namely, "to see the coming-into-being of an ethically satisfactory order of human together-existence" (*ethisch befriedigende Ordnung menschlichen Zusammendaseins enstehen zu sehen*).[51] The problem that Unger pinpoints in all non-metaphysical approaches to politics is that they lack a proper *organic* conception of the nature of the "communal." All non-metaphysical, merely empirical political programs operate on the assumption that a human community is composed of competing interests and that it is the responsibility of the governing regime to forge a compromise among these interests. By so doing, the "ethically satisfying order" is supposed to emerge. But such empirical politics is merely the balancing of various contending powers that otherwise would engage in war. Compromise is power masked as law (*Recht*). Compromise is simply the postponement of war and, therefore, "it bears all responsibility for the catastrophes that ensue from the postponement of power [*Macht-Verschiebung*]," the postponement of the inevitability of the reversion to sheer power after the collapse of the legal compromise among the warring interests. (We may surmise that Goldberg's "Logik und Macht" section of *Ontology* would have developed along similar lines in a critique of contemporary political practice.)

Unger contrasts the conception of the community in empirical politics and in metaphysical politics on the basis of two conceptions of whole-part relations. Compromises cannot form an authentic communal whole or togetherness; they are simply the mechanical balancing of the forces within disparate parts that maintain their distinct identities. An authentic whole is constructed out of a "system of forces" (*Kräfte-System*).[52] Unger's account of the nature of the "system of forces" is identical to the organicist explanatory model of force fields that was then coming to the fore in theoretical biology, as I described in chapter 1. Unger describes the difference between a compromise system of forces and an organic system of forces in the following terms:

> One can discover the compromise of forces in the sense of a balance of forces or a compound of forces throughout nature, even in quite arbitrary or chaotic arrangements. But the system of forces is only found in case of the "organism" [*Organismus*]. In the case of the balance of forces, each force works outward from itself and at a certain *meeting-point* it is influenced by the other force and either decreased or increased. The balance is effected *mechanically*. But in the case of the system of forces each force works as if the other forces were *already* involved with it. Each force works in such a way as if an *all-at-once* [*Auf-Ein-Mal*] reality of all the participating forces existed prior to any one of them and had effected a reality of the *together* [*Zusammen*] from out of which a tendency to differentiate and order the separate forces had emerged. It is as if each force straightaway from the beginning, at the very point of its originating, had experienced the effects and influences of all the other forces. Thus they arise straightaway in order. The balance works *organically*.[53]

Unger argues that an authentic organic political togetherness requires the domination of spirit (*Geist*) over the material conditions through which the community reproduces itself—the economy in other words. Economic forces or interests can be balanced through compromise arrangements, but this process will never produce an organic arrangement of the material conditions of communal life. Such an organic arrangement requires a unifying factor that can create a whole out of disparate political interests, and spirit alone is able to provide this. Only spirit is capable of exercising the "all-at-once" force that creates a real togetherness of parts. This "auf-ein-mal" principle clearly resembles Goldberg's description of the "positional value system" that constitutes a "uniqueness" (*Einmaligkeit*). An authentic human "togetherness-existence" cannot be a mere "series" of individuals or even just a finite collection or set. These are formed by division and not by the "interruption act." An interruption act works "all-at-once" to bring a new uniqueness into being.

Unger postulates that the political problem—how to create "an ethically satisfactory order of human together-existence"—is insoluble without a proper understanding of the psychophysical relationship of spirit and body. If spirit is to dominate over material economic interests, it must be more than a "superstructure" that merely reflects existing conditions. A truly organic political order requires the direct and immediate action of spirit on the material conditions of existence. So long as spirit merely lags behind material reality, the longed-for ethical order has no hope of realization. Where, however, does one observe such direct and immediate contact between spirit and matter? Is such a relationship even possible?

An example of the direct and immediate relationship between spirit and body does exist, Unger claims. It exists in *mathematics.* In mathematical intuition the spirit grasps the realm of the corporeal (*das Körperhaft*) given in sensation in the form of purely abstract multiplicities. "Law-conforming [*gesetzmäßige*] intuition is the activity of the spirit on the level of the senses; it is 'pure' sensibility [*Sinnlichkeit*]."[54] It is possible that Unger, although he had long believed that mathematics was at the basis of all experience, is here drawing from the phenomenological analysis of the difference between secondary and primary qualities that Edmund Husserl introduced in *Ideen: Allgemeine Einführung in die reine Phänomenologie* (*Ideas: General Introduction to a Pure Phenomenology*, 1913), the first major work he published after *Logische Untersuchungen* (*Logical Investigations*, 1900–1901).[55] In his *Ideas* Husserl explains that secondary qualities were traditionally understood to be only "subjective," the way an object appears to a perceiving subject, whereas primary qualities were "objective."[56] Primary qualities were thought to be the mathematically measurable properties of things in themselves (mass, spatial dimension, velocity, and so on). Husserl takes the step of making both secondary and primary qualities into the intentional objects of consciousness, although of two distinct "attitudes"—one the "natural" attitude of the "man in the street" and the other attitude the scientific one that "brackets" the sensible content of the natural attitude in order to focus only on abstract and formal "essences." Both attitudes bring consciousness into relationship with "the things themselves" through the mediation of the embodied Ego. When Unger says that mathematical intuition is "pure sensibility" and "the activity of the spirit on the level of the senses," he may mean, following Husserl, that the spirit (or consciousness) directly and immediately works on the body's senses to create a "bracketed" or "pure" intuition of how the sensible content of consciousness embodies mathematical structures and logical laws. Husserl calls the act of consciousness that intuits the mathematical structure of what is given in sensation *noesis.* Thus in *Ideas,* Husserl is returning to the Aristotelian psychology of the *nous poietikos* that his teacher Brentano had claimed held the key to understanding the operation of human consciousness as such. Recall that the same *nous poietikos* was for Brentano the cause of the step from animal fetus to human fetus.

Husserl in *Ideas* does not use the concept of noetic intuition to explain the way that the human organism achieves psychophysical unity, but Unger does take mathematical intuition to have something to do with the relationship between spirit and body: he claims that mathematical intuition is an example the operation of the "psychophysical sensibility."[57] For Unger, the only hope for a noncatastrophic politics is to discover a way for consciousness to directly and immediately work on the material conditions of collective human existence in exactly the same way that it works on the individual's sensibility to produce mathematical intuitions. For this process to take place, there must be a collective capacity for sensation, a collective psychophysical sensibility. "If there is no sensuousness [*Sinnenhaftigkeit*] in the realm of non-individual realities, if there is no field of law-conforming intuition in this realm, if there is no *sensation* [*Sinne*] of non-individual realities, then spirit is forever, in the literal sense, a free-floating schema that must eternally be at the mercy of the force of corporeal so-called 'reality.' "[58] If spirit is going to be able to transform the material conditions of a political community in such a way that it functions as an authentically whole organism and not merely as the inauthentic, catastrophe-prone aggregation of competing interests, then it must work through a corporate collective body sharing a collective capacity for sensation.

Unger thus calls for a new approach to the "psychophysiological problem."[59] He asks us to consider the possibility that, while the physiological basis of sensation exists at the individual level, the actual "psychic quantity" associated with conscious awareness may not be parceled out to individuals first and foremost. In other words, he asks us to consider the possibility that consciousness can be wider in scope than the single individual. The evidence that consciousness as a psychic quantity is not divided evenly and without remainder in relation to individual physiologies is first indicated by the fact that it is "too short" in respect of the unifying power that forms the individual into a single human organism enduring throughout the changes of his organic material substrate:

> For logical reasons (and not for historical ones), the individual's capacity for conscious awareness does not extend so far as the genetic origin of his body and it is not possible for it to extend this far. If an individual's consciousness were able to grasp its own materiality without any remainder—and this act would allow us to solve the psychophysiological problem—it would have to do this not in relation to the moment of its genesis in the biological cycle [of birth and death] but rather in relation to its moment of genesis in relation to its all-at-once causality. What I mean by "all-at-once causal genesis" [*einmalig-kausale Genese*] is something different from the biological causality that is constantly repeating itself [with every new birth] and in which the life-course

of the organism is presaged. What I mean, rather, is the cause of this presaging, the *construction-cause* that does not merely operate, as a naïve understanding of an individual cause would have it, in the "beginning," but rather *across the course of the life* as a concentrated cause [at every moment]. Consciousness cannot grasp this all-at-once cause in a moment of intuition within the circle of its individual awareness since this awareness does not possess a psychic magnitude commensurate with an event like that of a causality that operates at every point of the biological life cycle.[60]

Unger distinguishes between the cause of an individual's coming into being, the actual biological act in which an egg is fertilized, and the "all-at-once" cause that operates throughout the lifespan of the individual. The fertilizing cause happens only once, and that occurs in the beginning of the life of the individual. This fertilizing cause accounts for the coming into being of *this particular individual*, but it does not account for the coming into being of the species of which this individual is a member. In contrast, the "all-at-once cause" does not merely operate once in the life of the individual, at the point of conception. It operates throughout the life of the individual at every moment of that life. Consciousness can only grasp experience in the way it is presented to the senses as they are physiologically active through a certain duration of time. It cannot grasp the all-at-once organizing force operating in the organism at every moment.

If we put the "all-at-once cause" in relation to what Unger had said about the way that true organic wholes arise "all-at-once" as a "system of forces," we may understand better why Unger believes that only if a collective consciousness or sensation exists can there be a noncatastrophic politics. Consciousness, at least in its normal functioning in a single individual, is not able to experience the wholeness of the psychophysical reality of the individual: it only can grasp a fragment, a temporal portion, of this reality. We saw how Unger had argued that if a true community is to be created by a metaphysical politics, it can be only be formed through a spirit that can grasp the wholeness of the community. Anything less than this would at best produce a compromise among competing forces, merely a postponement of catastrophe. If spirit is going to be able to create a true organic community, it must do so by encompassing what normal individual consciousness cannot encompass: the "all-at-once" cause of the human psychophysical unity. This unity is not merely one that includes my own individual lifespan: it includes the whole of humanity, because it is the result of a force that makes this organic body into a *human* body. (Recall again Brentano's claim that the *nous poietikos* transforms the animal fetus into a human fetus.) The "all-at-once" cause of the unity of the individual as a human individual is part of a "transcendent reality"[61] that can only be encompassed within a "heightened" consciousness resulting from the "intertwining of originally foreign psychic factors into a singe consciousness."[62] These foreign factors involve the conjunction of the consciousness of an individual consciousness with that of others. This process, however, cannot be accomplished so long as consciousness remains at the level of what could be called the "surface" sensibility of the organism. It can only be accomplished at the level of the all-at-once causality that is the constructive principle of the human body as such. Collective consciousness would then, and only then, be truly coordinated with the collective constructive force of the organism. At this point the psychophysiological problem, the problem of how mind and body interact as a complete unity, would reach its *practical* solution.

If the psychophysiological problem is going to be resolved, there are two things that must in principle be the case:

> First: Consciousness of a specific physiological individual is not a constant magnitude, but it is capable of modification through psychic factors involving a multiplicity [*Vielheit*] for the members of which an unmetaphorical psycho-physiological connection exists.
>
> Second: With the potentiation [of this capacity for modification], whose rich documentation is the subject of an entire scientific area [i.e., anthropology and ethnology], there is an advance in the individual's capacity to experience his own materiality, that is, his own body, in the direction of its coming into being [*Zustandekommens*], that is, there is a conjunction and interpenetration of consciousness with the genetic, that is, the constructive forces of the organism (that normally fall outside consciousness); and this means nothing more and nothing less than the principle that these can be *manipulated* and that the limits of consciousness can be shifted into previously closed territories.[63]

Unger is here imagining the possibility that multiple consciousnesses could blend together at the level of the "all-at-once" (*einmalig*) unity of the multiple parts of the individual body. Recall that Goldberg's *Ontology* is based on the "uniqueness" (*Einmaligkeit*) ur-concept that "broke through" into a multiplicity of such uniquenesses, each a part of the transcendental organism in the form of a self-standing mathematical structure. We can now see that Unger has taken this basic idea and used it to explain, first, the constructive force of the individual organism as a unity, and, second, the level at which consciousness reaches into and beneath its material organic basis and there meets the transcendental reality that brings the individual's psychophysical reality into being.[64] "Just as our unmodified sensibility gives us access to the physical world, so our modified sensibility would in the same manner give us access to and make experienceable those transcendental relationships (those that are above and beyond the physical ones, that is, above and beyond the limits of one's own biological individuality). These are literally metaphysical relationships to which—however little one may have had an inkling of it—belong also our sociological relationships."[65] In this way, metaphysics is essential to politics. Only a metaphysical politics can grasp the possible unity of the multiplicity of humans. Metaphysical politics deals with the "totality problematic" that the human condition poses: "The animal is completed [*fertig*], the human being is incomplete [*unfertig*]: he must rise to the totality-problematic in order to be able to arrange his affairs."[66] Again, we can certainly hear echoes of Goldberg's *Ontology* in these words. Goldberg, we recall, argues that the task of philosophy is to produce a new reality and that this new reality can only be experienced at the point where the "not-yet-complete Being" is coming into existence. This Being, this "totality-problematic," is the human being in his sociological identity.

Unger published *Politics and Metaphysics* in 1921, and it shows clear evidence that its conception of a new organic community responds directly to the cataclysm of the First World War. "What lives today," he writes, "what the so-called civilized peoples have arrived at, is the n-tuple repetition of the individual and above him any real unity has as good as disappeared and in its place there is a metaphoric, 'historic,' i.e., living-dead unity in whose artificial bounds and decayed limits the peoples [*Völker*] twist in agony."[67] What is needed after the cataclysm of war are individuals who are capable of heightened consciousness that will allow them to manipulate and control the psychophysiological "apparatus" of a group and transform a disparate group of individuals into a real unity. In the ancient world, these individuals were the priests and ethnic eponyms (*Stammväter*). But how will such individuals be legitimized as a modern community's proper leaders? What signs will they display of their superior psychophysical abilities? This question goes straight to the problem confronting both Unger and Goldberg: How will the priest-eponym of the new community reveal his power? How can he be distinguished from a psychologically deranged dictator? Of course, Unger in 1921 cannot imagine the madness into which Germany will descend in the ensuing decades, but it is quite clear that he wishes to distance himself from any kind of race-based nationalism. In fact, the final sections of his work go beyond the psychophysical problematic to the sociological problematic. Although they do not bear as directly on the themes of *Ontology*, these later sections show the profound influence of Goldberg's thinking about the nature of the ancient Hebrew people as a "founded" people (rather than a racially created people). It therefore is valuable for us to follow *Politics and Metaphysics* to its end.

The metaphysical people whom the modern priest-eponym will help form will be a "people with a metaphysical *purpose*."[68] This is no distant, utopian dream, but "it is immediately possible."[69] It is immediately possible because it will not require, as in antiquity, a long period of time for thousands and thousands of descendants to create an ethnos that inherits the eponym's heightened psychophysical power. The new people will be "founded"[70] rather than united through genetic ancestry. Their unity will not be based on an appeal to a past ancestor, but instead to a future goal: the *completion of the human species*. And where will this people arise? Its members are not likely to be found among the upstanding citizens of any states, but among the displaced persons who are wanderers within Europe. The European states after the war experienced a heightening of the "centrifugal tendency" that had held their citizens in the unity, albeit a mechanical one, of the state.[71] In fact, the world-historical moment can be characterized as follows: "the wandering of peoples and groups as a whole."[72] At this moment, the state is no longer able to provide out of its own landmass the needs of so many people moving through so many borders. This dissolution of nation-states into unprecedentedly large displaced populations will, first of all, reconfigure the economic arrangements that will be needed to serve these people. The result, Unger says, will be the creation of a postnational noncapitalist economic system: "The spatial abandonment of the region of where capitalism rules [i.e., the territorial nation-state] is thereby the unavoidable first commandment of every social movement that seeks a new basis for its material existence."[73]

And what will be the social order within this new postnational order? This order will have at its center an individual with exceptional psychophysiological abilities. Calling on Max Weber's discussion of the charismatic leader, Unger describes the "societas" he envisions as one characterized by "prophetism" (*Prophetismus*). Unger makes it clear that the new order will break with previous economic practices based on the exploitation of the raw materials of a nation-state (or the imperialist exploitation of other regions' raw materials), but he does not believe that the new economic system will rely primarily on new technologies. Instead, the new system will be able to tap into the very source of the life energies of the collective. It will rely on "the interchange between spirit and matter" that is the essence of "metaphysics" and not the "technical manipulation of matter."[74] Finally, Unger argues that the new order will be one that fully reflects what he calls the "metapolitical universitas."[75] This is Unger's name for what Goldberg calls the "transcendental organism." The metapolitical universitas is the "universal origin-site" of a truly organic community, one that is not divided into fighting parts or *parties*. In *The Reality of the Hebrews*, Goldberg will claim that only the ancient Hebrews established a truly organic community in which the metapolitical universitas was reflected. All other peoples embodied only a part of the transcendental organism, a part of Adam Kadmon, in their particular pantheon. Although each such people was a "biological center" for a part of the transcendental organism, it was actually only a peripheral part of the transcendental totality.

Unger takes this idea over into his sociological analysis of the modern state. He calls the state the site of "ideologies all of them parties" that need to be destroyed "not in the name of some higher-order state totality which itself is nothing other than another party," but rather because "these ideologies rest always upon a *peripheral* principle, and because this peripherality can never constitute an actual totality of a sociological complex, which alone can be living, that is, catastrophyless and which can be ruled by a central point—this is no empirical state-totality, but it arises from a universal origin-site in which all imaginable peripheral viewpoints are not somehow bundled together, but rather overcome."[76] Unger has no doubt that a new sociological order will arise from the "metapolitical universitas" because such orders existed in the past of certain peoples and also in the present of "nature-peoples" (*Natur-Völker*). "There were cases of real unity only in ancient times (and in this respect one may find a much different approach to the 'mythological stories' and their otherwise endlessly confusing details) and also in the present moment one finds actual totality in the nature-peoples who lead a so-called 'historyless' existence, which only means that that they are part of an 'eternal ur-time.' With such peoples one can systematize and establish with certainly the psychophysiological data on whose basis a real binding together of a [new] folk can be accomplished."[77] Unger begins the task of assembling the archive of such psychophysiological data in his 1922 dissertation, but it is Goldberg who devotes himself to this task with the dedicated energy of an "ethnological experimenter" in *The Reality of the Hebrews.*

## Conclusion: The Mythic Imagination in 1925 Weimar

In 1925, four notable books dealing with the mythic imagination were published: Goldberg's *The Reality of the Hebrews*, Unger's *Against Poetry*, and two books by Ernst Cassirer, *Language and Myth* and *Mythic Thought*.[78] Before turning to Goldberg's book in chapter 4, I want to say a few words about the other three books.

The overlap between Cassirer's books and those of Goldberg and Unger is really quite remarkable. All three look toward ancient mythology to provide a different logic from that which applies in natural science. All three start with language itself as having a root in a *productive* power of the human mind, and all three find that this power is most forcefully concentrated in *the names of the gods.* The connection between Cassirer's theory of myth and Goldberg's did not escape Erich Unger's notice (Cassirer never refers to Unger or Goldberg, as far as I know). As I explained in the introduction, Erich Unger presided over a weekly lecture series under the auspices of what he called the Philosophische Gruppe in the late 1920s. At one of the evening meetings of this group, Unger delivered a presentation on Cassirer's myth theory. He concluded by saying that "everything would be perfect" if Cassirer "had gone so far as to grant to myth as much efficacy in reality as one must in the case of thinking in the natural science whose practical result are machines."[79] But to argue for the equally efficacious power of myth, one would have to turn Cassirer's relative assessment of the value of myth and science upside down, something that both Goldberg and Unger were quite willing to do. Cassirer believed that mythic thought lacks any connection to reality and lives on only in the imaginative worlds of poetry and in the power of metaphor (language's paradigmatic axis, we would say). Unger argues that poetry is merely the ineffectual shadow of mythic thought. The very title of his own 1925 book, *Against Poetry*, reveals the degree to which Unger opposes the purely aesthetic interpretation of the metaphor-creating power of the imagination. For in that power lies the essence of the "authentic imagination," that productive principle of *new* realities.[80] It is precisely by *reconfiguring the relationships of concepts and percepts on the basis of similarity* that a new world of experience comes to expression. For Cassirer in contrast, scientific thought rises beyond poetry by taming the wild associations of metaphor-generating imagination and reducing them to law-defining functions. Only the reductive power of functional thinking, according to Cassirer, permits humanity to comprehend nature and build new technologies that redirect its energies to serve our ends. So, if Cassirer were to grant efficacious power to myth, he would have to reverse his values and declare that the effective force of technological rationality is the mere shadow of mythic thought's power to create absolutely new forms of experience. Now this is certainly something Goldberg and Unger believe, but it is the very reverse of Cassirer's account of the trajectory of thought from myth to science. But, though the valences are the reverse of Unger's and Goldberg's, Cassirer's description of mythic thought can usefully serve to illustrate what Unger and Goldberg mean by "plunging into experience" in order to discover *new* forms of experience and *new* concepts.

Cassirer claims that mythic thinking is preceded by a stage where an immediately sensed experience of a specific object captivates and holds in thrall the individual. "The ego is spending all its energy on this single object, lives in it, loses itself in it."[81] Mythic *thinking* begins where language also begins: the attempt to break free of the thralldom of the particular object by *naming* it. The word is the beginning of the world as a place where the human has power over objects, rather than the other way around. Therefore, the word has a certain magical power in mythic thinking, and no word more so than the name of the god, the captivating presence of the immediate moment. As mythic thinking progressively frees itself from the momentarily overwhelming presence given in sensed experience, it generalizes these particular experiences and these particular names by giving each captivating experience its own distinct appellation, until it reaches the highest level of abstraction, the nameless "godhead." "The Divine, instead of entering into the world of properties and proper names—the gay kaleidoscope of phenomena—is set off against this world as something without attributes."[82] This is exactly where Goldberg and Unger would say that an "authentic" reality-linked concept has been exchanged for a "sterile" pure concept. But before making the transition to empty abstraction, mythic thinking organizes the "gay kaleidoscope" of its divinities in what Cassirer calls "analogy magic":

The articulation of the chaos of sensory impressions, in which definite groups based on similarities are picked out and specific series are formed, is . . . common to both logical and mythical thinking; without it myth could no more arrive at stable configurations than logical thought at stable concepts. But the similarities of things are . . . apprehended in different directions. In mythical thinking any similarity of sensuous manifestation suffices to group the entities in which it appears in a single mythical "genus." Any characteristic, however external, is as good as another; there can be no sharp distinction between "inward" and "outward," "essential" and "nonessential," precisely because for myth every perceptible similarity is an immediate expression of an identity of *essence*. This similarity is never a mere concept of relation and reflection but is a real force—absolutely actual because absolutely effective. All so-called analogy magic reveals this basic mythical view. . . . For where we see mere analogy, i.e. a mere *relation*, myth sees immediate existence and presence.[83]

The principle of "analogy magic" as revelatory of "immediate existence and presence" is central to Goldberg's conception of how *the new* is generated out of the manifold "universalia" in experience. Unlike Goldberg, Cassirer does not want to reactivate the mythic imagination, but rather to transmute it into the symbolic abstractions of science. Despite this fact, however, Unger was quite right to believe that Cassirer and Goldberg were indeed united about the nature of the mythic imagination.

Erich Unger also offered a theory of mythic imagination, largely based on Goldberg's *Ontology*, in a book provocatively titled *Against Poetry*.[84] Unger's goal in this book is precisely to defend imaginative creativity (*Dichtung*) against the charge that it merely generates fantasy or "poetry." In this book, Unger takes Goldberg's *Ontology* and offers a general theory of the aesthetic imagination. *Against Poetry* refers explicitly in a number of places to Goldberg's *Ontology* as the source on which it most heavily relies. The fact is that Unger's *Against Poetry* can be read a sort of companion to Goldberg's *Reality of the Hebrews*. Near the end of the book Unger refers to Goldberg's *Reality of the Hebrews* (and also his *Ontology*) as "presentations that are the primary object lessons for doing what this book has argued for," namely, to provide an analysis of the imaginative productions of the ancient world as containing "a representation of reality that is heterogeneous to that of our current concept of reality."[85]

Unger shares with Goldberg the conviction that philosophy's most pressing task is to provide the transcendental conditions of possibility for *an entirely new experience*. Unger, following Goldberg's *Ontology*, does not mean by this to refer to an experience that would be part of this empirical world of space and time, but rather to an entirely different form of experience. Also following Goldberg, Unger believes that Kant's system completely excludes the possibility of "the new":

Kant was forced from the outset to stifle a rebellion on the part of the drive towards knowledge, a drive that, when properly understood, finds its logical meaning in the concept of *new* knowledge. He saw quite clearly what was coming with his system: If the number of the highest concepts of the understanding were finite, if pure intuition and the transcendental forms in general constituted a narrowly defined structure, then thinking, looked at from the top down, had nowhere further to go. All experience that ought to have produced "endlessly new material and stimuli," would exhaust all its energies in the eternally self-identical edifice of the eternally same highest concepts and highest principles. The result is that in reality *never* can there be anything new brought forth. For however differently things may strike the intuition, however much the new and multifarious may appear to intuition, all this "newness" would be *annihilated by thinking* and turned into the same old and ever identical grist for its mill, that is, the forward movement of thought would actually be permanently closed off and stopped, if Kant's Critique of Pure Reason has its way. And that this is in fact Kant's deepest intention is brought to light in an entirely different aspect of his system: the famous division between analytic and synthetic judgments is Kant's way of opposing the concept of *the new.*[86]

Unger is arguing here that, given the way that Kant describes synthetic judgments as those that conform to the understanding's categories and analytic judgments as tautologous, there is no way for an experience to be entirely new and unexpected. Goldberg's *Ontology* makes precisely the same point in its criticism of the "sterility" of formal logic. And we have also seen that the central programmatic statement of the *Ontology* is that philosophy should not content itself with *explaining* experience. Its goal, rather, is "the production of another reality."

Goldberg's prescription for the "production of another reality" requires one to let go of the constancy and fixity of unitary objects and to let the sheer variability of experience emerge. This is Unger's prescription as well. To discover the new, "one must start out from the sensible manifold," he writes. But the new is not discovered *within* the sensible manifold of experience. Goldberg criticizes the intuitionist philosophers for seeking the new *immanently*, within the "sequence" of temporal experience. What one must search for is a site that opens out to an entirely different realm of experience: "If we seek *the new* correctly and authentically within the continuity of experience, then the *a priori* region must not be rigid and unmoving." He continues, "The source of the movement must already lie in the sphere of the categories which participate in the variability of experience and reality."[87] We are not talking about Kantian categories, Unger insists. The Kantian categories, as well as the forms of the intuition (space and time), are too distant from the variability of experience to allow for the emergence of a new experience. They are "foreshortened, that is, inauthentic, formal, and immobile."[88] The categories that Unger proposes are those that penetrate into the variability of sense experience and manifest themselves within it. They are, he explains, the "sensible qualities renderable in thought" (denkmäßige Sinnesqualitäten)[89]—that is, the universal qualia (*Quala*) that reappear identically in distinct acts of perception: the "green" that exists objectively that "is the condition of possibility for the eye" is "a reality which from its side makes possible the eye." Unger explains, "The eye and the specific, that is determinate, sense perception presuppose in their mutual relation the *universal* reality of their 'theme,' which is the medium and that which binds them together, that is, it effects the mutual adaptation of the specific, visible realities and the eye, since both have *the same universal*."[90] Unger here is claiming that the sense perception that is mediated by the sensory organ, the eye for example, and the sensory quality that is perceived—greenness, for example— are one and the same thing: *Every eye* sees *the same thing* (the universal) when it sees greenness. Unger's position was shared by a number of phenomenological psychologists who were students of Franz Brentano. This phenomenological viewpoint, as I explained in chapter 1, goes back, via Brentano, to Aristotle, and Unger is clearly indebted to the fundamental Aristotelian thesis that *the sense organ and the universal are united in the act of perception*. This is important for Unger because it allows him to show that by plunging into the variability of experience one reaches concepts or universals, objects "renderable in thought," rather than a purely chaotic manifold that must be ordered through a set of categories set apart from experience.

The sensible universals that are both objects of perception and "renderable in thought," Unger argues, have a logical structure of their own: *Greenness* is one of the species of the genus *color*, and *color* is a species of *quality*, and *quality* is one of the ways that *being* (*the real*) is expressed. Being is the "general concept" that Goldberg speaks about as "breaking down" and "pouring out" authentic possibilities. How these "authentic possibilities" emerge needs further explanation. That explanation depends on the premise that the independent reality of the sensible universals is accessible not only through direct perception but also through thought. After explaining that sensible appearances like greenness exist in reality as universals, Unger continues:

> This means that there must be a sort of universal sensible experience prior to the specific sense organs in order for there to be a specific sensible experience. And this implies that there must be sensible qualities renderable in thought, that is "a aprioristic" entities of thought which correspond to the individual specific forms of the senses (whose generality [*Allgemeines*] they contain) and as experiences they are grasped in thought. These experiences graspable in thought are given mythological garb in Platonism as the objects and acts of *anamnesis* [recollection], although Plato errs in making what is a structural apriority into something temporal ("before one's birth"). These experiences are in fact "covered over" by the earlier empirical sensations insofar as they are

rendered through consciousness. The collection of specific [sensations] into generalities forming "the general" happens in truth later. But the *legitimation* for the collection of these concepts is the universals ["greenness" and so on] that are entailed with them [the sensations], that is, the generality that makes the specific [sensation] possible. The general [as a universal] precedes the specific [sensation], although it first comes to consciousness after [the sensation]. This means that what provides the foundation for abstraction and what puts a limit to our arbitrary ability to form any possible abstraction whatever, are the co-entailed universals, in exactly the way that what puts a limit to our arbitrary ability to move one's sense organs in any direction whatever is—the shape of our empirical body. And finally it is wrong to think that any old concept relates to some pre-existing reality, the way it is in Platonism. It is clear that "light," "life force," "matter," have a transempirical actuality of an entirely different reality than such things as "the similar," "the greater," and the "the proportional decrease between the square of the distance and permeability" or "that which is unable to exist independently." The first are concepts and entities that are substances, the second are pure concepts, even if they might be accidents of the other entities.[91]

What Unger is arguing here is that there is a realm of universals that come to expression in sense experience, but that they are objects of thought preexisting any specific sense experience. As objects of thought, one can "collect" them and form higher-order genera with them, such as "light" or "life force" or "matter," and these entities are not "pure concepts." but are rather "transempirical entities" that come to appearance in experience.

Although Unger points to *The Reality of the Hebrews* as the complete working out of his argument in the case of the imaginative production (*Dichtung*) called the Pentateuch, he offers his own brief reading of another "mythology" that represents a reality heterogeneous to our own: Pythagoreanism. I want to conclude this chapter with a brief review of Unger's description of Pythagoreanism. It will allow us to gain further insight into one of the topics of chapter 2, the World-Root Club. For one way to describe this club's ultimate goal is *the revival of Hebraic Pythagoreanism*. Pythagoreanism is, besides the "Hebrew metaphysics" of the Pentateuch, another expression of the Semitic mythic imagination.

Unger claims that Pythagoreanism reveals a kind of thinking (his term is "concretizing thinking") that is radically at odds with the typical "abstracting cognitive style of Hellenism." Thus, Pythagoreanism belongs to the pre-Hellenic world and to the "Semitic and more precisely to the Hebrew cognitive world."[92] The connection between Pythagoreanism and the Hebrew "cognitive world" lies in this: both consider "quanta to correspond to actualities, that is, to inhomogeneous primordial givens." We saw in chapter 2 how Goldberg claims that Hebrew letters *are* numbers and that the "combinatorics" of the letters—the word roots— represent numerical structures. Indeed, one such numerical structure unfolds throughout the Pentateuch, the number 26, which is the sum of the four letters YHWH, the name of Israel's God. Unger also explains that, for Pythagoreanism, when one operates with numbers one does not merely "repeat" them, one actually "metamorphoses" them:

> Being-one, being-two, being-three, when taken as having more than a meaning as a relationship, have meanings in themselves, meanings that are equivalent to a metaphysical actuality. For just as "nothing" (whose "number" is zero) expresses a metaphysical reality with content, that is, a *quale*, the same is also the case with one, two and several other primordial numbers. . . . This means that there must be a metaphysical content to "twoness" that makes it possible for there to be a number two that is not just the mechanical repetition of one. In order to understand how there could be a "first repetition" that is different from all other mechanical repetitions, from the summative concept of two abacus counters or any other repeatedly postulated given object, there also needs to be a oneness with its own characteristic content, a oneness that is repeated— since there is a oneness that is not repeated. This first repetition is like the diversification of the living [*Spaltung des Lebendigen*] that is possible only on the ground of certain prior potentiality. Opposed to the purely formal number operation [of repeating a unit] is a number operation that connects with the first repetition and explains its "Why": the foundation of "the" two. And thus we may derive a structure of primordial metaphysical entities and their connections, such as: Nothing, Infinity, Substance, Matter, Spirit, Continuity, Discontinuity. These are not "concepts" but "experienceable" intuitions, that is, intuitions that can be completed [in concrete experience]. They serve as necessary intuitions, grounded in reality itself, corresponding to the primordial number operations. They are not "symbolic."[93]

The "first repetition" that is more than a mechanical repetition of a unit object is exactly what Goldberg is speaking about in *Ontology* when he talks about the "recurringness of Uniqueness." The first repetition is paralleled in the coming into being of the diversity of life, not on the empirical level of biology but in the "biology-productive" region of the transcendental organism. And not only animal species arise on the basis of the metaphysical number operations: *speech and writing* do so as well. Goldberg talks about the Pentateuch as the "numerical precipitate" of the metaphysical numbers, but Unger only hints at this: "What the precipitate of this universal combinatoric will be is not able to be foreseen [*ist im Vorhinein weder abzusehen*], nor does it lie within the provenance of this general outline of a logic of concretion to enter into a discussion of the foundation [of such a precipitate]."[94] Unger might simply have said this: to understand how number is productive of a living reality, read Goldberg's *Reality of the Hebrews*.

Unger's discussion of Pythagoreanism allows us to understand something about the World-Root Club, the group around Goldberg discussed in chapter 2. It now becomes clearer that its real goal was to take philosophy back to its Hebrew root. The World-Root, as we have seen, is YHWH, a name that infuses not only the whole of the Pentateuch but also the whole of reality with its "metamorphoses" into living forms, organic and textual. To learn how to see the patterns formed by these metamorphoses is to learn how to use what Unger calls the "authentic imagination," the same imagination at work in the mythic creations of antiquity. It is only through this renewal of the power of the imagination that we can break the stranglehold of the empty abstractions that have dominated philosophical thought from Plato to Kant. But the stakes are not merely theoretical. The givenness of the social and political forms of the empirical world cannot be altered from *within* the empirical: one requires metaphysical weapons, and this is the arsenal that Goldberg hoped to forge out of the "number structure" of the Pentateuch. The World-Root Club was nothing less than the revolutionary cell of a new *Hebrew* reality based on the foundation of a *Hebrew* metaphysics. The path to the recuperation of the world-transformative Hebrew metaphysics is through the Pentateuch—not merely its number system but also the content of its narratives and laws. It is this content, as it is interpreted by Goldberg, that I explore in chapter 4.

## Notes

1. The essay is published in Goldberg-*Aufsätze*, 69–122.

2. Erich Unger, "Nachts," *Der Sturm* 2, no. 57 (1911): 452, republished in Erich Unger, *Von Expressionismus zum Mythos: Schriften 1909 bis 1931*, ed. Manfred Voigts (Würzburg: Königshausen & Neumann, 1992), 26–28; quotation on p. 27. Unger's piece can profitably be studied in relation to the theme of the "night side" that was important for early Romantic Naturphilosophie. See, for example, Gotthilf Heinrich Schubert, *Ansichten von der Nachtseite der Naturwissenschaft* (Dresden: Arnoldische Buchhandlung, 1808). I return to the "night side" later in my discussion of *Reality of the Hebrews* and also in the conclusion.

3. One of Unger's clearest presentations of Goldberg's *Ontology* comes in Erich Unger, *The Imagination of Reason: Two Philosophical Essays* (London: Routledge & Kegan Paul, 1952). The second essay, "The Imagination of Reason," makes reference to Goldberg on pp. 115–118, but the entire essay is deeply informed by Goldberg's *Ontology*. For a sympathetic and well-informed appraisal of Unger's philosophy, see Heinz-J. Schüring, "Der Mythos als Seinsgrund der Erkenntnis (in memoriam Erich Unger, gestorben am 25. November 1950 in London)," *Zeitschrift für philosophische Forschung* 19, no. 3 (1965): 493–510. Unfortunately, apart from this one essay, there is no sustained treatment of Unger's thought. I hope in this book to offer at least a start toward a reassessment of Unger's philosophical importance, especially in the context of the recent "new materialism" of thinkers such as Jane Bennett and Elizabeth Grosz.

4. Goldberg, *Ontology*, in Goldberg-*Aufsätze*, 69.

5. Ibid., 70.

6. Ibid.

7. Ibid., 70–71.

8. Goldberg, "Eine Geheimschrift," in Golberg-*Aufsätze*, 379.

9. Hermann Cohen, *Ethik des reinen Willens* (Berlin: Bruno Cassirer, 1904); cf. 381–382: "uniqueness does not in the final analysis indicate an opposition to multiplicity, but to every other kind of reality."

10. Hermann Cohen, *Religion der Vernunft aus den Quellen der Judentum: Eine jüdische Religionsphilosophie* (Wiesbaden: marixverlag, 2008), 67.

11. On Adolf Bastian, see Klaus-Peter Köpping, *Adolf Bastian and the Psychic Unity of Mankind* (St. Lucia: University of Queensland Press, 1983); H. Glenn Penny, "Bastian's Museum: On the Limits of Empiricism and the Transformation of German Ethnology," in *Worldly Provincialism: German Anthropology in the Age of Empire*, ed. H. Glenn Penny and Matti Bunzl (Ann Arbor: University of Michigan Press, 2003), 86–126; Andrew Zimmerman, *Anthropology and Antihumanism in Imperial Germany* (Chicago: University of Chicago Press, 2001), 46–61 and passim; and Manuela Fischer, Peter Bolz, and Susan Kamel, eds., *Adolf Bastian and His Universal Archive of Humanity* (Hildesheim: Georg Olms, 2007). The disssertation of Klaus-Peter Buchheit, "Die Verkettung der Dinge: Stil und Diagnose im Schreiben Adolf Bastian" (Ruprecht-Karls-Univesität Heidelberg, 2002), offers a sympathetic and insightful treatment of Bastian's increasingly difficult writing style as itself being the expression of the logic of interconnected cultural phenomena that are constantly being generated out of primordial ideas.

12. For more on Adolf Bastian's views concerning ethnogenesis, see chapter 1, note 7.

13. Goldberg Nachlass, Kasten (box) 6, Deutsches Literaturarchiv Marbach.

14. Adolf Bastian, *Ethnische Elementargedanken in der Lehre von Menschen*, 2 vols. (Berlin: Weidmannsche Buchhandlung, 1895).

15. "The 'Infinitum creatum sive Transfinitum' [created or transfinite infinity] (besides the 'Infinitum aeternum sive Absolutum' [eternal or absolute infinity]) relates to the 'actual infinite number of the created individual beings' (see Cantor), as its final outcome (in the realm of the given)." Adolf Bastian, *Zur ethnischen Ethik* (Berlin: Ferd. Dümmlers Verlagsbuchhandlung, 1889), lx. Bastian's style is deliberately apophthegmatic and aphoristic often to the point of incomprehensibility. His reference to Cantor's transfinite numbers is a case in point. Perhaps he means that Cantor's transfinite number aleph-null stands between the infinite beings in the universe and the Absolute Infinite, God, as I explained in chapter 2.

16. Ibid., lxxxvii.

17. Adolf Bastian, *Der Mensch in der Geschichte: Zur Begründung einer psychologischen Weltanshauung*, 2 vols. (Leipzig: Otto Wigand, 1860), 1:10.

18. Goldberg-*Aufsätze*, 78.

19. Ibid., 82. The search for a point of identity or indifference from out of which polar relationships like subject-object emerge draws from Schelling's early Identity philosophy. As I have said, some of the early notebooks in the Goldberg Nachlass bear the unmistakable stamp of his reading of Schelling.

20. For a discussion of *Einmaligkeit* (and *Dauer*, lastingness), see Walter Benjamin, "Kleine Geschichte der Photographie," in *Gesammelte Schriften Bde. I–VII*, ed. Ralf Tiedemann and Hermann Schweppenhäuser (Frankfurt am Main: Suhrkamp, 1972–1989), II.1:368–386. For the opposition of mechanical reproduction and auratic uniqueness, see pp. 377–378. In "The Work of Art in an Age of Mechanical Reproduction," Benjamin defines aura as "the unique [*einmalige*] appearance of a distance, however close it may seem" (see *Gesammelte Schriften*, I.2, 479). Since Benjamin was very familiar with Goldberg's system through Erich Unger's *Against Poetry*, a book he thought very highly of, it is not at all implausible to suppose that Benjamin's concept of aura was influenced by Goldberg, as mediated by Unger.

21. The proximate source of the distinction between two types of multiplicity, one an aggregate of interchangeable, homogeneous units and another a multiplicity of unique, hetero-

geneous elements, is probably Henri Bergson, *Time and Free Will: An Essay on the Immediate Data of Consciousness*, trans. F. L. Pogson (London: George Allen, 1910). Bergson's book was originally published in French in 1889. It was certainly known to Benjamin (who adopts the phrase "empty homogeneous time" from it), and it was almost certainly familiar to Goldberg. Bergson's magnum opus, *Creative Evolution*, was published in French in 1907.

22. Set theory postulates that the set defined by any concept that has *no members* is a *unique* set, that is, there is only one unique way to be *no number at all*. Set theory calls this the "null set." Set theory is, one might say, the absolute contradiction of Cohenian and Goldbergian monotheism: Either YHWH is the Unique One or Nothing is. Set theory chooses Nothing. Not unlike Goldberg, mathematicians use the absolutely unique null set to construct all numbers as sets, thereby showing how, from uniqueness, infinite multiplicities can be generated. Goldberg precisely did not want pure uniqueness to produce multiplicities by any additive process that multiplied the uniqueness, but by an act corresponding to *divine creation* that maintains uniqueness as uniqueness. He called this nonadditive creation the "interruption act." In set theory, the unique set—the null set—is a subset of every other set. Mathematicians would deny that there is a difference between the null subset in one set and another. There is, in other words, only one null set but it is a subset of an infinite number of sets. Goldberg would likely find this to be at the very least a challenge to the uniqueness of the null set. The philosopher Alain Badiou makes much of the immanence of a unique (and therefore non-conceputalizable) non-being (null) within every structured whole as the condition of possibility of the emergence of a revolutionary breakthrough into a any given social arrangement or status quo, but Goldberg and Unger retain a concept of a transcendent Uniqueness (YHWH) to play this role. I have more to say about Badiou and Goldberg later in this chapter.

23. Goldberg-*Aufsätze*, 91.

24. Ibid., 86.

25. Ibid., 94.

26. Ibid.

27. Ibid., 95.

28. Bergson, *Time and Free Will*, 226.

29. Goldberg-*Aufsätze*, 97.

30. Ibid.

31. Ibid., 97–98.

32. Ibid., 97.

33. Badiou, *Logics of Worlds, Being and Event 2*, trans. Alberto Toscano (London: Continuum, 2009), 384.

34. Ibid.

35. Goldberg-*Aufsätze*, 98.

36. Richard Dedekind, *Stetigkeit und Irrationale Zahlen*, 2nd ed. (Braunschweig: F. Vieweg und Sohn, 1892).

37. Badiou, *Logics of Worlds*, 383.

38. Goldberg-*Aufsätze*, 100.

39. Goldberg, *Ontology*, 106.

40. Ibid.

41. Ibid., 109.

42. Erich Unger approaches the same problem in *Das Lebendige und Goettliche*, 59–61. The answer he provides is exactly what Goldberg suggests, but it is more clearly put. I quoted this passage in chapter 1: "The living in the world is an actual unitary object throughout all *biological* formations. It is reproduced in the living wave of the generations. This unity encompasses

all the species and forms of living things, and thus the living in the world is a total-object [*Gesamtgegenstand*]" (emphasis Unger's). It is possible, Unger argues, for consciousness to experience this single object through "the imagination of reason" that raises consciousness to a realm transcending normal experience but nonetheless conditions it as its originating source. He offers an account of the origin of life in the universe that attempts to imagine the way it is produced not only at one time in the past but in every living thing. See the next footnote for further discussion of this idea.

43. The turn inward to discover an intuition of the Becoming of transcendental Being into the world of experience shows the influence of F. W. J. Schelling's *Naturphilosophie*. Goldberg is wrestling with the problem of how to "get behind" the finitude of phenomenal experience and experience the emergence of the phenomenal realm as such out of infinity into finitude. This is the same problem that Schelling struggles with in his *Naturphilosophie*, at least according to the interpretation offered in Merleau-Ponty's 1956–1957 lectures on the philosophy of nature at the Collège de France. In the notes that recorded these lectures, we read that Schelling claimed that "we rediscover Nature in our perceptual experience prior to reflection." Merleau-Ponty explains that Nature, insofar as it is more than merely the givenness of the phenomenal world but is "the excess of Being over the consciousness of Being," can be accessed, according to Schelling, through a "mystical faculty specialized in this role." This faculty will not seek to penetrate any external phenomenon or even all external phenomena in their totality, but rather it will "retrieve our own nature in the state of indivision where we exercise our perception." Merleau-Ponty quotes from Schelling: "Because I am *identical* to Nature, I understand it just as well as my own life" (emphasis Schelling's). Merleau-Ponty puts Schelling's inward turn in these words, which capture Goldberg's basic position as well: "It is in my own nature that I find the originary state of the interior of things. This subjectivity inherent to Nature is not the result of a projection of a non-I outside of the I. We have to say, on the contrary, that what we call the I and what we call a living being have a common root in pre-objective Being." Maurice Merleau-Ponty, *Nature: Course Notes from the Collège de France*, trans. Robert Vallier (Evanston, IL: Northwestern University Press, 2003), 39–40. Both Goldberg and Merleau-Ponty were reading Schelling through the lens of phenomenology. The most fundamental difference between Goldberg and Merleau-Ponty is that Goldberg insists that when consciousness accesses the Becoming of transcendental Being into the world, it loses its limitation as a single consciousness and joins with a collective consciousness, a species-consciousness so to speak, that is also reflected in mythology. In this, Goldberg is closer to Schelling than is Merleau-Ponty.

44. In an early work, "Andeutungungen zur Kunst" (1909) (in *Von Expressionismus zu Mythos*, 1–7), Unger describes "knowing" in much the same terms that Goldberg describes imagination, as its own object and goal:

> Knowledge [*Erkenntnis*] does not so much consist in *result* (formulable in certain words) of a logical thought process, and also not in the *result* of a philosophical revelation, but much more in the psychic condition of the process of this revelation itself. Only so long as this condition of so-called intuition endures is there knowledge. As soon as it ceases, a deaf-and-dumbness enters and an impossibility of knowing. The formulation in words, the so called result that expresses the philosophical intuition, has no other value or purpose than to awaken again the condition that brought it into being in the first place, that is, to bring into being a new knowledge (identical with the intuitive condition). . . . The goal of all psychic activities should *not* be to achieve closed results, but to bring it about that humanity and all single individuals attain as long as possible to an intuitive condition. (3)

Unger quotes Spinoza in the opening of this piece. It would be valuable, but outside the scope of this book, to trace the importance of Spinoza's idea that the mind is the "idea of the body" not only for Unger and Goldberg but also for the neo-Naturphilosophie of the period and its concern for the "psychophysical problem."

45. Goldberg, *Ontology*, 112; emphasis Goldberg's.

46. Ibid.

47. Ibid., 104.

48. Another thinker who may have influenced Goldberg in addition to Brentano is Franz Joseph Molitor, the subject of Appendix II. I discuss there Molitor's theory of the imagination as the receptive organ of divine revelation.

49. Erich Unger, "Das Psychophysiologische Probem und sein Arbeitsgebiet: eine methologische Einleitung" (Inaugural-Dissertation der Erlangung der Doktorwürde der philosophischen Fakultät der Friedrich-Alexanders Universität Erlangen, 1922). I was able to examine a photocopy (from the original in the Unger Nachlass in the Deutsches Literaturarchiv) that Manfred Voigts provided to me.

50. Erich Unger, *Politik und Metaphysik*, ed. Manfred Voigts (Würzburg: Königshausen & Neumann, 1989).

51. Ibid., 4.

52. Ibid., 8.

53. Ibid., 12; emphasis Unger's.

54. Ibid., 16.

55. In "Andeutungungen zur Kunst" Unger emphasizes the mathematical nature of everything that takes place in space and time, and he argues that every sensation and feeling are the expression of "etwas Mathematisches" (4).

56. Edmund Husserl, *Ideas: General Introduction to a Pure Phenomenology*, trans. W. R. Boyce Gibson (London: Routledge, 2012), §40, 74–76.

57. Unger, *Politik und Metaphysik*, 16.

58. Ibid.

59. Ibid., 18.

60. Ibid., 19; emphasis Unger's.

61. Ibid., 20.

62. Ibid.

63. Ibid., 22.

64. It would take me too far afield to discuss it in any detail, but the ideas that both Unger and Goldberg are developing have their most significant and earliest precursor in Spinoza and his concept of the mind as the "idea of the body." So long as the individual's idea of his own individual body is the limit of his knowledge, he is the victim of happenstance and is never able to form a true community of minds with others. He can only form mechanical unities with others who are more or less like him, but he cannot rise to the level of understanding how his mind and other minds are joined together in the "idea of God," which is, like all ideas, the idea of a body—in this case the body of nature as a whole. Together with Leibniz, Spinoza is one of the two "presiding geniuses" of Naturphilosophie. His influence is so pervasive as to make it almost impossible to trace in any detail. Unger never mentions any thinker in *Politics and Metaphysics*, let alone Spinoza.

65. Unger, *Politik und Metaphysik*, 24. It would not be inappropriate to compare Unger with Durkheim, someone he was quite familiar with, as we can see from his discussion of the sociology of the collective consciousness in his dissertation. We could say that Unger rejects Durkheim's Kantianism and insists that the coming-into-being of the collective consciousness is accessible to a (heightened) consciousness that penetrates deeper into the physiological resources of the individual where the species-specific "universalia" latently reside. Unger would also argue that, with the exception of peoples who still are bound together by myth and ritual,

the collective consciousness of the society is not organic but purely atomistic. The task of metaphysical politics is not to return bourgeois society to its mythic past, but to open a path to a new organic collectivity that is transnational, as I explain in what follows.

66. Ibid.

67. Ibid., 26.

68. Ibid., 29.

69. Ibid., 35.

70. Ibid.

71. In chapter 4 I discuss a passage from Goldberg's *Reality of the Hebrews* that was not included in the final version of the book. In this passage, Goldberg argues that, during times when the state loses its hold on its population, there is an increase in paranormal phenomena associated with mediums and séances. He explains that such paranormal phenomena and the ectoplasmic outlines that emerge from them are small-scale versions of the collective fusion of consciousnesses that can produce actual effects in the physical world, such as are described in the mythologies of the ancient world.

72. Unger, *Politik und Metaphysik*, 47.

73. Ibid., 44.

74. Ibid., 48.

75. Ibid., 50.

76. Ibid., 54.

77. Ibid., 50. Unger's *Politics and Metaphysics* and its discussion of the "metapolitical universitsas" needs to be read in relation to Martin Heidegger's "ponderings" in the earliest Black Notebooks. Heidegger uses the term "metapolitical" in precisely the same context that Unger does, as giving another expression to the "end of philosophy" and another form of "metaphysics." Unger: "The field of operation of the metapolitical universitas can be delimited in the following declaration of goals [*Ziele*]: First of all, the reversal in the valuation of possibility—metaphysics. [Unger means that what had been considered impossible since Kant—a form of transcendental intuition—now needs to be considered possible, with the political possibilities it opens up.] Precisely the most far-reaching philosophical theoretics [*Theoretik*] exist not for the sake of 'pure knowledge,' but for the sake of the concrete mastery [Bewältigung] of all existence-pathologies including the sociological one, without however allowing itself to become a 'practical' 'prudence.' *The end* [*Ziel*] *of philosophy is not knowledge, but the mastery of concreteness—but this end is only achievable if it maintains itself in relation to pure knowledge*" (*Politik und Metaphysik*, 53; emphasis Unger's). Heidegger: "*The end* [das Ende] *of 'philosophy'*—We must bring it to an end and thereby prepare what is wholly other—metapolitics. Accordingly also, the *transformation of science.... Metaphysics as meta-politics.*" Martin Heidegger, *Ponderings II–VI: Black Notebooks 1931–1938*, trans. Richard Rojcewicz (Bloomington: Indiana University Press, 2016), 85; emphasis Heidegger's. It would take me too far afield to trace the various resonances between Heidegger's ponderings in the early 1930s and the work of Unger and Goldberg, but I hope to pursue this topic in another venue. See also chapter 4, note 67 for more on the parallels between Goldberg's and Heidegger's overall problematic in relation to "gods/worlds/peoples."

78. Ernst Cassirer, *Sprache und Mythos: Ein Beitrag zum Problem der Götternamen* (Leipzig: B. G. Teubner, 1925). English translation: *Language and Myth*, trans. Susanne Langer (New York: Harper and Bros., 1945); Ernst Cassirer, *Das Mythische Denken* (Berlin: Bruno Cassirer, 1925), vol. 2 of *Philosophie der symbolischen Formen*. English translation: *The Philosophy of Symbolic Forms*, vol. 2, *Mythical Thought*, trans. Ralph Manheim (New Haven, CT: Yale University Press, 1955).

79. I wish to thank Manfred Voigts for bringing this particular evening's presentation to my attention. He generously shared with me a photocopy of the Erich Engel Notizbuch containing notes about the lectures. The Engel Notizbuch is found in the Engel Nachlass in the Deutsches Literaturarchiv in Marbach.

80. Unger's account of the productive imagination, like Goldberg's, ultimately derives from Romantic Naturphilosophie. One can profitably compare their reception of the idealist Naturphilosophie conception of the productive imagination with that of Samuel Taylor Coleridge in *Biographia Literaria* (1817):

> The imagination then I consider either as primary or secondary. The primary imagination I hold to be the living power and prime agent of all human perception, and as a repetition in the finite mind of the eternal act of creation in the infinite I AM. The secondary I consider as an echo of the former, coexisting with the conscious will yet still as identical with the primary in the kind of its agency, and differing only in degree and in the mode of its operation. It dissolves, diffuses, dissipates in order to recreate; or where this process is rendered impossible, yet still at all events it struggles to idealize and to unify. It is essentially *vital* even as all objects as objects are essentially fixed and dead. (Samuel Taylor Coleridge, *Biographia Literaria; or Biographical Sketches of My Literary Life and Opinions* [London: George Bell and Sons, 1889], 144.)

81. Cassirer, *Language and Myth*, 33.

82. Ibid., 74.

83. Cassirer, *Philosophy of Symbolic Forms*, 2:67–68; emphasis Cassirer's.

84. Erich Unger, *Gegen die Dichtung: Eine Begründung des Konstruktionsprinzip in der Erkenntnis* (Leipzig: Felix Meiner, 1925) (hereafter *Against Poetry*).

85. Unger, *Against Poetry*, 189.

86. Ibid., 186–187 (emphasis Unger's).

87. Ibid., 142.

88. Ibid., 161.

89. Ibid., 166.

90. Ibid., 165–166.

91. Ibid., 166–167. Unger's logic of the general as containing *in potentia* the specific can be compared with Franz Joseph Molitor's "trinitarian logic" that I describe in Appendix II. It is also quite close to Husserl, as we have seen. It is nearly impossible to disentangle the sources of the phenomenological account of sensation and noesis in Husserl, but it is clear that Schelling, Hegel, and Romantic Naturphilosophie in general are among the earliest sources. As notes 44 and 64 also suggested, one would need to also add Spinoza's concept of the mind as the "idea of the body." A comparison of Unger's concept of *Quala* and the genera "light, life force, and matter" with the terms of Schelling's early Naturphilosophie (the 1799 *First Outline of a System of the Philosophy of Nature* has many points in common with both Goldberg and Unger) is certainly in order. Although limitations of space make it impossible to do justice to this rich intellectual history, I do hope to have shown that Unger's philosophical work deserves much closer study.

92. In a very interesting unpublished typescript (English) in the Erich Unger Nachlass in the Deutsches Literaturarchiv in Marbach (Kasten 4), Unger explains in greater detail that the early Kabbalistic *Book of Creation* (*Sefer Yetsirah*) does not, as was commonly believed, derive from Greek neo-Platonic and neo-Pythagorean speculations but in fact influenced those Greek traditions. (This was Robert Eisler's position in *Weltenmantel und Himmelszelt*, as I mentioned in chapter 2.) Unger's text can be read profitably in relation to what he writes

about Pythagoreanism in *Against Poetry*, but it also helps us understand Goldberg's *Ontology*. He argues that the

> contents of this book [*The Book of Creation*] may be regarded as the source of the basis of the following philosophical conceptions: (1) All being and developing is based on entities with the character of numbers. The Cabbalah calls the principle attributes of God and every being 'Sephirot' which means 'numbers.' Such numbers are not abstractions such as the common numbers which enable us to count the contents of the world which are something different from their formal expression, the numbers. But the 'Sephirot' as attributes of the infinite are contents in themselves such as being, nothing, force, etc., otherwise would not have been indicated by numbers. It is taken for granted that there is only a small quantity of such archqualities or archnumbers. On the first numbers express by themselves original ontological entities such as 'being one' or 'being two', the archnumber 'defining' the ontological state (quality condition, 'Sachverhalt'). (2) The logic unfolding (explicatio) of the realm of numbers up to its remotest regions is the ontological reason of the development of the infinitely varying phenomena out of the small number of the principle entities of being. (3) The letters of the Hebrew alphabet have the character of number symbols and take part as a kind of notional elements [sic] in the process of the development of the manifold phenomena. (4) The technical means by which the infinite variety of things are developed out of the small number of original qualities, is the theory of combination and permutation.

Unger then goes on to credit Goldberg's "ontology" for having explicated these principles, although he admits that Raymon Lull and Leibniz had earlier laid the foundations for this ontology of numbers. Interestingly, he does not mention Franz Joseph Molitor, although (as I explain in Appendix II) Molitor also speaks about "archqualities" (he calls them simply "qualities") as number elements in the Kabbalah's upper worlds.

93. Unger, *Against Poetry*, 178–179.
94. Ibid., 179.

# 4 *The Reality of the Hebrews* and YHWH's Battle for the Earth

In chapter 1 I described the neo-Naturphilosophie that nourished Oskar Goldberg's vitalism, and in chapters 2 and 3 I explored the mathematical and ontological foundations of Goldberg's thought. I explained how the Pentateuch was, according to Goldberg, the number system of the Name of God, Yahweh (the standard way to vocalize the four consonants YHWH). In this chapter I turn to Goldberg's magnum opus, his *Reality of the Hebrews*. I will explain how Goldberg accounts for the creation of the entire world through the operation of what he calls the "Y-Force" (*I-Kraft*, short for *IHWH-Kraft*). Opposed to the Y-Force is the "fixation" tendency of matter, a tendency to rigidification and stasis that can be found in both the inanimate and animate realms. The fixation tendency comes to the fore in the human world in the nation-state. I discussed Erich Unger's *Politics and Metaphysics* in chapter 3 to provide an avenue of approach to the difficulties of Goldberg's theory of the ontologically productive power of the imagination. We saw how Unger defined what he called metaphysical politics in opposition to the party politics of the state. With Goldberg's *Reality of the Hebrews*, we take the opposition to the state to another level. YHWH is the enemy not only of the state but also of the state's relationship to the earth, that is, to what had recently come to be known in Germany as *Geopolitik*, the staunchly nationalist precursor discipline to today's academic study of geopolitics. With *The Reality of the Hebrews* we move from metaphysical politics to an anti-statist metaphysical geopolitics. The Pentateuch as Goldberg understands it offers the blueprint for the renewal of a metaphysical geopolitics that can challenge the rising tide of state-based *Geopolitik* in Weimar Germany.

A word about my "voice" in the following pages is in order. Although I will frequently include phrases like "Goldberg argues" and "Goldberg claims" in what follows, to add such phrases to every sentence would be cumbersome and quite tiresome for the reader. It may therefore seem that, on occasion, I am not only explicating Goldberg's ideas but am actually affirming their validity. I have tried to be a sympathetic reader of Goldberg, but I am far from being one of his followers. Goldberg's interpretation of the Pentateuch, I hope to show, offers a powerful and imaginative response to the emerging ideology of state-based racism in Weimar Germany. And in regard to the validity of Goldberg's Pentateuch interpretation,

I am not at all concerned to do anything more in these pages than represent his interpretation with as much clarity as I can. I can say, however, that if one wants to assess the philological evidence that Goldberg brings forward to support his Pentateuch interpretation, one would need to examine all the passages that bear on Goldberg's basic thesis—that the Pentateuch asserts that YHWH was given a corporeal manifestation in the pillars of fire and smoke that rested on the desert tabernacle during the night and day, respectively. Focusing only on the basic thesis of YHWH's corporeal localization at the desert tabernacle, I believe that Goldberg's interpretation bears further scrutiny as a valid reading of the worldview behind at least some of the Pentateuch's central passages, especially those describing the construction and movement of the tabernacle in Exodus, Leviticus, and Numbers (attributed to the P or Priestly tradition). One of the most highly regarded books of biblical scholarship to appear in recent years has, in fact, argued for an understanding of the Priestly narrative of YHWH's descent into the tabernacle that shares Goldberg's emphasis on YHWH's corporeal immanence: "No priestly text . . . suggests that God is still in heaven after coming down to dwell in the tabernacle. On the contrary, the descent of God from heaven to Mt. Sinai in Exodus 19 and then into the tabernacle in Exodus 40 is so momentous precisely because the priestly authors are talking about God's one body, and hence about the decision of the transcendent God to become fully immanent."[1]

Therefore we can read Goldberg's *Reality of the Hebrews* as an attempt to explain God's "decision . . . to become fully immanent" in the midst of Israel's camp in the desert. This attempt takes Goldberg into speculative territory beyond the range of biblical philology. This chapter is devoted to charting the speculative path of Goldberg's attempt to make sense of the Hebrew Bible's portrait of YHWH as a corporeal presence within the tabernacle. While there are overlaps with today's biblical scholarship, Goldberg's *Reality of the Hebrews* deserves to be studied as an important but little-known attempt to construct a theology of divine embodiment as a head-on critique of the rising ideology of human embodiment defined through (and manufactured within) the racial nation-state. We might call this a *biotheology* in contestation with *biopolitics*.

## Transcendental Organisms as Life-Worlds

In the opening six pages of *The Reality of the Hebrews*, Oskar Goldberg lays out the "philosophical and cosmological foundations" of his interpretation of the Pentateuch. Much of this material was given a longer and more abstract treatment in his *Ontology*, the subject of chapter 3. Goldberg in *The Reality of the Hebrews* states that reality (*Wirklichkeit*) is divided into two parts: an infinite realm of possibilities and the finite realm of what actually comes to pass. The infinite realm of possibility is no less real than the finite realm: it is the realm of *latent reality*, whereas the finite realm is the *manifest reality.* The realm of latent reality comprises an infinitude of possibilities that *can* be experienced, but *are not actually experienced.* The finite realm is the empirical realm of actualized possibilities that have entered the spatiotemporal "here and now." The law of causality determines the sequential order of the latent possibilities that come into manifest being in this empirical world: it determines how one "world constellation," one "time moment," follows another.

The law of causality, Goldberg explains, is the necessary condition for the *temporal duration* of the world, preventing the emergence of all the possibilities at once. "The causal law relates to the preservation of finitude. It makes it possible for one finite world constellation to follow another.... This means that time itself is nothing other than the form that permits the entrance of possibilities out of infinity into finitude."[2] In addition to time and the law of causality, space is the third form in which infinity is measured out into the ordered structure of the empirical world. Finally, in addition to the *forms* of space, time, and causality, there are two "elements" that constitute the *content* of every finite world constellation: spirit (*Geist*) and matter (*Materie*). "They [spirit and matter] arise out of infinity and would collapse back into it if they had not been bound to finitude through the constitutive forms of finitude, namely, space, time, and the causal law."[3] We now have collected all the categories of Goldberg's metaphysics: infinity, finitude, latent reality (possibility), manifest reality (the empirical world constellation at every moment of time), space, time, causality, spirit, and matter. These are the same categories that we found in Goldberg's *Ontology.* As I explained in my discussion of this work in chapter 3, the infinite realm of possibilities comprises a multiplicity of "uniquenesses" (*Einmaligkeiten*): organized structures whose elements are not interchangeable and identical, but rather occupy "value-laden" (*wertbetonte*) positions within the encompassing whole of the larger structure. Each such structure possesses its own unique arrangement of parts. In *The Reality of the Hebrews,* Goldberg takes his *Ontology*'s abstract and mathematical descriptions of these uniquenesses and puts flesh on them: they are now described as "transcendental organisms," each a world in itself. The one, all-comprehending transcendental organism is Adam Kadmon, but each part is also able to be described as a transcendental organism (or, as Goldberg at one point says, "organ system"). They each possess what I have called "transfinite life."

How does transfinite life become finite, empirical life? Goldberg explains that "the endless number of self-enclosed worlds . . . are of an organic nature: they are biological centers that have both a cosmological and anthropological significance."[4] The *cosmological* significance of a biological center consists in the fact that each self-enclosed world has the potential to enter into empirical, finite reality in a variety of material forms. Goldberg speaks of fire as one of the "cosmic appearances" of the God of Israel, for example. The *anthropological* significance of the transcendental biological centers is that they can also be embodied within a biologically distinct part of the human species, that is, within a "folk group body" (*Volkskörper*). Each folk group body inherits certain unique psychophysical traits from its eponymic ancestor (the Moabites from Moab, for example) whose single body was the "discharge point" (*Entladung*) for the structured energy-field of a particular transcendental organism. The eponymous ancestor passes his uniquely restructured psychophysical capacity to his descendants, who finally allow the transcendental organism to inhabit the world in the ritual practice associated with their god (the transcendental organism).

The cosmological and anthropological significance of the transcendental organisms can only be realized for as long the "metaphysical age" of the world persists, that is, for as long as the bridge between the realm of transcendental organisms and the realm of finite actuality remains open for crossing. The metaphysical bridge, to be sure, is never entirely closed for traffic, but it ceases to be the driving force in human history when most folk groups are absorbed into larger imperial state structures. Israel's metaphysical bridge to YHWH Elohim was closed in the early monarchic period when Solomon built the Temple and transformed Israel into a (minor) Near Eastern empire. The time covered by *The Reality of the Hebrews* includes only the period when Israel's metaphysical bridge remained open and active.

Let us return to the opening pages of *The Reality of the Hebrews*. Goldberg explains that each of the "endless number of self-enclosed worlds" has its own transcendental configuration of space, time, and causality. Yet his conception of space, time, and causality differs from Kant's conception of these as forms of intuition and understanding. Contrary to Kant, Goldberg believes that every transcendental organism is defined by its own distinct way of apprehending possible objects of experience through its own configuration of space, time, and causality: "A different relationship between subject and object than the familiar one, the one represented in *this* world system, demands a *different* time and *different* causality. . . . From which it follows that there is an infinite number of self-enclosed worlds, each with its *own* space, its *own* time, its *own* causality, that represent transformations [*Abwandlungen*] of the world elements, spirit and matter."[5] Each transcendental organism defines its own conditions of possibility of experiencing the world; each represents a way of experiencing the world and therefore a *unique life-world*. A human folk group that gives one of the transcendental organisms an opportunity for material embodiment will reshape its psychophysical constitution in conformity with this unique experiential structure. It will bring this constitution into linguistic expression in its mythology. Its transcendental organism will be its god, and each god, as a biological center, will be represented as an animal, the totem of the folk group. The animal will be sacred, and the human body will be used as the metaphysical bridge to the god. The human, in other words, will be the center of the god's sacrificial cult. Human sacrifice is replaced by animal sacrifice, however, when the God of Israel seeks to create his own metaphysical bridge to the world. But I am running ahead of myself. Before discussing the conflict between the God of Israel and the gods of other folk groups, I want to discuss the nature of the transcendental organism as a life-world.

If we want to find the most immediate precursor to Goldberg's conception of the transcendental organism as a world constellation with its own space, time, and causality, it is Jakob von Uexküll's theory of the "Umwelt" and "Innenwelt" of the animal. In 1920 von Uexküll published his magnum opus, *Theoretische Biologie*. At the foundation of this work is a claim about the need to revise Kant's conception of space and time to include *all* animal life. "The task of biology consists in extending the results of Kant's work in two directions: (1) to take into consideration the role of our body, our sense organs and our central nervous system and (2) to examine the constitutive relations between other subjects (the animals) and their objects."[6] Goldberg accepts von Uexküll's revision of Kantian theory to include the possibility of multiple forms of experience beyond our own. While this approach does certainly depart from Kant's much narrower conception of the rigidly defined conditions of possibility of experience that all humans (and all animals) share, Goldberg and von Uexküll are actually returning to Kant's *pre-Critical* position, advanced in two of his earliest works: *Thoughts on the True Estimation of Living Forces* (1746) and *Universal Natural History and Theory of the Heavens* (1755).[7] These pre-Critical works had quickly dropped out of sight until they came to the attention of a new generation of scholars and thinkers when the philosopher (and "father of German science fiction") Kurd Lasswitz helped edit them and a number of other pre-Critical works in the first volume of Kant's *Gesammelte Schriften* (first published in 1902, with a second edition in 1910).[8] The publication of Kant's complete collected works was the major editorial project of what was then known as the Prussian Academy of Sciences. The entire project was supervised by Wilhelm Dilthey and was clearly one of the most important publication projects in German letters at that time, receiving a number of very positive reviews.[9] It is almost certain that Goldberg would have made himself familiar with the first volume of Kant's pre-Critical writings when it came out in 1902. But even if Goldberg was not directly influenced by the pre-Critical speculations of the early Kant (who remained largely under the influence of Leibniz), it is worthwhile taking a moment to summarize what Kant was proposing in these essays. The newly published pre-Critical essays gave additional impetus to the new reception of Kant as a precursor of Naturphilosophie.[10]

In the first essay that bears on the subject of space, time, and life, *Thoughts on the True Estimation of Living Forces*, Kant speculates about the possibility of the existence of many different worlds—each a whole unto itself and having no connection with any other world: "A substance that exists without any connection to anything in this entire world would not be a part of this world. If there were many such things that had a relationship with one another [but not with our world], then an entirely new whole would emerge that would make up a completely separate world [from ours]."[11] Kant goes on to suggest that it is unlikely that God would allow there to be a number of utterly disconnected worlds that had the potential for relating to one another but, only as a matter of *contingent fact*, did not do so. This would contradict the principle that the greater the complexity of the relationships among things, the more perfect they are as a whole. God would not have created a less than perfect order. However, God could have created worlds so unlike our world that they could not, *in principle*, have a relationship to ours. This would be the case if the nature of space itself were different in these other worlds. A different kind of space is a space of more than three dimensions. Our world has three dimensions, Kant says, because three-dimensionality is con-sistent with the Newtonian law that the strength of gravitational attraction between bodies is in inverse proportion to the *square* of the distance between them. To *dou-ble* the two-dimensional length of a side of a cube (or the radius of a sphere) is to *square* the volume of the three-dimensional cube (or the sphere). Such a propor-tional relationship—one that obtains between a length and the *square* of the length—only holds true for three-dimensional objects. Only in a three-dimensional space, therefore, would it be true that gravitational attraction between two bod-ies is in inverse proportion to the *square* of the distance between them. For four-dimensional objects, the proportion would be between two-dimensional length and the *cube* of the length. Therefore, if the attraction between objects changed in inverse proportion to the *cube* of the distance between them, rather than accord-ing to the *square* of the distance, as they do in this three-dimensional world, this law of attraction would hold true in a *four-dimensional world*. Kant argues that, despite the impossibility of our being able to conceive of spaces of more than three dimensions ("our soul is also able to receive impressions and also to affect external objects only under the law of the inverse square," he says), there is nothing to stop God from creating such hyper-dimensional spaces. Indeed, God very likely has already created such spaces, and it is in these spaces that other worlds (planetary systems) completely separate from ours most probably exist:

> Since it is possible that spatial extensions exist of different dimensions, it is very probable that God has somewhere brought them into being. His works are of whatever magnitude and manifold [*Größe und Mannigfaltigkeit*] that can be achieved. Spaces that are of different kind cannot possibly stand in relation with those of a different nature; therefore such spaces would not belong to our world, but would necessarily constitute their own worlds. In what I said before I argued that several worlds, in the sense of the word given in our metaphysical understanding [i.e., independent substances without relations to anything in this world], could exist simultaneously. And now, it seems to me, we have the sole condition under which it would be likely that many worlds actually exist.[12]

In this remarkable passage, Kant argues that there might be different worlds, with different kinds of rational beings with different kinds of material embodiments, in spaces with higher dimensions than ours.

In his 1755 work *Universal Natural History and Theory of the Heavens*, Kant allows himself to speculate about other worlds even within our three-dimensional space. He speaks about the different types of sensory experience that life forms, made up of different kinds of matter, may possess on different planets in our own solar system and in other solar systems. If we put the two essays together, we get a picture of self-enclosed worlds with different kinds of sentient and rational beings existing both in our space and also in spaces (and times, we might add) of higher dimensions than ours. Kant's pre-Critical essays can be read as metaphysical speculations that develop the Leibnizian theory that monads exist in hierarchies of ever more complex orders. Rather than monadic hierarchies, Kant proposes multidimensional hierarchies of life forms, each with its own configuration of space and time.

Having now gotten a better idea about the pedigree of Goldberg's theory of transcendental organisms within the tradition of Naturphilosophie from Kant to Jakob von Uexküll, let us now return to *The Reality of the Hebrews*.[13] Goldberg gives this theory a Kabbalistic twist, just as he does Cantor's theory of transfinite numbers and Hans Driesch's theory of the organism as an intensive manifold. Goldberg claims that the transcendental organisms are part of a larger transcendental structure, a transcendental macro-organism that the Pentateuch refers to as the *Zelem Elohim*, the "image of God": "Between infinite and finite reality there lies a region that represents the *finitization of the infinite* [*Verendlichung der Unendlichkeit*] or the *realization of the contradiction* [*Verwirklichung des Widerspruchs*]. It is the transcendental organism in which are 'compounded' [*einbezogen*] the totality of the self-enclosed worlds as the site of their 'preformation' [*Präformation*]. This region can be viewed as the site of origin for every *organic lawfulness* [*Lebensgesetzlichkeit*]; it is the biology-generative principle that is prior to every biology. In the Pentateuch, this site is the *Zelem Elohim*."[14]

Goldberg also designates the site of the transcendental macro-organism as the realm of "biology in itself" or the "Idea of Biology" or "Prebiology."[15] That is, the transcendental macro-organism is the source of the forms of life that exist in the finite world; it contains the ideal forms of all possible species of animals. Jakob von Uexküll called such ideal forms "Bauplans" or structural plans. But insofar as this entire realm embodies the "image of God," it serves as the pattern that will ultimately be used in the creation of one particular life form, the human being. As the pattern for the creation of the human being, the transcendental macro-organism is the Kabbalah's "Adam Kadmon," the "Ur-Human."[16] Adam Kadmon is the primordial form whose complete expression is found in humanity but whose parts (the separate transcendental organisms) serve as patterns for different animal species. Although Goldberg is obviously drawing from the

Kabbalah in his description of the transcendental Adam Kadmon, he is also carrying forward the central idea of Lorenz Oken's *Manual of the Philosophy of Nature*. I discussed this important document of idealist Naturphilosophie in chapter 1. Oken was persuaded that all living things could be divided into five large classes, each reflecting the prominence of a different sense organ. Only in the human are all five senses perfectly united. For Oken as for Goldberg, all animals are in some fashion *partial or failed humans*.

Before going further, I want to very briefly mention a possible Jewish source for Goldberg's conception of the transcendental macro-organism. I am referring to Nachman Krochmal's *Guide for the Perplexed of the Time*.[17] Nachman Krochmal (1785–1840) was a gifted young Galician talmudist living near Lemberg-Lviv who taught himself German and spent most of his life attempting to create a fusion of Jewish philosophy—especially as it was represented in the work of the medieval Jewish philosopher and biblical exegete Ibn Ezra (1089–1164)—with post-Kantian Naturphilosophie, including of course Lorenz Oken. It would be surprising, given Goldberg's similar interest in joining Naturphilosophie with an exegesis of the Pentateuch, if there were not points of overlap between Krochmal's Ibn Ezra–inspired Naturphilosophie and Goldberg's. Krochmal's discussion of Ibn Ezra's exposition of the various levels of creation comes in the seventeenth and final section of his book, "Gate Seventeen." There Krochmal explains that according to Ibn Ezra there is a "middle realm" between finite objects and the Infinite Wisdom of God, a realm populated by bodiless angels and the living spirits (*n'shamot*).[18] Like Goldberg, Krochmal identifies this realm, considered as a totality, with Adam Kadmon, the macrocosmic structure in whose image the human Adam was created.

Goldberg argues that Adam Kadmon, the macrocosmic structure of the transcendental organism, has not yet fully been realized in the world. Humanity has not yet achieved the condition of being the full embodiment of the "image of God." However, ancient Israel was able to give material shape to the formal pattern of the transcendental macro-organism in the unique arrangement of the tribes as they wandered through the desert after the Exodus from Egypt. The spatial order in which the Israelite tribes encamp around the tabernacle was an "image of the transcendental organism, that is, of the fixed and crystallized organic lawfulness as it emerges from the biology-productive principle." In other words, the encampment is not structured in relation to a particular transcendental organism, but in relation to the totality of the transcendental realm, *the* transcendental macro-organism. Goldberg explains that the Israelite camp is "the projection of the 'metaphysical' space into 'empirical' space, which means that it is the projection of the transcendental positional system [*Stellungssystem*] into the empirical positions of normal space."[19] The projection of the transcendental organism into empirical space is not a mere copying of a pattern (since the transcendental manifold is not "three-dimensional") but a spatial realization of a transcendental topology in the material conditions of our space. It also specifies how the transcendental organism preserves itself over time: "This means that the objects [of the tabernacle] and the sections of the folk group in their various positions are the various ways in which God comes to be concretely manifested."[20]

While ancient Israel was able to materialize the "image of God" within space and time, all the other metaphysical folk groups at the time were the sites for the manifestation of only a *part* of "the" transcendental macro-organism, Adam Kadmon. "Each god manifests itself as a center of organic lawfulness, that is *one* of infinitely many possible biological capacities, one that can be characterized this way: it is raised to such a high power [*so hochgradig potenziert*] and is able to be conceived of in its own right so that it becomes a self-enclosed 'world system.'"[21] Unlike the other metaphysical folk groups with their "part-gods," Israel was the site for the manifestation of the "prebiological" source—YHWH Elohim—of the totality of the organisms. Israel was the metaphysical folk group that thereby could be the vehicle for the final goal of history—when the *totality* of humanity will embody the image of God. Israel was never, of course, the full embodiment of the image of God, but in its encampment around the tabernacle Israel embodied this image as history's "teleological" goal. "While every [other] metaphysical folk group *must* serve its biological center if it hopes to preserve itself in existence, . . . the teleological folk group has *freedom of the will* to serve its chosen-God and goal-God [*Wahl- und Ziel-Gott*]."[22] The conflicts that arose between the folk group representing the *totality* of the (future) transcendental organism (Israel) and the surrounding folk groups representing only its (presently realized) *parts* constitute what Goldberg calls the ancient world's "transcendental politics" in *The Reality of the Hebrews*, and what he calls the "original form of geopolitics" (Urbild der Geopolitik) in a later essay, "Die Götter der Griechen" ("The Gods of the Greeks").[23]

In what follows I explain in more detail the way that Israel during its time in the desert embodied the pattern of the "image of God." But before I can do so, I need to explain why it was necessary for Israel to play its transcendental-geopolitical role in the world in the first place. I need to explain Goldberg's account of how other folk groups before Israel came to embody their own transcendental organisms, each specialized as one life function within the totality of the life activity of Adam Kadmon.


## Transcendental Colonialism: From Creation to the Primeval History

Each transcendental organism in its "preworldly" existence is composed of spirit and what Goldberg calls "transcendental matter." Transcendental matter is perfectly adapted to receive the organizing structure or topology of the transcendental organism. It is perfectly shapeable into heterogeneous configurations. Whatever transcendental matter is, it is as far as possible from the sort of matter that exists in what Bergson calls "empty homogeneous space." Composed of spirit (organizing force) and transcendental matter, the transcendental organisms exist along a gradient reaching from an apex point, where transcendental matter so closely approaches spirit as to disappear entirely, to the nadir point where matter is widely separated from spirit. The transcendental organisms are arranged, therefore, in a series of descending steps or stages as they become ever more distant from their source, the infinite power of YHWH Echad. On the second day of creation a division is made between "the waters above" and "the waters below" by something that in Hebrew is called *rakia*, the "firmament" (*Scheidewand*). Goldberg claims that the *rakia* should really be understood as a "limit concept" (*Grenzbegriff*) marking the division between the infinite transcendent worlds and our finite world. The *rakia* is the line at which the increasing gulf (*Kluft*) between spirit and matter becomes so great that there is no longer any unifying biological center (*biologische Zentrum*) on "this" side of the *rakia*. Matter here is separated from spirit. In this empirical world "beneath the *rakia*," *purposive*, organic lawfulness takes a back seat to *mechanical* lawfulness, the endless series of cause and effect. Matter here is as different from spirit as it is possible for it to be. Spirit therefore must struggle against matter to form organic forms. But "above the *rakia*" there are transcendental worlds upon worlds, each with a unifying "biological center," each, in other words, with a spirit that shapes its "transcendental matter" into the form of a unified "person." "The 'higher' that spirit 'ascends,'" Goldberg explains, "the more it approaches the infinite, and the smaller becomes the division, that is, the tension, between spirit and matter, and, consequently, the more does matter come to resemble spirit."[24]

According to Goldberg, the construction of this finite world takes place on days three through five of creation (which he does not take to be literal days). On days one and two, YHWH Echad (YHWH One), the infinite God, brings the transcendental world into being. It is not until day three that the finite, empirical world begins to be created—but the construction of the finite world no longer involves the direct creative power of YHWH Echad. YHWH Echad must "draw himself into [*hineinbegeben*] the finite part of the world" in order to participate, together with the transcendental organisms, in the construction of the empirical world.[25] YHWH Echad must himself enter into the realm of the transcendental organisms and become one of them. In entering this realm, YHWH Echad reveals himself as YHWH Elohim (YHWH [a] God). Only as YHWH Elohim is the absolutely infinite YHWH Echad able to enter into relationship with empirical reality:

When God enters the world—hinted at in the Bible in the words "I shall be seen in the cloud over the cover of the Holy Ark"—He cannot enter it in His whole perfection. Why not? Because He would thereby destroy the world, owing to its imperfection. . . . But now the question arises: Why has God, who is alleged to be omnipotent, not created a perfect world from the very beginning? The answer is: Because the truly perfect is unique. There are no two perfect essences, God and World. Such a fact would contradict the very idea of God. God does not create His uniqueness a second time.[26]

In discussing Goldberg's *Ontology* in chapter 3 I had occasion to talk about Goldberg's "ur-concept" of Uniqueness (*Einmaligkeit*). I explained that it corresponded to YHWH Echad in *The Reality of the Hebrews*. In the passage I just quoted we see that the creation of the world required, first, that the world be imperfect and, second, the loss of God's omnipotence as he assumes the identity of YHWH Elohim. In entering into league with the transcendental organisms to construct the empirical world, YHWH Echad limits himself and his power. YHWH Elohim is the way that the Pentateuch refers to YHWH Echad in his self-limitation as he faces the world.

YHWH Echad's self-limitation makes it possible for him to enter into relationship with the world, but it also offers an opening to all the transcendental organisms for "colonization": the establishments of organic outposts, sites of articulation, in the midst of inorganic matter. "Since they all have their own world [in the transcendental realm], the transcendental organisms represent 'colonial powers' in relation to this world."[27] The battle for ascendancy in this imperialistic land grab ("the original form of geopolitics") will be won by whichever transcendental organism or grouping of organisms is able to create a "biological center" (a sort of imperial metropole) on the earth from which the rest of the world can be governed. There is a problem, however: the biological center from which the entire world can be ruled must also be the center of the entire transcendental realm. It must possess, in other words, the organizing "totality function" of the transcendental macro-organism. But only YHWH Elohim possesses the totality function. Therefore, each of the separate transcendental organisms can only successfully colonize the earth if it can manage to create its own version of Adam Kadmon, the being who reflects the totality of the transcendental sphere. The struggle between YHWH Elohim and the other gods is, therefore, a struggle over what it means to be human, to reflect on earth the "image of God."

Let me explain why there is a struggle at all. Why is YHWH Elohim unable to simply impose his will over the other gods? Recall that YHWH Elohim has lost the full power of YHWH Echad. As one of the transcendental organisms, YHWH Elohim is compelled to establish harmony within the transcendental realm by confronting his "enemies" on earth as well as within the transcendental realm.

He must defeat the forces that seek to pull the world apart into warring colonial outposts:

> For this reason [because YHWH Elohim is the only God who is able to gain ascendancy over the other transcendental organisms], YHWH Elohim as the leading God undertakes the execution of creation [*Ausführung der Schöpfung*]. But, in order to construct the world, YHWH Elohim cannot prevent the most important "strategic" point in creation, the preformation region of the transcendental organism, from being the common possession of *all the gods*. And it is this region over which the war is fought. As long as YHWH Elohim is the "man of war," as long as he is a God who manifests himself as the leader who takes a folk group into battle, so long as YHWH is required to fight wars—like the war against Amalek—that extend throughout all time (*midor dor* [from generation to generation]) until its eschatological final point, *for so long YHWH is able to be defeated* [*solange kann YHWH auch unterlegen sein*]. If we translate this state of affairs into the terms of the problem of theodicy, we can put it this way: YHWH Echad cannot "dwell upon the earth" because he is the preworldly (and infinite) principle, but YHWH Elohim can dwell there, that is, YHWH Elohim can do this in so far as he is a God who is a principle that manifests itself in the realm of finitude. YHWH Echad is an absent God who is beyond space and time and bodily form, but YHWH Elohim, because he is found in space and time, necessarily possesses a (formless) embodiment [*gestaltlose Körperhaftigkeit*]. The transition from YHWH Echad to YHWH Elohim, that is, the unconditional, immediate, and "powerful" presence of the absolutely just God is the ultimate goal of *eschatology*.[28]

The Pentateuch, Goldberg explains, insofar as it describes the struggle of YHWH Elohim against the colonizing powers of the various transcendental organisms, is the "Book of the Wars of YHWH."[29] Goldberg's exegesis of the Pentateuch seeks to recover the principles on which the eschatological battle of YHWH to establish hegemony over the earth can be carried forward. The stakes are high. As Goldberg writes, YHWH Elohim *can be defeated*. He depends on human beings to wage a metaphysical war against the other gods and bring to completion the eschatological goal of creation. Israel is his chosen army. The metaphysical war is a war of liberation against the colonial powers—the transcendental organisms—who seek to impose their imperial hegemony over the earth. This is not a war on behalf of an even greater and more powerful colonial power, but on behalf of the metaphysical liberation of the earth from the rule of the biological laws imposed by the transcendental organisms: the rule that places every individual human being under the decree of death in the name of a species immortality, the only immortality that the partial power of a transcendental organism is able to attain. Only the totality function of the macro-organism, of Adam Kadmon, can lift the death decree from humanity and begin the eschatological reign of eternal life. Until that time, the metaphysical war on behalf of all humanity against the divisive forces of the partial biocentric gods (and the states that set themselves up as "ersatz gods," as we will see) remains one that every generation must fight. Unfortunately, the one record that humanity possesses of this metaphysical war—this authentic form of geopolitics—has been all but lost: the Pentateuch has been reduced to a collection of "sources," and its unifying metaphysical significance has been overlaid with a theological veneer (God as omnipotent Lord) that belies the real import (and the stakes) of the "wars of the Lord." Awakening the world to the metaphysical danger posed to the very identity of the human being by the false gods of the world's geopolitical states is the central task of *The Reality of the Hebrews.*

Let us then turn to the beginning of the metaphysical war against the colonizing attempts of the transcendental organisms. In the first chapter of Genesis we are told that the fish and birds were created on the fifth day and the land animals were brought into being on the sixth day. God creates humanity near the end of the sixth day. Goldberg offers a somewhat unusual interpretation of the creation of the animals. He takes the animals to represent failures on the part of the transcendental organisms to create, apart from YHWH Elohim, a biological center within the world or, differently put, to create a living human being. YHWH Elohim was not able to compel the transcendental organisms to completely submit their partial life forces to his totalizing will. YHWH Elohim could not compel the transcendental organisms to assist him in creating a living human being with all of the organic potencies that the transcendental organisms possess. YHWH Elohim was therefore forced to allow the other transcendental organisms to take their turns at attempting to create a being that could serve as the world's biological center. Having only a part of the biological power making up the whole realm of the "image of God," however, the transcendental organisms failed to fashion anything more than animal creatures with great but ultimately limited powers.[30] Only after these failed attempts at the independent creation of a single dominant life form on earth does YHWH Elohim manage to get the transcendental organisms to cooperate with him in fashioning Adam (a single being despite having male and female sides).

YHWH Elohim, although he finally succeeds in getting the other transcendental organisms to cooperate in the creation of the human Adam, is unable to prevent Adam from succumbing to the temptation placed before him by the serpent. Goldberg claims that the serpent is sent as the representative of all the other transcendental organisms. The serpent promises Adam—Goldberg assumes that the division into two separate beings with independent centers of self-consciousness was not finally achieved until *after* the "Fall"—that s/he will acquire the knowledge of good and evil and thereby become "like the gods," that is, like the transcendental organisms. Humanity forsakes the unifying Y-Force (the prebiological totality function of YHWH) that would have granted it the ability to triumph over the "demonic," disarticulating, force of empirical matter. In other words, Adam forsakes eternally renewable life. Having chosen to eat from the fruit of the tree of the knowledge of good and evil, humanity comes under the sway of the biological regime of sexual reproduction, the locus of the limited life-force possessed by the transcendental organisms. Each species and also every biological individual down to the level of the cell are alive only so long as they reproduce themselves. The division (*Zwiespalt*) within knowledge between good and evil is mirrored in the division between the sexes and the division of the cells. Partaking of the fruit of division, Adam is divided into two gendered beings and thus enters into the realm of biology.

When the human being falls under the lawfulness of the realm of biological reproduction, it is divided from the "regeneration source" (*Regenerationsquelle*) that is found within the "absolutely transcendental organism, the image of God." This regeneration source is the "unapproachable engine room [*unzugängliche Maschinenraum*] and dynamo that produces and sustains the organic lawfulness [*Lebensgesetzlichkeit*] of all the separate transcendental organism-worlds." The biologist Paul Weiss's first work, published in 1923, on morphogenetic fields was based, as I noted earlier, on the power of the salamander to regenerate an amputated limb. Regeneration, Weiss explains in his later *Principles of Development*, is a *"residue of the original capacities for growth, organization, and differentiation* through which the individual was first formed."[31] Weiss points out that the regenerative capacity is greatest among the "lower forms." Goldberg, in contrast, seems to have concluded that this regenerative capacity is at its fullest in the transcendental organism itself, the primal organism called Adam Kadmon whose various organ systems are realized in different animal species. The unapproachability of the regeneration source, Goldberg adds, guarantees the "indestructibility of this whole realm; it is in a word nothing else than the organic body *in so far as it is indestructible.*"[32] In choosing division over unity, Adam has divided himself as an individual from the "regeneration source" of the transcendental realm.

Having been unable to prevent Adam from losing his link to the biology-productive principle and thereby falling under the sway of reproductive biology (sexuality, birth, and death), YHWH Elohim also finds himself unable to prevent some of the transcendental organisms from assuming bodily forms and actually interfering in human reproduction, "mingling with daughters of men."[33] A new species, a species of giants (*nefilim*), is thereby produced. To save the unity of the human species, YHWH Elohim destroys these giants with the Flood.

After the Flood, YHWH Elohim was compelled to compromise again with the transcendental organisms, allowing them this time to forge connections with Noah's sons—Japhet, Shem, and Ham, the progenitors of the three "main races." After the Flood, the transcendental organisms no longer create new organic forms as they had done during the construction of the world (the animals), nor can they create bodies for themselves in order to have intercourse with humans. Rather, the transcendental organisms employ humankind's "capacity for metaphysics" (*Fähigkeit zur Metaphysik*) to enter into relationship with the spatiotemporal world.[34] They do so by taking advantage of the collective powers available in the human races and their offshoot folk groups.

Goldberg here may again be drawing some inspiration from Nachman Krochmal's *Guide for the Perplexed of the Time* (1851). I mentioned Krochmal earlier in this chapter as a possible source of Goldberg's conception of the "middle realm" between infinity and finitude as populated with transcendental life forms. In "Gate Seven" of his *Guide for the Perplexed of the Time*, Krochmal claims that various spiritual "prince-angels," members of God's "heavenly host" (the "middle realm" between God and the world), are associated with each of the various ancient folk groups.[35] Krochmal uses the philosophical framework of Hegelian idealism to explain the relationship between God and these lesser spiritual beings: "Consider how the Prophet [Jeremiah] announces and says: 'Their portion is not like the portion of Jacob, since he [God] is the creator of all, and Israel is his inheritance. His name is 'YHWH of hosts.' This means that he is the absolute spirit and there is nothing beside him; he is the source of all spiritual beings and he includes all things. But the individual manifestations of his spirit, taken by themselves, exist in dependency upon the hosts of heaven and earth and are finite and transitory, possessing no true existence truth and absolute being."[36] The "hosts" of heaven and earth are intermediary spiritual beings who lend their assigned folk group their spiritual characteristics. "For example, a folk group ['umah] that is ruled by the sword will have as its angel-prince, the spirit of force [ruach ha'gvurah]."[37] Only Israel has a relation to the "creator of all," YHWH. Krochmal's theory of folk groups and their corresponding "gods" or "angels" is quite possibly one of Goldberg's sources, but Goldberg gives his version a decidedly "biological" turn. He claims that Japhet, Ham, and Shem are each granted enhanced biological vitality by three distinct coalitions of transcendental organisms. That means that the three sons are able to use their psychophysical makeup not merely for exercising "normal" biological functions but also for entering into reciprocal relations with the transcendental organisms, whom they know as "gods."

The descendants of the three racial progenitors have different ways of displaying their enhanced metaphysical powers, all involving the alteration of the nature of the biological per se, namely, the relationship of spirit to matter. The Japhetic (or Aryan) race will seek to lift the spirit that enlivens matter upward toward the source of both spirit and matter in the Infinite. This requires "mastery over the form of spirit's state" (*Zustandsform des Geistes*) so that it approaches the point where materiality is almost entirely dissolved into pure feeling.[38] Echoing Schopenhauer's conception of the nature of Apollonian-Buddhistic aesthetics,

Goldberg says that music is the quintessential Aryan art form. The Semitic race will use its metaphysical power to create new complex manifolds within matter, that is, *new mathematical objects*. If we recall from chapter 2 that Goldberg considers the Pentateuch to be such a new mathematical object, it should not be surprising to learn that he claims that *writing (Schrift)* is the quintessential Semitic art form. Finally, the Hamitic race (also associated with the Negro and the Asiatic races according to Goldberg) will devote itself to manipulating *empirical* matter so that it can serve as the vessel into which spirit can descend (the Egyptian arts of mummification are paradigmatic cases of Hamitic metaphysics). Goldberg says that the plastic arts are the primary aesthetic field of the Hamitic races. In summary, Japhetic metaphysics engages in the practice of *purifying the spirit of empirical matter*; Hamitic metaphysics deals with *infusing empirical matter with spirit*; and Semitic metaphysics works to *mathematize matter*. (Recall in this context what Erich Unger in *Against Poetry* said about ancient Pythagoreanism—that it was of Semitic rather than Hellenic [Japhetic] origin.)

The transcendental organisms—three large coalitions of them, rather—employ the metaphysical capacities of Japhet, Ham, and Shem in their effort to colonize the empirical realm. In every generation there will be a descendent who inherits the psychophysical potential to enter into relation with the transcendental organisms. After a number of generations, descendants will be born who will become the eponym (eponymous progenitor) of the race's "metaphysical folk groups." The folk group ancestors who descend from each of the three main eponyms have a relationship to only a part of the coalition of transcendental organisms connected to the race. Goldberg's biological terminology encourages us to think of the development of the folk groups out of the eponym on the model of the differentiation of a "pluripotent" fertilized egg into a multitude of organ systems within a single mature organism. As I mentioned in chapter 1, each folk group is the vehicle of a transcendental "name" (*shem*), a sort of mathematical formula or function defining a transcendental organism's manifold or energy-field: "The *shem* signifies the *dynamic* relationship (the energetic *functions*) between a center, the god, and his periphery, the folk group, that represents the *force-field of the god*. The *shem* is also an *act of discharge* that occurs when the high level of tension of the force is spontaneously released and is forced into a condition of relaxation. . . . [T]he god represents the multifold potentiation of the folk group that is leveled out in its condition of relaxation where it is shared throughout the members of the folk group."[39]

Goldberg here describes a *shem*-folk group relationship as a dynamic relationship expressed in the higher energy level of the folk group that results in a discharge from a center (high tension) to the periphery. This tension-release dynamism is repeated over and over: each sacrificial act raises the tension of the center and creates the conditions for a new discharge throughout the group. How this is supposed to work is not clearly stated, but it is not too difficult to unpack what Goldberg means if we connect it to what I described in chapter 1 in relation to the theoretical biology of Gurwitsch and Weiss. Both researchers claimed that a species-specific "energy-field" governs the morphogenesis and physiology of the organism. In a much more speculative vein, Jakob von Uexküll argued that corresponding to every living species there is an abstract structure or *Bauplan* that exists independently of the empirical organisms whose life cycle and interactive relations with their *Umwelt* is determined by this structure and its perceptual "schemas."[40]

The morphogenetic field channels or contours the energy intake and output of the organism into self-restoring organic processes that use energy from external sources (food, light) to build new and more complex structures (morphogenesis) and ultimately sustain these structures by constantly recreating them (physiology). Rather than dispersing energy directly (as happens in what are called "open systems"), the field provides a template for trapping the energy in an ordered structure (a "closed system") so that it can be put to use at a later time. A simple example of this process is the way that ice crystals "grow": particulate matter in a cloud's water vapor provides the condition for the dissipation of heat energy in the cooling vapor (when it comes in contact with a colder air mass), to be restrained into hexagonal molecular patterns that form around the particles. These hexagonally structured molecular patterns hold the dissipating heat energy in place before it is completely lost to the surrounding air. We could say that "hexagonality" is an inorganic field that makes it possible for certain kinds of matter (water, in this case) to complexify into energy-trapping forms (ice crystals or snow). Indeed, we saw in chapter 1 that Paul Weiss, in a passage I quoted from his *Principles of Development*, explicitly compares the organic field to a crystal: "The organization of a field bears some remote resemblance to that of a crystal."

Now we can better understand Goldberg's energic descriptions of the relationship between a transcendental organism (*shem, elohim*) and its folk group. The transcendental organism is a morphogenetic field that allows the folk group to hold within its *shem*-patterned collective body a higher level of energy than an unstructured collective can hold. When an individual within such a high-energy structure "desecrates the *shem*" (i.e., uses the name of YHWH "in vain"), he or she causes the release of the energy, to the detriment of the collective and the individual: "This is why it is forbidden (in the third of the so-called ten commandments) to 'void' (*nassa*, bear, raise up, void) the *shem* YHWH without compelling necessity (*lashav* [in vain]), that is, to use it, because there are consequences (*lo yinakeh* [he will not be innocent]), in so far as it is *chilul ha'shem* [desecration of the name], which means, *making the shem into chol* ("making it into sand" is the ancient Hebrew expression for 'atomization'), which brings about or can bring about an *explosion*."[41] (Goldberg is referring to speculation in the 1920s that atomic energy could be used to construct a bomb.) The explosion of the *shem* into the world does not have to be destructive, however. It can also be "organizing": it can crystallize into a new pattern, as when the Pentateuch crystallizes into written number patterns, according to Goldberg.[42] But the crystalline structure can be shattered in a chain reaction that releases purely destructive energy when one of the elements of the structure loses its resonance with the other elements.

According to Goldberg, every metaphysical folk group stabilizes its dynamic "discharge" mechanism through its tie to a certain land. And what binds a metaphysical folk group to its land is its *cult*. The place of the cult is the center point linking god to the earth and across the surface of the earth to the outermost periphery of the folk group.

> A folk group—and this applies only to the metaphysical folk group!—requires a land not only within which to dwell, above all else, for the administration of its cult. The cult is the model of geopolitics. Every folk group confronts a question: *where* can the transcendental reality with which it is correlated make its breakthrough? For the life source of each folk group—its god—must feel in contact with the earth in much the way that that a man with a divining rod seeks out an underground stream. But discovering the proper cult site is not an easy matter. When one worships Zeus at Dodona, one can count on its effectiveness because there is a reality to which the site is related; had one tried to worship him at Memphis, it would have been a pointless game.
>
> One can express this state of affairs with the following equation: Folk groups = gods = lands. In so far as the god is concerned, once he has found his land, it requires "strategic occupation." If he succeeds, then he has become "chthonic" or "epichorios" [local]: he belongs to the earth, he is rooted to the land.[43]

Goldberg sums up the relationship between folk group, land, and cult in one sentence: "The cult is the original form of geopolitics." This sentence, which I quoted earlier, needs historical contextualization. In the 1935 essay, "The Gods of the Greeks," from which this passage comes, Goldberg goes on to describe the "metaphysical nationalism" of the ancient folk groups. He explains that it consisted in their aspiration for a "mastery over matter" and an "autarchy of life," that is, the rule of life over the inertial drag of the inorganic: "All mythical folk groups practice geopolitics and strive for autarchy—and they are the only folk groups who can ever succeed in this."[44] In contrast to current geopolitical theories in Germany, Goldberg did not view a people's relation to its land to be the result of a biologically inherent drive to expand the group's territory. Rather, he locates it in the transcendental organisms' struggle for metaphysical mastery over matter. This is not a sanctification of worldly geopolitics. Rather, Goldberg's analysis sets the stage for his audacious claim that *Israel and Israel's God are the only authentic geopolitical actors left in the world.* The ancient metaphysical folk groups associated with the mythic gods have lost their biological identity, but Israel's God does not require a genealogical lineage to operate in the world. Israel's God is a *chosen-God* (*Wahl-Gott*), and therefore an ethnically diverse population can act as the instrument of actualizing God in the world.

It needs to be noted that when Goldberg wrote his essay "The Gods of the Greeks," the term "geopolitics" was not as common as it is today. Coined by the Swedish jurist Rudolf Kjellén in an 1899 essay, the term came into prominence in Germany in the 1920s among political geographers who were looking to analyze the causes of the defeat of Germany in the First World War.[45] The German academic study known as *Geopolitik* was given its institutional imprimatur by the general-turned-professor Karl Haushofer, a proponent of Germany's recovery of its Pacific colonial possessions.[46] He founded the *Zeitschrift für Geopolitik* (*Journal of Geopolitics*) in 1924 and taught geopolitics at the University of Munich during the years that Goldberg was also teaching there.[47] In 1935 Hitler established the Reichstelle für Raumordnung und Raumforschung (Reich Institute for Spatial Order and Spatial Research), with an explicit acknowledgment of the central significance of Haushofer's plans for the new German empire. It makes sense, therefore, that in 1925 Goldberg did not use "geopolitics" in *The Reality of the Hebrews* (the term was not in wide use then). But *The Reality of the Hebrews* is nonetheless primarily concerned with geopolitics, albeit a transcendental geopolitics. The restoration of humanity's relationship to the metaphysical power of YHWH is, as we have seen, the eschatological goal of the "wars of the Lord." The sum and substance of Hebrew metaphysics is to serve as an instrument of what Goldberg calls "transcendental politics."[48]

As I mentioned earlier, Goldberg claims that the transcendental organisms looked on the earth as a site of *colonization*. The earth lacked a biological center, and therefore other biological centers could attempt to establish an outpost here from which to extend their control. The establishment of a cult center at which a folk group can worship its god (its transcendental organism) is the first expression of this imperial impulse. Cult foundation narratives are also narratives of the foundation of a political order (consider the foundation of Rome on the site where Romulus slew Remus). The Hebrew folk group is the instrument through which YHWH Elohim seeks to achieve his eschatological goal, namely, to overcome the land grab of the other gods and thereby reassert the unity of humanity (the "image of God") on the earth. "'Anthropology' has the following significance: to so direct the developmental process of history that every god has his own energy (his folk group) on the earth, the result of which is that once the gods have been separated from one another and earth divided up, *the war of the gods for mastership* (the real world history) can begin."[49] The Hebrew folk group failed to fulfill its task during the "anthropological" phase of the world. This failure, Goldberg says, was "the greatest fiasco of world history."[50] It was not that the other gods defeated YHWH Elohim; it was that Israel and, indeed, all other metaphysical folk groups drove the gods from the earth. Humanity sought its own form of geopolitics. In place of cults and metaphysical folk groups there arose *the state*. Geopolitics in a god-forsaken world is simply the degenerate cult of what Goldberg calls "humanity in general" (*Allgemein-Menschliche*).[51] The state has become the "administrator of an unmetaphysical normality."[52]

## The State as Fixation: Babel

The period in human history characterized by metaphysical folk groups is, in fact, anomalous. The inherent tendency is for humans to group themselves into non-metaphysical social and political structures with no bridging link to a transcendental organism. Goldberg explains that Cain, whose name is cognate with the Hebrew word meaning "possession," slew his brother Abel, the one whose line, Goldberg explains, is restarted with Seth and Shem, the line of metaphysics. Cain, the "tiller of the ground, *tool-maker* [*Techniker*], and city founder,"[53] stands for the fixation powers in history: "He murdered metaphysics."[54] Cain is the progenitor of those in history who rely on technology to master matter, rather than on the metaphysical psychophysiological power offered by the rituals of a cult. Not only do "tool-makers" seek an artificial mastery over matter but they also seek to create artificial organisms—*states*. That the state is an artificial organism is the thesis of Thomas Hobbes's *Leviathan*, so it should not come as a surprise to find that Goldberg considers the reference to the sea-monster called "Levyatan" in Isaiah (27:1) to be a reference to the "born enemy of metaphysics": "Fixation, the born enemy of metaphysics, is described in Isaiah as Levyatan and can only be eschatologically overcome by YHWH."[55] Although metaphysical folk groups manage for a time to overcome the human tendency to "unmetaphysical normality," they too ultimately collapse under the pressure of the impulse to state formation.

What can be salvaged from the "metaphysical" period in human history is the one great metaphysical insight from that period, the insight achieved by "Abraham, the greatest genius of ancient time"—namely, one can only ensure the survival of the metaphysical power of one's race not through forming a state but by *relinquishing the gods of biology and covenanting with the God of choice (Wahl-Gott)*.[56] There is only one God with whom one's relationship can be (and can only be) based on choice: the God who is not a mere part of the macro-transcendental organism, but who is the very source of all these organisms, the *prebiological* and *preworldly* God. To retain the metaphysical power that is associated with biological inheritance requires that one *universalize* one's race by choosing to be related to the God who is *beyond all biological races*. "Hebraism [*Hebräertum*]," the discovery of Abraham, "is the overcoming of race through race [*die Überwinder der Rasse durch die Rasse*]."[57] Goldberg in effect reverses the meaning of "chosen" in "chosen people." It is Abraham who chooses YHWH precisely because he is seeking to transcend the biological exploitation of peoples by the gods, an exploitation that necessarily decays over time as the biological connection weakens, whether due to genetic factors or to the rise of a new, state-based method of organizing the people. I explain in what follows how Abraham and YHWH entered into relationship for the purpose of overcoming race, but let me first describe in more detail the path from which Abraham broke, the path that all other races ultimately follow to preserve their waning metaphysical power: fixation through state formation.

The process of state formation, as I described, has its roots in the conditions under which world construction took place. World construction is the shaping of a material world within the constraints of space, time, and causality. In this world beneath the *rakia* (firmament), matter and spirit are divided, and spirit struggles as an alien presence in the world. World construction involves the release of the infinite reservoir of possibilities into finite actuality: *this* sequence of *these* events. Once released, the sequence runs on without interruption or discontinuity, unless some *new* object appears in the flow of time. This cannot happen except as a reorganization of the already present matter in the world. The "field energy" of the transcendental organisms serves precisely this purpose. Each new life form is a breakthrough of a new "world system" into finite actuality, for each transcendental organism represents its own self-enclosed organization, its own manifold in the transcendental space "above the firmament." But the shaping energy of the transcendental organism, derived from the *ruach* (spirit) of God, cannot perfectly mold matter into organic form:

> Matter throughout the cosmos is at home. Not so spirit. Hegel wanted to objectify spirit in order to guarantee its universal right of citizenship. His effort failed. Spirit can bind itself together with matter only under the most difficult conditions. This shows that it is not entirely at home. And this point has meant that we have failed to recognize the *sovereignty of life*, despite all of our vitalist theories. Life places spirit and matter into connection; it is the most independent and at the same most alien thing in the world that there is. Although life has entered into this world, the laws of biology have their origin *outside the world*, outside our experiential world. These origins, the sources of life, are the gods of the mythic time.[58]

The sovereign power of life within this world has a tenuous purchase on its material base. The weakness of spirit in relation to empirical matter is the origin of the political state.

The state represents the self-assertion of matter against the power of the mythic gods. It represents the "interest" of normalcy—that is, the unbroken continuity of the causal nexus of events—against the disruptive force of life. The state arises from a "destructive process" that undoes the relationship between god and folk group. Goldberg, as we have seen, calls state formation a "fixation process." Goldberg takes the term "fixation" from histology, the study of plant and animal tissues with which he would have been familiar from his naturopathic training. One histology textbook defines fixation as follows: "Fixation is the killing and conservation of the freshly living tissue with the help of so-called 'fixation media' in such a way that its structure is preserved as unchanged as possible."[59] The structure of the folk group is preserved—that is, the individual members remain intact and present—but the bond that unites them into a realization of the transcendental energy-field of their god(s) is lost. The fixation process is the result of the "powers that perpetuate the normal, unmetaphysical business operation of the world," making themselves independent and "forcing themselves between the biological center and the field of its biological developmental, the folk group, and thus cutting them off from their energy source."[60]

The state is the *technological* reassembly of the shattered crystalline structure of the once-vital metaphysical folk group. When the metaphysical bridge to the transcendental realm is closed, "individuals are then able to be viewed as the 'ruins' [*Trümmer*] of the dissolution process of their folk group."[61] The state imitates the unity of the metaphysical folk group, but the unity is purely artificial (as in Hobbes's "leviathan" state). While the ritual activities of the cult may continue, they are empty ceremonies without any ability to generate the heightened psychophysical powers of the folk group:

> As soon as the circuit between the biological energy source and its energy field (the folk group) is broken, there can be no further reciprocal action [between god and group]. Likewise our best technological inventions fail to function when there is no source from which they can be supplied with energy. Our most beautiful electric lights have no lighting power if there is no current present and the circuit is broken. In the same way the performance of religious acts is nothing but an empty ceremony as long as the most basic condition is not met, namely, that a *metaphysical* activity with a promise of effectiveness is at all a real possibility.[62]

The failure of the cult to have any metaphysical effectiveness in the world does not always lead, as one might expect, to the group's abandonment of its faith in its god. In the ancient Greek world, for example, the cessation of the people's metaphysical power came to expression in tragic theater's portrait of the hero's futile struggle against his fate: "Greek tragedy is the tragedy of [the passing of] the mythic era."[63] In the case of the Hebrews, their loss of metaphysical power led to a theological conception of God as a being who is not tied to any one group, but is rather the "general" God of "humanity in general." The God of the Hebrews is now understood to be all-powerful, the "most perfect being." This concept of a universal God with no direct connection to humanity emerges first in the Solomonic period and is announced in the words of Solomon after he built the Temple, a permanent structure for God: "Can God dwell among humans on the earth?" (1 Kings 8:27) Goldberg comments on this verse:

> Had Solomon been a little less "wise" and little less of a dandified aesthete devoted to his erotic "experiences," had he been possessed of a little bit more philosophical grounding, he would have been able to examine the entire past of Hebraism [*Hebräertum*] and found the answer to his question quite easily. The entire task of Hebraism had been to produce a dwelling for God, a *mishkan*, and thereby to bring about his presence [in the world]. The instinct created by this task is so deeply ingrained that even at a much later date, in the time of the Talmud and Midrash, it is common to describe God as "Shekhinah," which means "dwelling" and "presence," because originally one could not imagine God except as really present. When Solomon could no longer answer the question of such profound metaphysical import [whether God can dwell among humans on earth], when nothing wise occurred to him to say, he then spoke in the tone of a preacher bereft of any gift for metaphysics. "Open your eyes upon your house . . . and hear the prayer of your servant and when your people Israel calls out to you, hear them in the place where you dwell, in *heaven*, hear them and forgive. . . ." [1 Kings 8:29–30; Goldberg's rendering and emphasis.] A hard judgment needs to be spoken about this prayer, if we wish to clear the air: the "prayer of Solomon" in the First Book of Kings is merely the prattle of a dandy.[64]

What Solomon has forgotten is precisely that God's presence in the world is required in order to wage metaphysical war with the other gods. Solomon capitulates to the impulse to "normalize" Israel and assimilate to the universalizing tolerance (every god is as good as any other; all gods are reflections of the one supreme "heavenly" God) characterizing the religious syncretism of the surrounding kingdoms. "From the wise King Solomon to the assimilationist Maimonides there is a direct line that comes to its logical conclusion in the Maimonidean theory that sacrifice was a concession to the pagan instinct of the people."[65]

Solomon ushered in the loss of Israel's metaphysical power. The result, generations later, is the exile of Israel from its land. Israel is exiled to the very site where the anti-metaphysical tendency, the tendency to fixation, rules supreme: Babel (Babylon).

> In Babel, the classic land of fixation, the "gods" are nothing but *false gods*, idols of wood and stone without any sentience, exactly as in Rome (the successor to Babel and its "principle of the state"). The Babylonians have no gods [*Elohim*] because they cannot be described as a people. This is stated explicitly in the Pentateuch, although Babylon is not directly named, when it says: "You [Israel] have aroused my anger through a no-el [no god], you have stirred my wrath with your nothingnesses [*Nichtigkeiten*], and therefore I [YHWH] will rouse your anger through a no-people" (Deuteronomy 32:21).[66]

After the exile, Israel's metaphysical bridge to YHWH was broken. The triumph of *the normality of matter and technology* on the earth was assured. Without an ally on earth, God can do nothing to prevent the rise of the power of the state. Israel is the victim of the "principle of the state" as it comes to expression first in Babel, then in Rome. Israel's Temple is destroyed twice, snapping whatever metaphysical bond between Israel and God may remain. The rabbis erect a defense against the complete disintegration of the people by their insistence on the punctilious observance of the laws of the Pentateuch (except for those performed at the Temple), but these practices cannot protect the people. "The people begin to ask themselves how it came about that God no longer answers their prayers. . . . They descend into a condition of unconsolable loneliness. But they don't recognize that what is happening to them is part of a transcendental, world-political process, a war-like assault against metaphysics. God, even with the best of intentions, could not 'answer' them because he himself has been severed from his connection to his people by enemy powers [*feindliche Gewalten*]."[67]

Let us be very clear about what these "enemy powers" are that hold God himself in a state of impotence, preventing him from responding to the prayers of his people for salvation. "The metaphysics-hostile powers that bring about the fixation process," Goldberg explains, "arise from the biological 'intermediate layer' [*Zwischenschicht*] (the chasm [*Kluft*]) between spirit and matter)." These powers prevent spirit from conjoining with matter and thereby from forming novel organic forms. "Putting this in mythological terms, they are the same powers that maintain the *normal*, that is, the usual, unmetaphysical business of the world and that have an interest in the maintenance of 'normality.'"[68] As we have seen, Babel (Babylonia) is the ancient world's capital of "unmetaphysical business." Not surprisingly, it is also the capital of the ancient world's *technology*. "The Babylonians wanted, as the Bible explains it, to produce a *shem*, that is, they wanted to create an artificial *shem* through technological means, a technological world-system, a technological *organism*."[69] The "fixation powers" use the Babylonians because they are a "mixed folk group" composed of peoples who no longer possess an "authentic" (*echt*) identity. The fixation powers seek to replace metaphysics with brute technological *power* (*Macht*).

There is a revealing passage about fixation that Goldberg removed from the published text of *The Reality of the Hebrews*, but that is found in typescript in his Nachlass in the Deutsches Literaturarchiv in Marbach.[70] It describes the way that fixation in state formations often elicits counter-reactions that involve "revolutions" based on "folk-group-building powers" (*volksbildende Kräfte*). Such renewed powers arise when a state loosens its grip on its subjects, as when it launches colonies or suffers from civil war, or when its population is "decimated" in wartime. The upsurge of folk-building powers, Goldberg claims, can be observed in phenomena associated with "Spiritualism" (*Spiritismus*). Goldberg points specifically to what he claims is the "motherland" of spiritualism, occultism, and séance circles, namely "relatively youthful America" after the upheaval of the Civil War when there was, he says, an "epidemic" of such phenomena. He argues that the séance circle can produce a corporeal "outline" (*Aufriss*) that is a "bodily formation of a higher order" (*Körperbildung höherer Ordnung*). In this passage, Goldberg seems to be thinking about the appearance of "ectoplasm" that many paranormal researchers thought they could observe (and sometimes photograph) during a séance. Goldberg probably removed these pages from the final version of *The Reality of the Hebrews* because, as he himself admits, spiritualism has been "legitimately somewhat discredited" since it is associated with "murky motives" (*dunkle Triebe*) on its "surface" (he does not mention what these are, but he is probably thinking about mediums who make money off the gullibility of mourners).[71] But this excised passage offers a fascinating glimpse into Goldberg's early fascination with mediums and spiritualism, something that he will pursue when he arrives in the United States. It is also interesting to notice that he offers what could be called a "theory of ghosts" that correlates occult phenomena with the powers released in a nation-state whose hold on its population, for whatever reason, has been weakened.

While modern spiritualism offers evidence of the ability of a small group (a medium and the other members of the séance) to constitute a "body of a higher order," ancient folk groups could achieve this collective heightening of their psychophysical powers through their own form of séance—through gathering at the cult center to participate in the sacrificial rituals that brought a god into relation with their heightened biological forces. But there was one other way in antiquity to bring a new collective body into existence: a *covenant*. A covenant is a metaphysical bridge to the transcendental realm. Abraham was the first to discover the metaphysical power of the covenant.

## Transcendental Revolution: From Abraham to Mt. Sinai

Goldberg speaks of Abraham as the ancestor who inaugurates the metaphysical revolution that breaks with all the biological part-gods (parts of *the* transcendental organism, Adam Kadmon) and turns toward the "unbiological" God of "the human as such." Abraham thus begins the "making-universally-human" (*Allgemeinmenschlichmachung*) of the Hebrew folk group, a group that previously had its own part-gods.[72] As we will see, Abraham begins the process of splitting away from the biological part-gods, but it is only at Mt. Sinai that the break reaches a new, albeit not completely consummated, level. With the break with all part-gods and the beginning of a "universal" folk group, a new historical epoch begins. It begins by the fact that YHWH Elohim *founds* (*gründet*) Israel *at one time* at Mt. Sinai, rather than *generates it biologically* out of a single eponym

(*Stammvater*). To be sure, Israel must continue to purify itself of its remaining biological affiliations with earlier Hebrew and Semitic part-gods. This process is what the purity laws in Leviticus are meant to advance, a subject of considerable attention in *The Reality of the Hebrews*. Although the return to its biological past remains a threat, the founding of Israel at Mt. Sinai unifies the folk group in relation to a not-yet realized future. Israel thus possesses a "teleology," rather than a "genealogy." The teleological aspect of the folk group allows it to embody the *universal* aspect of the transcendental space (Adam Kadmon) that encompasses all of humanity, rather than the partial aspect that all the other folk groups embody.

The uniqueness of the relationship between Israel after Mt. Sinai and YHWH Elohim lies precisely in the fact that it is not biologically inheritable, as is the relationship between other metaphysical folk groups and their part-gods. That is, the resonant pattern or energy-field (*shem*) that lifts the Hebrew folk group into a heightened energetic condition is not inherited from a racial progenitor whose psychophysical constitution had been altered through contact with the "energetic function" of a transcendental organism. There is no animal avatar or totem associated with the Hebrew folk group.[73] Rather, the Hebrew folk group must give up its relationship with its biological god—it must give up its very life form as a single group and dissolve into individuals—in order to "choose" YHWH Elohim. The Hebrew folk group thus becomes Israel, a folk group that is "founded" through a "interruption act" on the part of YHWH Elohim, the God who possesses (or, more simply put, who *is*) the "totality function" that generates every single partial function within the whole transcendental realm:

> The Hebrews originally possess, as every other folk group does, a god, a descent-center, who is part of finite actuality. But because it is not possible to descend from YHWH Elohim as one would from a finite biological center, since he is prebiological, that is, he originates from the preworldly sphere and from the infinite actuality, the relationship between YHWH Elohim and the folk group is expressly one that relies upon an *act of choosing*. . . . Because of this, YHWH Elohim enters as a *biology-alien* [*biologisch-fremdes*] element in the folk group Israel. . . . In reality, something completely *counter to nature* is being demanded of the folk group Israel: it must give up its own "inherited" biological center. For an authentic folk group, this is tantamount to asking someone to exchange his body for that of someone else's. And this explains the constant backsliding: the golden calf in the desert and the later worship of bulls.[74]

To become Israel, the Hebrew folk group must, in effect, *die as one organism and be resurrected as another.* They must move from the security of an inheritable biological center to the terrible insecurity of *choosing to be responsible for recreating their collective life force through a covenant with their God.*

Abraham plays a significant role in the transition of the Hebrews from their relation to their part-gods to Israel's founding at Mt. Sinai. The Hebrew folk group had been prepared through Abraham for the radical demand on the part of YHWH Elohim to sacrifice their racial identity for an "anti-biological" relationship with a prebiological God. Abraham's relationship to YHWH Echad is mediated not through YHWH Elohim, but through El Shaddai, the name (or "formula") by which Abraham is said to have called on YHWH. YHWH Elohim is the principle that produces the unity within the many "world systems" of the transcendental realm. El Shaddai is the generative principle that creates the endless number of transcendental organisms (what Goldberg also calls "multiplicity-unities" or "uniquenesses" in his *Ontology*):

> One has to distinguish between relative and absolute transcendence. The individual self-enclosed organic worlds are relatively transcendent to one another, but they together constitute a continuum that encompasses the totality of all the worlds that are discontinuous among themselves. This continuum is an immanence system [*Immanenzsystem*] that correlates to the 'absolutely' transcendent organism, the biology-productive principle. . . . The way that the Pentateuch refers to how the doubly transcendent realm of authentic discontinuity [of elements among themselves and of the totality in relation to this world], that is, the *Zelem Elohim*—the effective instance of "prebiology" in "this" world—is able to undertake a process of abiogenesis [*Urzeugung*] in this world is El Shaddai.[75]

This is dense going, but it can be explained through the mathematics of infinity that Georg Cantor inaugurated. In chapter 2 I discussed Cantor's description of a "transfinite number" that totalizes the infinite series of finite ordinals. Cantor distinguished between two "principles" behind all ordinals: a "first generative principle" that produces one ordinal after another, each discontinuous with the earlier one, and a "totality function" that encompasses this entire series and forms a whole (Cantor calls it a "continuum"), the first transfinite ordinal. El Shaddai is the correlate of what Georg Cantor calls the "first generative principle," namely, the additive principle that creates the infinite series of ordinal numbers. It breaks off with one and adds a unit to form another. And YHWH Elohim is the "totality function" that produces the first transfinite number, the ordinal that totalizes the entirety of all finite ordinals.[76] The root of "Shaddai," according to Goldberg, is "shud," and like many such monosyllabic, biconsonantal roots, it has a "polar" meaning: its two opposed meanings reflect the dynamic tension of a single "indifference point" from out of which both centrifugal and centripetal forces derive. (Two magnets can both attract and repel one another depending on the alignment of their respective fields.) In the case of "shud," the root meaning is "multiply" (as in "be fruitful"), but there is also a polar opposite meaning (in the verb *shadad*) "to turn into a desert, to dry up, to make barren."[77] In other words, El Shaddai is the "function" that *discontinuously stops and starts an infinite additive series.* Each start is like the birth of something radically different. Goldberg calls this "abiogenesis," the emergence of a living structure not from a prior living structure but from some nonliving source. The origin of life on earth is generally believed today to be abiogenetic (arising from inanimate matter directly, rather than a previous life form). Goldberg takes the origin of the transcendental organism to likewise be abiogenetic, arising from a "prebiology" or a "biology-productive" principle. This is El Shaddai. The power that can gather the biological organisms into a totality—*Zelem Elohim*—is represented by YHWH Elohim.

El Shaddai breaks off Abraham's racial inheritance as a Semite, dividing him from the "gods of his fathers":

> As the effective indifference point of the origin of all organic lawfulness, that is, as the indifference point of the "image of God," El Shaddai has a *universal* significance that *leads beyond* "biology." This universalism, which is grounded in the unity of the human species, has been previously shown to be displayed in the fact that the human has the possibility for *all the gods*, that is, the human carries within himself the possibility for expressing all biological capacities. In so far as humanity is the creation of the gods taken severally, each human only expresses a specific and sharply delimited part-capacity, but humanity in so far as its source is YHWH Elohim, contains a *totality organ* that enables him to transcend biology and push all the way to the biology-productive principle itself. For this reason Abraham, in the bible passage introducing circumcision, which is an *anti-biological* sign and is directed *against* the other gods who are the originators of the "circle of life" (birth, death, etc.), Abraham is required to possess the *totality function*, namely, he is asked to be *tamim*, that is, "whole" as well as "ending" (the biological cycle) (*tamam* means both "to be whole" and to "bring to an end").[78]

Note the mathematical language in the final sentence. The "totality function" of YHWH Elohim is what Georg Cantor spoke of as the "totality function" that grasps as a unity the infinite series of units generated by the "first generative principle." To summarize, El Shaddai is the "indifference point" that infinitely generates one ordinal (the parts of the transcendental macro-organism seen as "multiplicity-unities") after another. Insofar as he *starts* a new additive series, El Shaddai is able to provide Abraham with the power to produce a new folk group. Insofar as he does so by creating a discontinuous series, he is able to begin the process whereby Abraham separates himself from the genealogical series that linked him to the racial gods of the Semites.

To better understand how Abraham can be the abiogenetic origin (spontaneously generated) of a new folk group, let us recall Goldberg's concept of life that I discussed in chapter 2 in the context of Georg Cantor's theory of transfinite numbers. Goldberg's definition of "being alive" is "to stand in a value-endowed [*wert-betont*], unexchangable position." If to be alive is to stand in that position, then to be alive is to be a part of a *world*. Every transcendental world is made into a world by the "biology-productive principle." Every transcendental world is also the finitization of the infinite, a "multiplicity-unity." Yet which side of this pair represents life? Goldberg says that the "biology-productive" principle is, in fact, neither *within* the multiplicity nor is it the unity or wholeness of a multiplicity. Both options miss the dynamic nature of being alive for Goldberg. Being alive is *to take one's unexchangeable place* within a world. But there is a qualitative intensity associated with life, that is, there are *degrees of being alive* corresponding to the degree to which one is connected to the biology-productive principle itself. What would the most intense form of living be for an empirical individual organism? Rather than simply occupying an unexchangeable position, one would make *oneself* unexchangeable. No longer a replaceable individual in a sequence of individuals, one *is* unexchangeable, simply by virtue of one's identity. Put in terms of the species as a living whole, one no longer lives by virtue of occupying a certain position in the "descent line"; instead, one *begins a new line*. This is the role of someone who can connect himself directly either to a transcendental world or to the transcendental biology-productive principle itself, the generative principle of *all* transcendental worlds. In creating a *new* descent line, the individual closes one descent line series and opens another, and thus he stands in relation to the past series as the transfinite number does to all the numbers that precede it. The new descent line will be a new folk group whose name will be taken from that of its eponym and will embody a different transcendental organism than did the prior descent line.

There are two possibilities for how a new descent line emerges from an ancestral founder. Either the ancestral founder starts a new line (a folk group) by differentiating a specific god or set of gods from out of a mixed-race connected group of gods, or (as with Abraham) the ancestral founder breaks with any partial grouping of gods and links himself directly with the biology-productive principle itself. Take the first case: the ancestral founder occupies a point of differentiation in the unfolding of one of the three "main races" in the way that, in embryological development, an organ system (the nervous system, for example) begins from a single cell that differentiates itself from the pluripotent cells that preceded it. The folk group that such an ancestral founder begins is, to be sure, "metaphysical" to the extent that it brings into concrete embodiment one or perhaps a set of transcendental organisms. But its metaphysical power is limited, just as the gods it serves are only a part of the total transcendental organism, Adam Kadmon. This is why such a folk group will imagine its gods in the form of totemic animals. This is also why such folk groups, according to Goldberg, will always *offer humans in sacrifice to their gods*. Connected to a transcendental organism that is only one biological center among many, the folk group imagines the human being to be equivalent to its sacred animal-god, the totem. Rather than sacrifice the sacred animal, the folk group sacrifices a human.

Take the second case where the ancestral founder connects himself directly with the biology-productive principle, going *behind* any transcendental organism to a site that is "prebiological." Only one ancestral founder ever attempted this: Abraham, "the greatest genius of the ancient world," as Goldberg describes him in his essay, "The Gods of the Greeks." Abraham recognizes the human as a universal being that transcends any animal form:

> The human can go beyond the animal. Is this not his most essential capacity? The general-human [*Allgemein-Menschliche*] is the idea of the totality of all the partial functions of life, of all the biological centers, that are merely the splinters of a whole. Could one not capitalize upon [*ausnutzen*] this whole—the idea of the human in itself—*without* ending up in a general humanity that is nothing else than the administrator of an unmetaphysical normality and of a new, even more terrible form of decadence, namely, technology? There was one [i.e., Abraham] who created a superior, anti-totemic ritual, one that is directed *against* the principle of descent lines. He thus became the only one to renounce human sacrifice and to replace it with animal sacrifice—the animals that were his folk group's totems.[79]

Abraham leaps beyond the partial animal-gods of all other folk groups. He does not merely differentiate out a new partial god from the mixture of gods associated with his race (the Semites) or his folk group, the Hebrews.

El Shaddai, as we have just learned, is the name in the Pentateuch associated with YHWH insofar as he creates discontinuities, including the discontinuity between prebiology and the transcendental organisms. Abraham's first relationship to the "prebiological" YHWH is through El Shaddai. But Abraham as an ancestral founder *could have been the point of differentiation* for another folk group branching off from the Hebrews had he not chosen to form a covenant with El Shaddai. Abraham, in other words, contains a pluripotent mixture of Semitic "partial" or totemic gods, and these must be separated off from his new descent line. Abraham's descent line divides between a lineage of a mixed Hebrew-Egyptian folk group (through Ishmael) and the lineage that will lead to Jacob-Israel. That latter lineage begins with a child, Isaac, whose birth breaks with the natural order: a child of the old age of both Abraham and Sarah. His name means "he will laugh" and signifies the "triumph of YHWH over the other gods," that is, the triumph of the "antibiological" God over the gods whose operation involves the use of sexuality and descent to "evolve" into their differentiated forms in their folk groups.[80] Abraham's relationship to El Shaddai is demonstrated in his willingness to sacrifice his biological descent line through Isaac and his sacrifice of an animal (a ram) in place of his son; it is demonstrated through his willingness to circumcise himself; it is demonstrated in the first place through the "unnatural" biological act of reproduction in old age: "All the antibiological acts of Abraham are supported by the late birth of Isaac."[81] Isaac himself cannot be the first of a new "antibiological" people because, in a word, he is not *adopted* but *conceived*.

Now in all the narratives concerned with Abraham's "antibiological acts" that Goldberg describes, it is not El Shaddai but YHWH who is named as the God with whom Abraham has dealings. This fact is not unknown to Goldberg. Goldberg, of course, does not distinguish El Shaddai and YHWH as two separate divinities. El Shaddai is only an aspect of YHWH, the aspect that is associated with discontinuity and rupture according to Goldberg's (admittedly fanciful) etymology of "Shaddai" from the verb *shadad*. The point is not to criticize Goldberg's lapses from the scholarly rigors of philology, but to understand the essential *antiracial* thrust of his exegeses. Goldberg's discussion of the relationship of YHWH to Abraham under the name El Shaddai is at the center of this important theme.

An "antibiological" folk group, one that breaks entirely with the principle of descent line inheritance of the metaphysical tie to its god, could never be the result of any continuous series of reproductive acts deriving from a single ancestral founder. But Isaac, at least, can be brought into relationship with El Shaddai. Furthermore, he occupies an important point in the separation of the lineage from the part-gods of the Hebrews. He has twins, and Esau will begin the process of separating out the "negative" side of the Hebrew gods, the side that seeks to retain its connection to the "natural" and "normal" order of biological inheritance. This is what Goldberg describes as the "night side" of the gods, their connection with the biologically *automatic*, rather than with what can be placed under volitional control.[82] The prophet Balaam seeks to use the night side that is intermixed with Israel (because it has not entirely separated out all the Hebrew part-gods from itself) when Balak asks him to curse Israel as they pass by his territory. YHWH turns his curses into a blessing through a form of "immune reaction" that turns the threat into a benefit. But this battle with Balaam is only one in an endless series of attacks that YHWH must suffer because of his necessary imbrication with a biological people. "He [YHWH] cannot permit his relationship with the negative side of Abraham to stand, but he must continually employ metaphysical means to undo the binding force of the [biological] causality that automatically works in Abraham; if that causality were ever to become entirely effective, it would be tantamount to God's constant submission to the compulsion of an alien natural lawfulness of another god."[83] The conflict between YHWH Elohim and the "night side" of the gods, the side most closely associated with the line of Esau-Balaam-Amalek, will only be consummated in the eschatological age. Until that time, "metaphysical means" must be found to counter the threat.

One of those metaphysical means that the Pentateuch describes is the act of blessing, *b'rachah*, passed from the father to the son, and it requires as its condition a prior act—the "cutting of the covenant," the *brit* or covenant of circumcision. The verb "cut" is used with the noun *brit* in all the contexts where covenants are made between two parties, but in the case of circumcision the verb takes on an additional significance. Goldberg explains that the word *brit* itself has a root meaning of *separation*:

> The transmission of El Shaddai (as distinct from the "making fruitful" of Ishmael) can only be successful on condition of the *brit*—a word that only secondarily carries the meaning of "covenant," but rather originally meant the "cutting off" or "breaking off" of a prior epoch or period of obligation and the beginning of a new one (hence the verb *karat* with *brit*, to "cut" a *brit*.) Applying this to the relationship between the folk group ancestor and YHWH, the *brit* should be understood to be the "cutting off" of the old biological connection to the other gods.[84]

Once the *brit* has "cut off" the son from the biological lineage of the other Semitic gods—transmitted to him in virtue of his participation in the Semitic race—the *b'rachah* (blessing) can then be given to him. The blessing, as Goldberg points out, is said to be the activity of a *nefesh* (as when Jacob tells Esau to bring him "savory meat" so that he might eat it and "that my soul [*nefesh*] may bless you before I die" Genesis 27:4). Now *nefesh*, although typically translated as "soul," is not some immaterial spiritual being, but refers "always and in every instance to the 'body,' not the body that can be divided into parts, which is called *basar*, but the indivisible bearer of the organic life functions that is maintained within the graspable-material body and in which the totality of the empirical organism is enclosed."[85] What the blessing transmits—indeed what the blessing *is*—is nothing less than what Gurwitsch and Weiss would call the *field energy* of the Hebrew folk group organism.

The *brit* and the *b'rachah* (covenant of circumcision and blessing) transmit from one folk group ancestor to another the *nefesh* that will ultimately become embodied within the folk group Israel. The embodiment of the *nefesh* at that point will still not be transmitted biologically. The preservation of the *nefesh* will require continuous performances at the cult center, a daily round of sacrifices. Abraham is the first to express his relationship with the anti-biological YHWH Elohim through sacrifice. Not only is he willing to circumcise himself (a form of sacrifice), not only is he willing to sacrifice his son, but Abraham also sacrifices *his earlier god*. The ram that Abraham sacrifices in place of his son, Goldberg says, is the Ur-ram, the transcendental organism that, according to tradition was "present since the first six days of creation" (Goldberg footnotes Rashi, the Tractate Avot, and the Mishna).

When the people of Israel offer God the blood and fat of the sacrificial animal, they are making it possible for the *nefesh* of YHWH Elohim to become materialized organically.[86] In contrast to the cults of the other metaphysical folk groups, that of YHWH Elohim has nothing to do with bringing the god into reality *in the very bodies of the people.* Other gods not only transmit their *shem* (morphogenetic field, entelechy) through sexual reproduction but also can be accessed directly through sexual activity itself. "Sexuality," as Goldberg explains, "is then no longer the means that makes it possible [for a folk group] to descend from god, but it also effects the *return* to the biological center."[87] YHWH Elohim rejects the entire "linking of sexuality with metaphysics" that characterizes many of the cults of the surrounding folk groups.

Since the blessing of El Shaddai can only be transmitted from individual to individual, during the "patriarchal" phase of ancient Israel there never was a possibility for YHWH Elohim to enter into the world and engage in the "transcendental political" task of doing battle with the other biological-sexual gods. The period of enslavement in Egypt makes it possible for the Hebrew folk group to move from separated individuals to one collective body. During the Hebrew people's time in Egypt, the division of YHWH's unity into a sheer multiplicity of person-units generates pressure on YHWH Elohim to reassemble himself into a single unified folk group. (It activates the totality function, so to speak). Had the person-units simply been dispersed into larger and larger spaces, there would have been no possibility of reassembly. This is why the descendants of Abraham were held in captivity in Egypt for four hundred years: "Their servitude [in Egypt] is the deliberate means taken by YHWH Elohim to compel the Hebrew folk group to discharge the metaphysical folk-group energies still remaining within it, an act that the folk group was able to accomplish only because of the high pressure [*Hochdruck*] under which it was placed. And this discharge act had as its goal that the folk group would cause a 'forced reaction' in God, the *innui* (in ancient Hebrew, to 'answer' or 'react') of God, so that *God himself is compelled into a reaction, into a manifestation.*"[88] The manifestation of YHWH Elohim that reassembles the divided person-units into a folk-group unity occurs on Mt. Sinai. Mt. Sinai is the founding act of Hebrew metaphysics, the revolutionary breakthrough that cuts the genealogical sequence of person-units initiated with Abraham and produces a new "organism" with no preexisting pattern in the transcendental realm of "preformation." This organism, this new folk group, is an "authentic beginning" (*echte Anfang*).[89] The act produces not only a "transversal structure" to unite the diverse person-units within the collectivity gathered at Mt. Sinai but also the two tablets on which the "ten commandments" are written.

The event of revelation at Mt. Sinai marks the transformation of a disarticulated collection of single individuals into a new structure, a new organism: "Since 'structure' and 'organism' are the same concept, from what has been said we can conclude the following: at Sinai there took place a spontaneous generation, an authentic beginning. A transversal structure [*Querstruktur*], the transcendental folk group-organism [*Volksorganism*] of the Hebrews was founded. This foundation was an act of simultaneity and suddenness involving an organizing explosion. The event at Sinai [das Ereignis am Sinai] was therefore an *eruptive* act of foundation [Gründungsakt]."[90]

The creation of the new folk group organism sets up a relationship of reciprocity between the "worldly" and the "preworldly" realms. The Hebrews (the name of whose eponymous ancestor, Eber, comes from a root that means "to cross over") now constitute the living passageway through which YHWH God can enter into relationship with humanity and complete its eschatological goal: the transcendence of all the limits imposed on humanity by biology (separation into races and folk groups, separation from the "regeneration source" of indestructible life). This passageway or bridge, whenever it is traveled on, ruptures the normal laws of causality that tie the "given" future to unbreakable chains to the past. Worldly fatalism is broken apart, and a new kind of future—one that is not predetermined but that is rather "produced" out of the "preworldly nothing"—becomes possible.[91] The principle of discontinuity, the principle that breaks in on every chain of events and inaugurates a new order, is at the heart of Hebrew metaphysics:

> The principle of discontinuity that was previously described as the goal and characteristic feature of Hebrew metaphysics has two sides which need to be emphasized: seen from one side, it is manifested as the sudden production of an authentic beginning, a new sequence that is qualitatively different from all prior sequential structures, a spontaneous generation and an act of foundation; seen from another side, it marks the possibility of making an abrupt cutting away of old sequences. In this way Hebrew metaphysics' principle of discontinuity, properly understood and given practical application, stands in opposition to every sort of fatalism and waiting for a redemption that is merely the termination of a certain sequence in so far as the application of the authentic principle of discontinuity signifies the interruptibility [*Durchbrechbarkeit*] of everything that happens with lockstep necessity. The opposition of Hebrew metaphysics to every other form of metaphysics can be articulated in relation to the problem of the future. There are two kinds of future: one that is "given" and fixed, the category of future found in "world-continuums" that are part of the finite reality; and another that is not fixed but is rather produced, the category of future that is found in Hebrew metaphysics.[92]

Goldberg goes on to explain that the metaphysics in which the future is only "given" underlies the predictive art of astrology practiced by the ancient Magi. In contrast, Israelite prophets "operated with the infinite reality and its principle of possibility in order to interrupt and transform the fixed form of the future."

Goldberg's notion of the discontinuity principle at the heart of Hebrew metaphysics is quite similar to what Alain Badiou calls "eventual trans-being" or "ultra-One."[93] Badiou, as I explained in chapter 3, note 22, has devoted much of his work to drawing out the implications of Georg Cantor's theory of infinite manifolds for philosophy. He has argued that Cantor showed that there is an essential "inconsistency" in mathematics, namely, the fact that all the possible sets of numbers cannot themselves be enumerated (matched in a one-to-one correspondence with any sequence of numbers). There is always an excess, a non-denumerable set, that *stands beyond the infinite sequence of numbers and inaugurates a new sequence of numbers.* Cantor, as I already explained, calls this the transfinite number $\omega$ and designates its cardinality as "aleph-null." I would argue on the basis of the passage I just quoted and also from the mathematics lying behind his description of El Shaddai that Goldberg takes his discontinuity principle from the mathematics of infinite sets. We saw in chapter 2 how important mathematics is for him. In this passage he speaks about breaks in the sequences and the production of qualitatively new sequences in much the way that mathematicians like Georg Cantor and Richard Dedekind describe the way that one infinite number sequence can be said to terminate and another one begin after a break in the apparent continuity of the series. These are the same mathematical ideas that inspire Badiou's notion of an "event" that ruptures any totalizing unity within Being. Badiou explains that "the event is of the order of trans-being: at once held within the principle of being (an event, like everything that is, is a multiple [i.e., a 'set' or 'manifold']) and in rupture with this principle (the event does not fall under the law of the count of the situation, so that, not being counted, it does not consist)."[94] Badiou rejects Cantor's appeal to an Absolute Infinite in God as a metaphysical capitulation to the principle of the One. We have seen, however, that Cantor's theological conception of the Absolute Infinite lies behind Goldberg's distinction between YHWH Echad and YHWH Elohim. But despite the presence of a notion of a divine Uniqueness (YHWH Echad) in Goldberg, the fundamental role it plays in Hebrew metaphysics is exactly what Badiou wants to capture by his "ultra-One." Goldberg's YHWH Echad (YHWH One or YHWH Unique) and Badiou's "ultra-One" serve to ground a "discontinuity principle" that can inaugurate an entirely new future, an entire new "event." Badiou describes the human collectivity that is created in response to the event as a "militant subject," a group (Badiou calls it a "body") connected by its "fidelity" to the event. It is precisely this *political* breakthrough of a new (communal) form of subjectivity in fidelity to its "grounding" event that Goldberg seeks to achieve. For Goldberg, such fidelity is what the Jewish people are called to display every Sabbath and every Yom Kippur when the revelatory event of Mt. Sinai is renewed. "Yom Kippur is an institution for the systematic incitement [*systematische Herbeiführung*] of a 'new revelation,' that is, the repetition of the moment of foundation [at Mt. Sinai]."[95] The sounding of the shofar (ram's horn) on Yom Kippur is done in imitation of the shofar sound heard by the folk group during the revelation at Mt. Sinai (Exodus 19:16). "When the spontaneous sounds heard at Mt. Sinai are imitated by the shofar, God is 'reminded,' that is, the [whole] transcendental organism is induced to become predisposed towards a *new* act of foundation."[96] Goldberg is aware that in his own day the rituals of Sabbath observance and Yom Kippur have lost their power of awakening or reminding God of the need for a new revelation, a new Mt. Sinai event. But he is convinced that there are enough folk groups left on earth with the metaphysical power necessary to call on YHWH Elohim and draw him down into this world once again, just as the ancient Hebrews had done during their enslavement to the Pharaoh in Egypt. In chapter 5 I discuss in more detail Goldberg's plan for a *new revelation*. But I want now to conclude this chapter with a few anticipatory remarks on this subject.

The hope of inducing God to renew his revelatory breakthrough into the empirical realm inspires Goldberg to write *The Reality of the Hebrews*. It is the manual for the renewal of the revolutionary power of Hebrew metaphysics. The Pentateuch, if it is properly understood, can give direction to the "production of the future" (*Zukunftsherstellung*). The fundamental question that the Pentateuch answers is, "How does one escape from the *limitation* of biological lawfulness, the limitation of biological energy sources that is inherent in the very system of finite reality?" This question, Goldberg continues, reduces to this: "How does one go from the 'rationing out' [*Kontingentierung*] of life to its unlimited capacity for being increased [*unbegrentze Steigerungsfähigkeit*]?"[97] This is the task that, according to the Pentateuch, does not fall on any individual to achieve, but is, rather, "the transcendental politics of a folk group." This folk group is the one founded with the revelation at Mt. Sinai.

In concluding this chapter's discussion of *The Reality of the Hebrews* I return to the theme of YHWH as the metaphysical enemy of the fixation of the state. Put differently, Hebraism is the metaphysical geopolitics that alone has the power to stand up to the technological geopolitics of the state. Let me put in the clearest possible terms the nature of the urgency impelling Goldberg to counter the ideology of the state. The organicist conception of the state was fundamental to Hitler's Darwinian understanding of the *völkisch* state as the instrument of the *Lebenskampf,* whose goal is the evolution of a master race—the Aryan race—on the earth. But where Hitler argues that the state can and should be the instrument of the racial evolution of a folk group with a racially pure and healthy "capacity for procreation" (*Zeugungsfähigkeit*), Goldberg would counter that the state is always a sign that a folk group has become "fixated" and has lost its authentic "capacity for metaphysics."[98] When a folk group becomes a *völkish* state it demonstrates that it has lost its transcendental "world-historic" significance. Goldberg's *Reality of the Hebrews* was published in 1925, and the second volume of Hitler's *Mein Kampf* was published one year later. Both, in quite opposite ways, seek to bring about the evolution of humanity to fully embody the "image of God," what Goldberg calls the "Urmensch" and "Adam Kadmon," and what Hitler calls the "Ebenbild des Herrn," the "image of the *Master*."[99] For Goldberg, the Urmensch reflects a "prebiological" reality incommensurate with sexual reproduction and "blood"; for Hitler, the image of the Master is the bio-state whose "most holy duty is to take every care that its blood remains pure."[100] In an unpublished manuscript in Goldberg's Nachlass (Manfred Voigts brought it to my attention) that dates to some time after 1926 (probably around 1933, when an essay that is close in tone and content was published), Goldberg writes:

> After the construction of the world it might have been possible that among the Germans at the time that the Wotan cult was flourishing a prophet would have arisen who would have said: "I see the future. We cannot worship Wotan forever. We are heading towards our decline. We are going to be cut off from our god in the course of time and we will not be able to renew ourselves any more. We want to *remain* a metaphysical folk group, but we want to universalize ourselves. We want to form a covenant with the preworldy God and help him enter into the world!" If such a prophet had arisen among the Germans, it could have been that today we had the true German bible and that the Germans were "the people of God." (Translation mine.)

Goldberg goes on to say that "among the Germans no such prophet arose, but one did arise among the Jews" (he means Abraham). Goldberg is not claiming Jewish racial superiority, but rather that the Jews *rejected racial gods for the one universal God in order to remain a metaphysical folk group*. Abraham's revolution failed, as I have said: this failure was the "greatest fiasco in world history." It is not on behalf of the Jews that Goldberg writes *The Reality of the Hebrews*, but humanity—and God. He wants to be the prophet in his generation who calls for a renewal of Hebrew metaphysics. Gershom Scholem, as I explain in chapter 5, considers Goldberg's claims on behalf of Hebrew metaphysics to be the signal example of the "hybris of the Jews" of his generation. If Goldberg is calling for the Jewish people to act in fidelity to the revolutionary breakthrough marked by the revelation at Mt. Sinai, Gershom Scholem seeks above all else to master the revolutionary potential of a breakthrough event and to bind it once again within the continuity of an unbroken tradition. Chapter 5 is devoted to explicating Scholem's lifelong antagonism to Oskar Goldberg. It also offers a close reading of Goldberg's revolutionary philosophy of Jewish history in his 1935 book *Maimonides: Critique of Jewish Religious Doctrine.*

## Notes

1. Benjamin D. Sommer, *The Bodies of God and the World of Ancient Israel* (Cambridge: Cambridge University Press, 2009), 98.
2. Goldberg, *Reality of the Hebrews*, 2.
3. Ibid., 3.

4. Ibid., 7.

5. Ibid., 4.

6. Jakob von Uexküll, *Theoretische Biologie* (Berlin: Gebrüder Paetel, 1920), 8–9.

7. Immanuel Kant, *Gedanken von der wahren Schätzung der lebendigen Kräfte und Beurteilung der Beweise derer sich Herr von Leibniz und andere Mechaniker in dieser Streitsache bedienet haben, nebst einigen vorhergehenden Betrachtungen welche die Kraft der Körper überhaupt betreffen* (Königsberg: Martin Eberhard Dorn, 1746), republished in *Immanuel Kants Gesammelte Werke [Akademie-Ausgabe]*, 23 vols. (Berlin: Walter de Gruyter, 1900–2006), 1:3–181; Kant, "Thoughts on the True Estimation of Living Forces" (1746–1749), trans. Jeffrey B. Edwards and Martin Schönfeld, in *Immanuel Kant: Natural Science*, ed. Eric Watkins, trans. Lewis White Beck, Jeffrey B. Edwards, Olaf Reinhardt, Martin Schönfeld, and Eric Watkins (Cambridge: Cambridge University Press, 2012), 1–155; Kant, *Allgemeine Naturgeschichte und Theorie des Himmels, oder Versuch von der Verfassung und dem mechanischen Ursprunge des ganzen Weltgebäudes, nach Newtonischen Grundsätzen abgehandelt* (Königsberg: Johann Friederich Petersen, 1755), in *Akademie-Ausgabe* 1:217–368; Kant, "Universal Natural History and Theory of the Heavens or Essay on the Constitution and the Mechanical Origin of the Whole Universe According to Newtonian Principles" (1755), trans. Olaf Reinhardt, in Watkins, *Immanuel Kant*, 182–308.

8. I wish to thank the anonymous reviewer for pointing out that Johann Gottfried Herder, a student of Kant's in the early 1760s, remained convinced that these and other early works deserved serious study and were unfairly overshadowed by Kant's later critical works.

9. For example, *Literarisches Centralblatt für Deutschland* (1903), 1204–1205; Ernst von Aster, "Die neue Kant-Ausgabe und ihr erster Band," in *Zu Kants Gedächtnis: Zwölf Festgaben zu seinem 100jährigen Todestage*, ed. H. Vaihinger and B. Bauch (Berlin: Verlag von Reuter und Richard, 1904), 321–341.

10. Two of the best examples of this new attempt to bring Kant into connection with Naturphilosophie are articles published in 1904 as part of the celebrations in the jubilee year of Kant's death (1804): Wilhelm Windelband, "Nach hundert Jahren," 5–20, and F. Heman, "Immanuel Kants philosphisches Vermächtnis," both in Vaihinger and Bauch, *Zu Kants Gedächtnis*, 155–195. Both essays make reference to the new edition of Kant's pre-Critical writings.

11. Kant, "Thoughts on the True Estimation of Living Forces," 22.

12. Ibid., 25.

13. One ought also to mention Edgar Dacqué (1878–1945), professor of paleontology at the University of Munich. He was removed from his teaching position in 1925 after he published in the prior year his speculative magnum opus, *Urwelt, Sage, und Menschheit: Eine naturhistorisch-metaphysische Studie* (*The Archaic World, Saga, and Humanity: A Natural-historical-metaphysical Study*) (Munich: R. Oldenbourg, 1924). Much like Goldberg with his theory of transcendental organisms, Dacqué claimed that all species reflect a certain number of "ideal types": "but the species in its deepest sense—identical with an 'ideal type'—is not an aggregate but rather the outward expression of an inwardly determined principle for the construction of a particular living form, a potency and not a mere conceptual abstraction" (291). Dacqué developed a rather imaginative picture of evolution. He thought that the dinosaurs represented a phase in the slow emergence of the human ideal type. Mammals developed as humanity sloughed off its reptilian stage. Thomas Mann refers to Dacqué's strange theory of evolution in the "Descent into Hell" section that begins the series of novels that are collectively known as *Joseph and His Brothers*. Thomas Mann (or, rather, the narrator of the novels) puts Dacqué's thesis this way (without mentioning its source): "man *qua* animal is the oldest animal and already during the later stages of prehistoric life, prior to any cerebral development, lived his life

on earth clothed in various zoological fashions, including amphibian and reptilian." Thomas Mann, *Joseph and His Brothers*, trans. John E. Woods (New York: Alfred A. Knopf, 2005), 19. The first volume of the novel, *Die Geschichten Jakobs*, in which this section is found, was first published in 1933, nearly ten years after Dacqué's *Urwelt, Sage, und Menschheit*. Dacqué was widely read, and Mann certainly was familiar with his work as well as with Goldberg's. I will discuss Mann's relationship to Goldberg in Appendix I. For the moment, I only want to suggest that Goldberg's notion of transcendental organisms was only one of a number of such theories in circulation at the time. Nor was his version the most fanciful.

14.  Goldberg, *Reality of the Hebrews*, 6; emphasis Goldberg's. Goldberg later clarifies this rather obscure statement, saying that the "contradiction" between "teleology" and "causality" is "actualized" in the "indivisible unity" of the living organism that manifests its own purposive "natural lawfulness" beyond mechanical cause-effect relations (137).

15.  Ibid., 76.

16.  Ibid., 75.

17.  Nachman Krochmal (1785–1840), *More Nebukhei ha'Zman* [Guide for the perplexed of the time] (Lemberg: Joseph Schnayder, 1851) [Hebrew, available at http://books.google.com /books?id=GtUFcSlkpKUC&pg=RA4-PT35&dq=inauthor:nachman+inauthor:krochmal#v =onepage&q&f=false]. German translation: Nachman Krochmal, *Führer der Verwirrten der Zeit*, trans. Andreas Lehhardt, 2 vols. (Hamburg: Felix Meiner, 2012).

18.  Krochmal, *More Nebukhei ha'Zman*, 323–324; in the German translation, 777–778.

19.  Goldberg, *Reality of the Hebrews*, 198.

20.  Ibid., 201. Goldberg's notion that a god (or YHWH Elohim) is given a *collective organic body* through the cult practices of a folk group can be traced to William Robertson Smith's *Lectures on the Religions of the Semites* (1889). Smith's book had been translated into German as early as 1899. (I thank Manfred Voigts for drawing my attention to the German reception of Smith.) Having argued that early Semitic sacrifice was always an act of commensality among kin, and that the animal offering was considered a clan totem, Smith describes god, humans, and animal as sharing one sacred life:

> Indeed, in a religion based on kinship, where the god and his worshippers are of one stock, the principle of sanctity and that of kinship are identical. The sanctity of the kinsman's life and the sanctity of the godhead are not two things, but one; for ultimately the only thing that is sacred *is the common tribal life*, or the common blood which is identified with the life. Whatever being partakes in this life is holy, and its holiness may be described indifferently, either as participation in the divine life and nature, or as participation in the kindred blood. (William Robertson Smith, *Lectures on the Religions of the Semites: First Series, the Fundamental Institutions* [New York: D. Appleton and Company, 1889], 271.)

Goldberg will infuse this anthropological conception with a metaphysical significance, attributing to sacrifice the power to create a metaphysical bridge between the transcendental organism and the empirical world.

21.  Goldberg, *Reality of the Hebrews*, 273–274; emphasis Goldberg's.

22.  Ibid., 89; emphasis Goldberg's.

23.  The essay is included in Goldberg-*Aufsätze*, 227–248; the phrase is found on p. 230. I believe it would be productive to place Goldberg's concept of the war between Israel's "choice-God and goal-God" representing the wholeness of the future and final human world system (*Weltsystem*) of YHWH Elohim and the other gods who seek to "colonize" the earth in relation to Martin Heidegger's discussions of the "strife between world and earth" in

*Contributions to Philosophy (of the Event)*, trans. Richard Rojcewicz and Daniela Vallega-Neu (Bloomington: Indiana University Press, 2012). Heidegger contrasts the "entirety of worlding (world)" and the "self-seclusion in the face of every projection (earth)," each of these two being "basic forms" of how Da-sein "measures up to beyng." Each of the two basic forms have different ways of articulating "the sensuous and non-sensuous," that is, "'body,' 'soul,' and 'spirit.'" Both basic forms of Da-sein (i.e., basic forms of human psychophysiology) appear "in strife, toward the en-counter of gods and humans" (Heidegger, *Contributions to Philosophy*, 379, 381). Whether or not Heidegger was familiar with Goldberg's *Reality of the Hebrews*, he, like Goldberg, was attempting to work out a metaphysical "geopolitics" that opposed the biologization of the realm of politics as sheer *Kampf ums Dasein* (struggle for existence) among racially distinct peoples. I hope to provide a fuller comparison of Goldberg and Heidegger in a future work.

24. Goldberg, *Reality of the Hebrews*, 15.

25. Ibid., 61.

26. Oskar Goldberg, "The Problem of God's Non-Ominipotence and Amalek," in Goldberg-*Aufsätze*, 339.

27. Goldberg, *Reality of the Hebrews*, 33.

28. Ibid., 70; emphasis Goldberg's.

29. Ibid., 36.

30. Ibid., 39.

31. Paul Weiss, *Principles of Development: A Text in Experimental Embryology* (Chicago: University of Chicago Press, 1939), 459; emphasis Weiss's.

32. Goldberg, *Reality of the Hebrews*, 73–74; emphasis Goldberg's.

33. Ibid., 39. The story of how the "sons of God" had intercourse with the "daughters of men" is told in Genesis 6:1.

34. Ibid., 44. Compared with Dacqué's theory that mammalian animal forms emerge from reptilian-like proto-humans, Goldberg's theory of transcendental organisms directly shaping empirical reality in the pre-Noah era seems rather tame.

35. For a discussion of the "gods of the nations," see Krochmal, *More Neboche ha'Zman*, 37–39; in the German translation, 100–102. For a general discussion of Krochmal, see Jay M. Harris, *Nachman Krochmal: Guiding the Perplexed of the Modern Age* (New York: New York University Press, 1993).

36. Krochmal, *More Neboche ha'Zman*, 37–38. English translation is mine, based on the Hebrew original and adapted from the German translation.

37. Ibid., 37.

38. Goldberg, *Reality of the Hebrews*, 37.

39. Ibid., 24.

40. Von Uexküll, *Theoretische Biologie*, 118.

41. Goldberg, *Reality of the Hebrews*, 24; emphasis Goldberg's.

42. Ibid., 285.

43. Oskar Goldberg, "Die Götter der Griechen" [The Gods of the Greeks], *Mass und Wert* 1, no. 2 (1937): 163–191; emphasis Goldberg's. Republished in Goldberg-*Aufsätze*, 227–247. Quotation is from pages 230–231 in the Goldberg-*Aufsätze* version.

44. Ibid., 234.

45. The essay in which the word "geopolitics" was first used was published in Rudolf Kjellén, *Inledning till Sveriges geografi* (Göteborg: Wettergren & Kerber, 1900).

46. For one of the best overviews of Haushofer's ideas, see Dan Diner, "'Grundbuch des Planeten': Zur Geopolitik Karl Haushofers," *Vierteljahrshefte für Zeitgeschichte* 1, no. 32 (1984): 1–28.

47. His magnum opus: Karl Haushofer, *Geopolitik des Pazifischen Ozeans* (Berlin: K. Vowinckel, 1924). In his CV, Goldberg says that he taught courses in medical anthropology in Munich after the war.

48. Goldberg, *Reality of the Hebrews*, 31, 171.

49. Ibid., 72.

50. Goldberg, "Die Götter der Griechen," 237.

51. Ibid., 237.

52. Ibid.

53. Goldberg, *Reality of the Hebrews*, 47.

54. Ibid.

55. Ibid., 46.

56. Goldberg, "Die Götter der Griechen," 237.

57. Oskar Goldberg, "Rasse und Ethik," unpublished manuscript (in the Deutsches Literaturarchiv Marbach Goldberg Nachlass, shared with me by Manfred Voigts).

58. Goldberg, "Die Götter der Griechen," 228; emphasis Goldberg's.

59. Ladislaus Szymonowicz, *Lehrbuch der Histologie und der microskopischen Anatomie* (Würzburg: A. Stuber, 1901), 385.

60. Goldberg, *Reality of the Hebrews*, 44–45.

61. Ibid., 141.

62. Ibid., 57; emphasis Goldberg's.

63. Goldberg, "Die griechische Tragödie," in Goldberg-*Aufsätze*, 268–285; quotation on p. 285.

64. Goldberg, *Reality of the Hebrews*, 50–51.

65. Ibid., 51.

66. Ibid., 53; emphasis Goldberg's.

67. Ibid., 57. Goldberg's discussion of the technological nature of the nation-state and its relationship to the loss of the ancient peoples' metaphysical connection to their gods may have influenced Martin Heidegger's very similar reflections about the need to overcome the loss of the gods and the world (what Goldberg called a *shem*) in the early 1930s. Heidegger refers only to Hölderlin as the source of his concept of history as the "venturing of the gods," and he gives no source for his concept of "world" and "worlding" as the establishment of a new, nontechnological relationship between a people and its god(s), but all this resonates closely with Goldberg's reflections on the interconnection of god, world, and people in *The Reality of the Hebrews*. It may not be merely coincidence that Heidegger emphasizes that "the gods indeed only those of a people: no general god for everyone, i.e., for no one" and that Goldberg insists on exactly this point, offering a similar description of the development of theology from the "immanent, effectively powerful god of the nation, the 'national god' representing a metaphysical folk-power" to the "barren, abstract, and general-human 'dearly beloved god'" of "world religion" (*Reality of the Hebrews*, 49). Martin Heidegger, *Ponderings II–VI: Black Notebooks 1931–1938*, trans. Richard Rojcewicz (Bloomington: Indiana University Press, 2016), 157. I mentioned in the introduction that Carl Schmitt was an avid reader of Goldberg. Schmitt very likely met Goldberg during one or more of the sessions of the Philosophische Gruppe in Erich Unger's home at which Schmitt was known to have been an attendee. Given the widespread interest in Goldberg's *Reality of the Hebrews*—evidenced, for example, in Thomas Mann's close reading of the work, which I discuss in Appendix I—it would not be at all improbable that Heidegger had read Goldberg's book. (I want to thank Mårten Björk for drawing my attention to Heidegger's discussion of "venturing the gods" in the Black Notebooks in a soon-to-be published manuscript he shared with me that contrasts Heidegger with Hans Driesch: "The Irritability of Being: Martin Heidegger, Hans

Driesch, and the Future of Theology," in *Heidegger's Black Notebooks and the Future of Theology*, ed. M. Björk and J. Svenungsson [New York: Palgrave Macmillan, 2018].)

68. Ibid., 44.

69. Ibid., 45.

70. The folder in which it is contained is titled "Einzelne Blätter zur Wirklichkeit der Hebräer" and is found in Kasten (box) 5.

71. I am not, of course, claiming that those mediums who were only interested in demonstrating their spiritual powers to paranormal researchers were not in fact frauds (I believe they were), only that their motives were not quite so "murky" as the mediums whose only motive was to make money from those who wished to communicate with loved ones "from the beyond." Goldberg, however, did believe that paranormal phenomena like the production of ectoplasm were authentic, as I will discuss more in the conclusion.

72. Goldberg, *Reality of the Hebrews*, 89–90.

73. In fact, the animals that the people are told to sacrifice represent the *former* totemic animals of the Hebrews before Abraham entered into a covenant with YHWH. The sacrificial rituals are intended to purify the people of the remnants of their biological inheritance as Hebrews.

74. Goldberg, *Reality of the Hebrews*, 88; emphasis Goldberg's.

75. Ibid., 77.

76. See chapter 2's discussion of Georg Cantor for details.

77. Goldberg, *Reality of the Hebrews*, 77.

78. Ibid., 78; emphasis Goldberg's.

79. Goldberg, "Die Götter der Griechen," 237.

80. Goldberg, *Reality of the Hebrews*, 80.

81. Ibid., 79.

82. Ibid., 229. The "night side" of God is not Goldberg's invention but is rather a Kabbalistic idea that appears frequently in Franz Joseph Molitor's exposition of the Kabbalah in precisely the sense that Goldberg ascribes to it (see Appendix II for a discussion of Goldberg's debt to Molitor). The phrase "night side" seems not to be found precisely in the Kabbalah, but is Molitor's suggested rendering of the term "back side" (*achor*) (connected with darkness, to be sure). Molitor also offers a more literal translation of *achor* as "back side" (*Hinterseite*), but he prefers "night side." The term "night side" (*Nachtseite*) comes from one of the most influential works of Romantic Naturphilosophie, one that Goldberg is almost certain to have known—Gotthilf Heinrich Schubert's *Ansichten von der Nachtseite der Naturwissenschaft*, a work I mentioned in a note connected to my discussion of Unger's "Nachts" (see chapter 3, note 2). The term "night side" ultimately comes from astronomy and refers to the side of a planet or moon turned away from the sun. Schubert himself was indebted to the Christian Kabbalistic tradition. On Schubert's debt to the Kabbalah, see Volker Roelcke, "Jewish Mysticism in Romantic Medicine? Indirect Incorporation of Kabbalistic Elements in the Work of Gotthilf Heinrich Schubert," *History and Philosophy of the Life Sciences* 16 (1994): 117–140. I return to the theme of the "night side" in the conclusion.

83. Goldberg, *Reality of the Hebrews*, 237.

84. Ibid., 81.

85. Ibid. Goldberg's claim that *nefesh* refers to the whole organism as the bearer in each part of an indivisible life principle is somewhat controversial, but it is exactly what Molitor says about the meaning of the term in the Kabbalah (see Appendix II). However, for an argument that this is in fact the meaning of the term in the Hebrew Bible, see Julien Harvey, "Is Biblical Man Still Alive?," *Biblical Theology Bulletin: A Journal of Bible and Theology* 3 (1973): 167–193.

More recently, Robert Alter has written about the difficulty of translating *nefesh*: "The primary meaning of nefesh is 'life-breath' (rather like Homeric psyche). By extension it is a term for 'life'; by metonymy it refers to the throat, the passageway for the lifebreath (the Psalmist says, quite concretely, 'the waters have come up to the throat,' not the soul). Perhaps the trickiest extension of this very common term is its use as an intensive form of the personal pronoun. There is no equivalent in English, and in some contexts I have represented it as 'very self,' but that does not always work." Robert Alter, "Translating from the Ancient: The Hebrew Bible," *Literary Imagination* 5, no. 2 (2003): 172–178; quotation on p. 177.

86. Goldberg, *Reality of the Hebrews*, 161.

87. Ibid., 130.

88. Ibid., 286; emphasis Goldberg's.

89. Ibid., 285.

90. Ibid., 288; emphasis Goldberg's.

91. Ibid., 292.

92. Ibid., 291–292.

93. See, for example, Alain Badiou, *Number and Numbers*, trans. Robin Mackay (Cambridge: Polity Press, 2008), 214.

94. Ibid., 214.

95. Goldberg, *Reality of the Hebrews*, 299.

96. Ibid., 300.

97. Ibid., 275; emphasis Goldberg's.

98. Adolf Hitler, *Mein Kampf* (Munich: Zentralverlag der N.S.D.A.P, 1936), 448.

99. Ibid., 445.

100. Ibid., 444.

# 5 Gershom Scholem, Oskar Goldberg, and the Meaning of Jewish History

I N THIS CHAPTER I discuss two diametrically opposed philosophies of Jewish history, those of Gershom Scholem and Oskar Goldberg. Let me first state the points on which both men agree. Both Scholem and Goldberg place Jewish history within the framework of the dialectical tension between revelation and tradition. Scholem writes, "The concepts of revelation and tradition constitute two poles around which Judaism has grouped itself for two millennia."[1] He explains that revelation refers to the "Written Torah," the Pentateuch most especially, and tradition refers to the "Oral Torah," the Written Torah's ongoing interpretation "dealing with the possibility of application and execution of the revelation in historical time."[2] Goldberg also understands revelation and tradition to be the twin poles of Jewish history: revelation is contained in the Pentateuch, and tradition is responsible for both preserving this revealed text and for explicating the meaning of its ritual laws. "The oral tradition exists solely for the purpose of transmitting the material and the key for the explication of ritual," the laws governing the life of Israel as they are laid out in the Pentateuch.[3] Scholem and Goldberg further agree that revelation points toward the time of redemption, the messianic era. Both men view tradition as offering the Jewish people a way to exist in the in-between temporality stretched out between revelation and redemption. Tradition connects the Jewish people to revelation in the past and also to a hoped-for redemption in the future. On all this Goldberg and Scholem agree.

The difference between Scholem and Goldberg has to do with how they judge tradition. For Scholem, tradition is not only the temporal unfolding of divine revelation but also the necessary *deferral* of redemption. Tradition protects the Jewish people from the temptation to "storm the Kingdom," to press God to manifest himself in all his redemptive majesty. Redemption must be deferred rather than hastened because, Scholem writes, "every attempt to realize it tears open the abysses which lead each of its manifestations *ad absurdum*."[4] For Goldberg, however, tradition's only value is to prepare for a new breakthrough of divine revelation in the world. Only a new revelation can redirect Jewish history (and all history) toward redemption. A tradition that only defers redemption has betrayed the meaning of revelation. Tradition must ultimately be put aside so that the link between revelation and redemption can be reestablished. Revelation must once again become a "creation within creation." A renewal of revelation is not "the end of the world, but a *renewal of the world*."[5] Redemption must not be deferred: the world must be transformed so the consummation of God's redemptive plan can be achieved.

It would be hard to find two more opposed philosophies of Jewish history. Scholem believed that Goldberg's position was dangerous, that it sought to "tear open the abysses" and release the demonic forces that, throughout the millennia, had been kept at bay by tradition. From the 1920s until the end of his life, Scholem never tired of attacking Goldberg when the opportunity presented itself. His attacks were often of an ad hominem nature. He sometimes ridiculed Goldberg as a *Hochstapler* (confidence man) who peddled in cheap magic tricks. At other times, Scholem would speak of Goldberg as nothing short of "Satanic." Goldberg for his part never directly confronted Scholem or Scholem's philosophy of Judaism. Rather than attack Scholem head on, Goldberg attacked what he believed Scholem represented: the "scientific objectivity" that refused to take revelation seriously in its power to reconnect humanity to redemption. One can therefore read Goldberg's 1935 work *Maimonides* as an assault on Scholem concealed within an attack on the rationalism and moralizing dogmatism of the medieval philosopher after whom Goldberg named his book. Although Erich Unger did write a lengthy defense of Goldberg against Scholem's earliest and most detailed critical attack, Goldberg himself never mentioned Scholem by name.[6]

This chapter falls into two parts. In the first, I trace the history of Scholem's critical stance toward Goldberg. In the second, I discuss Goldberg's philosophy of Jewish history in *Maimonides*, published in 1935 as part of the commemoration of the eight hundredth anniversary of Maimonides's birth. The conflict between Scholem and Goldberg brings to the fore the fundamental problem confronting the German-Jewish world in which both Scholem and Goldberg grew up: the sclerosis of tradition, that is, its failure to draw revelation into a meaningful relation to history. Both Scholem and Goldberg concluded that "life lived in deferment" was no longer an option for the Jewish people. Scholem opted for an entrance into history through the concrete tasks of building a Jewish homeland in Palestine; Goldberg advocated for the creation of new *prophets* and new *Messiahs* who would not reconnect a past revelation to history, but who would rather reconnect history to a new revelation.[7]

## Scholem contra Goldberg

In March 1928, Gershom Scholem (1897–1982) published the essay "On the Theology of Sabbatianism in Light of Abraham Cardoso" in which he linked Oskar Goldberg to the heretical seventeenth-century Jewish messianic movement known as Sabbatianism.[8] Later that same year, Scholem composed a five-page typed letter denouncing both the scholarship and the morality of Goldberg's *Reality of the Hebrews*.[9] He circulated the letter to Franz Rosenzweig, Leo Strauss, and Walter Benjamin and asked that they share it as widely as possible. Near the end of his life, in 1977, Scholem described his relationship with Goldberg in a letter to the historian Lionel Kochan (1922–2005). Scholem issued a rather scathing judgment of Goldberg's character, but he also revealed how significant was the place that Goldberg occupied in his own intellectual development: "I have assembled a great mass of information about the man and his career (consisting mostly of lies, some of them rather remarkable). Maybe I shall write some day a longer piece on this phenomenon. A diabolic Hochstapler [confidence man] with some luciferian sparks of genius joined to insanity. For me it represents the exact counterpoint to what I was doing in taking up the study of Kabbalism. You may call it a kind of negative fascination."[10]

It is clear from the letter to Lionel Kochan that Scholem's "negative fascination" with Oskar Goldberg was colored by intense personal feelings. It is not too much of an exaggeration to say that Scholem's lifelong antipathy to Goldberg indicates that Scholem saw himself as defending a Jewish identity that was the opposite of Goldberg's. I therefore want to remove Scholem's critique of Goldberg from the realm of personal animus—which is certainly at play—and place it in the context of the "Jewish Question" in German-Jewish life in the 1920s. Scholem's opposition to Goldberg was not merely personal, but responded to Goldberg's call for a revolutionary transformation in Jewish existence, a call articulated in *The Reality of the Hebrews*. Goldberg's revolutionary call to renew the Jewish people's metaphysical connection to YHWH Elohim stood in direct opposition to the decidedly non-mystical Zionist agenda embraced by Scholem. The "Goldberg sect," as Scholem called the group around Goldberg, wanted nothing to do with "normalizing" Jewish existence through the creation of a Jewish nation-state. Rather, they desired nothing less than a metaphysical transformation of the conditions of life itself. Scholem himself did not embrace Jewish statehood until after the outbreak of the Second World War, but he certainly believed in the real (and not metaphysical) construction of a Jewish homeland in Palestine. Despite Scholem's own early preference for a somewhat undefined "anarchic" revival of Jewish life in Palestine, he unqualifiedly rejected Goldberg's metaphysical "*a priori* Zionism," the phrase that Erich Unger, Goldberg's most important disciple, coined to describe the "stateless" world-historical, metaphysical task of the Jewish people.

The appeal for certain young German Jews of Goldberg's "*a priori* Zionism" (which I explain in detail later) reflected the profound upheaval caused by the First World War not only in German-Jewish life but also in European life more generally. In response to the trauma of the war and the ensuing revolutionary struggles in Russia and Germany (preceding the political stabilization marked by the establishment of the Weimar Republic), many young Jews wrestled with the most fundamental questions about the future of the nation-state and the role of the Jewish people in creating a post-state universal political order. The question of the future of the state was seen within the context of the emerging critique of technological rationality and positivist reductionism. The question was posed in the following terms: Is the state a spiritless machine, or is it a vital, organic expression of the human spirit? Goldberg, as we saw in chapter 4, had no doubt that the state is a technologically constructed machine without any connection to the vital forces of an authentic "metaphysical folk group." For this reason, the state cannot be part of the future of a metaphysically revitalized Jewish people. As someone with anarchistic leanings, Scholem was sympathetic with such criticisms of the state, but he would not let his antipathy for the state stand in the way of his commitment to rebuilding a Jewish homeland in Palestine. Scholem viewed Goldberg's "*a priori* Zionism" as, at best, magical thinking.

But Scholem went further than dismissing Goldberg's anti-statist conception of a metaphysical people as magic. He equated it with the most insidious danger that has confronted the Jewish people in different forms throughout their entire history: the effort to hasten the coming of the Kingdom through an embrace of antinomian irrationalism. Scholem might even have fought against Goldberg's "magical" version of a new Jewish homeland precisely because he saw in it the perverse extreme of some of his own views about the incompatibility of the nation-state with Jewish peoplehood. But, as I noted, Scholem abandoned his youthful anarchism for a tempered compromise with those Zionists who argued for a state in Palestine, insisting, however, that it not be an ethnically exclusive state. (As a founding member of *Brit Shalom*, Scholem opposed violence against the Palestinian Arab population aimed not only to take revenge for Palestinian violence against Jews but also to cause a large-scale exodus of Arabs from Palestine.) Despite his changing relationship to Jewish statehood, Scholem never wavered in thinking of Goldberg's "metaphysical" peoplehood as a flight from both reality and reason.

To trace Scholem's opposition to Goldberg we may aptly begin with the 1928 essay I mentioned earlier, "On the Theology of Sabbatianism in Light of Abraham Cardoso." In the final paragraph of that essay, Scholem appropriates the title of Goldberg's book *The Reality of the Hebrews* to name the deeply problematic situation confronting young German Jewish intellectuals in the interwar years: "At this great moment" of Jewish history "the reality of the Hebrews" is threatened with "melting into unpathetic babble [*Geschwätz*]."[11] In the essay, Scholem argues that Sabbatianism marks the beginning of the decline of modern Jewish existence into "unpathetic babble," that is, kabbalistically inspired "chimeras" of messianic redemption. The decline begins in the seventeenth century, but its consummation comes in the form of the metaphysical "*a priori* Zionism" of the Goldberg "sect" to which his comment alludes.

Scholem's essay is a report on his recent discoveries about the Sabbatian movement, but it distills a much longer period of reflection about the condition of modern Jews and Judaism that had consumed Scholem since his adolescence. The existential condition of modern Judaism was the frequent subject of Scholem's conversations with Walter Benjamin. In summarizing a memorable conversation he had with Benjamin in 1927 (just after having uncovered the manuscripts of Abraham Cardoso in the Bodleian Library in Oxford), Scholem captures the essence of the problem of modern Jewish life that was troubling him. Scholem describes the decline of Judaism's vitality and the ensuing critical question confronting the Jewish people: "Was Judaism still alive as a heritage or an experience [*Erfahrung*], even as something constantly evolving, or did it exist only as an object of cognition?"[12] Goldberg and Scholem both reject the view that the Jewish people are "alive . . . only as an object of cognition," but they stand at opposite poles in relation to how the Jewish people can reestablish a vital connection to history. For Goldberg, the living experience (*Erfahrung*) of the "reality of the Hebrews" can only be attained through a *metaphysical revolution.* This metaphysical revolution in the life of the Jewish people would inaugurate a new era in which YHWH Elohim would once again reveal himself in the world. For Scholem, in contrast, God's revelation in the world is "something constantly evolving." The life of the Jewish people in exile, according to Scholem, signifies a "life lived in deferment."[13] Exilic existence therefore marks a slowing if not complete standstill in the ongoing evolution of God's self-revelation. For revelation to regain the full expression of its evolution, the Jewish people need to enter history through the concrete acts involved in building a community in Palestine and, most particularly, returning to Hebrew as their everyday language, despite the dangers associated with reactivating this ancient language.[14] A renewal of the vitality of Jewish tradition, however, does not mean a renewal of Jewish messianism. Quite the contrary. Scholem sees the temptation of messianic fervor as one that will only lead into a tragic dead end. Sabbatianism, the modern expression of this messianic fervor, reveals clearly the tragic logic of all such expressions throughout Jewish history: in 1666, Sabbatai Zevi converted to Islam rather than be punished by death at the hands of the Ottoman sultan for proclaiming himself to be the King of the Jews.

Thus Goldberg and Scholem deeply disagreed about the way to revitalize "the reality of the Hebrews" in the modern era: Goldberg called on the Jewish people to embrace the *revolutionary* power of revelation, whereas Scholem asked them to kick-start an *evolutionary* change through a restoration of their ties to the land and language of their forebears. These recipes for the future of Judaism and the Jewish people were diametrically opposed. Scholem's "negative fascination" with Goldberg grew out of his conviction that the only way to save the "reality of the Hebrews" from sinking into "unpathetic babble" was to bring

Jewish life back into historical time by tying that life to the requirements of its national and cultural reconstruction in Palestine. Goldberg held out for the revolutionary alternative. For Scholem, Goldberg's revolutionary alternative was nothing other than a resurrection of Sabbatianism, and Goldberg nothing other than a modern Sabbatai Zevi, another messianic charlatan. For Goldberg, on the other hand, the Zionist movement, whether statist or anarchist or something in between, meant the complete betrayal of the Jewish people's metaphysical task to bring YHWH Elohim into the world.

Scholem's essay "On the Theology of Sabbatianism in Light of Abraham Cardoso" marks the beginning of Scholem's scholarly polemic with Goldberg, but Scholem's critical stance toward Goldberg and his "sect" began several years earlier. As early as 1921, Scholem had considered Goldberg to be a dangerous, Satanic figure. But only in "On the Theology of Sabbatianism" does Scholem articulate the position to which he will remain faithful for the next fifty years: Oskar Goldberg is a messianic charlatan cut from the same cloth as Sabbatai Zevi.

In the essay, Scholem describes how Sabbatianism's messianic antinomianism was given its most powerful theoretical articulation in the writings of Abraham Miguel Cardoso (1626–1706), an early follower of Sabbatai Zevi. Cardoso was a child of Marranos living in Portugal. Secretly identifying as a Jew, Cardoso grew up and was educated in medicine and theology in Spain. After leaving Spain, perhaps to escape the Inquisition, Cardoso converted to Judaism and began to study Kabbalah. After Sabbatai Zevi converted to Islam in 1666, Cardoso did not abandon his belief that Sabbatai Zevi was the messiah; he became the major spokesperson for an interpretation of Sabbatai Zevi's conversion that was shared by many other Jews of Marrano background.[15] Cardoso saw in Sabbatai Zevi's apostasy from Judaism a form of self-imposed "Marranism" that would bring redemption to all the Jewish people. Cardoso articulated the Kabbalistic explanation for the *necessary* apostasy of the Messiah and also for the coming abrogation of Torah law in the new messianic age, which will enable Israel to reestablish its proper relationship with YHWH. Cardoso, trained in Catholic theology, was familiar with the gnostic doctrines that early Christian heresiologists like Irenaeus battled. The early Christian Gnostics argued that the God of the Old Testament, the God responsible for the creation of this world, was in fact a despotic demiurge. The true God was the higher, hidden God who sent Christ to reveal to the world the knowledge of the true God. Cardoso appropriated this gnostic doctrine and turned it against the rabbis. He also reversed the relations between the higher God and the God of the Old Testament. Cardoso argued that the rabbis had forsaken the personal God YHWH who revealed himself in the Old Testament. In place of the personal God YHWH, the rabbis turned their prayers and the prayers of the Jewish people to a distant and impersonal First Cause whose existence was known through philosophical argument rather than through revelation. With the coming of Sabbatai Zevi, YHWH once again reveals himself in his personal identity. And with Sabbatai Zevi, the laws of the Old Testament will be overturned and replaced with a relationship between YHWH and the people that is one of perfect knowledge and therefore perfect obedience without the mediation of prohibitions. What was prohibited will be permitted.

In his essay on Cardoso's heretical Sabbatian theology, Scholem accuses Goldberg—not overtly but by that unmistakable innuendo in the final paragraph of his essay I quoted in which "the reality of the Hebrews" is threatened with becoming "unpathetic babble"—of being a modern-day antinomian messianic pretender (a "Hochstapler" as he will later call him) peddling a gnostic "remythologization" of Judaism. Like Cardoso, Goldberg wants to restore Israel to its authentic connection with the living power of YHWH. Like Cardoso, Goldberg wants to abrogate the present age's Torah for a new revelation. These are indeed points of similarity between Cardoso and Goldberg, but it would be unfair to characterize Goldberg as advocating gnostic antinomianism. The vehemence of Scholem's attack on Cardoso and Goldberg essentially comes down to accusing them of attempting to destroy the historic continuity of the Torah as an *evolving* revelation. Rather than working within the ongoing revelatory tradition of the Torah, Cardoso and Goldberg issue revolutionary calls to the Jewish people to be faithful to a renewal of the original truth of the revelation of YHWH in early Israel, a revelation that they believe has only been distorted in the process of its rabbinic transmission.

Scholem's essay was intended to have a significant impact. Published in a special issue of the journal *Der Jude* dedicated to celebrating Martin Buber's fiftieth birthday, "On the Theology of Sabbatianism in Light of Abraham Cardoso" was destined for the widest possible Jewish readership a scholarly article at that time could hope for. It was the culmination of Scholem's growing antagonism to Goldberg during the 1920s. The recurrent motif of that antagonism, a motif that Scholem also uses to characterize Sabbatianism, is Goldberg's "Satanic" or "Luciferian" character. In later years Scholem wrote two memoirs that include considerable material about his attitude toward Oskar Goldberg. In his autobiography, *From Berlin to Jerusalem*, Scholem describes a meeting in 1921 that he had with a young woman named Dora Hiller, the cousin of the prominent social activist and essayist Kurt Hiller (1885–1972), who was a close associate of Erich Unger and one of the founding members of the Neuer Club. Dora Hiller, Scholem explains, introduced herself as an "adherent" of the Goldberg circle. In fact, Dora Hiller was at that time either Goldberg's wife or his fiancé (they married in 1921, and we are not told the exact date of her visit to Scholem).[16] She came to visit Scholem in order to invite him to meet with Goldberg. She knew of Scholem's scholarly study of the Kabbalah, and she offered to introduce him to an actual adept of the Kabbalah. Scholem replied to Dora Hiller that he was not unfamiliar with

Goldberg, having heard "the strangest details" about Goldberg from a friend. Based on what this friend had told him, Scholem responded to Dora Hiller's invitation to meet Goldberg in this way: "Madam, I know who Oskar Goldberg is and I am inclined to regard him as the representative of the devil in our generation."[17] Scholem reports telling another friend around that time that Goldberg was "finding it impossible to realize his dreams of magical [world] dominance and therefore sought to make up for it through the subjugation and exploitation of human souls."[18] In his memoir about his friendship with Walter Benjamin, Scholem states (although without explaining how he knows this) that Goldberg experienced visions in "schizoid twilight states" before waking in which he claimed to have "revelations about the Torah." (Scholem admits that he never met Goldberg in person.) Scholem acknowledges in this memoir that Goldberg's ideas "did not lack a demonic dimension" and possessed "a certain Luciferian lustre."[19] Indeed, Scholem paid Goldberg the honor of characterizing his friends and students as making up one of the three "sects" of modern German-Jewish life. In a letter to George Steiner thanking him for sending him a copy of his introduction to Benjamin's *Origin of German Tragic Drama*, Scholem names the three most important "Jewish sects" (Scholem is alluding to Josephus's characterization of the three sects of Judaism at the time of the Roman uprising: the Pharisees, the Sadducees, and the Essenes) that German Jewry had produced: the Warburg Institute, Horkheimer's Institute for Social Research, and the Oskar Goldberg "sect."[20]

Scholem was repelled by Goldberg's apparent use of Kabbalah to style himself as someone with supernatural powers. In chapter 2 I described how Goldberg's Gymnasium friend, Erwin Loewenson, had once told Kurt Hiller that Goldberg was capable of amazing feats, including "seeing" the numbers (*gematria*) of the Pentateuch. He even suggested that Goldberg, at certain "prophetic" moments, would emanate a sort of light. Whatever we make of such reports, it is clear that Loewenson and Goldberg's other friends in the World-Root Club of those years had nothing but respect and affection for Goldberg. His friends from later years, and he had quite a few, agreed that Goldberg was unusual, but they were hardly repelled by him. However, it is easy to understand how others may have felt quite differently about him. Scholem never met Goldberg, but he had clearly heard reports about him from people who were put off by Goldberg's self-presentation. But was the animosity that Scholem obviously felt to Goldberg merely due to Goldberg's alleged Kabbalistic chicanery?

I believe that Goldberg earned the appellation "Luciferian" from Scholem in large part because of Goldberg's revolutionary brand of "metaphysical" or "*a priori*" Zionism. Goldberg's metaphysical Zionism must have seemed like a major threat to Scholem's own *concrete* Zionism. Scholem in fact spoke about certain adherents of Goldberg's group who were once active Zionists, but then turned away from their Zionist commitments under pressure from Goldberg. Scholem targeted Erich Unger's *The Stateless Upbuilding of a Jewish People* (1922) as being a particularly provocative attack on contemporary Zionism. Unger was one of Goldberg's most prominent disciples, and Scholem regarded him, correctly I would argue, as someone who possessed "considerable philosophical gifts." His *Stateless Upbuilding of a Jewish People*, Scholem writes, "was really quite something":

> It censured practical Zionism, which the author rejected, for being deficient in "metaphysics," but what Unger meant was not so much metaphysics as magical power (not intended metaphorically) which, according to Goldberg's doctrine, should be possessed by metaphysically charged "biological entities." Instead of learning how to work magic, the Zionists—according to the author—were wasting their energies on the building of villages, settlements, and similar nonsense that could not promote that Jewish "magical faculty" which needed renewal. All this was somewhat obscured by the elegant language in which the lecture was couched, but intelligent readers could not help noticing that it was the salient point of this remarkable essay. Later on, in Goldberg's own writings, the point was expressed rather more bluntly and with appropriate invective.[21]

Unger and Goldberg, as Scholem would have it, were encouraging young Jews to practice magic rather than go to Palestine and build villages and settlements. Scholem called Unger's essay "remarkable," but one would hardly know why from his précis. If we take a moment to examine Unger's essay, which is written under the influence of Goldberg from beginning to end, we may better understand why Scholem felt so strongly about the "Goldberg sect" to characterize its leader as "the representative of devil in our generation."

In *The Stateless Upbuilding of a Jewish People*, Unger argues that Zionism's commitment to the "corporeal [*körperhaft*] reality" of the Jewish people within a territorial nation-state in effect reduced Jewish identity (*Judentum*) to a race (*Rasse*).[22] Zionism, Unger declares, "emphasizes the physiological or, better put, the genetic component of the complex nature of Jewish identity and out of this genetic specificity it draws the conclusion that is generally drawn throughout the world from a group's genetic kinship, namely, that the group belongs together as a nation with its own territory." Unger calls his own version of Zionism "*a priori*" because it attempts to address the goal of Zionism without assuming that there is only one particular empirical means to reach this goal. The goal of Zionism is this: "to take Jewish identity [*Judentum*] into the realm of the corporeal powers that act decisively in the world."[23] *A priori* Zionism asks this question: What are the conditions of possibility for the decisive action of the Jews in the corporeal realm? Unger argues that "empirical" Zionism assumes that there is only one condition under which this is possible, namely, through a Jewish *state*. This assumption necessarily emphasizes one aspect only of Jewish identity, its racial or genetic basis. Empirical Zionism places Jewish identity "on par with a hundred other raceoid [*sic*] organized groups, but this means that it also places Jewish identity's ineradicable and necessary claims to possess some kind of pre-eminence, exclusivity, and uniqueness because of its spiritual and religious content on par with every other group's claims." Along with other nation-states, the Jewish state could certainly include "religion" as one component of its national life, but like most advanced nations, it would deem it a "private affair." The Jewish state, insofar as it ranked as one of the modern nation-states, would be a state with "freedom of religion" (meaning in this case, freedom to choose to follow Jewish *halachah* or not). But this would not give concrete material power to Jewish identity, only to "the Jewish race." And if one tries to give *cultural* content to Zionism, once again this results in placing Jewish identity on par with other national cultures. These other cultures, however, have no final or highest goals that define them: "Germanness [*Germantum*], Englishness, Americanness, and Frenchness are expressions of ethnic groups but they are not commanding imperatives nor are they conceptions of the world that can be given exact formulation."[24] It is only chauvinism that ranks one such culture above another. If the power manifestation of Jewish identity in the corporeal world is not simply to be another chauvinistic cultural formation, then its commanding imperative and world conception must emerge from within and not be modeled on anything extrinsic to Jewish identity. Jewish culture should not simply be a Jewish version of other national cultures; it must possess its own organic articulation of spiritual activities and aims. Only on this condition can Jewish identity give complete expression to the identity of the Jewish people. Only then will Jewish identity possess a "life-encompassing universality." "Otherwise," Unger concludes, "it is a 'religion'—one among other religions."[25]

Having established that *a priori* Zionism seeks to give corporeal power to a spiritual totality and not a mere aggregation of cultural "spheres," Unger goes on to ask how this goal is to be achieved in practical terms. One cannot assume that the European model of binding individuals together to form an "abundance of numbers" (*Zahlenreichtum*) is the way to give Jewish identity its proper corporeal power in the world. Nor can the unifying factor of this corporeal power be based on genealogy, as it is with other peoples. "Genealogy alone does not create a people," Unger states.[26] "A *task* however is a means through which to *found* kinship."[27] A spiritual totality is unified through an overriding task [*Aufgabe*] that creates a corporeal cohesion among individual that transcends the merely biological givens of inherited traits. The kinship of Jews is ultimately a *founded* one, not one based on genealogy. As we have seen, the distinction between genealogical peoplehood and founded peoplehood is central to Goldberg's understanding of the way that YHWH Elohim interacts with Israel not through biological inheritance but through *choice*. A founded people is one whose members choose to share in a goal and a task that transcend the mere biological survival of the group.

Goldberg in *The Reality of the Hebrews* discusses what he calls the "*a priori* history" of the Jewish people in terms that clearly reflect Unger's discussion of *a priori* Zionism in *Stateless Upbuilding*, published three years earlier. But Goldberg's discussion of *a priori* history goes well beyond Unger's argument. Goldberg explains that *a priori* history differs from empirical history by virtue of the logical necessity governing *a priori* history versus the merely contingent relations among the events of "normal" history: "While normal history contains facts that could be imagined as having happened quite differently, *a priori* history contains facts that exceed the mere principle of causality and have a logical necessity, that is, they follow certain specific laws (in their specificity they far exceed the generality of the causal law) in such a way that they must happen in that specific way."[28] Goldberg argues that *a priori* history takes place during an "Ur-time" in which the physical world was more closely connected to the transcendental world system of the gods. In this Ur-time, the psychophysical makeup of an individual was capable of providing corporeal manifestation of a transcendental organism: "In the Ur-time the prominent living individuals were not like the ancestors and descendants of later peoples because *they themselves were these very people*."[29] The founding of the Jewish people happens at the point when the metaphysical power of such prominent individuals was on the wane. YHWH Elohim breaks with the biological descent principle contained within prominent individuals and *founds* a metaphysical people who take conscious responsibility for concretizing their God in the world, and they do this for the sake of a world-historical task: to lead humanity beyond races and folk groups to a unity grounded in the "biology-productive" principle of YHWH. Only when humanity as a whole is linked to this principle will it finally overcome the "catastrophic" history of wars sparked by competition over scarce resources. The biology-productive principle is an endlessly productive source of life and energy. It is the task of the Jewish people to assist YHWH in his struggle to overcome the empirical limits of nature's diminishing energies.

Unger calls for a reexamination of the primary documents of Judaism, most importantly the Pentateuch, to rediscover the method with which to "found" a people. That method can only be based on the combined psychophysical power of exceptional individuals who still hold within themselves the capacity to spiritually master their corporeal nature: "to drive the spirit onward for the sake of the corporeal: to cultivate the spirit in a deeper, more expressive, more subtle and more abstract way—precisely in order to finally reach a level of maturity that is suited to the challenges of corporeality, to be spiritual *out of love for materiality*, to be ready for the tension [between spirit and matter] in its deepest expression, this is perhaps where the power and the definition of Jewish identity are found."[30] Unger describes this "disciplining" of the spirit for the sake of the corporeal as the "goal of messianism" and the "task of Judaism."[31]

Scholem cannot accept Unger's *a priori* Zionism as the "task of Judaism" in world history. To accept Unger's anti-empirical Zionism would mean to plunge the Jewish people into the worst excesses of messianic frenzy, or so Scholem believed. It would lead inevitably to the excesses of orgiastic sexuality that marked the Frankist movement in the eighteenth century (see the later discussion on this movement). Furthermore, Scholem vehemently disagreed with Unger that Zionism ("empirical Zionism" as Unger called it) is nothing more than racial nationalism. As David Biale has argued, at the heart of Scholem's commitment to Zionism is his belief that Zionism in fact offers the only way for Jewish identity in *all its facets* to attain its fullest historical expression. Therefore, Scholem entirely rejects Unger's denunciation of Zionism as the reduction of Jewish identity to biology. He further rejects Unger's call for a revolutionary, metaphysical Zionism that would be the "agent of the coming era and the germ cell of new and unheralded phenomena that have life-encompassing universality."[32] Such a revolutionary conception of the relationship between Jewish identity and history is anathema to the Zionist in Scholem, who hoped that Zionism would provide a means to channel the apocalyptic forces at work in Jewish history away from destruction and place them in the service of real but *gradual* transformation: "apocalyptic energies moderated by tradition" is Biale's succinct way of capturing Scholem's anti-revolutionary Zionist program.[33]

To unleash the latent antinomian apocalypticism within Jewish messianism is, for Scholem, precisely to open the gates of Hell. This accounts for the recurrent characterization of Goldberg as "demonic," "Luciferian," and "the representative of the devil in our generation." As I have mentioned, Scholem used similar terms to characterize Sabbatianism. Describing the transformation of the Kabbalah after the Expulsion from Spain in 1492, Scholem wrote that the "flames which flared up from the apocalyptical abyss" swept across the Jewish world "until they seized upon and recast the mystical theology of Kabbalism" and ultimately led "to that further catastrophe which became acute with the Sabbatian movement."[34] In the Sabbatian movement, and once again in the Oskar Goldberg "sect," Scholem believed he could see the visage of Lucifer tempting the Jewish people to leap into the flames of destruction as they vainly pursue what they take to be the footsteps of the Messiah.

Scholem's critique of Goldberg in "The Theology of Sabbatianism" is largely hidden from view, however. As I have noted, it is only in the final paragraph that we learn that the "reality of the Hebrews" remains threatened by "unpathetic babble" even today. In contrast, Scholem's critique of Goldberg as a modern-day Sabbatai Zevi forms the outright content of a letter he wrote in August 1928 to Sonja (Rosa) Okun, a friend of his wife, Elsa Burchardt.[35] As I already mentioned,

Scholem wrote five typed pages (one copy is preserved in the Franz Rosenzweig Archive of the Leo Baeck Institute in New York) in answer to Rosa Okun's request for his opinion about Goldberg's book. In that letter, Scholem tells Rosa that Goldberg and his circle are involved in an effort to create a new "folk group center [*Volkszentrum*] with its own so-called 'metaphysical'-imperialistic goals," with Goldberg serving as its messianic prophet. In his later memoir about his friendship with Benjamin, Scholem repeats this claim: "What Goldberg aimed at was the restoration of the magical bond between God and His people (of which he viewed himself as the biological center)."[36] Scholem adds in his Benjamin memoir that the Goldberg circle, although it publicly identified its cause with "social-revolutionary movements," in fact had a different ambition: "the realization of a new worldwide theocracy, and Goldberg believed he was pulling the strings." This "worldwide theocracy" is what Scholem refers to in his letter when he writes that the Goldberg circle has "metaphysical-imperialistic goals."

In his letter to Rosa Okun, Scholem makes it clear that Goldberg is promulgating a modern-day version of the most extreme form of Sabbatianism. He tells her that he appended to the title page of his copy of *The Reality of Hebrews* the following subtitle: "Or Why We Should All Become Frankists." The Frankists were the most radical of the Sabbatians. They gathered around Jacob Frank (1726–1791), a man who declared himself to be the incarnation of the male side of the Godhead (and, as such, Sabbatai Zevi redivivus). He was, Scholem says, a "figure of tremendous if satanic power" who "will always be remembered as one of the most frightening phenomena in the whole of Jewish history."[37] "Here was a man who was not afraid to push on to the very end," Scholem declares, "to take the final step into the abyss, to drain the cup of desolation and destruction to the lees until the last bit of holiness had been made into a mockery."[38] Jacob Frank is simply the final, historically inevitable endpoint of the Sabbatian theology that Abraham Cardoso had unfolded in the prior century. This is the danger, then, that Goldberg poses: in reviving the gnostic antinomianism of Cardoso, he will forge a new and powerful Jewish sect devoted to Satanic destruction. Scholem is playing the role of historian-cum-heresiologist of antinomian messianism. Like the late antique Christian heresiologists who fought against Gnosticism in the Church, Scholem will focus on the *orgiastic* side of the Jewish heresies of the modern period.

In his letter to Rosa Okun, Scholem explains his appended subtitle ("Or Why We Should All Become Frankists") after referring to what Goldberg calls "the night side of God." Scholem claims that "the night side of God" section of Goldberg's book contains a sort of "inner circle" revelation about the *real* nature of God.[39] The "night side of God," as Goldberg explains it, corresponds to the time that YHWH Elohim granted temporary ascendancy to the "other gods," the gods whose power is revealed in "sexuality, somnambulism, and the dimming of the sense of reality."[40] Although Goldberg makes it perfectly clear that the metaphysical power of YHWH Elohim lies in the conscious, voluntary, and non-automatic system of the daytime, Scholem wants Rosa Oken to believe that Goldberg is particularly interested in the ritual power of nighttime ecstasies, especially of a sexual nature. This assumption would make sense of Scholem's claim that Goldberg is really offering a "polytheist commentary" on the Pentateuch. Yet, while Goldberg explains that the "night side of God" is the time of sexual abandon, the time when the "other gods" are invoked in orgiastic rituals, YHWH Elohim seeks precisely to free Israel from this "night side." YHWH Elohim relates to the people through the "day side" of the transcendental organism, the side that places the body's functions under the control of the conscious spirit. Of course, Jacob Frank's Kabbalah demanded precisely the opposite—"strange acts" of sexual release—from his followers. In his study of Frankism, Scholem writes, "It would be pointless to deny that the sexual element in this outburst was very strong: a primitive abandon such as the Jewish people would scarcely have thought itself capable of after so many centuries of discipline in the Law joined hands with perversely pathological drives to seek a common ideological rehabilitation."[41] Without the least bit of evidence, Scholem insinuates in the letter that the Goldberg circle is engaged in nighttime orgies, apparently with Goldberg as their "biological center."

Scholem concludes his letter to Rosa Okun with a clear statement of the fundamental continuity between Cardoso's gnostic reinterpretation of Judaism and Goldberg's alleged attempt to uncover the mythic elements in "Urjudaism." The statement makes clear Scholem's own position as the polar antithesis to all such remythologizing efforts:

> The remythologization of the central theological concepts of Judaism by means of which it first broke free from the mythic world in order to reach the "pathetic" world of justice [*des Gerechten*] about which myth knows nothing, has been attempted again and again in the history of religion. These attempts, when they appear the writings of many Kabbalists, might deserve to be considered rather remarkable, but when they are offered as the positive truth about the real structure of the world, they cannot but lead to disappointment and they deserve to be combatted. That is my position in regard to Goldberg's theories.

We see that Scholem's polar opposition to Goldberg went very deep. Scholem wanted to uphold reason against what he took to be the continuing antinomian threat of mythologically tinged Kabbalistic messianism. Scholem, of course, knew that Goldberg himself would refuse to be characterized as an enemy of reason in favor of orgiastic abandon. The very term "*un*pathetic" is key to Goldberg, and Scholem was quite aware of this fact. "Unpathetic" is meant to capture the sober and objective approach of Goldberg's "experimental ethnology" in contrast to any appeal to Nietzschean emotionalism. And Scholem was also aware of Goldberg's mathematical exegesis of the Pentateuch in *The Five Books of Moses.* How could this dry accumulation of numbers and number patterns reflect orgiastic irrationalism? To understand the source of Scholem's characterization of Goldberg as an enemy of reason in favor myth, we need, strange as it may seem, to know something about Scholem's training in mathematics.

Scholem knew that Goldberg attempted to link mathematics with the Kabbalah. For Scholem, this attempt went hand in hand with the rejection of reason. Long before he encountered Goldberg, Scholem expressed an almost visceral response to German Romanticism's linkage of mathematics and Kabbalah in the works of Novalis, Schelling, and Oken. In his earliest studies in mathematics, Scholem sought to protect the rational integrity of mathematics from the symbolic excesses of the Romantic imagination. To appreciate how far Scholem's opposition to Goldberg extended, it is useful to take a moment to examine Scholem's philosophy of mathematics, such as we are able to make it out from his youthful diaries and letters. We shall see that it is of a piece with his philosophy of Judaism. Characterizing Scholem's aversion to the Cantorian mathematics of the infinite (about which I will have more to say in a moment), Peter Fenves writes that "his [Scholem's] aversion to new theories of the infinite is of a piece with a more general tendency, which can also be discerned perhaps in his relation to Judaism. Despite a certain rhetoric of radicalism, which requires that the roots of the current crisis be exposed, his primary interest lies in discovering overlooked connections to a vibrant past in the midst of a confounding present."[42] In other words, Scholem was focused on the *tradition* pole of the *revelation-tradition* grouping. In mathematics as in Judaism, this meant resisting the revolutionary power of the breakthrough of the infinite into the realm of the finite.

Scholem was very well informed about mathematics, including the Cantorian theory of transfinite numbers that is at the heart of Goldberg's theory of transcendental organisms. In his essay "Walter Benjamin," Scholem even made use of Cantor's transfinite numbers to describe the relationship between Benjamin's interpretive essays and their target texts: "The reader—if I may use a mathematical simile—finds himself between two transfinite classes reciprocally related, though not by a one-to-one correspondence."[43] Scholem studied mathematics at the universities of Berlin, Munich, and Jena. He was deeply interested in the foundations of mathematics, and he even studied with Gottlob Frege.[44] Scholem wrote that Frege's *Grundlagen der Arithmetik* (*Foundations of Arithmetic*, 1884) was one of the books that "greatly fired my imagination."

Scholem's opposition to Goldberg was so deep that it was reflected even at the level of the philosophy of mathematics that each man embraced. Scholem accepted his teacher Frege's conception of mathematics as having its grounding in the purely logical operations of thinking.[45] For Scholem, mathematics needed to be "wholly purged of mysticism." According to Scholem, mathematical computation was the polar opposite of "mystical symbolism."[46] In his 1928 critical letter about Goldberg's *Reality of the Hebrews*, Scholem describes it as based on "ontology by fiat" (*Konstatier-Ontologie*). This criticism is directed against Goldberg's penchant for writing as if he were in direct contact with the metaphysical source from which the Pentateuch itself crystallized. However, we may also connect Scholem's criticism to Goldberg's Cantorian (Platonist) approach to mathematical objects. Indeed, for Goldberg the Pentateuch is itself a numerical concretization of a transcendental mathematical reality. Cantor argued for the real existence of any newly imagined mathematical objects, such as the transfinite numbers, so long as they were consistently defined and compatible with previously defined mathematical objects. Indeed, he claimed that the transfinite numbers could offer a pathway for the human intellect to approach the Absolute Infinity of God. Frege would have none of Cantor's mathematical Platonism. As Michael Hallett points out, Frege "rejected the position that showing the non-contradictory nature of a concept is enough to establish that an object falls under it." Hallett quotes from the final page of Frege's *Grundlagen der Arithmetik* the following passage in which Frege "with damning intent" speaks about mathematical theorization like the kind Cantor favored: "This theory imagines that all we need do is make postulates [*Forderungen*]; that these are satisfied then goes without saying. It conducts itself like God, who can create by his mere word whatever he wants."[47] Frege in effect characterizes Cantor's mathematical Platonism as "ontology by fiat."

To preserve mathematics from anything "foreign" to its purely logical and abstract set of concepts is the goal of Frege's work, and it is also the reason why Scholem entirely rejected the reception of the Kabbalah by Romantic thinkers, which formed one of the foundations of the mathematical Naturphilosophie of Novalis, Schelling, and Lorenz Oken (whose views I described in previous chapters as providing the basis for much of Goldberg's thought). Scholem offers his most pointed criticism of such mixing of mathematics and Kabbalah in relation to Novalis who, as I noted in chapter 2, was seen by Erwin Loewenson (one of the members of Goldberg's World-Root Club) as Goldberg's only real precursor. In a letter of 1917 Scholem writes, "Novalis's thesis that 'pure mathematics is religion' has for nearly a year now caused me to shudder. . . . The real evil of it does not lie so much in its enthusiasm for mathematics as in the way it pushes mathematics beyond its proper sphere."[48] It is no wonder that Goldberg also caused Scholem "to shudder."

Scholem sensed that the purity of reason itself was at stake in the fusion of mathematics and Kabbalah. Logic was the only safeguard against the "mythological" dimension of Kabbalah. If reason and logic were abandoned to mystical "enthusiasm," then the essence of Judaism—justice (*das Gerecht*)—would be lost. Mathematics is the self-enclosed world of signs to be logically manipulated, whereas Kabbalah is the poetic manipulation of symbols to create a radically distinct self-enclosed world, the world of myth. The Torah, however, is an ongoing revelation and is precisely not self-enclosed; it is neither mathematics nor Kabbalah. "The Torah *cannot* be a symbol . . . since any transmission of the truth is, by its nature, unsymbolic. Justice is not a symbol."[49] When Scholem disparages Goldberg's theoretical claims in *Reality of the Hebrews* as "ontology by fiat" (*Konstatier-Ontologie*), he is correctly identifying Goldberg as a follower of Cantor's mathematical Platonism—someone committed to the ontological (and theological) reality of mathematical objects (for Goldberg, the transcendental organisms).

I have so far traced the political (Zionist) and mathematico-philosophical (Fregean) dimensions of Scholem's opposition to Goldberg and his circle. There was also a deeply personal aspect to Scholem's antipathy to Goldberg, and it had everything to do with Scholem's friendship with Walter Benjamin. To understand the personal dimension of Scholem's opposition to Goldberg, I first need to describe Benjamin's relationship with the Goldberg circle.

Scholem raises the charge of "ontology by fiat" not only against Goldberg but also against Benjamin.[50] Benjamin's "ontology by fiat" is not reflected in his mixing of Kabbalah and mathematics, as with Goldberg, but rather in his mixing of Kabbalah and Kantian epistemology. I explain this in more detail soon, but let me now state clearly what was at stake for Scholem personally in his opposition to Goldberg. Benjamin's mixture of "mythological" symbolism and philosophy, his tendency toward "ontology by fiat," meant that Benjamin *was in danger of falling under the spell of Oskar Goldberg*. In his Benjamin memoir Scholem makes a telling remark about Benjamin's relationship to the Goldberg circle: "Benjamin's interest in this Jewish sect, if I may so describe it, accompanied him right into the Hitler period."[51] Goldberg embodied everything negative that Scholem feared might ultimately come to dominate and destroy Benjamin. Goldberg's "unpathetic babble" posed not only an existential danger to the future of the Jewish people but Scholem believed that it also threatened the psychic stability of his closest friend.

Since his first enthusiastic reception of Erich Unger's *Politics and Metaphysics* in 1921 ("the most important book of our time on politics," Benjamin wrote in a letter to Scholem[52]), Benjamin was drawn to Unger and some other members of the Goldberg circle, although he was repelled by what he called Goldberg's "impure aura." Benjamin noted in his first letter to Scholem about his encounter with Goldberg (he knew many members of the circle, including Unger, from his Gymnasium years, although they were not students together) that Goldberg's views on Zionism clashed with those of Scholem: "You are obviously right to meet the

Zionist tendencies of these people with complete indifference. The Hebraic side of these people goes back to a Mr. Goldberg—to be sure, I know very little about him, but his impure aura repelled me emphatically every time I was forced to see him, to the extent that I was unable to shake hands with him."[53] But despite his personal antipathy to Goldberg, Benjamin continued to meet with him at the homes of mutual friends who were close to the "Goldberg circle." Benjamin remained particularly close to Erich Unger, Goldberg's philosophical expositor. Benjamin's relationship to Unger will help us better understand what Scholem meant when he referred to Benjamin's penchant for "ontology by fiat."

Benjamin and Unger shared an interest in a number of philosophical themes. Both men attempted to provide a consistent framework for thinking beyond the Kantian stricture on the necessary finitude of experience. Scholem summarizes Benjamin's philosophical goals quite well when he writes that "he expected that an experience of infinitely greater richness would still have to be fitted into what was basically Kant's frame of reference, however great the necessary modification."[54] One of the texts in which Benjamin describes how to reach this "infinitely greater richness" of experience is *One-Way Street*, published in 1928 but written earlier in the decade. The concluding section, "To the Planetarium," bears the unmistakable imprint of Unger (and, consequently, of Oskar Goldberg as well).[55] Scholem points to this text as the first appearance in Benjamin's work of his "ontology by fiat."

In "To the Planetarium," Benjamin summarizes the "teaching of antiquity" as "they alone shall possess the earth who live from the powers of the cosmos." He goes on to explain that the ancients did not have an "optical connection" to the cosmos as an object of scientific investigation as do we moderns. Rather, "the ancients' intercourse with the cosmos had been different: trance [*Rausch*]." Furthermore, this intercourse was not that of an individual but of a group: "Man can be in ecstatic contact with the cosmos only communally." And the ancient human's communal experience was not limited to objects within space and time that constitute the subject matter of the physical sciences. "The paroxysm of genuine cosmic experience," Benjamin explains, "is not tied to that tiny fragment of nature that we are accustomed to call 'Nature.'" Benjamin claims that the Great War was the symptom of a new communal birth and a new human relation to the cosmos. Its "wooing of the earth" through new technologies that built great "sacrificial shafts" in the earth and lifted humans into the sky and took them into the ocean depths, however, was subverted by the ruling classes who sought only to profit from these new human relationships to the planet. Benjamin claims that these new technologies, if they can be wrested from the hands of the capitalist ruling classes, augur a new stage in human evolution, one that recreates the ancient experience of the cosmos with a new human subject: no longer "men" [*Menschen*] in "nations and families" but all of "mankind" [*Menschheit*]: "in technology, a *physis* is being organized through which mankind's contact with the cosmos takes a new and different form from that which it had in nations and families. . . . In the nights of annihilation of the last war, the frame of mankind was shaken by a feeling that resembled the bliss of the epileptic. And the revolts that followed were the first attempt of mankind to bring the new body under its control." Finally, Benjamin connects "mankind" with the proletariat: "The power of the proletariat is the measure of its [i.e., mankind's] convalescence."

Erich Unger in *Politics and Metaphysics* had similarly argued that a new political subject is in the process of emerging after the "catastrophe" of the Great War and that it will be a new collectivity of human individuals with a heightened power of consciousness and an intensified physiological capacity. Unger, borrowing from Goldberg's mathematical ontology, calls this new collectivity a "real unity." "The existence of such a unity [*Einheit*] of a specific, empirical multiplicity [*Vielheit*]," Unger writes, "is the fundamental element and condition of a catastrophy-less sociological order." In other words, Goldberg's "multiplicity-unity" (corresponding to what Cantor calls a transfinite number) is the condition of possibility of any real political transformation of the present order. Unger says that the complete destruction of all such unities "is what this generation experienced in the continuous explosions that shattered the nations." The contemporary postwar sociological reality is that of "the individual in n-multiple repetition [*n-fach Wiederholung*], and aside from this the real unity has as good as ceased to exist; its place has been taken by a metaphorical, 'historical' unity, that is, a living-dead unity, in whose artificial limits and in whose dead boundaries the nations twist in spasms [*in Krämpfen winden*]."[56] Soon after reading *Politics and Metaphysics*, Benjamin invited Unger to be a contributor to a new journal he was planning, *Angelus Novus*. In a statement announcing the goals of this journal, Benjamin almost quotes directly from Unger: "Nothing appears more important to the editor than that the journal should forgo all appearance and simply express the truth of the situation, which is that even the purest will and the most patient labor among the different collaborators *will prove unable to create any unity* [*Einheit*], *let alone a community* [*Gemeinschaft*]. The journal should proclaim through the mutual alienness of their contributions *how impossible it is in our age to give a voice to any communality*."[57]

One can certainly understand why Benjamin thought that Unger's *Politics and Metaphysics* was so important: in Unger's work Benjamin found a conception of political action that imagined not only a new configuration of social relations (a new "unity") *but also an entirely new way of experiencing the world*. Since his early essay, "On the Program of the Coming Philosophy," this new form of experience had been Benjamin's hope as well. Indeed, the practical implementation of the new social "real unity" can only begin with a theory that imagined the possibility of a new experience. For Unger and for Benjamin, the critical *political* issue was *how to imagine the possibility of the impossible*. As Unger puts it, "At the beginning of every attempt to comprehend a social, that is, a political problem one must necessarily attain to the following insight: everything is possible and impossibility in human affairs is only blindness in regard to the means. Thus, concrete existence and the most extreme point of theorization are situated in immediate proximity to one another."[58]

We therefore see that Scholem's polar opposition to Goldberg was not only about the "catastrophic temptation" of antinomian messianism within the Jewish mystical tradition, it was also about Benjamin's tendency to fall prey to this temptation. In this section I tried to show the roots of Scholem's animosity toward Goldberg. I did not try to refute Scholem's criticisms of *The Reality of the Hebrews* because many of them, if not most, are based on sound philology and historical scholarship—the documentary hypothesis, the late origin of Kabbalah, several doubtful etymologies—that I do not want to question. But more importantly, my goal is not to defend Goldberg but to understand him on his own terms. Scholem sent his letter about Goldberg to Franz Rosenzweig, and we may take his response to the letter as perhaps the final word on Scholem's critique of Goldberg. Rosenzweig wrote to Buber and discussed Scholem's letter soon after receiving it. After describing Scholem's critique as coming down to a "liberal ideology" that stresses the morality of the Bible, Rosenzweig concludes, "If the realm of 'ritual' and the realm of 'the moral' were able to be divided with a clean slice of the knife, then there would indeed be no Goldberg, but there would also be no Judaism."[59] Rosenzweig does not deny Scholem's specific historical and philological claims, but he does question whether Scholem has fully appreciated how Goldberg's work might reveal, however filtered by metaphysical theorizations alien to the Bible, something that authentically captures the imaginative and literary power of the Pentateuch.

Now that we have understood the broad contours of Scholem's opposition to Goldberg and the Goldberg circle, including its personal dimension in relation to Walter Benjamin, it is time to turn to Goldberg and his 1935 exposition of his philosophy of Jewish history, *Maimonides*. As I have said earlier, this can be read on one level as a response to Scholem's critique of his *The Reality of the Hebrews*. But, more than this, it is Goldberg's frontal assault on all modern forms of Judaism, including the academic study of Jewish history represented by Scholem.

## *Maimonides*: Oskar Goldberg's Philosophy of Jewish History

In 1935, the eight hundredth anniversary of the birth of Moses Maimonides, Oskar Goldberg published *Maimonides: Kritik der jüdischen Glaubenslehre* (*Maimonides: Critique of Jewish Religious Doctrine*).[60] In this book, Goldberg offers a broad overview of the history of Judaism. The first half concentrates on

Maimonides and on the developments leading up to him; the second half lays out Goldberg's own interpretation of the Pentateuch in a series of fourteen "theses" (*Sätze*), which can be taken as replacing Maimonides's thirteen articles of faith (*Glaubensartikel*). The book concludes with a section titled "The Future" in which Goldberg describes his vision of the paths confronting the Jewish people at the present moment. Let me begin with a brief overview of the first half of the book.

As I mentioned in the opening of this chapter, the fundamental poles of Scholem's and Goldberg's philosophies of Judaism are *revelation* and *tradition*, as represented by the Written and Oral Torah, respectively. We have seen that Scholem views tradition as the evolutionary unfolding of revelation. For Goldberg, tradition is at best the faithful preservation of revelation. Goldberg, not unlike Abraham Cardoso, looks forward to *a new revelation*. Unlike Cardoso, however, Goldberg does not rely on the Kabbalah for guidance in understanding the nature of the new revelation. The Pentateuch, when properly understood as the expression of the "reality of the Hebrews," itself offers the key to inaugurating a new revelation and a new set of laws for a new Jewish people. I discuss how an understanding of the Pentateuch as the "reality of the Hebrews" can become the basis for a new revelation when I come to the second half of *Maimonides*. In the first half of the book, however, Goldberg is concerned primarily to show how tradition succeeded in preserving the text of revelation (the Pentateuch), but failed to keep intact the memory of it as the unique repository of what the Jewish people need to know about the relationship between God, the world, and themselves.

Goldberg explains that, before Maimonides, the "Talmudists" concentrated on transmitting the text of the Torah and on interpreting the laws of the Pentateuch so that they could be practiced in the different historical circumstance in which the Jews found themselves. Most Talmudists accepted the fact that they essentially did not understand the reasons why the text was written in exactly the way it was (why some words were written differently than they were pronounced, for example). Nor did most Talmudists claim to understand fully the reasons for all the laws that they interpreted. However, over the centuries, the Talmudists began to systematize the Bible's commandments in order to bring them under a single overarching worldview. This led them ultimately to step beyond the limits of their calling as textual tradents, that is, preservers of the Written Torah. In their systematizing zeal, they became confused about the nature of God. The majority of Talmudists accepted the Psalms as their guide to interpreting the nature of God. Among the writings of the Hebrew Bible, the Psalms represent the theology of the Solomonic Temple priesthood. In chapter 4 I explained that, according to Goldberg, the building of the Solomonic Temple led to the loss of Israel's intimacy with YHWH Elohim during its time of wandering in the desert. According to Goldberg, the fundamental attitude of the Psalms toward God is that he is remote from the world and only accessible through prayer and self-humbling. For the Talmudists who based their understanding of God on the Psalms theology, God was thought to be so far beyond heaven and earth that he could have no unique place or abode in the world. They tended to downplay the significance of spatiotemporally limited forms of God's glory, for example, the pillars of smoke and fire that accompanied the Israelites through the desert.

The Talmudists, according to Goldberg, made two fundamental mistakes regarding the Pentateuch itself: they did not understand how God's glory could be uniquely present within the world at the cult site of the tabernacle, nor did they understand the *goal* of God's presence in the world and Israel's *task* in relation to that goal. For the Psalms-oriented Talmudists, the goal of God is fundamentally completed with creation, and Israel's task is to *praise* God's glory (and obey his revealed law just as the world obeys natural law). When the Talmudists systematized their worldview to explain the relationship between God, the world, and Israel, they lost sight of what the Pentateuch's authentic teaching came down to, namely, that God had revealed his glory *at a particular place and time and to a particular people.* Only when this fact is acknowledged can the question of God's goal and Israel's task be properly answered.[61]

The obscuring of the Pentateuch's teaching that began with the Solomonic priesthood and continued with the Talmudists reaches a new level with Maimonides. The Talmudists remained connected to authentic inner-Israelite traditions. These traditions are neither fully in tune with what Goldberg calls "Urjudaism," the Judaism of the ancient Hebrews, nor are they altogether foreign to it, based as they are on the worldview of the book of Psalms. Maimonides, however, buries the authentic teaching of the Pentateuch under the foreign categories of Aristotelian philosophy. And while Maimonides claims to be offering nothing incompatible with the Psalms-based worldview of his fellow Talmudists, he draws a new and sharper line between God and the world than they ever had. According to Maimonides, there is an unbridgeable gulf between God in his essence and the mutable world that we inhabit. Reason can understand God's essence only as the negation of all the properties that characterize this world in whole and in part: finitude, change, movement, passive affectability, and so on (God is *not* characterized by any of these qualities, but human reason cannot assert any *positive* attribute that is true of God's essence). Reason can grasp God in his positivity only through the *effects* he causes, namely, the rational order of nature and the rationally justified (as propaedeutic to moral virtue) commandments of the Pentateuch.

Maimonides argues that the teachings of the Talmudists that do not conform to Aristotelian philosophy—the creation of the world out of nothing, the resurrection of the dead, the reward and punishment of the soul in the afterlife— can be defended as articles of *belief* precisely because these teachings can neither be demonstrated nor refuted by reason. Aside from these articles of belief,

Maimonides draws the interpretation of the Pentateuch completely within the ambit of rational scrutiny and contemporary scientific knowledge (Ptolemaic astronomy rather than Aristotelian, the theories of the four humors, and so on). The laws of kashrut, for example, serve hygienic goals. The pig is forbidden because its flesh is the source of disease. Miracles are merely "knot points" in the unalterable causal sequence of the natural world. When the time comes when these knot points are reached, a "pause" in the sequence occurs. These pauses look like miracles, but they are only complications in the same causal nexus that governs all the events of the world: "Divine interventions in the natural order simply do not exist."[62]

Maimonides's Aristotelianism, Goldberg concludes, divides Jewish religious doctrine into two parts: those propositions that conform to reason (and Aristotelian philosophy) and those whose truth or falsity is beyond reason's capacity to adjudicate (*creatio ex nihilo*, resurrection, and so on). (Goldberg aptly compares Maimonides to Kant on this score.) The propositions that can neither be proved nor refuted by reason constitute the articles of Jewish belief or dogma. Among the dogmas is the coming of the messianic kingdom when Jews will return to Zion. Maimonides teaches that the messianic age will arise at the conclusion of a continuously progressing historical development. When it arrives, there will be no break in the natural laws of our present world. The beginning and the end of the world as we know it are the only points where miracles can be said to occur: creation from nothing and the resurrection of the dead. Finally, Maimonides overturns the open-endedness of the Talmudic tradition. Rather than remaining faithful to the transmission of conflicting viewpoints in the Talmud, Maimonides codifies his interpretation of the appropriate resolutions of conflicts in his *Mishnah Torah*. In effect, he makes the Talmud an object of study, but not of living tradition.

Goldberg concludes the first half of his book with an assessment of Maimonides's role in Jewish history. Maimonides, Goldberg says, can be considered the progenitor not only of the Jewish Enlightenment (insofar as he subjects the Pentateuch and its laws to a rational exegesis governed by contemporary scientific norms) but also of Orthodoxy (in his insistence that Judaism has dogmas that cannot be rationally refuted and in his zeal to codify Talmudic law rather than engage in its open-ended development). And Maimonides is the progenitor of Zionism, the practical project of creating a Jewish state within the framework of the natural and historical laws governing all the world's peoples. Last but certainly not least, Maimonides, Goldberg claims, is the father of the Jewish cultural assimilationists by bending revelation into the mold of the culturally foreign categories of Greek philosophy and science.

The second half of *Maimonides* is devoted to the explication of Goldberg's own fourteen theses and a discussion of the possibilities confronting the Jewish people in his day. The fourteen theses are essentially condensations of the major points advanced in *The Reality of the Hebrews*. Having analyzed Maimonides as the source of all the modern forms of Jewish malaise, Goldberg now offers his therapy. Goldberg's theses begin with a preamble in which he lays out the Pentateuch's fundamental philosophical problem: how to reconcile God's omnipotence (*Allmacht*) with the imperfections of the world, imperfections that are felt as *injustices*. "The problem of God's omnipotence is the authentic problem of the Torah. For directly upon acknowledging God's omnipotence the question arises as to his justice. If God is omnipotent, why has he created such an imperfect world? Why has he burdened humanity with such a frail and fragile body? Why does he permit it that humanity must struggle with a natural world that is not merely unsuited to humanity's designs but downright inimical to them?"[63] The central problem facing the Torah, Goldberg declares, is the problem that produces the theological genre known as "theodicy," the "defense case for God." Traditionally, theodicy attempts to reconcile the omnipotence of a God who can create the world out of nothing (only infinite power could accomplish this) with the injustice of the created world as we experience it in our frail, fragile, and frustrated existences. Theodicy is unwilling to abandon the doctrine of the omnipotence of God, and therefore it denies the reality of the world's injustice. As Leibniz put it, "this is the best of all possible worlds." Goldberg is radically opposed to this form of theodicy. He refuses to deny the reality of the world's injustice. The need to work out an adequate concept of God's omnipotence as Creator that is compatible with an acknowledgment of the world's real injustice is Goldberg's first "thesis." He says that it is the guiding problem of his philosophy. His answer is simple: God, insofar as he is present within the world, is *not* omnipotent in his dealings with humanity (Goldberg views the war with Amalek, God's "eschatological enemy," as a signal example of God's limited power).

Goldberg accepts the claim that creation ex nihilo is not possible without an infinitely powerful God. Goldberg sides with the Talmudists against the Kabbalists on the question of whether God created the world from nothing or emanated it out of his infinity. The Talmudists are right that creation from nothing is possible if God is omnipotent. An infinitely powerful God can produce something out of nothing; this is simply a matter of logic. But also as a matter of logic, the world created by God's infinite power is necessarily imperfect. The created world cannot be as perfect as God for then it would not be separate (created as different) from God; in effect the world would then be a second God (Spinoza used this logic to claim that God and world are one substance). The created world, therefore, must be imperfect, simply by virtue of its createdness. The Kabbalists account for the imperfection in various ways, including, for example, Rabbi Isaac Luria's doctrine of the breaking of the vessels. This is not the path that Goldberg takes. For him, it is simply a matter of logical necessity that the created world is imperfect. But the logical necessity of the world's imperfection means that the created order must be unjust. Disease, death, and frustrated aspirations are constitutive elements of *this* world but not of a *perfect* world. Rather than place the blame for the injustice of the world on a sinful humanity or some cosmic catastrophe like the breaking of the vessels, Goldberg describes it as a constitutive feature of any world that truly is "outside God."

Given the constitutive nature of the world's imperfection and injustice, the question of theodicy—how an omnipotent God can permit the world's injustice—must be restated as follows: How can an omnipotent God reconcile his sense of justice with the necessity that a created world is an unjust world? It is not the injustice of the world that is the essential problem that theodicy must solve; it is the *existence of the world as such*. There is, according to Goldberg's reasoning, only one condition under which God could have reconciled himself to creating a necessarily imperfect and therefore unjust world: "He must himself enter into the world as surety for its justice. God must have reserved a right to enter the world." The existence of the world is incompatible with a conception of the Creator who will not descend to the level of what he has created. This is Goldberg's second thesis.

The Creator's descent to the level of the created world is his entrance into time: he cannot have a perfect world *all at once*. The Creator's descent into the world and temporality is his *revelation*:

> Therefore God, who wants to have a world, is constrained to respond to and undo the limitation on his omnipotence. From which it follows that God's goal for the world and also the meaning of the world is this: *to allow the omnipotence of God to enter into the world*. This can only be achieved if *God himself* enters the world. The entrance of God in the world is called: revelation. And now we understand the meaning and purpose of revelation: the limitation upon God's omnipotence that was a consequence of the creation of the world must be once more undone through revelation. That is the third thesis.[64]

Creation, therefore, logically demands revelation. For Goldberg, this means that *God himself* must enter the world, which in turn means that God must reveal himself in and through living corporeality, but one that is not subject to the necessity of death. Unlike the Christian doctrine of the divine Word becoming *mortal* flesh, Goldberg claims that God's incarnation is not bound by the strictures governing "normal" biology. This is expounded in the following three theses.

The entrance of God into the world requires that he conform to some set of rules or laws because "if the preworldly God [i.e., the infinite God before creation] were to storm into the world without rules [*regellos*], he would simply destroy it."[65] (This is the fourth thesis.) However, God cannot merely accommodate himself to the rules of inorganic matter if he hopes to allow his omnipotence to enter the world fully. God must "construct an order through which he can place himself into relationship with both living and dead matter, and therefore *this order must be an organism*."[66] (This is the fifth thesis.) Of course, God's organism cannot be just another organism among many others. It must be an organism that is not limited in its functioning as are other organisms; it must contain the virtual power of *all biological functions*. In the Pentateuch this is called *temimut*, wholeness, or "the wholeness function" (*die Ganzheitsfunktion*). The divine organism must provide the basis for bringing an imperfect natural order into conformity with God's omnipotence. It must be a vehicle, in other words, for the *continuous revelation of God*. "One can characterize it as the *transformation-schematism between revelation and nature*."[67] (This is the sixth thesis.) In chapter 4 I described this organism as a topological energy-field instantiated within Israel's encampment and marching order during its desert wanderings. The cult practices at the tabernacle circulated the energy into camp and in turn drew from Israel new energy through the daily sacrifices with which to sustain the presence of the glory of God in the pillar of fire by night and the pillar of cloud by day. This continuous production of the divine organism can be considered a continuous miracle, but it is better understood as the *production of a new natural order in the midst of the old one*. "A miracle is what conforms to the natural law of the progressing idea of divine omnipotence."[68] (This is the seventh thesis.)

Goldberg's concept of a continuous miracle operating according to a higher natural law is based on the assumption that "nature is not an impenetrable, closed whole."[69] (This directly contradicts Maimonides's position.) He explains that the "negative properties" of nature—the properties it possesses insofar as it is a limited structure created out of nothing—are what permit the breakthrough of a new order into the old order, beginning with the emergence of life itself in the universe. With each breakthrough act, "the manifestation expanse of the Godhead goes from one power realm [*Machtbereich*] to another in the direction of All-Power [i.e., omnipotence, *Allmacht*]."[70] I cannot resist hearing in this description of the increasing powers of God a reference to the number classes ("cardinalities") of Georg Cantor, each the "power set" or *Mächtigkeit* of the previous one, whose limit is the Absolute Infinite of God himself. Thus, revelation is the means to *increasing the transfinite life of God*.

Goldberg now is ready to lay out the interpretive principles guiding his explication of the Pentateuch. The narrative in the Pentateuch is not about humans; it is about God. References to God's relationship with humans in the Pentateuch describe God's progressive entrance into the world and the stages that lead up to his revelation. Humans are, to be sure, necessary participants in the process of God's overcoming the limits imposed on his omnipotence at creation. But God does not act on behalf of humans; he acts on behalf of himself. "All the expressions (of a terminological nature) and all descriptions that deal with the relationship of God to humans relate to God himself and are propositions that deal with God himself. The covenant—the *Brit*—between God and Israel is a covenant for the sake of God."[71] (This is the eighth thesis, and it directly contests Maimonides's doctrine that all predicates attributed to God in the Bible express the *human* perspective on God.) The ritual laws regarding sacrifice in the Pentateuch, for example, are designed to maintain the divine organism in its functioning. The holiness and purity laws are designed to separate the organism from contact with foreign organisms (the gods of the other peoples). These other organisms do not have the same goal as God's organism: they are not seeking to increase the power of God in the world to the point of omnipotence, but to *thwart it*. They are therefore on the side of the existing natural order. (Here Goldberg follows Maimonides, who believed that pagan polytheism was the worship of natural objects, the stars, which Aristotle took to be organisms with an ethereal corporeality.) They represent the biological functions of already existing animal life, not the totality function of the virtual source of all biological functions. These gods employ cultic sexual practices (the *hieros gamos* or "holy marriage" ceremony, for example) and also the sacrifice of humans (subordinating the human to the partial biological function of an animal.) The Pentateuch's purity laws are practices that maintain the divine organism's immunity against these foreign bodies.[72] Even the so-called ethical prohibitions like that against murder are designed to protect the divine organism from the incursion of impurity from the blood of the victim staining the land where God's organism dwells.

Goldberg's explication of the Sabbath commandment brings to the fore the meaning of the divine organism's presence in the world in its negative relationship to the world's natural (and imperfect) order. We have so far considered how the manifestation of God in Israel's cult is designed to increase God's power and decrease the imperfection of the natural order. This is not a simple matter of forward progress. The natural order, like every order, has a tendency to harden into fixity. In chapter 4 I explained how the nation-state is the fixation of the order of the "unmetaphysical" peoples who have lost their connection with their "biological center." All of nature hardens itself against the pressure of revelation. And, insofar as the divine organism is itself a part of the larger natural world, it also has a tendency to fixity. The natural order of God's organism "however high it may be, always contains elements of *normal* nature."[73] The Sabbath prohibition of work is designed to preserve the distinction between the *miraculous* order of the divine organism (all the activity of the cult continues on the Sabbath) and the *normal* order of nature. In particular, the work that is prohibited is any work that was done in the construction of the tabernacle. This work was not miraculous, but employed material nature in accordance with its basic order. This work was *technological*. The Sabbath commandment is designed to draw a bright line between God's goal of bringing justice through the transcendence of the imperfect natural order of the world and the attempt to master the natural world through the deployment of its own limited power. "The God who has taken himself into the world is the implacable foe of technology."[74] He is the enemy of the present natural order of the world. He is the enemy of every stable normality. (This is the ninth thesis.)

God's purpose as it relates only to himself is to bring the world to perfection so that he no longer needs to limit himself in relation to the created world. (This is the tenth thesis.) He can do this only in a slow process of battling against the natural order of the world in its imperfection and its tendency to stabilize itself against revelation. In the end, the world's natural order will no longer be limited, and it will be fully adequate to hold God's presence (his glory) within itself. Since "glory" in Hebrew (*kavod*) has the same root consonants as the adjective "heavy" (*kaved*), the full presence of God in the world means that the laws of three-dimensional space will give full expression to "the principle of gravitational force."[75] Space will hold the "coagulation [*Verdichtung*] of the divine organism in its efficacy [*Wirksamkeit*]." The "force coagulation" of the divine organism was in ancient times effected at the tabernacle during Israel's wilderness wandering: "The tent represented a dynamic system whose goal was to make Elohim present. It contained a *motor* that worked day and night (the sacrifices with their fire, spices, and animal offering) and that united physics and biology (and therefore cosmology and anthropology). . . . The clouds of YHWH's glory there were the 'force coagulation' of YHWH."[76] Thus, the goal of God's engagement with the world: to install within it an indestructible tabernacle, a site within the finite realm where a "power can dwell that belongs to a wholly heterogeneous grade of reality."[77] When God acquires this permanent site for his power, his revelation will be brought to completion. He will have made it possible for the world to contain his glory. And when the world contains God's glory, God will have restored the proper relationship between his omnipotence and his justice. This is God's "self-justification" (*Selbstgerechtigkeit*).[78] (This is the eleventh thesis.)

God's self-justification can be understood to be the polar opposite of traditional theodicy, the "defense case for God." God does not want humanity to offer a defense of "the ways of God" in the midst of an unjust order. God instead wants humanity to work together with him to build a new tabernacle where his glory can dwell in the midst of the world. Humanity, and only humanity, is able to break through the present natural order and bring a new order into being because humanity, made in the image of God, possesses a share of the "totality function" of the divine organism. In fact, humanity is the "master of the natural order" (*Herr der Naturordnung*).[79] But humanity is also a part of the natural order and, as such, can conceive of its mastership in purely natural terms, as a function of harnessing the "normal" order of nature to serve human needs. "If humanity works with the normal order of nature, it creates technology." But in this way, humanity will betray the essence of its authentic mastership, which consists in *going beyond* normality. Humanity will become the servant of nature rather than its master. To transcend the order of nature through metaphysical rather than technological means is the "world goal of humanity," which Goldberg characterizes as humanity's ethical task. To fail to fulfill humanity's ethical task is not only to become a slave to technology but also to *increase the imperfection of the natural world*: "If the human being does not fulfill his ethical demand, which is to become the enemy of technology in the *same* way that the Godhead itself is, then there will arise all the natural catastrophes, economic failures, and sociological deformities [*Ungeheuerlichkeiten*] that are part of the grim inventory of an unethical world order."[80] However, if humanity does fulfill its ethical world goal, there will be two results. First there will be a transformation in human biology itself, "the removal of all the compulsion [*Zwang*] in which nature's inertia and fixity holds humanity by virtue of the fragile constitution of the organic functioning of the body." Second, the ethical world order will be expressed sociologically as the unification of power and justice: "The immanently present God stands surety for the ethical world order *in which power and justice are united*."[81]

Goldberg reiterates in *Maimonides* the claim that was central to *The Reality of the Hebrews*: the revelation of God in the world can only take place through a *people*, and never through separate individuals. "The people correspond to the organism of God. Both together—God and people—constitute the *Brit*, the covenant, in other words, a system of mutual exchange." The exchange relations established between God and people define a *ritual* system that is opposed to mere *technology*. Unlike technology, which merely perpetuates the unjust order of nature by using its power to maintain the given order, ritual joins a people and God together "in order to create an actuality of a higher order."[82] The individual is charged to assist in this creation. He or she must become a prophet, one who is "the master of the miracle" (*Herr des Wunders*). All peoples within whose population there resides some residual capacity from the earliest period of humanity for wonder working, a residual capacity for ritual, should join with one another in a new "universalism." "There is a Jewish tradition," Goldberg writes, "that says that the Torah was offered to *all* peoples. Therefore the *ethical* imperative is clear that is addressed to all ritual-capable peoples: Perform Hebrew ritual!"[83] (This is Goldberg's thesis number 13.) When all ritual-capable peoples express their wonder-working capacities together, the order of nature as it is now imperfectly constituted will be altogether transformed. "The *Kavod*, the manifestation sphere of the immanently present [*anwesende*] Godhead, will encompass the entire earth—and then the world is redeemed [*erlöst*]."[84]

Finally, Goldberg turns to the role of the Jewish people in the redemptive process of bringing God's *kavod* into the world. He points out that when Israel's "nationalists" used their "technological architectural skills" to construct the Solomonic Temple, Israel as a whole was doomed to be driven into exile from the land in which God had hoped to manifest himself through "metaphysical" ritual rather than through natural technology.[85] In *The Reality of the Hebrews*, Goldberg explained how the tabernacle was intended to be a mobile instrument used in the "wars of YHWH" against the cults of the other gods ("stability cults" dedicated to the limited powers of the natural order) and also against the fixation state institutions of peoples who had either lost their connection to their gods or had never possessed one (Babylon). Instead, the Temple rendered God's presence immobile, and the divine organism lost its capacity to maintain its dynamic "exchange system" with the people. Exile was inevitable.

A change in direction (*teshuva*, "turning about") is needed if the Jewish people are to assume their place among the peoples of the world in the "wars of YHWH." The first element of this change is to discern the true reasons for the laws of the Pentateuch. The laws are not "rational" in the way that Maimonides believed, namely, insofar as they are consonant with Greek philosophical morality (virtue ethics) and contemporary science. Rather the laws are rational *to the degree that they can reconfigure the natural order and create a new one.* The ritual laws in ancient Israel had this power, but they were limited to one people. Today, rituals need to be crafted that can fit a universal peoplehood. The need today is for people who can use their reason to forge new rituals. Goldberg explains that in Hebrew a person who has such a power is called a *navon*, the sort of person that Moses in Deuteronomy (1:13) commands the people to select to assist him in governing and judging Israel. Actually, Moses tells the people to select both "wise men" (*chachamim*) and *nevonim*, "men of discernment." Goldberg refers to the medieval French exegete Rabbi Solomon ben Yitzchak (Rashi), who comments on this verse that the *navon* is the one who has a "logical ability" to discover what the "wise" know immediately, without a need for logical reasoning. Rashi further states that in his day (in the time of exile, in other words), *no one is wise.* Goldberg adds, "And now we have the *content* of the change in direction that is the ethical imperative of the time of exile. The time of the exile belongs to the *Nevonim*. These are the logicians who are able to discover the background of ritual through their reason."[86] (This is Goldberg's final thesis, number fourteen.)

Goldberg now brings his section titled "Theses" to an end. He states that the final thesis stands in direct opposition to Maimonides's ninth article of faith, "the Torah is unique." If the ritual laws of the Torah were the only laws that expressed God's "world goal" in relation to a people, then God's glory would never be able to be manifested in the entire world. "The Torah in accordance with its own intention leads beyond itself. All the theses together are encapsulated in this one: The Torah that had previously been the only Torah does not have to remain so. *For one must anticipate a new revelation with the character of the Sinaitic one, that will give to the people new laws with the character of the Torah.*"[87]

Goldberg opens the third and last section of *Maimonides*, "The Future," by excoriating the Jewish people for their failure to live up to the revolutionary demand of their God to transform the world order. He finds it ironic that anyone had ever attributed a revolutionary spirit to Jews. "The immanently present God who had once been the God of the Hebrews, he is revolutionary, not they."[88] The Jewish people are always making accommodations to history, even in the midst of the most terrible persecution. "Always in the course of Jewish history there is someone to write a graceful poem of lamentation for every pogrom. The Jews would have been able to learn a lesson from the Sioux Indians."[89]

Goldberg has nothing but scorn for all the current movements within Judaism. He counts them all as having one and the same goal for the future of the Jewish people: their transformation into a "normal" people. The modern Orthodox who espouse "Torah together with Derech Eretz [the customs of the world]" want only to be able to enjoy all the benefits of modern civilization's technological advances. The Zionists play the game of international power politics so that Palestine can be the site of "industry, financial markets, and land speculation."[90] Finally, there are the Jews who fall into neither the Orthodox nor the Zionist camp but are "the compromisers at any price, the ones who profess that they await the Messiah, the ones who are Bible scholars but who do not take the Bible seriously, and the ones who stand Thou to Thou with an absent God."[91]

Goldberg thus stands opposed to all the "parties" of modern Judaism. Like a Jewish Immanuel Kant breaking with rationalism and empiricism, Goldberg calls for an investigation into "the conditions of possibility of revelation."[92] Like a Jewish Hegel breaking with the static nature of Kant's conditions, Goldberg acknowledges that the conditions of possibility of revelation have a history. In the beginning of the world, the active forces were "abiogenetic powers" (*Urzeungungskräfte*) through which God created the world out of nothing and then created living organisms out of inorganic matter. The abiogenetic powers (those that bring about spontaneous generation) are described in all the "works" of God in the first six days of creation. The creation of inorganic matter and of living organisms were acts involving the "breakthrough" (*Durchbrechung*) of infinite power into the limited sphere of the empirical realm. As Goldberg had earlier explained in *Maimonides*, the goal of creation is to allow God's infinite power to find expression within the finite realm so that his justice can be reconciled with his omnipotence. For some time, the abiogenetic powers held sway within the world, and God's presence in the world grew. New life forms proliferated. The creation of living beings from inorganic matter was an ongoing process. And after each new work of creation, there was a divine Sabbath. "The Sabbath is not only the conclusion of the six days of God's work after which the rule of the abiogenetic powers is supposed to begin, it is also the 'act of interruption' [*Unter-brechungsakt*], the Nothing, from which God brought forth the world."[93] The Sabbath is not a day of rest, but a day marking the transition between one natural order and a new one that supervenes as God's presence (his *kavod* or glory) progressively fills finitude. The Sabbath is the reinsertion of Nothing into the world, so that infinity can once again break into finitude and inaugurate a higher order. The Hebrew word Sabbath means not only "rest" but also "stop." In speaking of the Sabbath as an act of interruption equivalent to the Nothing that is the source of creation, Goldberg, as noted in earlier chapters, is appropriating the set-theoretical interpretation of number theory as developed by Dedekind, Cantor, Frege, and others. The Sabbath is like Cantor's higher cardinality or "power" (the cardinal number of the set of all subsets of finite numbers) that breaks through the series of finite numbers and starts a new "higher order" series. It is, in other words, a principle of discontinuity that disrupts every possible closure of the system of nature and opens the possibility of the new.

The Sabbath with its disruptive and creative power began to fall under the sway of the natural sequence of time after the event that the Pentateuch calls the Flood. Goldberg quotes the verse that concludes the narrative of the Flood: "Seedtime and harvest, cold and heat, summer and winter, day and night, shall not stop" (Genesis 8:22). Because the verb "stop" in this verse has the same root consonants as Sabbath, Goldberg concludes that the Flood marks the beginning of a new era, the "general stabilization of the powers of nature." Hence arises the necessity of a people who would be able to disrupt the sequence of time and preserve the power of divine creation within the world. "Only one people, the people who possess the revelation, are able to repeat the act of creation and go from one creation to another."[94] This people was able to hold itself in relation to the original "abiogenetic power" by forming a covenant with the God who is the "biology-productive" source of this power. Unlike all other peoples, the covenanted people of revelation retain in the Torah a power to repeat the breakthrough act of creation. The Torah can never entirely succumb to the natural forces of stability and normality. There lies within it the infinite power that can repeat "creation within creation." This power must be rediscovered by the "logicians" (*nevonim*) of the Jewish people. They in turn must take their discoveries and bring them to other peoples who retain some of their ancient capacity for ritual. Goldberg believes that these peoples will not be found among the nations of Europe, which have entirely succumbed to the rule of technology over ritual. Only in the Far East and in Africa can remnants of ritual-capable peoples be found. These peoples still perform rituals that draw on the abiogenetic powers of the "Urtime." The logicians of the Pentateuch can show how these rituals can be connected to the ultimate creative source of all abiogenetic power, YHWH.

It is, therefore, the task of Jews today to take the lead in a mission to the non-European world. Jews must break entirely from their racial conception of their chosenness and accept the racial principle at work in the Pentateuch, namely, that the people of God are not defined by their racial makeup. "A ritual-capable Mongolian ethnicity [*Mongolenstamm*] who is brought into the service of YHWH Elohim thereby become the 'people of YHWH' and a member of this ethnicity becomes anthropologically full Jews in the sense of Urjudaism."[95]

At the conclusion of *Maimonides*, Goldberg makes his final appeal to his Jewish readers to reject the Maimonidean "assimilationist" theology in accordance with which God is omnipotent and perfectly just, and humanity is charged only to obey God's will and await the coming of the Messiah. Goldberg rejects the passivity of waiting for the Messiah: "The flaw in all forms of waiting for the Messiah is this: it places the initiative for change in God's hands. *God does not legitimize this world order*, but he rather wants to break through into this world in order to let a higher world order enter. God has done everything he can on his side: he has created the possibility of his entrance, but it is up to humans to seize it."[96] We must not sit passively waiting for God to send his Messiah, but must, like Job, reject the idea that the world as it stands is just and that it is God's will that we simply accept this order and wait patiently for our salvation. The book of Job's essential message is that "Zidduk ha-din, the justification of the given, is a crime."[97] But the book of Job is unable to solve the problem of theodicy, of how to reconcile the justice of God with the injustice of the world, and Goldberg explains why: "The problem of theodicy is insoluble so long as one accepts the uniqueness of the Torah."[98] The Torah is misunderstood if it is taken to be not only a historic record of Israel's past metaphysical power but also as a closing of the door on any future rebirth of that power *on the initiative of the people*. Goldberg does not want Jews to rebuild the Temple (whose construction, as we saw in chapter 4, is the beginning of the end of Israel's metaphysical power) nor even to recreate the tabernacle with its sacrificial cult. The sacrificial cult and the tabernacle allowed Israel to win its battle against the Amalekites in the desert and against the Canaanite cities in the time of Joshua. Today what is called for is, indeed, a "new revelation on the scale of the Sinaitic revelation and a new Torah."[99] As we have seen, this new revelation will require the work of "logicians" and the cooperation of remnants of the ritual-capable peoples. It will require Jews who are "simple people" without partisan commitments to one or another historical tradition descending from the Hebrew Bible. They must be willing to "abandon the 3,400 years of Jewish history as a fiasco and write it off just as if it were a business loss." These Jewish simple people "must be willing to be historyless [*geschichtslos*], since historyless means: to be supersensory-revolutionary [*übersinnlich-revolutionär*]."[100]

Goldberg condenses the articles of his new Jewish belief structure down from the Maimonidean thirteen to five: (1) In place of expecting a Messiah, expect a new Torah; (2) free yourselves from the canonical status of the "Holy Bible" and accept only the Pentateuch as the revelation of the metaphysical power of God; (3) recognize this world order as unjust; (4) understand that the Torah is opposed to the "normal" natural order of the world and the laws governing it; and (5) recognize that all the "world religions" are religions that celebrate unwittingly God's impotence.[101]

Contrary to what Scholem had claimed, these five theses in no way constitute a gnostic mythologization of Judaism. There is no talk of a hidden God and a tyrannical demiurge, or some reverse formation with a good "worldly" God and a distant "universal" God of world religion and philosophical theology. Goldberg's "supersensory-revolutionary" theses articulate a theology in which humanity and God must join together in bringing justice into the world and, by making God's "biology-productive" power present in the world, transcend the limits imposed on humanity by the "normality" of nature's laws. In this world, a "supersensory-revolutionary" revelation would do battle with every form of racism and ethnic particularism, including Jewish particularism. There can be no talk of a "Jewish state," but only of a "stateless upbuilding of a Jewish people," to use the title of Unger's book that I discussed earlier in this chapter. Significantly, Unger speaks of "a" (*eines*) Jewish people, not "the" Jewish people. Since "the" Torah is not unique, neither is "the" Jewish people: only the God of Israel is unique. The task incumbent on the present Jewish people, Goldberg declares, is to become "a" Jewish people, that is, a people who can bear responsibility for realizing God's justice in the world.

The final pages of *Maimonides* address the historical conditions that make a new revelation necessary *now*. Goldberg refers to his two most prominent disciples, Erich Unger and Adolf Caspary, who together offer what he believes is a compelling account of the present sociological and economic condition of humanity. According to Caspary's *Maschinenutopie*, the supply of raw material that provides the energy to run the machinery of the capitalist economy (coal and oil) will run out in approximately two centuries, but before this occurs the high cost of these raw materials will make production no longer economically feasible.[102] (He did not, of course, take into account the dangers of global warming due to fossil fuel consumption, which seriously reduces this two-century limit on coal and oil use.) Goldberg acknowledges that rumors circulate of new sources of energy (he mentions "smashing the atom"), but he dismisses these as unable to supply the needs of a rapidly growing world population. Erich Unger, he says, has argued that technological inventiveness has reached a final limit. No new transformative inventions like the steam engine are possible, Unger posits. Goldberg explains why: technology reaches the limit of its power to transform matter when it runs up against the limits of human biology. Goldberg states that a spaceship to other worlds might be technologically possible, but such travel "is incompatible with the organic laws" governing human life in its current form. Goldberg does not deny the need to escape the earth's limits and reach out for a "piece of the cosmos" (*Stück vom Kosmos*), but he does not believe that humanity can sever its ties to the earth.[103] Therefore, humanity must connect to the cosmos without space travel. The cosmos, Goldberg believes, holds within itself the biology-productive power that once brought life into existence on this planet. This power remains untapped, but it is present within the collective power of the human species. This biology-productive power is not accessible through technology, however. It is only accessible through new rituals that will bring about a wholly new way of living, one that frees humanity from the imperfections of its "normal" organic existence. The "simple people," and in particular the Jewish proletariat, must defend themselves against the technological hubris of European humanity that will inevitably lead to their greater and greater immiseration. Goldberg warns against the Zionist goal of "Europeanization" of the "Orient," a goal that he says will only spread a new and virulent "Oriental" anti-Semitism that will make Jewish life in the region impossible. "But what possibilities lie in an ambitious religious *Orientpolitik*," he declares. The Jewish European proletariat must bring to non-European peoples, especially those who still possess some remnants of their ancient metaphysical powers, the logic of revelation, that is, the understanding of the Pentateuch whose foundations Goldberg himself laid bare in *The Reality of the Hebrews*. The religious *Orientpolitik* is a form of Jewish missionary activity that cannot only save the Jewish people, but all people:

> This [the religious *Orientpolitik*] is the affair that the little man needs to concern himself with now. He needs to know that he must not allow the last remnants of the mythic cults to disappear and the transformation of all people into "Europeans." The little man must ward off all talk of sensational new technological discoveries: they disappear into the mist the minute they appear. He needs to acknowledge that without supersensory means [*übersinnliche Mittel*] there is neither progress nor salvation, because with these humanity cannot go beyond the limits of the earth. And he must go beyond the earth's limits because there is more needed from the earth than the earth possesses. To use supersensory means to go beyond the earth's limits is the true world revolution, not any kind of socialism.[104]

The world revolution will require, Goldberg goes on to say, "the untapped forces of life" (*die bisher unausgenutzten lebendigen Kräfte*). These forces are latent within the peoples who have not yet lost their capacity for cultic ritual. "To activate these forces is to work with the forces of organic matter. This is what it means to produce a revelation [*Offenbarungsherstellung*]."[105]

Goldberg concludes *Maimonides* with a dire warning: either the Jewish people will live up to the demands of a metaphysical world revolution, or they will be left out of the revolution and thereby lose their last opportunity to represent

Hebraism in the world. Other peoples will assume the task that the Jews forsake. Neither in Europe nor in the East is there any other future for the Jewish people.

What do we make of Goldberg's rather negative final judgment concerning the place of the Jewish people in world history, coming as it does in the same year that the Nuremberg laws were promulgated (1935)? Goldberg's conception of the failure of the Jewish people to live up to their metaphysical task (*Aufgabe*) can be compared to two other negative evaluations of the metaphysical status of the Jewish people, those of Carl Schmitt and Martin Heidegger. I have had occasion to speak about Schmitt's recommendation of Goldberg's *Maimonides* to his friend Ernst Jünger. Together with Bruno Bauer's *Die Judenfrage* (*The Jewish Question*), Schmitt described *Maimonides* as essential reading for anyone who wants to understand the Jewish people in the modern world.[106] Schmitt thought that Goldberg had correctly diagnosed the malaise confronting the modern world, namely, its capitulation to technorational administration in all spheres of social and political life. Schmitt, however, believed that Goldberg had grotesquely misrepresented the Jewish people as having the latent capacity to renew a *cultic* rather than a *technological* relationship to the earth. Dismissing Goldberg's entire reconstruction of the revolutionary "Hebrew metaphysics" of the Pentateuch, Schmitt judged the Jewish people to be the purveyors of rootlessness and calculative rationality. Heidegger, in his recently published Black Notebooks, offers the outlines of a theory of the "gods" and their return to the earth through a renewal of the German people's former metaphysical encounter with "Seyn" (Being, in an archaic spelling) in their "poetic" (i.e., mythic) dwelling on the earth. Heidegger never refers to Goldberg, but there are striking parallels in some of his formulations to those of Goldberg in *The Reality of the Hebrews*.[107] Whether or not Heidegger was familiar with Goldberg is really not to the point, however. The question is: Was Goldberg aligned with the reactionary political philosophies of Schmitt and Heidegger?

The answer is complicated. First of all, Goldberg was adamantly opposed to the nation-state as the vehicle of any metaphysical peoplehood. But there is evidence that Schmitt and Heidegger, despite their early embrace of Adolf Hitler and National Socialism, became (privately) critical of the power structures of the single-party state apparatus invoked by Hitler to tighten his grip on German society. Second, Goldberg was adamantly opposed to any biological or racial basis of metaphysical peoplehood. Indeed, it was his central contention that YHWH Elohim was the unique God who sought to triumph over the biological gods of the other peoples. But it would be unfair to accuse Schmitt or Heidegger of having advocated Aryan racism or the need for the biological purification of the German people. On one issue, however, the difference between Goldberg on the one hand and Schmitt and Heidegger on the other is unequivocal and stark. Never, at any time, did Goldberg seek to stigmatize one particular people as characterologically tainted by its penchant for technorationalism. Never did he single out any one group when he discussed the distancing of European modernity from the metaphysical gods of antiquity. Never did Goldberg scapegoat one people as the purveyors of technorational corruption. Both Schmitt and Heidegger, however, fell in line with the prevailing anti-Semitism of their culture, recycling its tropes in their reflections on the need for the German people to distance itself from the Jews' metaphysical "rootlessness." They recycled these tropes from the time when they actively participated in the National Socialist de-judification of their institutions (university and judiciary) to the time when they knew that the regime had put into operation a vast machinery of genocide. Goldberg had no part in the intellectual and moral failure that afflicted not only Schmitt and Heidegger but many of Germany's leading intellectuals. I believe that Schmitt (and most likely Heidegger) appropriated Goldberg's ideas but failed to be touched by the force of his anti-racist and anti-statist positions. Schmitt called Goldberg a "Jewish philosopher," and this allowed him to dismiss his "Hebrew metaphysics" as mere special pleading.

Goldberg seems to have given little or no thought to Judaism or to the Jewish people after he arrived in the United States in 1941. He did not seek out Jewish leaders or Jewish intellectuals. Rather, he undertook to establish "proofs of immortality" by photographing ghosts and recording poltergeist activity. This seems like quite an abdication of Goldberg's revolutionary goals as they are laid out in *The Reality of the Hebrews* and *Maimonides*. I will argue in the conclusion that there is a deeper logic that connects world revolution through Hebrew metaphysics to spirit photography.

## Notes

1. Gershom Scholem, "The Crisis of Tradition in Jewish Messianism," in Scholem, *The Messianic Idea in Judaism and Other Essays on Jewish Spirituality* (New York: Schocken Books, 1971), 50.

2. Ibid.

3. Goldberg, *Maimonides: Kritik der jüdischer Glaubenslehre* (Vienna: Heinrich Glanz, 1935), reprinted in Goldberg-*Aufsätze*, 123–217. Quotation is found on p. 160. All further references will be to the reprint in Goldberg-*Aufsätze*.

4. Scholem, "Toward an Understanding of the Messianic Idea in Judaism," in Scholem, *The Messianic Idea in Judaism*, 35.

5. *Maimonides*, Goldberg-*Aufsätze*, 203.

6. Erich Unger, "Der Universalismus des Hebräertums: Philosophie und Kabbalah, dargestellt aus dem Gesichtspunkt der Goldbergschen Schrift 'Die Wirklichkeit der Hebräer.' Eine Entgegnung auf G. Scholems 'Die Theologie des Sabbatianismus im Lichte Abraham Cardosos,'" in Erich Unger, *Vom Expressionismus zum Mythos des Hebräertums: Schriften 1909 bis 1931*, ed. Manfred Voigts (Würzburg: Königshausen & Neumann, 1992), 97–143. Unger's essay

was first published in Voigts's collection of his essays. An English translation is found in Esther Ehrman, "Erich Unger's 'Der Universalismus des Hebraertums,'" *Journal of Jewish Thought and Philosophy* 4, no. 2 (1995): 271–314.

7. For a detailed treatment of the controversy between Scholem and Goldberg, see Manfred Voigts, "Eine nicht ausgetragene Kontroverse: Die Beziehung Gershom Scholem zu Oskar Goldberg und Erich Unger," *Ashkenas* 25, no. 2 (2015): 313–364, reprinted in Manfred Voigts, *Jüdische Geistesarbeit und andere Aufsätze über Jakob Frank bis H. G. Adler* (Würzburg: Königshausen & Neumann, 2016), 329–379. My reading of the controversy differs from Voigts's, but does not contest it. I focus not only on the early essay on Cardoso and Sabbatianism (where Goldberg is figured as bringing a new form of Sabbatianism into the Jewish world) but also on Scholem's critique of Goldberg's and Unger's anti-Zionism and his wish to draw Benjamin away from the Goldberg circle. David Biale has also recently discussed Scholem's criticism of Goldberg in Biale, "Gershom Scholem on Anarchism and Nihilism," *Rethinking History* 19, no. 1 (2015): 61–71. Biale offers a nuanced interpretation in this article of Scholem's ambivalent relationship to political Zionism, especially to the goal of creating a Jewish state. See also David Biale, *Gershom Scholem: Kabbalah and Counter-History*, 2nd ed. (Cambridge, MA: Harvard University Press, 1982), 107–111. Biale's discussion of Scholem suggests that, perhaps, his rejection of Goldberg's ideas about the future of the Jewish people stems from his attempt to distance himself from some of the more radical implications of his own theories. Voigts also points to the possibility that Scholem saw in Goldberg (or projected onto Goldberg) a life path that, as we know from early diary entries, he himself felt tempted to take, namely, that of modern-day Messiah.

8. Gershom Scholem, "Über Die Theologie des Sabbatianismus im Lichte Abraham Cardosos," originally published in the journal *Der Jude* (1928): 123–139. The essay is reprinted in Gershom Scholem, *Judaica*, 6 vols. (Frankfurt am Main: Suhrkamp, 1968), 1:119–146. Page references in what follows are to the original publication, available at http://sammlungen.ub .uni-frankfurt.de/cm/periodical/titleinfo/3110818.

9. Gershom Scholem, *Briefe: Band I, 1914–1947*, ed. Gershom Scholem and Theodor Adorno (Munich: C. H. Beck, 1994), 235–239.

10. Scholem, letter 145 to Lionel Kochan (in English), in *Briefe: Band III, 1971–1982*, ed. Itta Schedletzky (Munich: C. H. Beck, 1999), 161.

11. Scholem, "Über Die Theologie des Sabbatianismus," 139. In what follows I discuss how "unpathetic" is also a direct reference to Goldberg's book.

12. Gershom Scholem, *Walter Benjamin: The Story of a Friendship*, trans. Henry Zohn (New York: Schocken Books, 1981), 136.

13. The phrase "life lived in deferment" is found near the end of Scholem's essay, "Toward an Understanding of the Messianic Idea in Judaism"; quotation is found on p. 35.

14. In a letter to Franz Rosenzweig written in 1926, Scholem writes: "A language is composed of names. The power of the language is hidden within the name; its abyss is sealed therein. After invoking the ancient names day after day, we shall no longer be able to hold off their power." Scholem, *On the Possibility of Jewish Mysticism*, trans. Jonathan Chipman (Philadelphia: Jewish Publication Society, 1997), 27–28.

15. For a detailed exposition of Abraham Cardoso's theology, see Bruce Rosenstock, "Abraham Miguel Cardoso's Messianic Theology: A Reappraisal," *Association of Jewish Studies Review* 23, no. 1 (1998): 63–104.

16. It seems likely that Scholem would have known of the personal connection between Dora Hiller and Goldberg, and it is a little strange that he does not mention it in his memoir. Perhaps he does not want to give the impression of being impolite to Dora Hiller in the remark he makes

about Goldberg—that he is "the representative of the devil of our generation." If she is only an "adherent," the remark is pointed but not impolite. If she is Goldberg's wife, the remark does not reflect very well on Scholem's sense of propriety about what a "decent" German is permitted to say to a wife about her husband, especially if she has just extended an invitation to their home.

17. Gershom Scholem, *From Berlin to Jerusalem: Memories of My Youth* (New York: Schocken Books, 1980), 147.

18. Ibid.

19. Scholem, *Walter Benjamin*, 96–97.

20. Scholem, *Briefe: Band III, 1971–1982*, 140.

21. Scholem, *From Berlin to Jerusalem*, 147–148.

22. Erich Unger, *Die staatlose Bildung eines jüdischen Volkes: Vorrede zu einer gesetzgebender Akademie* (*The Stateless Upbuilding of a Jewish People*) (Berlin: David, 1922).

23. "Das Judentum auf die Ebene auf der Welt entscheidenden körperhaften Gewalten zu bringen." Ibid., 7.

24. Ibid., 12.

25. Ibid., 13.

26. Ibid., 17.

27. "Wohl aber ist eine *Aufgabe* ein Mittel, Verwandtshaft zu *begründen*." Ibid., 18; emphasis Unger's.

28. Goldberg, *Reality of the Hebrews*, 255.

29. Ibid., 256.

30. Unger, *Die staatlose Bildung*, 28.

31. Ibid., 28, 32.

32. Ibid., 13.

33. Biale, *Gershom Scholem*, 109.

34. Gershom Scholem, *Major Trends in Jewish Mysticism* (New York: Schocken Books, 1947), 247.

35. Scholem, *Briefe: Band I, 1914–1947*, 235–239.

36. Scholem, *Walter Benjamin*, 97. Scholem's repeated use of the apparently derogatory word "magical" in reference to Goldberg is perhaps influenced by the usage of that word in the work of Franz Joseph Molitor, the author who first inspired Scholem to pursue his own study of the Kabbalah. See Appendix II for a fuller treatment of Molitor's work in relation to Goldberg and a brief description of Scholem's discovery of Molitor. If Molitor's use of "magical" is indeed behind Scholem's use of it to characterize Goldberg, this somewhat tempers the entirely negative connotation the word seems to bear. It is one thing to say Goldberg practices "magic," the tricks of a confidence man, and another thing to say that he wants to resuscitate the theurgic power attributed to the Kabbalah by Molitor. Perhaps Scholem wants to say both things about Goldberg.

37. Gershom Scholem, "Redemption through Sin," in Scholem, *The Messianic Idea in Judaism and Other Essays* (New York: Shocken Books, 1971), 78–141; quotations on pp. 127 and 126.

38. Ibid., 127.

39. Scholem would certainly know that Goldberg had a secure basis in the Kabbalah for describing a "night side" of the supernal world because Franz Joseph Molitor, someone with whom Scholem was very familiar, describes this concept in his work on the Kabbalah. See Appendix II for more on Molitor.

40. Goldberg, *Reality of the Hebrews*, 218.

41. Scholem, "Redemption through Sin," 123.

42. Peter Fenves, *The Messianic Reduction: Walter Benjamin and the Shape of Time* (Stanford, CA: Stanford University Press, 2011), 114. Fenves's book covers an aspect of Benjamin's

thought that brings him very close to the Goldberg circle, especially Erich Unger. Fenves offers a fascinating window on Benjamin's engagement with both Cantorian mathematics and vitalism, the twin sources of Goldberg's thought.

43. Gershom Scholem, "Walter Benjamin," in Scholem, *On Jews and Judaism in Crisis: Selected Essays* (New York: Shocken Books, 1976), 172–197; quotation on p. 183.

44. Scholem, *Walter Benjamin*, 21.

45. For a detailed exposition of Scholem's Fregean philosophy of mathematics as a sphere of formal logic without any possible relationship to mystical or Kabbalistic symbols, see Daniel Weidner, *Gershom Scholem: Politisches, esoterisches und historiographisches Schreiben* (Munich: Wilhelm Fink, 2003), 176–180.

46. Scholem, *Walter Benjamin*, 49.

47. Gottlob Frege, *Die Grundlagen der Arithmetik: Eine logisch mathematische Untersuching über den Begriff der Zahl* (Breslau: Wilhelm Koebner, 1884), 119. Quoted (and translated) in Michael Hallett, *Cantorian Set Theory and Limitation of Size* (Oxford: Clarendon, 1984), 20.

48. Quoted in Weidner, *Gershom Scholem*, 179.

49. Quoted in ibid., 178.

50. Gershom Scholem, "Walter Benjamin and His Angel," in Scholem, *On Jews and Judaism: Selected Essays* (New York: Shocken Books, 1976), 198.

51. Scholem, *Walter Benjamin*, 98.

52. Gershom Scholem and Theodor W. Adorno, eds., *The Correspondence of Walter Benjamin*, trans. Manfred R. Jacobson and Evelyn Jacobson (Chicago: University of Chicago Press, 1994), 172. The letter is dated January 1921.

53. Ibid., 173.

54. Scholem, "Walter Benjamin," 180.

55. Walter Benjamin, "One-Way Street," in Benjamin, *Selected Writings*, vol. 1, *1913–1926*, ed. Marcus Bullock and Michael W. Jennings (Cambridge, MA: Harvard University Press, 2002), 444–488. German in Walter Benjamin, *Gesammelte Schriften Bde. I–VII*, ed. Rolf Tiedemann and Hermann Schweppenhäuser (Frankfurt am Main: Suhrkamp, 1972–1989), IV.1, 83–148. Quotations are from the English translation, pages 486–487.

56. Erich Unger, *Politik und Metaphysik*, ed. Manfred Voigts (Würzburg: Königshausen & Neumann, 1989), 30.

57. Walter Benjamin, "Announcement of the Journal *Angelus Novus*," in Benjamin, *Selected Writings*, 1:292–296; quotation on p. 296; emphasis Benjamin's. German in Tiedemann and Schweppenhäuser, *Gesammelte Schriften Bde. I–VII*, II.1, 241–246.

58. Unger, *Politik und Metaphysik*, 35.

59. The letter is quoted in the annotations to the Goldberg letters. See Sholem, *Briefe: Band I, 1914–1947*, 407.

60. A brief but insightful review was published by Goldberg's close friend, Adolf Caspary: "Theologie der Selbstgerechtigkeit Gottes," in the journal *Grenzbote* (Bratislava, 1936). A digital version of the transcript is available through the Leo Baeck Institute/Center for Jewish History, www.europeana.eu/portal/search?q=what%3A%22http%3A%2F%2Fdata.dm2e.eu%2Fdata%2Fconcept%2Fcjh%2Flbiarchive%2FTheology%22.

61. Goldberg believes that the Kabbalists, a small group among the Talmudists, were more faithful to the authentic teaching of the Pentateuch, although they do not transmit the full "reality of the Hebrews." The Kabbalistic tradition actually *predates* the Pentateuch, according to Goldberg. It goes back to a mythic period in which the Hebrews were still under the thrall of Semitic part-gods and had not yet covenanted with the unique YHWH Elohim. This accounts for the Kabbalistic focus on the sexual element within the Godhead and the unification of the male and female aspects of the Godhead.

62. *Maimonides*, Goldberg-*Aufsätze*, 138.

63. Ibid., 162.

64. Ibid., 164–165; emphasis Goldberg's.

65. Ibid., 165.

66. Ibid.

67. Ibid., 167.

68. Ibid.

69. Ibid.

70. Ibid.

71. Ibid., 168.

72. Ibid., 180. I have not dwelled on Goldberg's detailed exposition of the Levitical laws of purity as an immunological means to protect the Israelite camp and the *mishkan* from the pollution of the biological gods, pollution that is both extrinsic to Israel (in its confrontation with other peoples, such as the Moabites and Amalakites) and internal to it (its inheritance of a propensity to revert to earlier Semitic gods like Baal, with their tincture of sexuality). This exposition in *The Reality of the Hebrews* deserves a closer reading, especially in light of Jacob Milgrom's magisterial commentary on the book of Leviticus, in which he argues that the Levitical purity legislation reflects the attempt to "eviscerate" the realm of the "demonic" from the Temple and bring it under direct, conscious, and human control. The points of overlap between Goldberg's viewpoint and Milgrom's (apart, of course, from Goldberg actually crediting the "demonic" with a definite "reality") are numerous. Milgrom achieved his insights by allowing himself to imagine, in all its power, the "mythological" perspective reflected in the book of Leviticus. For an accessible presentation of the basic points of the multivolume commentary, see Jacob Milgrom, *Leviticus: A Book of Ritual and Ethics* (Minneapolis: Fortress Press, 2004).

73. *Maimonides*, Goldberg-*Aufsätze*, 172.

74. Ibid., 174.

75. Ibid., 170.

76. Goldberg, *Reality of the Hebrews*, 176.

77. Ibid.

78. *Maimonides*, Goldberg-*Aufsätze*, 177. Goldberg was not unaware that the Christian theology of divine incarnation reworked the biblical concept of indwelling of God's glory in the world (in the tabernacle/Temple), but he believed that he was restoring it to its authentic meaning. In a piece published in 1933, Goldberg argued that Christianity sought to "stabilize" the relationship between God and humanity by grounding it in a single instance of divine incarnation rather than in an "authentic people," but that it thereby reduced both God and humanity to "fictions." Oskar Goldberg, "Missionierendes Hebräertum," in Goldberg-*Aufsätze*, 219–226; quotations from p. 224.

79. *Maimonides*, Goldberg-*Aufsätze*, 177.

80. Ibid.

81. Ibid.

82. Ibid., 178.

83. Ibid., 179.

84. Ibid.

85. Ibid.

86. Ibid., 181.

87. Ibid., 182; emphasis Goldberg's.

88. Ibid., 183.

89. Ibid., 183–184.

90. Ibid., 186.

91. Ibid.

92. Ibid.

93. Ibid., 190.

94. Ibid.

95. Ibid., 198.

96. Ibid., 205.

97. Ibid., 206.

98. Ibid.

99. Ibid., 207.

100. Ibid.

101. Ibid., 207–213.

102. Adolf Caspary, *Die Maschinenutopie: Das Übereinstimmungsmoment der bürgerlichen und sozialistischen Ökonomie* (Berlin: David, 1927).

103. *Maimonides*, Goldberg-*Aufsätze*, 216.

104. Ibid.

105. Ibid.

106. See introduction, note 39 for the bibliographic details.

107. For details on Heidegger's "ponderings" about the interconnection of people, god, and world in the Black Notebooks, see chapter 4, note 67 and, in relation to Heidegger's use of the term "metapolitical" in the Black Notebooks as evidence of his familiarity with Unger's *Politics and Metaphysics*, see chapter 3, note 77.

# Conclusion:
# Ghosts and the Vitalist Imagination

> What is remarkable is not that one person should enable another person to see
> a ghost (for this seldom happens), but that one person should routinely enable
> another person to see the inside of his or her consciousness.
>
> —Elaine Scarry, *The Body in Pain*

I OPENED THIS book with a story from the *New Yorker* about Oskar Goldberg's project to photograph ghosts in haunted houses in the New York area. I close the book by returning to Goldberg's interest in ghostly hauntings because I want to understand how that interest connects to his broader vitalist metaphysics. There has been a great deal of work on ghosts, spirit photography, and spectrality in recent decades.[1] While I have learned a great deal from this work, the question of how spirit photography might relate to the rise of vitalism has not been the subject of much discussion. Tom Gunning's essay, "To Scan a Ghost: The Ontology of Mediated Vision," is an exception to the general lack of attention to vitalism in discussions of spirit photography.[2] Although Gunning mistakenly assumes that early German Naturphilosophie had been securely overturned by positivist science and had become an "untimely system of thought" by the early decades of the twentieth century, he does draw attention to the importance of Romantic Naturphilosophie in the scientific presentation of a certain Professor Bulwer about the "night-side of Nature" in the opening scenes of Friedrich Murnau's 1922 *Nosferatu.*[3] Bulwer's lecture is intercut with clips from scientific films of that period, including one taken of a microscopic polyp with its moving tentacles. "As the microscopic monster's tentacles grasp another cellular creature and seem to devour it, this glimpse into an invisible world made possible by the conjunction of two emblematic optical devices (the microscope and the movie camera) still compels our wonder," Gunning writes.[4] The intertitle speaks of the polyp as "transparent, almost ethereal, . . . but a phantom almost." The scientific lecture of Professor Bulwer posits a universal life force operative throughout nature, unifying microcosmic and macrocosmic levels. The belief in the unity of nature is, as Gunning explains, a staple of Romantic Naturphilosophie. Gunning goes on to argue that the emergence of cinema in the early twentieth century with its interest in "the play between the invisible and visible" can be linked to spirit photography, the practice of capturing mediumistic materializations of ectoplasm on film that had begun six decades earlier and was, in the 1920s, gaining wide notoriety among parapsychological researchers. (Goldberg, as we will see, claims to have studied among some of the most well known of these researchers.)

The common link joining Naturphilosophie, spirit photography, and early cinema is the *phantasm*, and Gunning's essay offers what might be called a "phantasmatic phenomenology." Phantasms, Gunning explains, are "images that oscillate between visibility and invisibility, presence and absence, materiality and immateriality, often using transparency or some other manipulation of visual appearance to express this paradoxical ontological status."[5] The paradoxical ontological status of the phantasm suggests that life itself, as viewed through the lenses of Romantic vitalism, cinema, and spirit photography, is irreducible to the purely material components of its organic makeup. There is something else, a vital principle, that expresses itself *through* the body and can sometimes appear as a "phantasmatic body" whose ethereal nature can leave its traces on film. Gunning argues that the visual technologies used in the production of the phantasm aimed at "reenchanting the disenchanted world."[6] Modern media phantasms "enact basic fantasies of release" from "the constraints of mortal physiology."[7] These fantasies, Gunning suggests, answered the particular historical exigencies of an increasingly technologized world.

Gunning does not mention the paradox that the reenchantment of the technologized world was brought into being through a technological invention, the camera. Goldberg, as we noted in the introduction, proudly described to a *New Yorker* writer how he developed an "infra-red" camera for photographing ghosts. The paradoxical nature of a *technology for world-reenchantment* can perhaps be understood in relation to what Gunning calls the "paradoxical ontological status" of the *phantasm*, an image that "oscillates between visibility and invisibility." The phantasmatic image can be compared to the optical illusion: both are more than a mere effect of light falling on the optic nerve; both are "intentional objects," objects at the intersection of the electromagnetic force of light on a sensitive medium and the *play of the imagination*. The camera, especially the movie camera, Gunning is suggesting, is a technology for the production of illusions, the transformation of light into the play of presence and absence, the visible and the invisible. As such, it exemplifies the paradoxical logic of Derrida's *pharmakon*: it is a technical supplement to and for the natural capacity of the human imagination to produce *phantasmata*, but it also reveals the always already *supernatural* (more than natural) structure of the imagination.[8] The imagination is precisely the psychic capacity that releases the human from the constraints of the givenness of sensation, or, in Gunning's words, "the constraints of mortal physiology." To the extent that the imagination seems to be a natural endowment of the human being that *exceeds* nature (by presenting what is absent), it opens the space for "fantasies of release" that include, perhaps most saliently, *postmortem life* together with the whole realm of the "supernatural" and paranormal.[9]

In what follows I build on Gunning's suggestive phenomenology of the *phantasm* as an embodiment (or, perhaps better, *disembodiment*) of humanity's "basic fantasies of release" in an era characterized by technological rationality and the disenchantment of the world. Drawing on the work of a number of different theorists, I sketch the outlines of a phenomenology of the imagination that helps to explicate how the imagination can function as the common source of both vitalism and spirit photography. First, I introduce a neurophysiologist and psychiatrist with deep grounding in Drieschian theoretical biology and the phenomenological tradition, Kurt Goldstein (1878–1965). Goldstein developed a theory of the organism within the framework of a theory of biological knowledge more generally. Goldstein argued that anti-reductionist "holism" was the only appropriate method for acquiring knowledge when the object of inquiry was a living organism, but, even more significantly, it was also a way of "biological being." Holism, Goldstein further argued, also provides the basis for a new psychiatric therapy of *Angst*-ridden patients who have lost their capacity to engage creatively, and imaginatively, with their environment, a capacity that is the hallmark of every healthy organism. Goldstein exercised a major influence on the historian of science George Canguilhem (1904–1995), another thinker I rely on for my theory of the vitalist imagination. Canguilhem's vitalist epistemology extends Goldstein's insights and grounds them in a discussion of the dialectical relationship between machinal artifact and living organism. As critics of vitalism who happen to have very interesting things to say about ghosts, I also invoke Max Horkheimer and Theodor Adorno. Horkheimer and Adorno's "Notes and Sketches" section in the final pages of *The Dialectic of Enlightenment* include not only one of the most trenchant critiques of vitalism in the modern period, it also presents a related "Theory of Ghosts" with a fascinating discussion of the rise of spiritualism. Finally, I invoke the work of Elaine Scarry in *The Body in Pain* on the phenomenology of the world-shaping imagination and its power to guide the creation of "disembodying" artifacts.[10] Goldstein, Canguilhem, and Scarry together provide the scaffolding for a theory of the vitalist imagination that offers a nuanced response to the critical challenge posed by Horkheimer and Adorno. Since all of this theoretical material is in the service not only of constructing a phenomenology of the vitalist imagination, but also of offering a better understanding of Goldberg's ghost photography, let me begin with a brief description of Goldberg's account of how he came to be interested in ghosts. This account appears in a short piece titled "Metaphysical Education in Tibet" that he published in the *New York Spiritualist Leader* in 1945 when he was living in the United States.[11]

In "Metaphysical Education in Tibet," Goldberg describes how he learned to see ghosts during a visit to the city of Srinagar in the Kashmiri valley of the Himalayas. As I explained in the introduction, Goldberg seems to have persuaded German and Ottoman authorities in the early years of the First World War to allow him to represent their interests there. The real reason that he appealed for permission to travel to Nepal, however, was to learn whether some people there could, as he had heard, communicate with the dead in "haunted temples."[12] In Srinagar, Goldberg met with a widely known yogi, Sri Agamya Guru Parahamsa, who had visited the United States and Europe in the early years of the twentieth century and made a considerable impression on many of those whom he met.[13] After more than six months of following a strict vegetarian diet, engaging in breathing exercises, reciting a mantra given to him by Sri Agamya, and meditating on a geometric pattern drawn by the guru, Goldberg finally felt ready to ask his teacher for the examination that would determine if he finally could enter a haunted temple and see the ghosts that gather there. Sri Agamya took Goldberg to a gorge and had him look down into it while reciting a mantra. While he was doing this, Goldberg says that he visualized a large eye that seemed to blink at him. Sri Agamya told Goldberg, "Now you may work for the redemption of the world. The metaphysical treatment of Hauntings is the lowest step of salvation: the release of earthbound souls. If you have resolved on it, travel to Patan in Nepal. The temple of Min Nat is haunted. I shall announce your arrival to the priests."[14] In another short piece, "The Apparition in the Temple of Min Nat," Goldberg explains what happened when he arrived at that haunted temple.[15] Goldberg first was taught a special mantra that allowed him to "prepare the own body [*sic*] to emanate rays" that will affect the ghost so that it can be released from its earthbound condition. He also learned how to prepare a sketch of the lines of force emanating from his body and also from the ghost in order to "lay the apparition" and hold it in place for the time it takes to recite the mantra. Assisted by one of the monks, Goldberg entered the temple just before midnight with the aim of releasing a ghost that had been haunting it. A second monk arrived on the scene, but no ghost appeared. The monk who had accompanied Goldberg into the temple, however, informed Goldberg that the second monk was, in fact, the ghost that had been haunting the temple. Goldberg took out paper and sketched the ghost monk standing beside him. Not long after, the ghost monk vanished. The living monk informed Goldberg that he was ready to pronounce the mantra that would permanently free the ghost, but it would require another visit to the temple. At the appropriate time, Goldberg again confronted the ghost monk: "I spoke the prescribed closing mantra, the Mantra of Release. The priest [the ghost monk] was no longer seen. He was free. This was the first case of my research on hauntings."

We do not have to trust in the veracity of Goldberg's autobiographical report to appreciate the value of its testimony about his self-understanding. Goldberg begins his "metaphysical education" as a curious researcher with little or no interest beyond either demonstrating or debunking the reports of "haunted temples" in Tibet. What his metaphysical education teaches him is much more than how to see ghosts, it reveals to him his life's task: to work for the redemption of the world. In *The Reality of the Hebrews*, Goldberg hoped to show how a renewal of Israel's "metaphysical war" might bring about or at least begin a transformation of the "organic lawfulness" that holds humanity in subjection to the cycle of birth, reproduction, and death. In the United States, Goldberg's goal remains the same as in his theoretical writings, but its scale has changed: it is now to release "earthbound souls" from their unhappy imprisonment in the material bonds of this world.

An earlier piece (1943) that Goldberg published in the *New York Spiritualist Leader* was titled "Rules for Research in Hauntings." It begins, "Since we live in a technical culture, we must prove immortality by technical means. Newest developments in infrared and ultra-violet photography provide this opportunity."[16] Goldberg explains that he had worked with two of Europe's most well-known researchers of paranormal phenomena, Osty (Dr. Eugene Osty) and Schrenk-Notzing (Baron Albert von Schrenk-Notzing).[17] Although Osty and Schrenk-Notzing had worked only with mediums, Goldberg writes that he wants to avoid the doubts that surround mediumistic materializations of ectoplasm ("we cannot *prove* that these are dead people, though doubtless they are"), and he therefore plans to investigate only "spontaneous phenomena," namely, sounds and moving objects caused by poltergeists and the apparitions of ghosts. The research he is undertaking is of paramount importance for humanity: "The time will come when all cases of spontaneous phenomena will, by law, have to be reported for investigation." The stakes are too high to allow individuals for any reason to conceal such phenomena for fear of being thought credulous: "Anyone concealing hauntings, for any reason, must know that he is acting unethically by preventing research in proofs of immortality."[18] But the benefit of paranormal research is not limited to providing proof of immortality. There is also an ethical and religious obligation to free the ghosts from their "earthbound condition" and allow them to continue "their proper progression." Finally, Goldberg describes ghosts that do not wish to be released from their connection to this world. "If these cases are properly treated," Goldberg concludes, "we may expect, in the future, a close connection, and permanent communication, between this world and the beyond."[19]

One cannot help but be struck by the overwhelming optimism of Goldberg's "Rules for Research in Hauntings." Goldberg seems to be proclaiming the coming of a new human era, a time when humans will have no doubt about the possibility of postmortem existence and when there will be a permanent link between this world and the next. If Goldberg were one of only a few persons who happened to be interested in proving immortality and creating a permanent line of communication between the living and the dead, it would be easy to dismiss him as an eccentric whose loss of his homeland had driven him to some rather strange and extreme attempts to find a place for himself in the world, at the intersection of this world and the beyond. No doubt there is something like this at work in his psychological makeup, but it cannot be the whole story. To appreciate more clearly how Goldberg's interest in proving the existence of ghosts connects with his vitalist metaphysics, we need to look beyond his personal psychology and examine the wider context of both his vitalism and his interest in ghosts, namely, the cultural and historical conditions that called forth new ways to imagine and theorize life's irreducibility to purely physico-chemical processes. I turn now to Kurt Goldstein and his theory of holism as a form of both biological knowledge and creative biological functioning. This theory is, like all other vitalist theories of the period, a product of surrounding cultural and historical conditions, but it also reflects on the deeper sources of vitalism in the "biological being" of the theorist. It therefore provides an apt starting point for a phenomenology of the vitalist imagination.

In chapter 1, I situated the fundamental axiom of vitalist epistemology—the principle that to know organic phenomena one must grasp the whole and not merely the parts—in relation to the emerging movement of phenomenological psychology inaugurated by Franz Brentano. Brentano's phenomenology argued for a holistic relationship between consciousness and its intentional objects and claimed to offer a non-reductivist account of the "psychophysical problem." Phenomenological psychology viewed consciousness as more than the aggregate of neuronal activity in the brain, however complex it may be. Rather than happening at the level of the cell or cellular structures, consciousness, it was argued, orients the *whole organism* in relation to the world as a field of possibilities for self-organizing activity. As Kurt Goldstein puts it his phenomenologically informed magnum opus, *Der Aufbau des Organismus* (*The Construction of the Organism*, translated by Goldstein himself into English more simply as *The Organism*), "We are always dealing with the activity of the whole organism, the effects of which we refer at one time to something called mind, at another time to something called body."[20] The organism conceived of as a whole does not only respond to external stimuli in preset ways, it also selectively filters and interprets stimuli in relation to its own self-regulating constraints. Goldstein, following Jakob von Uexküll, argued that the organism actively transforms its "world" (*Welt*) into an "environment" (*Umwelt*). For Brentano and those who were influenced by his ideas, consciousness helps the organism construct a self-perpetuating and ordered whole in the midst of environmental thermodynamic processes that otherwise tend to dissipate energy (entropy).[21] Sigmund Freud, who had studied with Brentano in Vienna, shows the influence of phenomenological psychology in his theory of the ego's conscious system (Cs) as the holistic "mental projection" of the sensations arising from the body's surface.[22] The phenomenological approach of the Berlin school of psychology (led first by Carl Stumpf, a Brentano student, and later by Wolfgang Köhler) considered consciousness to be an active shaper of external stimuli into holistic patterns (*Gestalten*). Goldstein makes frequent reference to the work of the Berlin school of Gestalt psychologists as evidence for the need to use a holistic methodology in the study of living organisms.

In *The Organism*, Kurt Goldstein developed a methodological defense of his biological holism that rested on the triple structural correlation that obtains between (1) biology and the objects of its study, (2) consciousness and its intentional objects, and (3) the organism and the objects of its environment. Goldstein argued that the holistic methodology in biology correlated with the way that consciousness apprehends its intentional objects as *Gestalten* (patterns) and also with the way that the organism as a whole shapes the world into its "adequate" environment. Goldstein writes in *The Organism*:

> The attainment of biological knowledge we are seeking is essentially akin to . . . the capacity of the organism to become adequate to its environmental conditions. This is a fundamental biological process by virtue of which the actualization of organisms is made possible. Whenever we speak of the nature, of the idea, picture, or conception of the organism we have in mind these essentials for the realization of adequacy between the organism and its environment. And these are the principles of compositions of that picture that biology has to grasp. *In so doing, the cognitive process of the biologist is subject to practically the same difficulties of procedure as the organism in learning;* he has to find the adequacy between concept and reality.[23]

We might say, following Goldstein, that biological holism is *life's native theory of itself.* The deepest source of vitalist holism is *life itself as a problem-solving activity.*

In describing vitalism as life's native theory of itself as a problem-solving activity, I am drawing not only from the work of Kurt Goldstein but also from one of the twentieth century's foremost historians of the life sciences, George Canguilhem.[24] Canguilhem was deeply influenced by Goldstein's claim that biological knowledge was "adequate" to its object only to the degree that it gave expression to the same methods that allowed the organism to construct an adequate environment for its flourishing.[25] Canguilhem went so far as to argue that vitalism in all its forms is "an expression of the confidence the living being has in *life,* of the self-identity of life within the living being conscious of living."[26] Canguilhem's study of the history of vitalism in *Knowledge of Life* demonstrates that vitalist and mechanist accounts of life stand in a dialectical relationship with one another. The modern scientific examination of life begins with a Cartesian assumption that living things function like machines. But, as Canguilhem shows, the reduction of organisms to machines cannot ultimately succeed, since the machine is itself only comprehensible as a sort of prosthetic organ, that is, a machine is a tool created and operated by an organism. Thus, a machine is a way to solve a problem, but it is not itself the product of a machine. How could a *new* problem be solved by an *old* machine? There is, it is clear, a limit to the explanatory power of a theory that seeks to reduce the organism to a machine: what will correspond to the creator-operator of this machine? The organism possesses "a vital originality irreducible to rationalization."[27] When the knower uses the model of the machine-automaton to force the phenomena of life within the bounds of the explanatory principles of the physico-chemical sciences, the knower herself as a *living organism* is out of synch with the object she desires to know.

Canguilhem points out that the Greek term *mêchanê* reflects the dialectical tension between vitalist and mechanist models of explanation. The Greek term *mêchanê* can mean both "ruse" and "machine," both the unpredictable trick and the product of a rule-governed skill. But a *mêchanê* is always already more than a machine. A reductivist explanatory model of life reduces *ruse* to *machine*, vital originality to mechanical replication. As Canguilhem succinctly puts it, "A machine does not create anything."[28] Vitalism, Canguilhem argues, attempts to reverse the priority of machine over life. It asserts the irreducibility of life's inventiveness to an algorithm or program and "translates a permanent exigency of life in the living."[29] Put differently, vitalism reflects a fundamental need at work within the knowing subject (the biologist, for example) to transgress methodical-mechanical thinking for the sake of coming back into synch with life. *Vitalism is itself a ruse of life* that is called into being as the voice of life speaking through the knowing subject: "I, Life, know ruses that transcend the artifice of any mere machine." To know life, the knower must employ the analytical tools that divide a whole into constituent parts while at the same time acknowledging the inescapable limitation of such a partitive methodology. Just as an organism cannot adequately engage with its environment if its responses are entirely disconnected from its self-regulating center, biological knowledge cannot adequately grasp its object except through a synthetic and holistic methodology. This is a lesson that Canguilhem admits he learns from Goldstein.

Canguilhem describes vitalism as arising from "life's permanent distrust of the mechanization of life" and also as "an expression of the confidence the living being has in life."[30] Goldstein, looking back thirty years after the original publication of *The Organism*, claimed that his holistic theory of the organism was "a form of biological being."[31] We may take this claim to be saying exactly what Canguilhem says about vitalism more generally. Goldstein's holism offers a perfect example of *life's consciousness of itself.* What makes Goldstein's holistic biological way of knowing the organism also, and more essentially, "a form of biological being" is that it fashions its theoretical concepts in the image and likeness of the living and changing organism itself. Goldstein, to put it most boldly, situates his holistic method of biological knowing *within the context of the evolution of life and consciousness.* As Canguilhem puts it in relation to all vitalist theories:

> It must . . . be acknowledged that it is neither without interest nor entirely false to think of the offensive—or defensive—returns of vitalism as tied to bourgeois society's crises of confidence in the efficacy of capitalist institutions. Still, this interpretation of the phenomenon may appear too weak, in the epistemological sense, rather than too strong. It may appear too weak inasmuch as it presents *a phenomenon of biological crisis within the human species*—a phenomenon that is a matter of a technological philosophy and not only a political philosophy—as a phenomenon of political and social crisis. The rebirths of vitalism translate, perhaps in discontinuous fashion, life's permanent distrust of the mechanization of life. In them we find life seeking to put mechanism back into its place within life.[32]

How does Goldstein's and Canguilhem's wider contextualization of vitalism (and holism, one of vitalism's expressions) as an evolutionary exigency of life itself help us to understand how vitalism is related to spirit photography? This question takes us, finally, back to the central theme of this chapter, the phenomenology of the imagination. Vitalism is not simply a tendency within the history of the biological sciences, it is also an *expression of the imagination.* Canguilhem speaks of the way that the mechanist biologist faults vitalism for its "nebulousness" and "vagueness." Rather than considering this to be a fault, Canguilhem instead attributes these qualities to what he calls "the fecundity of vitalism."[33] Canguilhem rightly stresses the central importance of life's productive exuberance for vitalism; vitalism itself, Canguilhem explains, is "life's proper spontaneity."[34] As a form of cognition, vitalism, however much it may seek to express itself in the language of "normal" biological science, retains a close tie with the creative imagination, the "proper spontaneity" of both life and consciousness. The objects of the imagination transcend the concrete immediacy of what is given in sensation. Vitalism by its very nature will always see more in the objects of its study than any assemblage of empirical data could possibly reveal.

Kurt Goldstein also helps us to understand the relationship between vitalism and the phenomenology of the imagination. According to Goldstein, when the biologist employs a holistic methodology to study the organism, this is best understood to be an act of *empathic imagination,* that is, a way of understanding another organism as the organism itself shapes the world. In a fascinating essay, "The Smile of the Infant and the Problem of Understanding the 'Other,'" Goldstein argues that any "adequate" human relationship to the world must be constituted against the background of a fundamental confidence that the world as a particular human being sees it is also the world that others see: "This is the structure of the mutual smiling of friends in encounter. This experience of the same adequate world is the presupposition of the understanding of the other one, of all our knowledge of what is taking place in the 'other.' This is the foundation of understanding language. It is the basis of all friendship, of all love, where with surprise and astonishment we recognize that what is taking place in the 'other' is identical with what is taking place in us."[35]

Goldstein argues that the task of the psychiatrist is to help the patient reestablish an adequate and confident relationship to the world by reactivating his diminished imagination. Kurt Goldstein began his career as a neurologist working with brain-injured veterans of the First World War. He understood that his brain-injured patients were trying to do what all humans (indeed, all organisms) do, namely, restore their confidence in a reliable milieu or environment in which to actualize the fullest range of their behavioral possibilities. His patients, however, had suffered such brain damage that their responses to the "normal" environment were "catastrophic." Goldstein described catastrophic reactions as those that are "disordered, inconstant, inconsistent, and embedded in physical and mental shock." When his reactions are catastrophic, the patient's condition, Goldstein explains, is that of "anxiety" (*Angst*), a concept that figures prominently in Goldstein's phenomenology of catastrophic reactions. Anxiety consists precisely in the loss of all intentional relations to objects in the world. It is a state "without reference to any object" and is therefore "contentless" (*inhaltlos*).[36] The subject's consciousness is trapped within itself with only an awareness of an existential threat to its existence whose source it cannot identify. The patient in anxiety

> experiences the utter impossibility of establishing any reference to the world without knowing the cause of that experience. He experiences a breaking down or dissolution of the world and a shattering of his own self. Just as little as he can render to himself a conscious account of an object, just as little can he become conscious of his self. To be conscious of one's self is only a correlate to being conscious of objects. The patient experiences the dissolution of the existence of his personality as anxiety. This shock, in terms of subjective experience, is what we call anxiety.[37]

Patients whose brain damage makes them prone to catastrophic reactions feel constantly threatened by a sense that they might at any moment descend into a condition of anxiety. As a result, they hold desperately to the security afforded by the concrete objects that surround them. This focus on the concrete is reflected in a reduction of their language skills, which deprives them of the power to transcend the literal and concrete description of an object and to see it in more abstract ways and in relation to other categories beyond its sensory qualities: "Whenever the patient must transcend concrete (immediate) experience in order to act—whenever he must refer to things *in an imaginary way*—he fails."[38]

Goldstein's therapy did not seek to repair the damaged brain, but rather to help the patient learn how to *imagine new possibilities* for "self-actualization." Goldstein, in effect, became, at least in the beginning, his patients' *substitute imagination*. His holistic therapeutic practice informed his holistic theoretical approach to life: as doctor and also as biological knower Goldstein sought to understand how living organisms transcend concrete givens and create—*imagine*, if they are conscious—new possibilities for action. A fully flourishing human being's consciousness resides not so much in the consciousness of the concrete immediacy of the world, *but in her imagination of new possibilities for action in the world.* If we want to appreciate the deepest source of vitalism, therefore, we will need to understand how *the imagination is humanity's self-therapy against the threat of anxiety, the loss of the world of objects.* Anxiety, we might say, is the condition of being in the world while being unable to connect meaningfully to it; it is a condition of self-immersed stasis, a sort of death-in-life. Imagination is the condition of possibility of reconnecting not only to the objects of the world but also to the future of the world beyond its present givenness. If we can understand more fully the deep phenomenological structure of the imagination as opening up a possible world of shared objects, we will also understand the deepest source not only of vitalism but also of research into ghosts and spirit materializations. Both respond to the cultural and historical *Angst* induced by the threat of a mechanization of life itself, the reduction of life to a technologically manipulable *dead thing.*

Kurt Goldstein's holistic theory of biological knowledge led me to invoke the work of George Canguilhem. His holistic therapy of his *Angst*-ridden patients leads me to invoke the work of Elaine Scarry. That the imagination functions most essentially as a therapy against the threat of contentless consciousness (Goldstein's *Angst*) is the basic insight of Scarry's phenomenology of the imagination and its "world-making" power. She develops her phenomenological theory of imagination in her pathbreaking book *The Body in Pain: The Making and Unmaking of the World.* Scarry to my knowledge never mentions Kurt Goldstein, yet her work has much in common with his. Scarry, like Goldstein, takes as her starting point the basic thesis of Brentano's phenomenology (which she takes over from Sartre), namely, that all consciousness is intentional, that all consciousness is related to an object. Scarry, like Goldstein, offers a phenomenological approach to the radical disabling of human consciousness into a condition of "contentlessness" that Scarry identifies with overwhelming bodily pain inflicted through torture and that Goldstein calls "anxiety." Scarry, also like Goldstein, associates the loss of the connection to the world with the loss of the power of the voice or language to give expression to one's experience. Goldstein's patients were not driven into the condition of contentless consciousness by the deliberate infliction of pain, as were the torture victims who were the focus of Scarry's analysis of the "unmaking of the world." Rather, Goldstein's patients had suffered serious brain injuries in war that left them prone to catastrophic reactions and anxiety, the "breakdown or dissolution of the world and the shattering of the self," as Goldstein describes their condition in terms quite similar to those of Scarry in her characterization of torture victims.[39] Goldstein's therapeutic intervention against anxiety consisted of helping his patients gain confidence in their own creative ability to imaginatively reshape the world, rather than merely be victims of their catastrophic reactions to it. It involves the cultivation of what Goldstein calls "genuine courage," which "requires the ability to view a single experience within a larger context" and to assume "the attitude toward the possible."[40]

If Goldstein as a psychiatrist acts temporarily as a substitute imagination to enable his patients to see beyond their entrapment within the limits of the concrete, Scarry calls for interventions against torture like that of Amnesty International, whose "deluge of letters and telegrams" constitute a deluge of "voices speaking in the voice of the person silenced," by means of which the prisoner is given back "his psychic content and density." The *substitute voices* of the Amnesty letter writers are "almost physiological in their power of alteration."[41] One such substitute voice that Scarry recounts came to a prisoner hidden on a scrap of paper in a loaf of bread: "Corragio!" "Take courage!"[42] It is with these words that Scarry concludes her book, calling them the "universal salutation" of Amnesty International.[43] As we have seen, it is precisely "genuine courage" that also Goldstein describes as the necessary antidote to the debilitating effects of war's catastrophic traumas. In turning to Scarry for guidance in understanding how the imagination serves as the deepest source of both vitalism and the interest in spirit materializations as verifications of life after death, I am not departing from the phenomenological study of vitalism begun by Goldstein and Canguilhem. What is more, Scarry will lead us directly back to Oskar Goldberg and *The Reality of the Hebrews*.

Scarry's book is divided into two sections, the first devoted to the "unmaking of the world" in torture and the second to the "making of the world" though the imagination. Where torture seeks to deprive the victim of her world through the infliction of pain, the imagination makes it possible to bring a world of objects into being that heals bodily pain. Torture is the enemy of the imagination. The imagination, in turn, is the enemy not only of torture but also of pain in all its forms. Scarry argues that the "making of the world" begins with a state she calls "aversiveness," that is, a *turning away* from the world.[44] Aversiveness is a psychic state brought on by pain, and it most frequently results from a traumatic wound having been inflicted on the body. As I have mentioned, Scarry discusses in the first half of her book (the section devoted to the "unmaking" of the world) the condition of aversiveness that is deliberately brought about through torture or war. In the second half of the book (devoted to the "making of the world"),

Scarry makes it clear that aversiveness is a more much general phenomenon; indeed it is one of the most fundamental structures of human sentience. Aversiveness has the identical phenomenological structure to the condition that Kurt Goldstein called "anxiety." Aversiveness reduces human consciousness to pure objectless sentience (the interior sensation of pain detached from any representation of its cause). To overcome aversiveness, the imagination brings forward figurations of objects that can heal or ameliorate the pain. Most frequently it is not the sufferer herself who can engage in this healing work of imagination but someone else who observes her condition, empathizes with it, and seeks to relieve it. The healing imagination guides the suffering consciousness out of its entrapment within the aversive interiority of pain. Imagination leads the sufferer back into relation with the world. The imagination makes possible the labor of fabricating objects—tools and artifacts—that will assume the burden of the body's pain (like the chair that relieves the pain of a too-long-held standing posture). Scarry claims that this projection of the imagination into fabricated tools and artifacts is part of the basic drive on the part of human beings "to deprive the external world of the privilege of being inanimate."[45] Scarry explains how an artifact is fabricated as if it were itself capable of experiencing and absorbing the aversive sentience of the sufferer: "A chair, as though it were itself put in pain, as though it knew from the inside the problem of body weight, will only then accommodate and eliminate the problem. A woven blanket or solid wall internalize within their design the recognition of the instability of body temperature and the precariousness of nakedness, and only by absorbing the knowledge of these conditions into themselves (by, as it were, being themselves subject to these forms of distress), absorb them out of the human body."[46]

Scarry describes the imaginative animation of the inanimate world as the "disembodiment" of aversiveness. A coat, Scarry explains, can remake the body of the one who otherwise would suffer the pain that drives sentience deeper into the body and away from the world. A coat will assume the sufferer's embodiment ("corporeal engulfment," as Scarry frequently puts it) and "will bring about her disembodiment, divesting her body of its vulnerability to external temperatures and therefore also freeing her mind of its absorption with this problem."[47] The imagination, according to Scarry, heals an aversive sentience that is "engulfed" in the body by creating "disembodying" imaginative solutions to the pain that ultimately take the concrete shape of tools and artifacts. This is, she says, the way that the human imagination animates the world.

We find in Scarry's phenomenology of the imagination the basis for an explanation of the deep conjunction of vitalism and the rise of an interest in ghosts and mediumistic materializations in Germany before and after the First World War. In a perceptive essay on Kurt Goldstein, the historian of science Anne

Harrington describes the wider cultural and historical context of his biological holism within Germany from 1800 onward:

> Against a longstanding background of national fragmentation and political instability, the larger resonances of ideals of "wholeness" had long held a deep attraction for many Germans, going back at least to the Romantic era. Later, in the hard wake of industrialization, these older ideals would again capture the cultural imagination, albeit retooled to the new concerns of the day. By the time we reach the second decade of the twentieth century, the German-speaking countries had managed to lose a war, lose an empire, and lose the respect of the world. That these years should also have represented a peak in holistic reformist agitation is no coincidence.[48]

Harrington manages in these few sentences to succinctly describe the immediate causes of the immense appeal of holistic thinking and its power to "capture the cultural imagination" in Germany in the decades before and after the Great War. In her monograph *Reenchanted Science*, Harrington speaks at length about the widespread complaints in Wilhelmine Germany about the "hard wake of industrialization" and the threat of the "Machine" more generally.[49] In the years leading up the First World War, the Machine seemed to have acquired a frightening independence from its human creators, a sort of artificial life force that threatened the authentic vitality of the nation. After the war, overconfidence in the (foreign) Machine rather than in Germany's native *Geist* was identified as one of the major causes of the nation's defeat.[50] To many German thinkers vitalism seemed to provide an antidote to the earlier worship of the Machine. The holistic axiom on which vitalism rested—that the whole organism is greater than the sum of its parts—offered hope that a spiritually rejuvenated Germany might one day rise above the partisan conflicts that divided the nation in the postwar period.

Anne Harrington's succinct description of postwar Germany's loss of belief in the power of its technological achievements—the artifacts that should have saved it, but instead propelled it only more quickly into the destructive fury of world war—captures perfectly the essence of what could be called a form of *cultural* aversiveness, to adopt the language of Elaine Scarry. Cultural aversiveness is the condition where the collective social body is wounded rather than healed by its artifacts. It is precisely marked by a society's loss of belief in the power of its artifacts to fulfill their mission of rescuing the social body from its suffering. Scarry frequently uses the term "materialization" to describe the way that the imagination heals the pain of the suffering body through the creation of tools and artifacts.[51] She also describes this as a process of "disembodiment." In her discussion of Marx's *Capital* in the second part of her book, Scarry argues that the tools and artifacts of a social world can lose their valence as products of a healing imagination, becoming freestanding objects in a system of production no longer anchored to the exigencies of human need: "If the monumentally complex substance of *Capital* were to be described in a single sentence, it could be described as an exhausting analysis of the steps and stages by which the obligatory referentiality of fictions ceases to be obligatory: it is an elaborate retracing of the path along which the reciprocity of artifice has lost its way back to its human source."[52] The "referentiality" of an artifact (arising from an imagined solution to suffering sentience) is the human "body in pain." When an artifact enters into a system of exchange relations as a commodity, however, the laborer who created the artifact "has not only ceased to be the recipient of his creation's beneficent disembodying powers but, in some ways more radically, has even ceased to be recognizable to himself and to others as the 'creator.'"[53] In such a system of production and exchange, the artifact's relation to human sentience is severed. Rather than seeing their bodily suffering "disembodied" and healed in the artifacts that surround them, the members of what I am calling a culturally aversive society see only commodities whose value seems to be determined through the self-regulating operations of the "free" market independently of any relation to their human makers and their suffering sentience. The suffering sentience of the members of such an aversive society hovers like a disembodied ghost over the commodities that now seem to have acquired an independent life of their own.

Although Scarry does not put it this way, I believe it is not going too far to say that a social world whose made objects no longer heal aversiveness but rather participate in the dehumanization and atomization of the society's members is a milieu that is *haunted*.[54] A haunted house, for example, is an artifact whose once healing power of disembodiment (to shelter the fragile body) has become the very power of aversiveness itself, the entrapping power of an inexpressible pain. The ghost is the materialization of a pain-suffused, aversive sentience.[55] In seeking to demonstrate the reality of life after death through documenting spirit materializations, the paranormal researcher investigates, indirectly to be sure, the wider society's aversiveness, that is, its severance from its world of artifacts. Here is my thesis in a single sentence: *Vitalism and also paranormal research seek to restore belief in the power of the imagination to animate the world.* They reflect the effort of the imagination to reassert its right to "deprive the external world of its privilege of being inanimate," that is, to reclaim its recuperative and healing function against the dominance of the machine (and the economic machinery of capitalism) over the living. Or, as Thomas Gunning puts it, vitalism and spirit photography are forms of "reenchanting the disenchanted world." It is true, as Harrington has shown, that vitalism (and paranormal research as well) is always a culturally and historically specific response to the "Machine," but its source is the imagination itself as the human's essential response to aversiveness in all its forms.

My account of the deeper source of vitalism and paranormal research complements and expands on Scarry's own description of the more "benign" ways that a society responds to its loss of faith in its world of made objects. Before explaining these benign forms, let me say a word about the forms that are not benign: torture and war. Scarry argues that when a culture loses its belief in its world of shared objects, it regains its belief by reconnecting the imagination to the sentience of the human body. She describes sentience and the objects of sentience (consciousness and its intentional objects) as the "two locations of selfhood."[56] Normally, these two locations "occur together and imply one another,"[57] as phenomenology has long claimed. "But the two can also become utterly split off from one another," she explains. When this happens to an entire society, we have what I call a condition of cultural aversiveness but what Scarry calls "a political situation," which for her is "almost by definition one in which the two locations of selfhood are in a skewed relation to one another or have wholly split apart and have begun to work, or be worked, against one another."[58] As we have just seen, Scarry turns to Marx to explain how the working class in nineteenth-century industrialized economies came to bear the burden of suffering sentience while the capitalist claimed ownership of the objects produced through that pain. This was a skewing of the two locations of selfhood into two separate classes. In its radical separation of the workers' suffering sentience from the objects that were produced as "disembodiments" of such suffering, nineteenth-century capitalism created a form of social aversiveness and a "political situation" that could not be sustained. Scarry suggests that the First World War can in large part be seen as a deliberate rebalancing of the "skewed relationship" that placed the burden of suffering sentience on one class only. By mobilizing millions of men from working-class and bourgeois households, the warring nations could at least present the fiction of a unified social body. Each nation sought to verify this fiction *in the willingness of its soldiers to submit their bodies to the extremes of physical violence.* Scarry describes how modern authoritarian regimes use torture as a means to verify the reality of the objects of the beliefs that sustain their regime (order, security, national honor, and so on) by increasing the sheer objectless sentience (i.e., pain) of the victim. Torture is the most extreme form of the skewed relationship between the two locations of selfhood: sentience and its objects. The torturer verifies the reality of the objects of the regime's belief by forcing the "objectified pain" of the victim to confess to the truth of the words that the regime demands.

But the infliction of pain on others—whether one's enemies in war or the torture victim—is not the only way a society can overcome the skewing of the relationship between sentience and its objects. Scarry describes the "affirmative" form of translating pain into a world of shared objects:

> Every act of civilization is an act of transcending the body in a way consonant with the body's needs: in building a wall . . . one overcomes the body, projects oneself out beyond the body's boundaries but in a way that expresses and fulfills the body's need for stable temperatures. Higher moments of civilization, more elaborate forms of self-extension, occur at a greater distance from the

body: the telephone or the airplane is a more emphatic instance of overcoming the limitation of the human body than is the cart. Yet even as here when most exhilaratingly defiant of the body, civilization always has embedded within it a profound allegiance to the body, for it is only by paying attention that it can free attention.[59]

Scarry's analysis of the way that civilization can and ought to maintain a "profound allegiance to the body"—precisely by forging artifacts that extend it in such a way as to alleviate its suffering—presents an optimistic and hopeful picture of the role of the imagination in human culture. She tempers this optimism in her discussion of how the infliction of pain on the body of others is often used to reinforce the reality of the values that sustain an unjust social order.

We may measure the optimism of Scarry's analysis by comparing it to another treatment of the way that the body and its pain lie at the basis of civilization, that of Max Horkheimer and Theodor Adorno. Horkheimer and Adorno are, unlike Goldstein, Canquilhem, and Scarry, quite critical of vitalism and vitalist phenomenology. But their critique offers us important insights, not at all unrelated to Scarry's reflections on the "disembodying" role of the artifact in a capitalist society. Horkheimer and Adorno title one of their "Notes and Sketches" at the end of *Dialectic of Enlightenment* "Interest in the Body." In these few pages, Horkheimer and Adorno describe the "love-hate" relationship with the body that "colors the whole of modern culture." The ruling classes have always appropriated the power of the imagination to create ideological systems to sustain their power and at the same time produce ever more technically refined means to alleviate themselves of the burdens of their embodiment. Their hatred of the body is projected out onto their slaves and then the wage laborer, and the love for the body is figured as "forbidden."[60] In the modern world, the ruling capitalist class is itself enslaved, "no longer . . . by the sword, but by the gigantic apparatus which, to be sure, ultimately forges the sword."[61] At this point, the hatred of the body that characterizes the entirety of bourgeois culture comes to expression in the sadism of those who are used by the governing power to destroy those who would oppose the capitalist system: "The murderer, the killer, the brutalized colossi who are used by the ruling powers, legal and illegal, great or small, as their clandestine enforcers, the violent men who are always on hand when there is someone to be dispatched, the lynchers and clan members, . . . in them the love-hate for the body is crude and direct; . . . in blind rage they repeat against the living thing what they cannot make undone: the splitting of life into mind and its object."[62] Horkheimer and Adorno in this sentence come very close to describing what Scarry refers to as the "unmaking of the world," namely, the attempt to once and for all separate the pain-prone sentience of the body in one realm from the made world of artifacts in another. The production of artifacts in a capitalist system only places the burden of suffering sentience on the working class, it does not relieve sentience of suffering. Reacting against this injustice, murderous "brutalized colossi" turn their "rancor against reification" against the living bodies of their victims.

For Scarry, the attempt of torturers ("the violent men who are always on hand when there is someone to be dispatched," as Horkheimer and Adorno call them) to wrest the world away from their victims runs counter to "the natural reflex of sympathy" that would normally seek to alleviate the pain of the other. Where Horkheimer and Adorno join a Marxist analysis of reification with a psychoanalytic understanding of reactive symptom formation, Scarry situates her reading of Marx within the wider frame of phenomenology—that is, the structure of sentience in relation to its objects—and for her the basic human drive is not ressentiment but empathy, the result of the imagination's capacity to place itself in the position of another human. We have seen how this is also the fundamental frame of reference and fundamental human drive for Kurt Goldstein. Perhaps there is no way to decide which frame of reference, the phenomenological or the psychoanalytic, is the truer. I choose to adopt the phenomenological frame of Scarry and Goldstein. At the very least, this frame offers a better fit for the work of Oskar Goldberg that I am attempting to explicate in this book.

Horkheimer and Adorno's "Interest in the Body" sketch not only helps us to see more clearly the ultimately optimistic and affirmative cast of Scarry's phenomenology of the imagination, it also provides a contrast to Canguilhem's analysis of the nature of vitalism as an exigency of life itself. Horkheimer and Adorno, like Canguilhem, identify a "perennial process" to reduce "nature into stuff, material."[63] They find in the fascist glorification of the muscular male body a reflection of that same perennial process; the fascists "see the body as a mobile mechanism, with its hinged links, the flesh upholding the skeleton." The fascist fascination with the body is nothing else but a sublimated hatred of the vitality of the body: "They measure the other with the eye of the coffin maker."[64] The fascist cult of death is already presaged in the "renaissance of the body in the nineteenth and twentieth centuries" that only "idealized something dead and mutilated." Thinkers like "Nietzsche, Gauguin, George, and Klages" recognized the underlying decadence of bourgeois culture's idealization of healthy living, but they "did not denounce the wrong as it is but transfigured the wrong as it was." Rather than find a real alternative to the "mutilated" condition of bourgeois culture's relation to the body, these thinkers and artists exalted "paragons of vitality, from the Blond Beast to the south-sea islanders."[65] In this way, "the rejection of mechanization became an embellishment of industrial mass culture" that leads inevitably to "advertisements for vitamins and skin cream."[66] Horkheimer and Adorno see nothing else in the upsurge of vitalism in the late nineteenth and early twentieth century but a dressing up of a corpse much the way a funeral director would present the deceased for viewing: a denial of a moribund reality in the name of a faked beauty.

Canguilhem offers a vastly different picture of the resurgence of vitalism in this period. To be sure, Canguilhem is fully aware of the way that vitalist thinking can feed fascism. But in taking a longer view of the history of vitalism, Canguilhem argues, one must acknowledge that it cannot be reduced to an ideological construction that masks the "mutilated" condition of the society in relation to its bodily incarnation. Canguilhem, like his teacher Kurt Goldstein, does not view all civilization as the product of an essentially diseased or "inadequate" relationship between the human organism and its internal and external environments. He does not deny the capacity of a society to fall into pathology; it is simply that, for Canguilhem in contrast to Horkheimer and Adorno, society is not by its very nature pathological. And vitalism, he argues, can be one of the ways that society expresses its *health*. Canguilhem's perspective differs from the approach of Horkheimer and Adorno because he understands the history of science—and therefore the history of civilization in general—as an expression of the same evolutionary principles that govern life itself, and these are not nor could they be *unnatural*. For Horkheimer and Adorno, however, civilization is, at its core, *at war with nature*.

One of the other "Notes and Sketches" at the end of the *Dialectic of Enlightenment* is titled "The Theory of Ghosts." I have so far only disagreed with Horkheimer and Adorno's extremely negative portrait of civilization and of vitalism more specifically, contrasting it with the views of Goldstein, Canguilhem, and Scarry. Yet we may learn something valuable from Horkheimer and Adorno's "theory of ghosts." According to Horkheimer and Adorno, the condition of modern experience is that of death-in-life: "Individuals are reduced to a mere sequence of instantaneous presents which leave behind no trace, or rather the trace of which they hate as something irrational, superfluous, utterly obsolete."[67] In the modern experience of life, the sense of the valuelessness and impermanence of each moment of time results from the way that no commodity lasts beyond its present fashion ("any book which has not been published recently is suspect"). I spoke earlier of "cultural aversiveness," the condition that arises when made objects no longer are sensed as products of the imagination's capacity to materialize pain in inanimate objects so that the body can be rescued from its engulfment in suffering sentience. I suggested that cultural aversiveness leads to a sense that the painful sentience that ought to be embodied in and healed through the artifact now somehow hovers over it in a disembodied state of pure painful sentience. Such cultural aversiveness, I argued, can lead to a sense that the world is haunted. Horkheimer and Adorno offer an alternative but complementary analysis of the way that the commodity can strip the living person of her relationship to the continuity of life. The commodity itself, they suggest, has no permanence, but is created only to be replaced. Yet Scarry argues that the artifact, insofar as it is designed to rescue painful sentience, is made to have greater resilience than the human body. A coat can bring warmth to a body for a much longer time than the energy resources of a naked body could ever achieve. What the commodity's short "shelf life" means is that its power to rescue the body from pain is diminished; it dies before its time, so to speak. If Scarry is right that our pain is transferred to the *artifact*, then Horkheimer and Adorno allow us to understand that our mortality is transferred to the *commodity*. We sense ourselves as living in a world where we seem to be surrounded by dead objects that have passed their "use by" date. And, Horkheimer and Adorno claim, we see ourselves in the image of objects made for obsolescence: "What someone was and experienced earlier is annulled in the face of what he is now, or of the purpose for which he can be used."[68] We are all living beyond our "use by" date. This makes us fear those who really have died. They remind us of our own death-in-life existence. This "disturbed relationship with the dead," Horkheimer and Adorno write, "is the modern counterpart of the belief in ghosts which, in unsublimated form, continues unabated in spiritualism."[69] In other words, the modern individual who lives in what I call an aversive culture where commodities no longer are sensed as, in Scarry's terms, "disembodiments" of their pain, will revert to a fear and even an envy of the already dead. And this fear and envy, Horkheimer and Adorno claim, is the source of the belief in ghosts, whether or not that belief is sublimated (into a sense of one's own life as a merely ghostly survival past one's use-by date) or unsublimated (in actual research into ghostly apparitions).

Horkheimer and Adorno's "theory of ghosts" is one with which I am sympathetic. However, as in the case of their entirely negative assessment of vitalism, I want to give spiritualism a little more credit than being merely an unsublimated fear of the dead. Goldberg, as we saw, considers freeing ghosts from their earthbound existence a part of the redemption of the world. He neither fears nor envies ghosts. Rather, he *empathizes* with them. Spiritualism and occultism are not necessarily projections of our "disturbed relationship with the dead," but can be, as ghost photography is in Goldberg's case, a symptom of the disturbed relationship of the empathic imagination to the world as a whole: its work of redemption is frustrated by the economy of obsolescence and the injustice that sustains it. But although I disagree with their entirely negative assessment of spiritualism, I agree fully with Horkheimer and Adorno's analysis of what a "proper relationship to the dead" would entail. They write, "Only when the horror of annihilation is fully raised into consciousness are we placed in the proper relationship to the dead: that of unity with them, since we, like them, are victims of the same conditions and of the same disappointed hope."[70] What I take them to mean is that we should neither fear nor envy the dead; these emotions only reinforce our experience of ourselves as existing in a state of death-in-life. Instead we should recognize that we and the dead are both "the victims of the same conditions and of the same disappointed hope." I recognize in Horkheimer and Adorno's call to acknowledge "the horror of annihilation," a call to redeem the world of the living and the dead from this horror and to create a new and fuller life for both.

Let me draw some of the threads of this discussion together before turning again to Scarry and her reading of the Hebrew Bible. Vitalism and paranormal research, if not in all cases then at least in those that this book has studied, should be regarded as products of the imagination in response to a condition I call cultural aversiveness. Like the civilizational artifacts that Scarry analyzes, vitalism and paranormal research into ghosts are "exhilaratingly defiant of the body" while at the same time remaining "embedded within it." Each is an artifact of the imagination that is, as Scarry says, an "act of transcending the body." Each affirms, as one of the foremost vitalist theoreticians of the early twentieth century, Georg Simmel, put it, the "transcendence of life": "the grasping for what is beyond [*Hinausgreifen*] the current condition of life towards something that is not found in its present actuality but that causes it to become actual, this is nothing that is a mere addition to life, but it is rather the essence of life itself as we see in growth, reproduction and finally brought to completion in the sphere of consciousness."[71] Vitalism and paranormal research, both expressions of faith in the resources of life to transcend the death-in-life of contentless sentience (pain and *Angst*), are reactivations of the imagination as one of life's irrepressible resources. Unfortunately, neither vitalism nor paranormal research is able to replace torture and war as ways that a culture overcomes its collective aversiveness, although we saw in chapter 1 that Hans Driesch believed that a verification of life after death would have a transformative power unequaled by any previous scientific discovery. Goldberg, as we saw earlier in this chapter, also held out great hope for the power of a scientific proof of immortality to transform human life. Although we are justifiably skeptical of Driesch's and Goldberg's hopes for paranormal research, I believe we may add it, along with vitalism, to Scarry's list of ways that civilization can display its "profound allegiance to the body," that is, its profound allegiance to—or "confidence in," as Canguilhem would say—*life*.

I promised that Scarry would lead us back to Oskar Goldberg and his vitalist metaphysics of the Hebrew Bible. Scarry devotes a considerable amount of time in *The Body in Pain* to the Hebrew Bible, but it may seem strange to place her into relation with Goldberg, someone who insisted on the embodiment of Israel's God in the midst of the encamped Israelites. Scarry has recently been accused by Benjamin Sommer of seriously misinterpreting the Hebrew Bible because she characterizes the God of Israel as first and foremost revealed through a *bodiless* voice when, as in the story of Garden for example, God seems fully embodied.[72] How useful then can Scarry be for understanding Goldberg, whose whole project depends on the idea of an embodied God? I believe she is eminently useful in clarifying Goldberg's thought. Sommer's presentation of Scarry's discussion of God's bodiless voice is rather selective. Sommer, in his one-page portrait of Scarry's ideas, does not situate her characterization of the Hebrew Bible's God as bodiless voice within the frame of her book's overarching theme—the nature of the imagination and its connection to the human body's vulnerability to pain. Scarry understands the Hebrew Bible to be an act of imaginative creation "so monumental and majestic (however problematic) that it perhaps has no peer in any single artifact invented by another people."[73] The Hebrew Bible, she argues, presents nothing less than a complete representation of the human imagination itself as the creator of a world that can become a site of redemption from suffering. But the imagination can create this world only if the healing artifacts that constitute the redeemed world do not acquire such power over human beings that they themselves become sources of suffering and oppression. For this not to happen, the power of the imagination, "the pure principle of creating . . . on which nothing less than the fate of humanity depends," must be recognized to transcend any given artifact: the artifact is always only a means to the redemption of the body from suffering and never an end in itself.[74] When an artifact is created by Israel (a "graven image") that draws the focus of worship to itself and away from God as the sole source of Israel's redemption, God repudiates this artifact and insists—or tells a prophet like Isaiah to insist—that it is he alone who possesses sentience: "He now not only reminds his people that he is alive, that he sees, hears, moves, breathes (and by implication even eats, for the absence of this attribute is included in his denunciation of wooden and stone objects), but even that he experiences the most passive, extreme, and unselfobjectifying form of sentience, physical pain."[75] Thus Scarry does not deny that God is described as possessing a sentient body in the Hebrew Bible, but rather insists that he possesses such a body *in a paradigmatic way*—in the precise sense that "having a body means having sentience and the capacity to sense the sentience of others, reciprocity, compassion." Fully supporting Sommer's description of the localization of God according to the Priestly source in the Hebrew Bible, Scarry writes that "having a body means being not everywhere, but somewhere, no longer hidden."[76] We may wish to join with Sommer in problematizing some of Scarry's statements about the way that the New Testament gives full expression to the Hebrew Bible's portrait of the sentient, indeed suffering, God of Israel, but it would not be fair to characterize her, as Sommer does, as merely recirculating "medieval Christian supersessionism."[77] Nor is Sommer attentive to Scarry's description of the tabernacle as "God's material form" where Israel's "longing for His observable presence" is satisfied.[78] At the very least, a careful reading of Scarry on the Hebrew Bible—and a contextualization of that reading within her larger theme of the imagination as seeking to relieve suffering sentience through placing the burden of pain on the artifact to bear—complicates Sommer's dismissive and disparaging critique of her work. It is therefore appropriate to bring her interpretation of the Hebrew Bible into relation with Goldberg's.

In the second section of *The Body in Pain*, Scarry argues that the Hebrew Bible describes a society caught in the grips of a cyclical alternation between belief in the primal object of its imagination (its "primal Artifact," God) and the loss of this belief. For Scarry, the Hebrew Bible is the West's classic ("monumental and majestic") meditation on the making and unmaking of the world. Israel's God is something like the Platonic Form of the Artifact, the "Original Artifact" or "prime Artifact."[79] God's essential function in relation to Israel is to create a world of objects through which Israel's "bodily engulfment,"[80] its enslavement to voiceless and objectless embodiment (pain and *Angst*, in other words), can be relieved. God as the West's "Original Artifact" is, first of all, the projection of the imagination as pure expressive power, as *voice*. In the beginning, God has no body through which he acts upon the world. His world-making power lies only in his speech and his *ruach*, his enlivening breath. When God uses his voice in the first six days of Genesis to create living beings, his speech authorizes (blesses) the fecundity of life, commanding that the animal species of air, sea, and land should "be fruitful and multiply." Scarry seems perfectly to grasp in all its concreteness the significance of Goldberg's description of YHWH as the "biology-productive" principle, the "totality function" of the "transcendental organism." And like Goldberg, Scarry knows that the real drama emerges only in the creation of human biological fecundity:

> What is to be noticed here [in the passages where God promises offspring as numberless as the sands and the stars to the already aged Abraham and Sarah] is that however more powerful the Word of God is than the Body of man, it is within these stories always the case that the Word is never self-substantiating: it seeks its confirmation in a visible change in the realm of matter. The body of man is self-substantiating: iteration and repetition (the material re-assertion of the fact of their own existence) is the most elemental form of substantiating the thing (existence, presence, aliveness, realness) that is repeated. But the body is able not only to substantiate itself but something beyond itself as well: it is able not only to make more amply evident its own existence, presence, aliveness, realness, but to make ever more amply evident the existence, presence, aliveness, realness of God. With each successive increase (yesterday there were five hundred people and today six hundred: here are their names, the space they fill, the presence that can be seen, the garments that can be touched, the laughter and conversation that are audible), they reassert not only the sensorially confirmable realness of their own existence (We are. We are. We are. We are.) but the *sensorially confirmable realness of God's existence* (He is. He is. He is. He is.), or in the voice that is attributed to him, "I am. I am. I am. I am." Although the invented Artifact [Scarry's way to refer to the God of Israel] allows a people to experience itself in the capacity of spirit rather than

matter, it is here not a diminution of the body but its amplification that sponsors the increased apprehensibility of the spirit. An extreme change in the visible world now has a referent in the invisible world; *the body in its most intense presence becomes the substantiation of the most disembodied reality.*[81]

Goldberg would not describe YHWH Elohim as "the invented Artifact," but he would entirely agree with Scarry that the Hebrew Bible imagines God to be "apprehensible" in the amplified intensity of the collective and vital body of the people. He would use exactly the same terms to describe the conjunction of spirit and matter (*Geist* and *Materie*) as they come together in the cult practices and cult objects of the people, especially the tabernacle and the sacrificial altar, which for both Goldberg and Scarry are construed to be materializations of spirit.

Scarry points out that human fecundity (the embodiment of God's disembodied reality) is revealed in the genealogies that bring the various peoples into being and also in the stories where birth functions so centrally, as in the narrative of the contest within the womb of Rebekah that presages the future struggle between the lineage descending from Jacob and that of Esau, whose descendants include the Amalekites, Israel's quintessential enemy. In chapter 2 we saw how Goldberg found numerological significance in the list of descendants of Shem in Genesis. And in chapter 4 we saw how Goldberg attended to the power of individuals to carry within themselves the futurity not only of a people but of a whole "race." Scarry is not interested in *gematria*, but she does give the genealogical lists in Genesis their due weight. In noting how they punctuate stories of "the successful bringing forth of children," Scarry claims that "each of the two contains within itself what is withheld from view in the other: the men and women in the stories contain within themselves not the singular children specified in the narrative, but the tiers and tiers of offspring contained in the lists; so in turn the formal tiering in the lists conceals what only becomes manifest in the stories, the extremity of physical and imaginative work required of human continuity and connection."[82]

The fact that Abram is chosen by God to become the progenitor of "a multitude of peoples" is for Goldberg a sign of his heightened psychophysical capacity for metaphysics; however, for Scarry, it is the revelation of his heightened capacity for *belief*, for imagining that the human body—that *his* body—can be the vessel for the world-making power of God, the "prime Artifact." According to Scarry, humanity's biological fecundity as it appears in the genealogies and stories of Genesis is a sign of the fecundity of *belief*, the creative power of an imagination that is large enough to "make the world." She argues that the power of belief—the power of the imagination—is precisely the power to project the interior of the body outward, to build a world of artifacts in which the body's shapes and functions are amplified and translated into a world of artifacts. After Abram is told by God, "I will make your descendants as the dust of the earth, so that if one can count the dust of the earth your descendants also can be counted" (Scarry's rendering), he builds an altar to demonstrate his belief in the "prediction of man's incomprehensible plenitude."[83] Yet building an altar is not just a believing response to God's promise of incomprehensible fecundity; it is the very expression of how belief (imagination) works to project the body into the world. The altar's surface, Scarry argues, is "the reversed lining of the body," a claim she supports by referring to the fact that blood is poured across its surface. The altar, therefore, is an artifact constructed by "turning the body inside-out."[84] It is the act of belief made visible: "Belief in the scriptures is literally the act of turning one's body inside-out—imagining, creating, the capacity for symbolic and religious thought begin with the capacity to endow interior physical events with an external non-physical referent."[85] Goldberg would call this *the capacity for metaphysics.*

The Hebrew Bible, according to Scarry, reveals in its own ideal artifact, God, the very nature of artifactuality as such. When the God of the Hebrew Bible rejects graven images as forbidden artifacts, Scarry argues, this is because the Hebrew Bible understands that God, as an ideal artifact, is only effective as a healer of pain as long as he activates the healing power of the imagination in the sufferers themselves. God prohibits any attempt on the part of Israel to fabricate a body for him because it is he (the power of the imagination itself) who precisely unburdens human sentience of its aversive engulfment in the body. It is not that God is somehow "pure Spirit." Quite the contrary. God is the power that heals and redeems the body's aversive sentience through the materiality of the artifact. The prohibition against graven images refuses the equation of divinity with the human body not because divinity has nothing to do with the body, but because it *lifts the body out of its suffering through the instrumentality of the made object.* Graven images *freeze pain in place* and reinforce what Scarry calls humanity's "bodily engulfment." In effect, the prohibition on graven images is the *perpetual assertion of the exuberant power of life over the machine.* The machine (the artifact) has its rightful place in human culture only if it serves to redeem sentience from suffering, only if it redeems the body from its enslavement to pain. The prohibition against graven images, to return to Canguilhem's formula for vitalism, is an expression of "life's permanent distrust of the mechanization of life."

It is Scarry's profoundly *bodily* understanding of God that links her to Goldberg. Like Goldberg, she understands that God's worldly existence is mediated through the body's fecundity, whether in the extraordinary reproductive power granted to the aged bodies of Abraham and Sarah or in the extraordinary reproductive power of the Israelite slave population in Egypt. Also like Goldberg, Scarry understands that this collective biological exorbitancy is materialized in the ritual objects and ritual practices of the people. Goldberg turned to the Pentateuch to find another model for the relationship between spirit and matter, a model where artifacts (the Pentateuch itself, the Tabernacle, and the rituals of animal sacrifice) could serve as the instruments through whose operation spirit and matter come together to create (and continuously recreate) the Hebrew people's animated world (their *shem*, as Goldberg explains). Without in any sense endorsing Goldberg's vitalist metaphysics of the transcendental organism, Scarry, too, turns to the Pentateuch for her founding model of how the projective imagination "makes" a world. In uncannily similar terms to those used by Goldberg, Scarry describes the artifacts of the Pentateuch and the Pentateuch itself as materializations of God's otherwise invisible body. For Scarry, the artifacts that God commands the Israelites to build are instruments that give back to the people their greatest act of projective imagination—the projection of the imagination's own creative power on an invisible being (only able to be imagined), "their first artifact."[86] All the artifacts that God instructs the Hebrews to build are what Scarry calls "passover artifacts." A passover artifact works like the blood on the doorpost of the Hebrews in Egypt: it "depossesses one of the consequences of having a body."[87] In other words, it transforms the burden of inexpressible pain into a medium of redemptive healing in the face of imminent death.

Goldberg's Hebrew metaphysics is the theory and practice of the manufacture of "passover artifacts." As such, it is a form of healing, nothing less than a form of metaphysical medicine. It is therefore not surprising that Goldberg is a student of naturopathy, a practice premised on giving back to the body its own power of healing.[88] Nor is it surprising that Goldberg would search out sites of hauntings. With incontrovertible proof that spirit is more than an arrangement of organic matter, Goldberg hoped to heal the West of its burden of metaphysical pain, its severance from the sources of its own creative imagination. And, if that goal were made temporarily impossible because of the rise of Nazism, he would at least heal those unhappy spirits who were trapped in their own private hauntings. One way or another, Goldberg would perform his metaphysical duty to redeem the world. As an exponent of Hebrew metaphysics and as a spirit photographer, Goldberg gave his life to the cause of the vitalist imagination.

## Notes

1. For an overview of this literature, a good place to start is María del Pilar Blanco and Esther Peerenn, eds., *The Spectralities Reader: Ghosts and Hauntings in Contemporary Cultural Theory* (London: Bloomsbury, 2013). Another important book is Clément Chéroux, Andreas Fischer, Pierre Apraxine, Denis Canguilhem, and Sophie Schmit, *The Perfect Medium: Photography and the Occult* (New Haven, CT: Yale University Press, 2005). This book is the catalog issued in conjunction with the exhibition of the same name at the Metropolitan Museum of Art in New York in 2005.

2. Tom Gunning, "To Scan a Ghost: The Ontology of Mediated Vision," in Blanco and Peeren, *The Spectralities Reader*, 207–244.

3. The title of the lecture refers to a book I mentioned in chapter 4, note 82, in which I discussed the origin of Goldberg's concept of the "night side" (*Nachtseite*) of God. The book, Gotthilf Heinrich Schubert's *Ansichten von der Nachtseite der Naturwissenschaft*, went through four editions from 1808 to 1850 and was one of the most influential Romantic Naturphilosophie texts ever written. Schubert's book influenced the English novelist and spiritualist Catherine Crowe who wrote a book titled *The Night Side of Nature, or Ghosts and Ghost-Seers* (London: T. C. Newby, 1848). Crowe's book was also incredibly popular, influencing, among others, Charles Baudelaire. The Murnau title of Professor Bulwer's lecture seems to be a reference to both Crowe and Schubert. Crowe's key concept is what she calls a "vital force" that expresses itself through the "constructive imagination," which in turn is able to materialize forms externally in the surrounding "ether." In the following pages I am interested to explore why vitalist thought is drawn to the imagination as a productive or constructive principle.

4. Gunning, "To Scan a Ghost," 208.

5. Ibid., 212.

6. Ibid., 230.

7. Ibid., 232.

8. One of the most interesting attempts to offer a phenomenology of the imagination informed by Derrida's logic of the *pharmakon* is found in the work of Bernard Stiegler. See especially the section "Pharmacology of the Imagination," in Stiegler, *What Makes Life Worth Living*, trans. Daniel Ross (Cambridge: Polity Press, 2013), 15–18. Stiegler's entire project can be described as a "pharmacology of the imagination," but this section at least offers a focused introduction.

9. This "natural-supernatural" exorbitance of the imagination is what makes it so central to Romantic aesthetic theory and to Romantic vitalism. In speaking of the imagination as "natural-supernatural," I am alluding to the classic work by M. H. Abrams, *Natural Supernaturalism: Tradition and Revolution in Romantic Literature* (New York: W. W. Norton, 1971). The phrase "natural supernatural" was first used in Thomas Carlyle, *Sartor Resartus* (1831), a mock testament of a young German Naturphilosoph named Diogenes Teufelsdröckh. Carlyle, like his friend Samuel Coleridge, was deeply steeped in Naturphilosphie.

10. Elaine Scarry, *The Body in Pain: The Making and Unmaking of the World* (New York: Oxford University Press, 1985). The philosopher most frequently invoked by Scarry in this book is Jean-Paul Sartre whose *Psychology of the Imagination* is obviously of considerable importance for her. Her entire approach to the nature of pain depends on the phenomenological understanding of consciousness as intentional (pain lacks an intentional object). Scarry's discussion of the making of the world and the creation of the artifact as the product of the "excessive" expressivity of the body can be understood to be a vitalist alternative to Marx's discussion of the alienated commodity. Scarry's key term in her discussion of the imagination is "vivacity." For a largely sympathetic but nonetheless balanced account of Scarry's work, see Geoffrey Galt Harpham, "Elaine Scarry and the Dream of Pain," *Salmagundi* 130/131 (Spring–Summer 2001): 202–234.

11. Republished in Goldberg-*Aufsätze*, 321–325.

12. My colleague in the Religion Department at the University of Illinois Urbana-Champaign, the Sanskritist and Hindu religion scholar Rajeshwari Pandharipande, assures me that the belief in "haunted temples" is quite widespread in this region of India and Nepal. The practice of seeking to release the spirits of the deceased from their entrapment in this world continues to this day, and it is thought to demand training in a special "siddhi" or paranormal, "metaphysical" power.

13. See, for example, Paul Zillman, "Sri Mahatma Agamya Guru Parahamsa in Berlin," *Neue Metaphysische Rundschau* 11, no. 2 (1904): 67–74.

14. Goldberg-*Aufsätze*, 325.

15. The piece is in the Goldberg Nachlass but, to the best of my knowledge, was never published in *New York Spiritualist Leader*. It is not reprinted in Goldberg-*Aufsätze*.

16. Goldberg-*Aufsätze*, 305–308; quotation on p. 305.

17. For an overview of the work of Osty and Schrenk-Notzing, see Andreas Fischer, "'The Reciprocal Adaptation of Optics and Phenomena': The Photographic Recording of Materializations," in *The Perfect Medium: Photography and the Occult*, ed Clément Chéroux, Andreas Fischer, Pierre Apraxine, Denis Canguilhem, and Sophie Schmit (New Haven, CT: Yale University Press, 2005), 171–215, with accompanying reproductions. On the Institut Métapsychique de Paris that Osty directed, see M. Brady Bower, *Unruly Spirits: The Science of Psychic Phenomena in Modern France* (Urbana: University of Illinois Press, 2010).

18. Goldberg-*Aufsätze*, 307.

19. Ibid., 307–308.

20. Kurt Goldstein, *Der Aufbau des Organismus: Einführung in die Biologie unter besondere Berücksichtigung der Erfahrungen am kranken Menschen* (The Hague: Martinus Nijhoff, 1934). For a discussion of Goldstein's holistic theory of neurology, see Anne Harrington, "Kurt Goldstein's Neurology of Healing and Wholeness: A Weimar Story," in *Greater than the Parts: Holism in Biomedicine 1920–1950*, ed. Christopher Lawrence and George Weisz (Oxford: Oxford University Press, 1998), 25–45. See also Anne Harrington, *Reenchanted Science: Holism in German Culture from Wilhelm II to Hitler* (Princeton, NJ: Princeton University Press, 1996), 140–174. Kurt Goldstein published his own English translation of *Der Aufbau des Organismus* in *The Organism: A Holistic Approach to Biology Derived from Pathological Data in Man* (New York: Zone Books, 1996). The translation first appeared in 1939. The 1996 republication contains a foreword by Oliver Sachs. Translations are from Goldstein's English version. Quotation is from pp. 264–265.

21. A typical holistic definition of the organism is found in Erwin Bauer, *Die Grundprinzipien der rein naturwissenschaftlichen Biologie und ihre Andwendungen in der Physiologie und Pathologie*, vol. 26 of *Vorträge und Aufsätze über Entwicklungsmechanik der Organismen* (Berlin: Julius Springer, 1920). Bauer writes, "Every living being has the defining characteristic of being a system that is not in a condition of equilibrium with its environment and that has transformed the sources and forms of the energy of its environment into such forms of energy that entering into equilibrium with the environment is prevented" (10). Bauer goes on to define consciousness as *etwas qualitativ Neues* ("something qualitatively new") that reflects a more complicated relationship between the system of the organism and its environment (see pp. 144–160, a section titled "Körper und Geist").

22. Sigmund Freud, *The Ego and the Id*, trans. Joan Riviere (New York: Norton, 1960; orig. pub. 1923). "The ego is first and foremost a bodily ego; it is not merely itself a surface entity, but is the projection of a surface" (16).

23. Goldstein, *The Organism*, 307–308; emphasis Goldstein's.

24. If space permitted, I would have begun my discussion of Goldstein and Canguilhem with Ernst Kapp's *Grundlinien einer Philosophie der Technik* (*Outlines of a Philosophy of Technology*) (Braunschweig: George Westermann, 1877). Kapp's work argues for a theory of the machinal artifact as the imaginative projection of the human body (*Organprojektion*). The living organism (specifically, the human organism) is the condition of possibility of the machine, and therefore the machine cannot serve as the model for understanding the organism. This argument is central for Canguilhem (who refers to Kapp's work), but it also informs the work of Elaine Scarry (who may not have read Kapp and does not refer to him) to whom I turn in the following pages.

25. Canguilhem discusses Goldstein at length in the introduction to George Canguilhem, *Knowledge of Life*, trans. Stefanos Geroulanos and Daniela Ginsburg (New York: Fordham University Press, 2008), xvii–xx.

26. Canguilhem, *Knowledge of Life*, 62.

27. Ibid., 93.

28. Ibid., 63.

29. Ibid., 62.

30. Ibid., 73.

31. Goldstein, "Author's Preface" to the republication (1963) of the English edition of *The Organism*, 22.

32. Canguilhem, *Knowledge of Life*, 73; emphasis added.

33. Ibid., 66, 67.

34. Ibid., 73.

35. Kurt Goldstein, "The Smile of the Infant and the Problem of Understanding the 'Other,'" in Kurt Goldstein, *Selected Papers/Ausgewählte Schriften*, ed. Aron Gurwitsch, Else M. Goldstein Haudek, and William E. Haudek (The Hague: Martinus Nijhoff, 1971), 482.

36. Goldstein, *The Organism*, 231.

37. Ibid., 232.

38. Ibid., 43; emphasis added.

39. Ibid., 232.

40. Ibid., 240.

41. Scarry, *The Body in Pain*, 50.

42. Ibid.

43. Ibid., 326.

44. Ibid., 290.

45. Ibid., 285. I mentioned in note 24 that Scarry's notion of the artifact as the bearer of human sentience could be related to the classic work of Ernst Kapp, *Die Philosophie der Technik*. In one passage Kapp explains that "inorganic matter, despite the fact that it remains the same as it originally was when it is assembled into a machine, nonetheless is transformed into an organic extension [*organische Bestand*] and for as long as it shares in the activity of a living will it has become organic and no longer remains what it had been." Kapp offers the following example: "The telegraph, a lifeless machine composed out of the inorganic material, becomes through the act of the human will a bearer of thought and speech" (290). Kapp, unlike Scarry, does not emphasize the way that the artifact is first and foremost a vicarious bearer of *pain*.

46. Scarry, *The Body in Pain*, 288.

47. For the expression "corporeal engulfment," see Scarry, *The Body in Pain*, 50, 167, 184.

48. Harrington, "Kurt Goldstein's Neurology of Healing and Wholeness," 25.

49. Harrington, *Reenchanted Science*, 19–33.

50. If one runs a Google ngram-viewer search for "*deutscher Geist*" (German spirit) one finds a fourfold increase in the appearance of this phrase from 1906 to 1918. A critical appraisal of the widespread postwar retrenchment around the concept of a "native" German Geist can be found in Georg Friedrich Nicolai, *Die Biologie des Krieges*, 2 vols. (Zürich: Orell Füssli, 1919); see especially 2:402–414 for Nicolai's defense of a cosmopolitan conception of German Geist.

51. Scarry, *The Body in Pain*; for "materialization" see, for example, pp. 188, 190, 215, 223.

52. Ibid., 258.

53. Ibid., 259.

54. This is a point that Pheng Cheah makes in *Spectral Nationality* in relation to both colonial and neocolonial culture as depicted in the novels of the Indonesian author Pramoedya. As

Cheah points out, the colonial and neocolonial state are *doubly* haunted, both by the "abstract state alienated from living human work" (a negative specter) and the not-yet-born national spirit of the people's freedom and self-determination, a "good" specter. Pheng Cheah, *Spectral Nationality: Passages of Freedom from Kant to Postcolonial Literatures of Liberation* (New York: Columbia University Press, 2003), 355–356.

55. If it is not entirely clear, let me state that I am not asserting the existence of haunted houses or ghosts, although I take quite seriously as a symptom of cultural aversiveness the proliferation of discursive and other practices (séances, spirit photography, and so on) that seek to demonstrate the reality of hauntings and ghosts.

56. Scarry, *The Body in Pain*, 37.

57. Ibid.

58. Ibid.

59. Ibid., 57.

60. Max Horkheimer and Theodore Adorno, *Dialectic of Enlightenment: Philosophical Fragments*, trans. Edmund Jephcott (Stanford, CA: Stanford University Press, 2002), 193.

61. Ibid., 194.

62. Ibid., 195.

63. Ibid., 194.

64. Ibid., 195.

65. Ibid., 194.

66. Ibid.

67. Ibid., 178.

68. Ibid., 179.

69. Ibid., 178.

70. Ibid.

71. Georg Simmel, *Lebensanschauung: Vier metaphysische Kapitel*, 2nd ed. (Munich: Duncker & Humblot, 1922), 12.

72. Benjamin D. Sommer, *The Bodies of God and the World of Ancient Israel* (Cambridge: Cambridge University Press, 2009), 5.

73. Scarry, *The Body in Pain*, 221.

74. Ibid., 222.

75. Ibid., 230.

76. Ibid., 233.

77. Sommer, *The Bodies of God*, 5.

78. Scarry, *The Body in Pain*, 256.

79. Ibid., 244.

80. Ibid., 184.

81. Ibid., 193–194; emphasis mine.

82. Ibid., 187.

83. Scarry, *The Body in Pain*, 190.

84. I mentioned earlier the classic work of Ernst Kapp, *Die Philosophie der Technik*. Kapp in various places in the book explains that the creation of tools and artifacts is the objectification of the interior of the body.

85. Scarry, *The Body in Pain*, 190.

86. Ibid., 185.

87. Ibid., 238.

88. In the Goldberg Nachlass in the Deutsches Literaturarchiv Marbach there is a fully worked-out curriculum for a new naturopathic College of Medicine to be established in San

Francisco (through the auspices of the National Naturopathic Society headquartered in that city). Goldberg was elected to chair the educational committee. We do not know how far these plans went toward completion. We also know that Goldberg was selected by the International Society of Naturopathic Physicians to represent them at the World Health Organization's annual meeting in Geneva in 1951. Goldberg received naturopathic medical training in Munich some time before the outbreak of the First World War.

# Appendix I: Thomas Mann's Critique of *The Reality of the Hebrews*

Thomas Mann paraphrased (and in part lifted direct quotations from) some of the key passages of Oskar Goldberg's *The Reality of the Hebrews* for his 1948 novel *Doctor Faustus*. Mann introduces a certain Dr. Chaim Breisacher as one of a motley group of characters who would gather regularly at a fashionable aristocratic salon in the days just before the outbreak of the First World War. What these characters shared, despite their vastly different backgrounds and viewpoints, was contempt for the "philistinism" of German bourgeois culture. Mann's narrator, Serenus Zeitblom, describes Chaim Breisacher as "a racial and intellectual type in high, one might almost say reckless development and of a fascinating ugliness."[1] Breisacher preaches a reactionary (but also revolutionary) attack on modern "progressive" civilization, contrasting it with the earlier, "mythic" period in history when, like other folk groups, the ancient Hebrews worshipped an "effectively present national god" whose very body was "fed" with the "blood and fat" of the sacrificial animal. Breisacher complains of the "weak water-gruel" of the modern "abstract" God of the Jews (and of liberal Protestant Christians too). "Folk and blood and religious reality [*Wirklichkeit*]" have, Breisacher argues, disappeared from modern culture.

Soon after the publication of *Doctor Faustus*, Thomas Mann wrote a letter to Ludwig Lewisohn, a founding faculty member of Brandeis University and critic of American Jewish assimilationism.[2] In that letter Mann explains that Breisacher is meant to represent a "Jewish fascist" and that the character is based on the figure of Oskar Goldberg.[3] Thomas Mann's identification of Breisacher-Goldberg as an exponent of fascism has been criticized as a misunderstanding, indeed a deliberate falsification, of Goldberg's clear and unambiguous rejection of fascism. In one of the essays he published in Thomas Mann's own anti-Nazi journal, *Mass und Wert*, Goldberg attacks both George Sorel's and Alfred Rosenberg's "myths" as leading to nothing more than an "ecstasy [*Rausch*] of tragic proportions" in which "the masses are roused to pseudo-bacchantic frenzy."[4] But to say that Mann misunderstood or deliberately misrepresented Goldberg's notion of the Hebrew folk group is really not the point. Mann read every page of *The Reality of the Hebrews* very carefully and he fully understood that Goldberg was in no way a mystagogue peddling a Jewish version of Alfred Rosenberg's "myth of the blood."[5] Mann does not represent Breisacher as a Jewish fascist because of his racial views or because of his valorization of myth. Mann identifies the Goldberg of *The Reality of the Hebrews* as a "fascist" because of his "anti-humanism," which for Mann means that *Goldberg refused to abandon his "national" religion for a "universal" world religion.*

In his letter to Lewisohn, after explaining that much of what Breisacher is given to say comes directly out of Goldberg's *Reality of the Hebrews*, Mann asks Lewisohn if he is acquainted with the book and whether he "*loves* it" or has an "antipathy to its snobbish-spiteful anti-humanism." Breisacher's "anti-humanism" is what particularly impresses the narrator of *Doctor Faustus*: "It was at the Schlagenhaufens' [the hosts of the salon], and through this very Breisacher, that I first came in touch with the new world of anti-humanity, of which my easy-going soul till then had known nothing at all."[6] The narrator explains that the fact that a Jew introduced him to the "new world of anti-humanity" confirmed for him his belief that, despite his "general profession of friendliness toward the Jewish people," there were "some pretty annoying specimens" among them. One cannot, of course, identify Serenus Zeitblom, the narrator of *Doctor Faustus*, with Thomas Mann himself. But it is telling that Mann asks Lewisohn whether he *loves* Goldberg's book or rather rejects its "snobbish-spiteful" anti-humanism. Is this Mann's *litmus test for whether a Jew is an "annoying specimen"*? That Serenus Zeitblom makes a decided point of linking his first encounter with "the new world of anti-humanity" to one such "pretty annoying" Jew raises this question: Is there, for Mann himself, something that connects "the Jewish people" to anti-humanism, something that is also connected to a "snobbish spitefulness" that can make some "specimens" among the Jews "pretty annoying"?

The answer to this question requires us to examine in more detail just what Mann means by the "anti-humanism" of Breisacher-Goldberg. Thankfully, we know with some degree of precision what Mann found to be "anti-humanistic" in *Reality of the Hebrews*. The phrase "the new world of anti-humanity" appears as a marginal note in his copy of the book. In the sentence that it glosses, Goldberg describes the decline from the "national God" of the Hebrew "folk group" to "the God of the world religion who 'can do everything and owns everything.'" The "folk group" God is the "effectively present God," but the "world religion" God is the "bland, abstract, and generically-human 'loving God'" who "is everything and therefore nothing."[7] Parts of this sentence are incorporated verbatim into *Doctor Faustus*.

We may put the nature of "anti-humanism" this way: *The anti-humanism that Mann finds in Goldberg is his rejection of humanity's world religion of a loving God.* It makes sense for Mann to link anti-humanism to a Jew because Judaism, insofar as it is a "national" religion, precisely refuses to be "superseded" by a "world religion" that claims to overcome the limitations of Jewish "chosenness." Rejecting this world religion, Jews can certainly seem "snobbish" and "spiteful" (for what would lead them to reject their own Messiah except spite?). In other words, Thomas Mann finds in Goldberg the same "misanthropy" that has been attributed to the Jews since the Hellenistic period, a misanthropy that made "the Jews and their religion" into a "constant threat to the civilized world, which by definition is Greek."[8] Let us be clear: Mann does not find Goldberg to be a "Jewish fascist" because he identifies the ancient Hebrews as a "race." In fact, Mann *agrees* with "the fascist Goldberg" on this point.[9] Instead, *Goldberg is an anti-humanist because he believes that his "national" religion is superior to the "world religion" it spawned.* Because Goldberg-Breisacher clings to his "national God" and rejects the "loving God of generic humanity," he is condemned as an "anti-humanist." Mann is saying that, while National Socialism may be the full flowering of the "new world of anti-humanity," *the Jews themselves are its precursors.* It makes perfect sense, then, that when Mann in *Doctor Faustus* wants to place in Breisacher's mouth a social policy that would offend bourgeois sensibilities, he relies on the elimination of undesirables for the sake of racial eugenics.

(Goldberg never espoused eugenics.) "By placing an argument for genocide in the mouth of a repulsively ugly Jew," the literary scholar Todd Kontje recently argued, "Thomas Mann suggests that the Jews are indirectly responsible for their own misfortune."[10]

Another Mann scholar, Christian Hülshörster, has sought to defend Mann's representation of Goldberg in *Doctor Faustus*. He acknowledges that the fact that "Breisacher is a Jew may be confusing at first and can be the source of misunderstanding." Hülshörster argues that Breisacher's attack on world religion's "abstract and generically human God in Heaven" displays a dangerous antipathy toward "the theological universalism" that is the "foundation of Christian-Jewish [*sic*] ethics."[11] Hülshörster thus correctly identifies the reason why Mann calls Goldberg a "Jewish fascist," namely, his "anti-humanist" rejection of "Christian-Jewish" theological universalism. We may perhaps wish to disagree with Mann's (and Hülshörster's) belief that the rejection of "Christian-Jewish" theological universalism is tantamount to an embrace of anti-humanism, let alone fascism. But whatever we may think about this equation, Mann as a creative artist certainly has every right to create a fictional character who attacks this theological universalism and every right to associate this attack with a radical undermining of "Christian-Jewish ethics" that will ultimately lead to genocide. But it is indeed "confusing" and a potential "source of misunderstanding" to have a *Jewish* character serve as the major spokesperson for this attack on theological universalism. Hülshörster attempts to clear up this confusion by saying that "in the novel [*Doctor Faustus*] the Jewish [*das jüdische*] serves always as the mirror for and is the *alter ego* of the German [*das deutsche*]."[12] But this only begs the question. It is obvious that "the Jewish" is figured as the *alter ego* of "the German," but the question remains: Why is the Jew the alter ego of the *negative* side of "the German," the side that drives the nation forward toward moral bankruptcy and genocide? Mann, in other words, identifies "the Jewish" as *the "alter" ("other") of the "ego" of "the German."* "The Jewish" is, in effect, the German *Id*. We confront the paradox that Todd Kontje aptly sums up as follows: "Mann identifies German fascism in *Doctor Faustus* simultaneously and paradoxically as a specifically German malady and as an infection of the foreign. By a reversal of the same logic, the Jew becomes not only the foreign body in the German *Volk*, that is, that which is most alien and must be expelled, but also that which is most intrinsically German, the latent illness that can break out at any time."[13]

The paradoxical logic of "the most alien as the most intrinsic" makes it dangerous to draw any conclusions about the *real* Oskar Goldberg from Mann's portrait of Dr. Chaim Breisacher. Mann himself certainly thought his representation of Goldberg in *Doctor Faustus* was a faithful one (otherwise he would not have called Goldberg a "Jewish fascist" in his letter to Lewinsohn), but what would a "faithful" portrait of a *Jew* look like when it is meant to represent the deepest and most consequential conflicts within the *German* psyche? Mann uses Goldberg as a figure for "the most alien and the most intimate" identity of the *German* people, but he cannot be trusted to give us a faithful portrait of what the rejection of "humanism" and "theological humanism" would mean for a *Jewish* writer. In chapter 4 I argued, and I hope adduced sufficient evidence to demonstrate, that Goldberg's *Reality of the Hebrews* directly challenges the racialized concept of the state. I also argued that

"Hebrew metaphysics" is not limited to one "national" folk group, but is precisely a revolutionary interruption in the world of such national folk religions in order to establish the presence in the world of the *universal* God of "humanity in general." Whatever we may wish to say about his fictionalization of Goldberg, it seems clear that Mann, like the narrator of *Doctor Faustus*, found something particularly distasteful ("annoying") in a *Jewish* critique of the "world religion" theology of the loving God of "humanity in general."

Since this point is at the heart of Mann's charge of Jewish fascism against Goldberg, let me restate very briefly why Goldberg's criticism of "world religion" was, in fact, neither a rejection of universalism nor of humanism. Given his own deeply ingrained assumptions about the fundamentally "Western" nature of universalizing humanism, Mann was unlikely to understand how Goldberg's "Hebrew metaphysics" could possibly serve as the means for realizing the moral values of what Goldberg called "the human in itself" (*Mensch an sich*). Goldberg claims that the "universalism" of the Pentateuch lies precisely in its rejection of every form of *völkisch* "ancestral biology" (*angestammte Biologie*) in favor of *choosing* to align oneself with the God in whose image humanity's oneness is grounded.[14] Goldberg stresses that his interpretation of all the injunctions of the Pentateuch as linked to a national *ritual*, including the commandment against murder, in no way makes it impossible to discover universal *moral* value in some of those injunctions. "In contrast with the moral laws of the other metaphysical folk groups which must be different because each folk group has its own reality, . . . the biological universalism of Hebrew metaphysics (based upon the control of the biology-productive principle) leads to 'moral' laws that retain their meaningfulness when they are abstracted from their ritual context; indeed, they contain within themselves the possibility of their universal application."[15] Goldberg's Hebrew moral universalism rejects entirely the idea that the world of "Joseph and his brothers" needs to be superseded by a purified myth of the birth, death, and resurrection of the "enlightened" hero. Because Goldberg insisted that the Pentateuch *and only the Pentateuch* transcended all *völkish* mythologies of "ancestral biology," Mann could only find in Goldberg another "annoying" embodiment of *Jewish "snobbish-spitefulness."* Thomas Mann's charge that Goldberg is a "fascist" cannot be sustained. Granted, Goldberg's universalism and humanism are certainly neither "Western" nor "Christian," nor even particularly "spiritual." It is this fact that allowed Mann to treat Goldberg's *Reality of the Hebrews* as the "mirror" in which one could discern the lineaments of the "anti-humanism" of National Socialism. This mirror, however, distorts Goldberg's explicit claims on behalf of Hebrew metaphysics as the authentic form of theological universalism.


## Notes

1. Thomas Mann, *Doctor Faustus*, trans. H. T. Lowe-Porter (New York: Random House, 1991), 279.

2. Lewisohn's parents had converted to Methodism, and he had been raised as a Christian. He returned to Judaism when he confronted anti-Semitism among the faculty at Columbia University where he hoped to pursue a doctorate in English literature. See Kim Alegretto,

"Biographical Note," for the Finding Aid for the Ludwig Lewisohn collection at Brandeis University, available at http://archon.brandeis.edu/index.php?p=collections/findingaid&id=79.

3. "Kennen Sie es? *Lieben* Sie es? Oder haben [Sie] einen Widerwillen gegen seinen snobbisch-boshaften Anti-Humanismus?" Quoted in Christian Hülsthörster, *Thomas Mann und Oskar Goldberg's "Wirklichkeit der Hebräer"* (Frankfurt am Main: Vittorio Klostermann, 1999), 227 (emphasis Mann's).

4. Oskar Goldberg, "Die griechische Tragödie," in Goldberg-*Aufsätze*; quotation on p. 285. "Die griechische Tragödie" was originally published in *Mass und Wert* 1, no. 5 (1938): 728–752. At the conclusion of the essay (page 752 in the original; pages 284–285 in Goldberg-*Aufsätze*), Goldberg contrasts his view—that Greek tragic drama deals with the closing of the mythic age and the rise of the "metaphysics-alien" age—with the view of Nietzsche that Dionysus was a vital part of early Greek tragedy and that Socrates and Euripides "rationalized away" this vital reality. Goldberg's critique of Nietzsche is worth quoting in full:

> Socrates and Euripides thought more profoundly than did Nietzsche. They understood that when myth comes to an end, one cannot recreate it artistically. When is myth an artistic invention? When no reality—no world of gods—stands behind it. This artistic myth is the one that Nietzsche speaks of. When myth calls upon groups of people [*Völker*] in a metaphysics-alien age to sieze the thyrsus staff and enter into an ecstasy of tragic proportions, this is not the old and true myth, but that myth of Sorel's, the "Myth of the twentieth century," from which nothing can be expected except that it drives the masses into pseudobacchantic frenzy.

Goldberg correctly saw that Alfred Rosenberg's 1935 *Der Mythus der 19. Jahrhunderts* was deeply influenced by George Sorel's theory of social myth.

5. For the documentation regarding Mann's detailed annotations in *Reality of the Hebrews*, see Hülshörster, *Thomas Mann*, 131–133.

6. Mann, *Doctor Faustus*, 284.

7. Goldberg, *Reality of the Hebrews*, 49.

8. See Peter Schäfer, *Judeophobia: Attitudes towards the Jews in the Ancient World* (Cambridge, MA: Harvard University Press, 1998), 175–178.

9. In a diary entry of October 1945, Mann notes how the word "race" in regard to Jews has been "compromised." But he asks, "What should you call them? For there is something about them and not just that they are Mediterranean. Is it anti-Semitic to notice this? Heine, Kerr, Harden, Kraus *up to the fascist Goldberg*—it is after all a *single* race" (Mann's emphasis). The entry is quoted in Todd Curtis Kontje, *Thomas Mann's World: Empire, Race, and the Jewish Question* (Ann Arbor: University of Michigan Press, 2011), 7. Kontje explains that the word he translates as "race" is "Geblüt" and that this is literally "a single blood-type or species, more broadly, a distinct ethnic or cultural group."

10. Ibid., 172.

11. Hülshörster, *Thomas Mann*, 241.

12. Ibid., 243.

13. Kontje, *Thomas Mann's World*, 172.

14. Goldberg, *Reality of the Hebrews*, 79–80, 140.

15. Ibid., 140.

# Appendix II: Franz Joseph Molitor's *Philosophie der Geschichte* and Oskar Goldberg's Kabbalah Interpretation

Franz Joseph Molitor (1779–1860) devoted the last forty years of his life to defending the claim that the teachings of the Kabbalah can provide the basis for a world-historical renewal of Christian theology. Kant, he argued, had defended the ideas of God, the immortal soul, and freedom against the critical assault of fatalistic materialism, but had denied that the objects corresponding to these ideas could be intellectually intuited. Molitor found in the Kabbalah evidence that the human spirit could attain a direct intuition of the supersensible realm. Of course, Molitor was hardly alone in thinking that the ultimate challenge to philosophy after Kant was to explicate the conditions of possibility of the intellectual intuition of supersensible objects. He believed that the new conceptual apparatus of post-Kantian German idealism, Schelling's Naturphilosophie in particular, had prepared the necessary philosophical groundwork for humanity's ultimate redemption through a perfect synthesis of knowledge (*Wissen*) and faith (*Glaube*), philosophical reason and revealed scripture. Idealistic Naturphilosophie would serve as the theoretical skeleton for this new synthesis of knowledge and faith, and the Kabbalah was to be its flesh and sinews.

The result of this grand synthetic interpretive effort is a four-volume, 2,500-page work titled *Die Philosophie der Geschichte* (*The Philosophy of History*), published between 1827 and 1857.[1] "Despite his Christian theosophic leanings," Gershom Scholem wrote, "Molitor's work remains unsurpassed by any previous attempt, both in speculative depth and familiarity with Jewish sources."[2] As Scholem points out, Jewish historians of the *Wissenschaft des Judentums* school dismissed Molitor's work both for its apparent lack of interest in philologically informed text criticism and its emphasis on the mystical tradition as the key to understanding Judaism. Scholem frequently acknowledged his own profound debt to Molitor. Scholem describes how, after having stumbled on Molitor's first volume "at Poppelauer's," a renowned Judaica bookshop (associated with the Moritz Poppelauer publishing house) in Berlin, he decided that he would devote his life to uncovering "the metaphysics of the Kabbalah."[3]

Oskar Goldberg mentions Molitor in a programmatic outline, preserved in his Nachlass, for the foundation of a research group devoted to the study of the Kabbalah and its reception by Christian theosophists from the Renaissance through the nineteenth century. Although Molitor is the last-named figure in Goldberg's outline of history of the Christian Kabbalah, he is not singled out for special attention (Franz von Baader and Schelling receive more attention). Despite this fact, it does seem that Molitor played a not insignificant role in Goldberg's interpretation of the Kabbalah. I have had occasion in footnotes to remark on Molitor's likely influence on Goldberg's conception of God's "night side" and also on his interpretation of the meaning of the

Hebrew term *nefesh*.[4] Beyond such specifics, however, one could say that Goldberg's *Reality of the Hebrews* attempts to do for Jewish theology what Molitor attempted for Christian theology, namely, to synthesize Kabbalah and Naturphilosophie (or, in Goldberg's case, neo-Naturphilosophie) to provide a basis for a new era in which science and revelation could together lead humanity toward redemption. The goals of Molitor's and Goldberg's Kabbalah interpretation share much in common, as do many of the details of their expositions of the Kabbalah. It is difficult, however, to be entirely sure exactly where Goldberg drew directly from Molitor and where their common goals and common building blocks (Kabbalah and Naturphilosophie) lead them to similar conclusions. The positions that divide them are perhaps more illuminating for our purposes than those that they share. A complete account of Goldberg's relation to Molitor is beyond the scope of this book, but a few remarks are certainly in order. In what follows I first briefly describe what I see as two major points of convergence between Molitor and Goldberg: their conception of the organic-mathematical nature of the "upper worlds" and their theory of how Universality (*Allgemeinheit*) unfolds into a qualitatively differentiated multiplicity (*Besonderheit* for Molitor, *Vielheit-Einheit* for Goldberg). Molitor's theory of how this unfolding process can be grasped by intuition is perhaps the single most significant point he and Goldberg share in common. It seems likely that Goldberg in his *Ontology* was influenced by Molitor's theory of the productive power of the imagination, although it is true that this theme is central to all of Romantic Naturphilosophie. After discussing these possible points of congruence between Molitor's and Goldberg's systems, I turn to several points where Goldberg definitively parts company with Molitor. The first such point lies in Goldberg's understanding of Pentateuchal revelation as signaling a radical break with the earlier Semitic system of revelation to which, according to Goldberg, the Kabbalah bears witness. The second point where Goldberg diverges from Molitor is his insistence that the Pentateuch decisively rejects the Kabbalah's emphasis on masculine-feminine cosmic harmonization as the key to redemption.

In discussing Goldberg in relation to Molitor, I add nothing of substance to this book's presentation of Goldberg's ideas. But comparing Goldberg with Molitor allows me to highlight the way that Goldberg reads the Pentateuch as precisely a critical response to the Kabbalistic conception of redemption as Molitor expounds it, replacing the restoration of masculine-feminine *harmony* with the establishment of divine *power* (*Allmacht*) over the machinal forces of the racialized geopolitics of the state. Molitor, whose views were largely defined by the political and social conditions in Germany during the first quarter of the nineteenth century, could not have imagined how myths of racial purity and the organic state could together put an end to his dream of a renewal of Christianity through the revivification of the Jewish mystical tradition.

Let us begin, then, with some points of convergence between Molitor and Goldberg. This requires a brief description of Molitor's general Kabbalah interpretation. Despite the fact that it is spread across four volumes published over thirty years, Molitor's interpretation of the Kabbalah is remarkably consistent. In every aspect of the Kabbalah, Molitor finds two interwoven themes at work: a trinitarian logic and a masculine-feminine dynamism. In the Kabbalah's anthropology, for example, the human is understood to be a combination of the intellective spirit (*Geist, n'shamah*), the willing-expressive soul (*willende auswirkende Seele, ruach*), and a body-formative soul (*leibbildende Seele, nefesh*).[5] This trinity of souls, descending from universal-spiritual to particular-corporeal, reflects the general trinitarian logic governing the ontological unfolding of the ideal realm into the realm of concrete, embodied reality. The terms of this trinitarian logic are Universality (*Allgemeinheit*), Specificity (*Besonderheit*), and Concreteness (*Concretheit*).[6] The highest ideal form, Universality, is unitary but potentially expandable into a multiplicity of qualitatively differentiated kinds or species. Specificity (*Besonderheit*) arises when Universality expands into a multiply differentiated structure. (The root of the German word is the same as that of the verb *sondern*, to assign something to a separate category or kind.) Finally the two ideal realms of Universality and Specificity are concretized in embodied, physical reality when a specific kind or species (a horse or dog, for example) is instantiated in a spatiotemporal individual. As ideality is unfolded into concrete reality, two countervailing forces are always at play: a feminine principle of receptivity and a masculine principle of expressivity.[7] Thus, applying the trinitarian logic and the masculine-feminine dynamic to an understanding of the human psychic constitution, a unitary and universal spirit (*n'shamah*) finds outward diversification in the expressive will of the soul (*ruach*), and both together achieve concrete individual reality in the living activity of the corporeal organism (*nefesh*). At every stage of this unfolding process we find two dynamic, mutually interacting forces at work: an outward-expressive masculine principle and a receptive feminine principle. At the highest ideal level, the masculine principle of unitary universality seeks to express itself in outward specificity in the soul's will; the feminine principle within the lower level of the will seeks to receive and conform itself to the unifying force of the upper level of spirit. In the harmonization of the masculine and feminine principles, upper and lower levels are balanced. This trinitarian logic, together with the masculine-feminine dynamic of countervailing active-receptive principles, is expounded again and again in Molitor's four volumes. Here is an exemplary passage from the last volume to be published, an expanded second edition of volume 1:

> The being and life of every created thing rests upon the indivisible unity of the universal, the specific, and the concrete and their constant reciprocal action upon each other. The inner, universal, and unitary aspect of every thing has, on the one hand and in accordance with its nature, the desire for itself as a unity and, on the other hand, the desire for the specific and the concrete aspect of itself as what is opposed to itself. The latter desire is a desire to externalize itself as an objective being and at the same to spiritualize [*begeistigen*] this being and to draw it upward toward itself. In like manner, the lower aspects of the external, specific, and concrete have the desire on the one hand to persist in their selfhood [*in seiner Selbstheit zu verharren*], but, on the other hand, there lies within them also the desire to conform themselves to the higher aspect and to be lifted up to it and to be fulfilled within it.[8]

The same two themes—trinitarian logic and the masculine-feminine dynamism—are developed also in the totality of creation, with the two ideal "upper worlds" of the Kabbalah's theosophy (*b'riah*, Creating and *y'tsirah*, Contructing) corresponding to the intellective spirit and expressive-willing soul of the human being, respectively, and the "lower" corporeal real world (*asiyah*, Making) corresponding to the body-formative soul (the names of the three worlds are taken from the different verbs used in the Hebrew Bible to describe God's creative activity):

> The Kabbalah describes the two upper worlds as that which is inner, ideal, masculine, and outpouring [*einfliessende*] and the lower world of *asiyah* as that which is external, real, feminine, and receptive. The lower world is characterized as the body of creation's immense totality. In and through this body the upper ideal beings achieve their complete reality through the external and objective reflection of themselves. As I have intimated, the ideal, upper, and outpouring aspect needs and desires the lower and receptive aspect and the former seeks to lift the latter to itself and also to give itself to it, just as the lower, receptive aspect needs and desires the higher, ideal masculine aspect in order to let itself be taken and held by it and drawn up to it.[9]

We thus see that Molitor's trinitarian Kabbalistic cosmology is crisscrossed by the mutually attractive forces of a masculine, outpouring aspect and a feminine, receptive one. The mutually desiring aspects of the masculine and feminine bring about the unending emanation of differentiated specificity (*Besonderheit*) out of infinite universality (*Allgemeinheit*). The first such emanation is, according to the Kabbalah, that of Adam Kadmon (whom Molitor also refers to as the Son) from out of the Eyn Sof (Infinity, whom Molitor also calls Father):

> The differentiating emanating birth of the Son, the bringing forth of creation, which is the image of the eternal immanent generation of the Son, is, according to the true meaning of the Kabbalah, the work of the progressive divine self-limitation, and it takes place as the Father, as the infinite will of universality negates himself in his infinite universality and through this self-negating magical [*magisches*] act, brings forth out of himself the Not [*das Nicht*] of himself, namely, the form of externality, in the level of the specificities that had been present within him. . . . The Kabbalists express it this way in their realistic fashion: "When it occurred to the Eyn Sof to bring forth the worlds, he drew back his infinite light that extended in all directions and left a single place where there remained traces of his holiness, and this is why this place was not an actually empty nothingness; and into this place, which was set aside to be the space for all the worlds, he emanated Adam Kadmon."[10]

The Father (the principle of universality) emanates the Son (the principle of specificity), and the Son in turn, through another act of self-limitation, emanates the Holy Spirit, the principle of concreteness. The figure of Adam Kadmon, however, consists of ten elements, formed in the following manner: The trinitarian structure of Father, Son, and Holy Ghost is crossed at each level by the dynamic interaction of the masculine-feminine principles, thus doubling the three elements, making six separate elements out of the original three. Each element remains in a condition of unity, however, so the total of all elements (as unities and as dynamically divided into masculine and feminine aspects) is now nine. Finally, the whole doubled trinitarian structure is also a single complex unity, a tenth element beyond the nine: Adam Kadmon.

We are now in position to note some of the points of convergence between Molitor and Goldberg. The first point is the mathematico-organic nature of Adam Kadmon. The following passage of Molitor seems quite close to Goldberg:

> The trinitary Godhead is an absolute one-and-allness that contains within itself, in a state of indifferentiation, its infinite tenfoldness (*Zehnfachheit*), positing itself as the identity of universality, specificity, and concreteness and conceiving all of its infinite qualitative oppositions in harmonious balance. The Godhead, while it is all in all and is eternally self-sufficient, has outside of itself another object, the created world. The created world is the reversed negative image of the trinitarian Godhead arising from out of the separatedness (*Schiedlichkeit*) of the decad (*Zehnzahl*) and the opposed relations of the universal, specific, and concrete as they divide apart from one another. The created world is a partitioned (*gegliederte*) infinite unity made up of purely relative active-passive mutually interacting unities. Each such unity is *a single determinate number* or, *an objectively expressed quality of the divine will*, which expresses in its own way a completed ideality which, in the relativity of its reflected image, mirrors in this small part the whole totality of the universe. All these number-qualities in their living *magical* reciprocal action upon one another form a single unity in their multiplicity (*Einheit in der Vielheit*) or one great *organism*, representing the reversed negative image of the divine absolute unity.[11]

The mathematico-organic structure of the upper world of Adam Kadmon contains the specific "qualities" that make up God's infinite thought. These number-qualities, Molitor claims, are the patterns of the souls found in animals and humans. Again, this seems close to Goldberg's concept of the transcendental "world systems" as structures of "organic lawfulness." Molitor, like Goldberg, considers all these number-organisms to be the constituent elements of one total structure, Adam Kadmon (or the Son). Of course, Goldberg never would present his Kabbalistic cosmology in the terms of Christian trinitarianism. In fact, Goldberg downplays Molitor's trinitarian logic and seems to almost completely replace it with a straightforward dualism of the infinite and the finite, the former consisting of all possible world systems and the latter being the actual empirical world. Despite this difference, however, we may acknowledge a fundamental agreement between Molitor and Goldberg about the mathematico-organic nature of the upper or transcendental realm that serves as the model of the empirical world's diverse animal species.

The second point of convergence between the Kabbalistic systems of Molitor and Goldberg that I draw attention to is the mediating power of the imagination (*Phantasie*). One of the fundamental concerns of Goldberg's *Ontology* is to explain how the imagination can both directly experience *and produce* something that exceeds the limits of this empirical world's possibilities. Goldberg, in a passage I discussed in chapter 3, describes how the imagination can break open the "universal concept" (*Allgemeinbegriff*) into an infinity of new possible experiences: "Out of the *content* of the broken up universal concept there pours out the sort of sequences [of possible experiences] that exceed the [current] law governing causal sequences: the totality of authentic possibilities."[12] The imagination, according to Goldberg, has the ability to reach beyond the apparent solidity and constancy of the experiential content of the empirical realm. Beyond this world of apparently fixed causal sequences, the "hinterground of the imagination" (*Hintergrund der Vorstellung*) opens on a realm of pure becoming.[13] As I argued in chapter 3, this "hinterground" is the point of psychophysical suture between mind and body, the point where human consciousness itself emerges from out of its organic matrix. Here is also where the divine image enters into the world (as the human "image of God"), and it is here that Goldberg believes that mythic images once congealed into real biological forces are shared throughout a folk group's collective psychophysical existence. It is at an individual's psychophysical suture point that the imagination in the present-day world can rediscover the "metaphysical" bridge that can lead it back to God. At the conclusion of his *Ontology*, Goldberg writes that "the imagination strives for an identity with its object and it thereby strives for pure Being through the act of completing the infinity of possibilities."[14] Properly understood, the imagination is the site of a continuous but mostly unnoticed interchange between the transcendental realm as the "universal concept" (Goldberg's *Allgemeinbegriff*, Molitor's *Allgemeinheit*) and our spatiotemporal world with all of its diverse qualitative specificities (Molitor's *Besonderheit*, Goldberg's *Vielheitseinheit*). The individual's imagination, once its authentic power is awakened, strives for what Goldberg calls a "completion act," an act that intuits a wholly different configuration of possible experiences. This completion act is, in effect, the coming into being of a new revelation and, therefore, a new embodiment of God's presence in the world.

Molitor's concept of the imagination (*Phantasie*) as the spiritual organ that mediates between upper and lower worlds is very similar to what we find in Goldberg's *Ontology*. Molitor begins his account of the mediating power of the imagination by distinguishing between the *form* and *matter* of the human individual. He argues that the image of God is reflected within the human spirit (*Geist, n'shamah*) as a "self-active" formal principle:

> The *formal* aspect of the divine is the absolute, autonomous, self-positing unity and eternal self-equivalence [*Selbstgleichheit*]. The *real* aspect of the divine, however, is the unity and harmonious self-equivalence of the *infinite qualities*. The absolute form of unity and self-equivalence with which the Godhead posits itself at the same time forms the generic principle of unity of every relative, finite existence. The human spirit bears this form in an inner, self-active manner within itself and this is what makes it alone of all existing things the *image of the Godhead*. This self-active formal principle grants to the human spirit its capacity to raise itself to its creator, to recognize the divine in God as what is similar to itself in its absolute expression. It is what gives the human spirit the ability to as it were become configured within the Godhead [*in die Gottheit eingestaltet zu werden*].[15]

All three levels of the human psychic makeup—*n'shamah, ruach*, and *nefesh*—have a self-active and a receptive aspect. In addition to the self-active formal principle, there is also a receptive principle that is open to influences from the outer world. While the receptive aspect is usually attuned to the outer *physical* world, there is a receptive organ that is attuned to the *higher* world. One such receptive organ is the imagination (*Phantasie*). The passage where Molitor describes the receptive organs of the three psychic levels of the human being is lengthy, but it is worth quoting in full:

> Correlated to the self-active principle of form there exists in every creature a receptivity in relation to its embodiment in matter. This correlation is at the basis of the entire existence of every creature. It is what regulates all the parts and levels of life, and it is found, as has been noted, in every body [*Leib*], in every soul, and in every spirit. Just as the organic body, with all its ways for assimilating objects within itself, and the soul, with all its manifold sense organs, are able to stand in relation with the external earthly world and to receive its influences and actively work upon them, so also does the human being possess within his deepest, most inward center, or, one might say, *in the hinterside of his body-soul-spirit nature [in der Hinterseite seines leiblichen, seligen, und geistigen Wesens] a similar sort of organ. To be sure, this organ, during most of our usual earthly life, is mostly covered over but it is never entirely closed off. It is an organ found in different gradations. At its highest level, it is an organ for the higher, invisible, spiritual world. It is able to directly grasp the spiritual and the divine in proportion to the level of its inward openness. It is able to perceive within itself in a living way the manifold manifestations of the higher world as actual realities.* As the receptive organ of the spirit, it offers the unmediated perception of the spiritual and the divine. At the next lower level, as the receptive organ of the soul, it receives from above (by means of the spirit) impressions through its imagination [*Phantasie*] of variegated content. In this way the power of the creative imagination [*Einbildungskraft*] constitutes the passageway [*Uebergang*] between the infinite and the finite. But at the same time it is the pinion [*Schwinge*] on which the being that is enchained to the earth can lift itself to the heavens. Finally, at the lowest level of the body-forming soul or *nefesh*, bodily life possesses a receptive organ, in accordance with whatever its original nature is, that allows the influences from the higher world to be transformed into real concreteness within the living body.[16]

Molitor goes on to say that the human's receptive organ for the higher world enables him to experience a "supernatural clairvoyance" that in our modern era of "disbelief" has largely disappeared.[17] However—and here we may note another point of convergence with Goldberg—in the earliest eras of humanity there had been "an original purity in which the human being stood in trusted relationships with higher beings."[18] This leads us now to consider the points where Goldberg significantly departs from Molitor. In fact, these are the very points where Goldberg breaks with the Kabbalah entirely.

Molitor's idea of revelation, as we have just read, is based on the analysis of the human psychic apparatus as possessing both active and receptive aspects, the first transforming into specific imagistic forms what the second provides as content from the upper world. The basic content of all revelation is the harmonious, active-passive, masculine-feminine Godhead.[19] The sin of the first human couple, Adam and Eve, corrupts humanity's ability to receive revelation, but it does not altogether destroy it.[20] Revelation occurs whenever the human's psychic apparatus is properly reattuned to the higher world's influence, when its "deepest, most inward center" grounds the whole existence of the human and places him in proper balance with the organizing, creative center of the upper worlds. In ancient Israel, "as it were the central point of the entire whole [of humanity],"[21] the human capacity for the reception of revelation was most powerfully expressed. Molitor believes that after a millennium, ancient Israel's revealed tradition (Kabbalah) lost its spiritual force and became hardened in custom and outward ceremony. Christ came to renew Israel's receptivity for revelation, but the time had passed when Israel could recognize the inward spiritual truth of its revealed traditions. Remarkably, Molitor goes so far as to say that Christ's coming would not have been necessary had Israel remained able to experience the inward force of its revelation. "The rebirth of humanity would in that case have taken place through the course of time in a gentle but more accelerated fashion. . . . Afterwards, salvation through the triumphant Messiah would have finally arrived and the mystical kingdom of David would have been instituted in its full brilliance, and Israel would have been established with all her outward glory, something that could only occur when the entire human in spirit, soul, and body is reborn and has become a new, supernatural creature."[22] Israel, however, was incapable of recognizing Christ as the renewer of its revealed tradition and so ceased being the spiritual center of humanity's redemption. Christ's teaching was carried outward to the nations, but Christianity itself took a turn away from Christ when it *overspiritualized* his teaching. In the course of history, an overspiritualized Christianity fell prey to the Enlightenment's religion of reason. Once again, although for reasons quite the opposite of what happened to ancient Israel, humanity's organ of revelation became atrophied. Molitor thus returns to the Kabbalah to reawaken humanity's capacity to experience revelation and to restore humanity on the path toward salvation.

While the general thrust of Molitor's interpretation of the history of revelation seems not unlike Goldberg's (with the exception of his conception of Christ, however downplayed it may be), Goldberg's account of the nature of revelation is entirely different from that of Molitor. Goldberg sharply distinguishes the revelation that is reflected in Kabbalah (the only kind that Molitor is interested in) from the revelation that is vouchsafed to the people of Israel in the desert and preserved in the Pentateuch. Goldberg explicitly denies that the earliest revelation to humanity was one of "original purity." The revelation that mythic humanity received from the upper worlds was deeply tainted by *biology*. The upper world of Adam Kadmon was riven by competing world systems that sought a colonial mastery over the empirical world.[23] The means whereby these world systems sought to establish their hegemony over this world was through the psychophysical potency of ancient folk groups. The cult performances of these folk groups offered metaphysical beachheads from which the world systems could engage in "transcendental geopolitics." The gods—the transcendental world systems—did not represent the totality of Adam Kadmon, but only particular organ systems. Each organ system found its heightened concrete expression in an animal: Each animal has its peculiar strength and character that depend on the organ system most developed in it. Since mythical religions and their cults likewise expressed only parts of Adam Kadmon, they were intimately connected with a certain animal, the folk group's totem or sacred biocenter. Only with the descendants of Shem did God (YHWH Elohim) find an entrance point to offer a revelation that could challenge the power of these colonizing gods. But even so, at first, YHWH Elohim's revelation needed to be couched in the imagery and language of the other revelations: the organism and its processes of birth, death, alimentation, and reproduction. Where other revelations had offered a particular animal as the totemic embodiment of the divine organism, with Shem and his descendants the revelation offered the complete human organism as the image of the divine. This divine organism is pictured not as having two separate genders but as the harmonious union of both genders: Adam Kadmon as the balanced union of active masculine expressivity and passive feminine receptivity. This is the image that, according to both Molitor and Goldberg, underlies the whole of the Kabbalah. For Molitor, the Kabbalah is the fullest expression of divine revelation ever granted to humanity. Christianity's historical mission is to prepare the groundwork for a more spiritual and idealized interpretation of the Kabbalah, one that Molitor himself provides in his *Philosophie der Geschichte.*

For Goldberg, on the contrary, the revelation of the Kabbalah is superseded by the revelation given to Moses, the Pentateuch. The Pentateuch is the revelation of the *pre-biological source of biology, the power that transcends organic existence and interrupts the principle of biological inheritance to create a people constituted through free choice rather than genealogy.* The Kabbalah, according to Goldberg, was a revelation granted to individuals with a *racial* (Semitic) metaphysical capacity. Its imagery remains at the level of biology (masculine-feminine harmonization). The Pentateuch, however, is a revelation that breaks with the principle of race entirely and bases itself, for the first time in human history, on the power of a people to consciously shape its biology and to wield the power of the productive source of life itself against the geopolitics of race-based cults. The Kabbalah, Goldberg acknowledges, has efficacious power, but only at the level of the individual who encapsulates a racial metaphysical power. To wield power at the level of transcendental geopolitics, another kind of revelation is necessary, one that connects a voluntarily united people to the transcendent source of biology itself.

Molitor, unlike Goldberg, is mostly concerned with the efficacious power of revelation in the life of the individual. His image of salvation focuses on the rebirth of the "spirit, soul, and body" of the individual. Perhaps the sole reference to the "folk group" as the subject of interest in the Pentateuch comes in volume three's discussion of impurity, and it does indeed remind one of Goldberg: "Just as it is the duty of the Israelite to do nothing to disturb his inner salvific order [*die innere Heilsordnung*], so in like manner is he strictly enjoined to do nothing to voluntarily alter the ordered organism of the holy people [*das angeordnete Organismus des heiligen Volks*], which serves as the precondition [*Bedingniß*] for the stability of that order of salvation [*Ordnung des Heils*], or to hand over the holy people to the power of impurity."[24] While he does discuss the danger that an individual poses to the integral order of the people, Molitor clearly sees the people as primarily the "precondition" for the purity of the individual.

This reverses Goldberg's priorities and is the major point of divergence between him and Goldberg. Where Molitor stresses the unification of the masculine-feminine aspects within the individual as the highest goal of revelation, Goldberg focuses on the restoration of divine justice within all humanity. Goldberg focuses entirely on the power of the people to serve as a collection center (*Ladung*) for the metaphysical energy of YHWH Elohim. Divine justice can only be achieved if God transcends the limitations imposed on his power that creation imposed on him. (As we saw in chapter 5, Goldberg argues that an imperfect creation could only be justified if God himself reserved the right to enter into the world to overcome its fundamental imperfection.) We may aptly conclude both our discussion of Molitor and Goldberg and the book as a whole with one of Goldberg's most forceful statements about the difference between Kabbalah and the Pentateuch, a statement that encapsulates the entire thrust of his thought:

> The Kabbalah says: the world is constructed in a polar fashion. It is comprised of opposed forces, positive and negative, masculine and feminine. It is concerned with unifying these countervailing forces and thus to bring about the equipoise of the world: *the harmony of the forces.* . . .
>
> The Pentateuch says: equipoise is harmony, harmony is beauty—beauty, however, is not justice. The Torah concerns itself with justice. The Torah's task is to escape from rounded completedness [*Abgerundetsein*], from beauty, and from equipoise. The world goal of the Torah is to bring the world out of its dead center-point of polarity. The world goal of the Kabbalah can only be realized in the life of the individual human—even if he is a supernaturally powerful individual; but the only goal of the Torah is the Godhead itself. Only God can transcend the finite-limited field of forces, insofar as he breaks through these forces and thereby permits his infinity, that is, a path towards his total mastery [*Allmacht*], to enter the world.[25]

## Notes

1. Franz Josef Molitor, *Philosophie der Geschichte, oder Über die Tradition*, part 1 (Frankfurt am Main: Hermannschen Buchhandlung, 1827); part 1, 2nd ed. (Münster: Teissing'sche Buchhandlung, 1857); part 2 (Münster: Theissing'sche Buchhandlung, 1834); part 3 (Münster: Theissing'sche Buchhandlung, 1839); part 4, vol. 1 (Münster: Theissing'sche Buchhandlung, 1853). For a study of the Kabbalistic sources of Moltior's work, see Katharina Koch, *Franz Joseph Molitor und die jüdische Tradition* (Berlin: Walter de Gruyter, 2006).

2. Gershom Scholem, "Franz Josef Molitor," in *Encyclopaedia Judaica*, vol. 14, 2nd ed., ed. Michael Berenbaum and Fred Skolnik (Detroit: Macmillan Reference USA, 2007), 426.

3. On Scholem's relation to Molitor, see David Biale, *Gershom Scholem: Kabbalah and Counter-History*, 2nd ed. (Cambridge, MA: Harvard University Press, 1982), esp. 31–33 where Biale discusses an unpublished manuscript in which Scholem describes how Molitor served as an inspiration for his own study of Kabbalah. See also Bram Martens, *Dark Images, Secret Hints: Benjamin, Scholem, Molitor and the Jewish Tradition* (Bern: Peter Lang, 2007), and Christoph Schulte, "'Die Buchstaben haben ihre Wurzel oben': Scholem und Molitor," in *Kabbala und Romantik: Die jüdische Mystik in der romantischen Geistesgeschichte*, ed. Eveline Goodman Thau, Gert Mattenklott, and Christoph Schulte (Tübingen: Niemeyer, 1994), 143–164.

4. For Molitor on the "night side" of God, see *Phil.* 2.80. For the discussion of *nefesh*, see the later discussion where I explain Molitor's understanding of the relationship between *n'shamah*, *ruach*, and *nefesh*.

5. *Phil.* 1².508–510.

6. The trinitarian logic of Universality, Specificity, and Individuality (*Einzelhiet*) is given its classic form in Hegel's "Subjective Logic" in the second volume of his *Science of Logic* (1816). See Georg Wilhelm Friedrich Hegel, *Wissenschaft der Logik*, 2 vols. (Frankfurt am Main: Suhrkamp, 1969), 2:273–300. For a discussion of Hegel's trinitarian logic, see Christian Iber, "Hegels Konzeption des Begriffs," in *G. W. F. Hegel Wissenschaft der Logik*, ed. Anton Friedrich Koch and Fridrike Schick (Berlin: Akademie, 2002), 181–201.

7. For the fullest exposition of the masculine-feminine dynamism in the Kaballah, see *Phil.* 3.297–304.

8. *Phil.* $1^2$.510.

9. *Phil.* $1^2$.511.

10. *Phil.* 2.157. See also on the *zimzum, Phil.* 4.313–315.

11. *Phil.* 2.100–101; emphasis Molitor's.

12. Goldberg, *Ontology*; Goldberg-*Aufsätze*, 118: "aus dem *Inhalt* des aufgelösten Allgemeinbegriffs diejenigen Abläufe ergießen, die über das Gesetz der erfahrbaren Ablaufsfolge hinausgehen: die Gesamtheit der echten Möglichkeiten."

13. Ibid., 122.

14. Ibid.

15. *Phil.* 2.176; emphasis Molitor's.

16. *Phil.* 2.178–179; emphasis Molitor's.

17. *Phil.* 2.182.

18. *Phil.* 2.185.

19. *Phil.* 4.170.

20. *Phil.* 4.144.

21. *Phil.* 4.169.

22. *Phil.* $1^2$.236–237.

23. Molitor discusses the dissolution of the unity of the upper worlds in *Phil.* 3.305–311. The discussion centers on the Kabbalistic notion of the *kitzutz ba'netiot*, the "uprooting of the plants."

24. *Phil.* 3.339.

25. *Maimonides*, in Goldberg-*Aufsätze*, 194.

# Bibliography


Abrams, M. H. *Natural Supernaturalism: Tradition and Revolution in Romantic Literature.* New York: W. W. Norton, 1971.

Adler, H[ans]. G[ünther]. "Erinnerungen an den Philosophen Erich Unger." *Eckart* 3 (1960): 182–185. Reprinted in *Erich Unger: Politik und Metaphysik*, edited by Manfred Voigts, 65–69. Würzburg: Königshausen & Neumann, 1989.

———. *Theresienstadt, 1941–1945: Das Atlitz einer Zwangsgemeinschaft.* 2nd ed. Tübingen: J. C. B. Mohr, 1960.

———. *Vorschule für eine Experimentaltheologie.* Stuttgart: Franz Steiner, 1987.

Adler, Jeremy. "February 8, 1942: H. G. Adler Is Deported to Theresienstadt and Begins His Life Work of Writing a Scholarly Testimony to His Experience." In *Yale Companion to Jewish Writing and Thought in German Culture 1096–1996*, edited by Sander L. Gilman and Jack Zipes, 600–605. New Haven, CT: Yale University Press, 1997.

Agutter, Paul S., and Dennis N. Wheatley. *Thinking about Life: The History and Philosophy of Biology and Other Sciences.* Dordrecht: Springer, 2009.

Albertazzi, Lilliana. *Immanent Realism: An Introduction to Brentano.* Dordrecht: Springer, 2006.

Alter, Robert. "Translating from the Ancient: The Hebrew Bible." *The Literary Imagination* 5, no. 2 (Spring 2003): 172–178.

Antliff, Mark. *Inventing Bergson: Cultural Politics and Parisian Avant-Garde.* Princeton, NJ: Princeton University Press, 1993.

Ardoin, Paul, S. E. Gontarski, and Laci Mattison, eds. *Understanding Bergson, Understanding Modernism.* London: Bloomsbury, 2013.

Aster, Ernst von. "Die neue Kant-Ausgabe und ihr erster Band." In Vaihinger and Bauch, *Zu Kants Gedächtnis*, 321–341.

Badiou, Alain. *Briefings on Existence: A Short Treatise on Transitory Ontology.* Translated by Norman Madarasz. Albany: State University of New York Press, 2006.

———. *Logics of Worlds, Being and Event 2.* Translated by Alberto Toscano. London: Continuum, 2009.

———. *Number and Numbers.* Translated by Robin Mackay. Cambridge: Polity Press, 2008.

———. *Theoretical Writings.* Edited and translated by Ray Brassier and Alberto Toscano. London: Continuum, 2005.

Bastian, Adolf. *Der Mensch in der Geschichte: Zur Begründung einer psychologischen Weltanschauung.* 2 vols. Leipzig: Otto Wigand, 1860.

———. *Ethnische Elementargedanken in der Lehre von Menschen.* 2 vols. Berlin: Weidmannsche Buchhandlung, 1895.

———. *Zur ethnischen Ethik.* Berlin: Ferd. Dümmlers Verlagsbuchhandlung, 1889.

———. *Zur Lehre vom Menschen in ethnischer Anthropologie.* Berlin: D. Reimer, Hoefer & Vohnsen, 1895.

Bauer, Erwin. *Die Grundprinzipien der rein naturwissenschaftlichen Biologie und ihre Andwendungen in der Physiologie und Pathologie.* Vol. 26 of *Vorträge und Aufsätze über Entwicklungsmechanik der Organismen.* Berlin: Julius Springer, 1920.

Beiser, Frederick C. *Late German Idealism: Trendelenburg and Lotze.* Oxford: Oxford University Press, 2013.

Beloussov, Lev, John M. Opitz, and Scott F. Gilberg. "Life of Alexander G. Gurwitsch (1874–1954) and His Relevant Contribution to the Theory of Morphogenetic Fields." *International Journal of Developmental Biology* 41 (1997): 771–779.

Benjamin, Walter. "Announcement of the Journal *Angelus Novus.*" In *Selected Writings,* vol. 1, *1913–1926,* edited by Marcus Bullock and Michael W. Jennings, 292–296. Cambridge, MA: Harvard University Press, 2002. German in *Gesammelte Schriften Bde. I–VII,* II.1: 241–246.

———. *Gesammelte Schriften Bde. I–VII.* Edited by Rolf Tiedemann and Hermann Schweppenhäuser. Frankfurt am Main: Suhrkamp, 1972–1989.

———. "Kleine Geschichte der Photographie." In *Gesammelte Schriften Bde. I–VII,* II.1: 368–386.

———. "One-Way Street." In *Selected Writings,* vol. 1, *1913–1926,* edited by Marcus Bullock and Michael W. Jennings, 444–488. Cambridge, MA: Harvard University Press, 2002. German in *Gesammelte Schriften Bde. I–VII,* IV.1: 83–148.

Bennett, Jane. *Vital Matter: A Political Ecology of Things.* Durham, NC: Duke University Press, 2010.

Bergson, Henri. *Time and Free Will: An Essay on the Immediate Data of Consciousness.* Translated by F. L. Pogson. London: George Allen, 1910.

Bertalanffy, Ludwig von. *General Systems Theory: Foundations, Development, Applications.* New York: George Brazillier, 1968.

Biale, David. *Gershom Scholem: Kabbalah and Counter-History.* 2nd ed. Cambridge, MA: Harvard University Press, 1982.

———. "Gershom Scholem on Anarchism and Nihilism." *Rethinking History* 19, no. 1 (2015): 61–71.

Bivort, Benjamin de. "Cellular Level Gene Regulatory Networks: Their Derivation and Properties." In *Systems Biology for Signaling Networks,* edited by Sangdun Choi, 429–446. New York: Springer, 2010.

Björk, Mårtin. "The Irritability of Being: Martin Heidegger, Hans Driesch, and the Future of Theology." In *Heidegger's Black Notebooks and the Future of Theology,* edited by M. Björk and J. Svenungsson. New York: Palgrave Macmillan, 2018.

Blackmore, John T. *Ernst Mach: His Life, Work, and Influence.* Berkeley: University of California Press, 1972.

Blanco, María del Pilar, and Esther Peeren, eds. *The Spectralities Reader: Ghosts and Hauntings in Contemporary Cultural Theory.* London: Bloomsbury, 2013.

Bolzano, Bernard. *Parodoxien des Unendlichen.* Berlin: Mayer & Müller, 1889.

Botar, Oliver A. I. "Defining Biocentrism." In *Biocentrism and Modernism,* edited by Oliver A. I. Botar and Isabel Wünsche, 15–46. Surrey, UK: Ashgate, 2011.

Bower, M. Brady. *Unruly Spirits: The Science of Psychic Phenomena in Modern France.* Urbana: University of Illinois Press, 2010.

Brentano, Franz. *Aristoteles Lehre vom Ursprung des menschlichen Geistes.* Leipzig: Veit & Comp., 1911.

———. *Aristoteles und seine Weltanschauung.* Leipzig: Quelle & Meyer, 1911.

———. *Die Psychologie des Aristoteles, insbesondere seine Lehre vom Nous Poietikos.* Mainz: Franz Kirchheim, 1867.

Bryant, Levi, Nick Srnicek, and Graham Harman, eds. *The Speculative Turn: Continental Materialism and Realism.* Melbourne: re.press, 2011.

Buchheit, Klaus-Peter. "Die Verkettung der Dinge: Stil und Diagnose im Schreiben Adolf Bastian." Ph.D. diss., Ruprecht-Karls-Univesität Heidelberg, 2002.

Canguilhem, Georges. *Knowledge of Life.* Translated by Todd Meyers. New York: Fordham University Press, 2008. Originally published as *La connaissance de la vie.* Paris: Hachette, 1952.

Cantor, Georg. *Grundlagen einer allgemeiner Mannigfaltigkeitslehre: Ein mathematisch-philosophischer Versuch in der Lehre des Unendlichen.* Leipzig: B. G. Teubner, 1883. Also published as "Ueber unendliche, lineare Punktmannichfaltigkeiten," *Mathematische Annalen* 21 (1883): 545–591. English translation by George A. Bingley available at http://formandformalism.blogspot.com/2011/06/georg-cantors-1883-grundlagen-article.html.

———. "Über verschiedene Theoreme aus der Theorie der Punktmengen." *Acta Mathematica* 5 (1885): 105–125.

Caspary, Adolf. *Die Maschinenutopie: Das Übereinstimmungsmoment der bürgerlichen und sozialistischen Ökonomie.* Berlin: David, 1927.

———. "Theologie der Selbstgerechtigkeit Gottes." *Grenzbote.* Bratislava, 1936. Available at www.europeana.eu/portal/search?q=what%3A%22http%3A%2F%2Fdata.dm2e.eu%2Fdata%2Fconcept%2Fcjh%2Flbiarchive%2FTheology%22.

———. *Wirtschafts-Strategie und Kriegsführung, wirtschaftliche Vorbereitung, Führung und Auswirkung des Krieges in geschichtlichem Aufriss.* Berlin: E. S. Mittler, 1932.

Cassirer, Ernst. *Das mythische Denken.* Vol. 2 of *Philosophie der symbolischen Formen.* Berlin: Bruno Cassirer, 1925. English translation: *The Philosophy of Symbolic Forms,* vol. 2: *Mythical Thought.* Translated by Ralph Manheim. New Haven, CT: Yale University Press, 1955.

———. *Die Begriffsform in mythischen Denken.* Leipzig: B. G. Teubner, 1922.

———. *Leibniz' System in seinen wissenschaftlichen Grundlagen.* Marburg: N. G. Elwert'sche Verlagsbuchhandlung, 1902.

———. *Sprache und Mythos: Ein Beitrag zum Problem der Götternamen.* Leipzig: B. G. Teubner, 1925. English translation: *Language and Myth.* Translated by Susanne Langer. New York: Harper and Bros., 1945.

———. *Substanzbegriff und Funktionsbegriff: Untersuchungen über die Grudfragen der Erkenntniskritik.* Berlin: Bruno Cassirer, 1910. English translation: *Form and Function & Einstein's Theory of Relativity.* Translated by William Curtis Sawbey and Marie Collins Sawbey. Chicago: Open Court, 1923.

Cheah, Pheng. *Spectral Nationality: Passages of Freedom from Kant to Postcolonial Literatures of Liberation.* New York: Columbia University Press, 2003.

Chéroux, Clément, Andreas Fischer, Pierre Apraxine, Denis Canguilhem, and Sophie Schmit. *The Perfect Medium: Photography and the Occult.* New Haven, CT: Yale University Press, 2005.

Chrudzimski, Arkadiusz, and Barry Smith. "Brentano's Ontology: From Conceptualism to Reism." In Jacquette, *The Cambridge Companion to Brentano,* 197–219.

Cohen, Hermann. *Ethik des reinen Willens*. Berlin: Bruno Cassirer, 1904.

———. *Religion der Vernunft aus den Quellen der Judentum: Eine jüdische Religions-philosophie*. Wiesbaden: marixverlag, 2008.

Coleridge, Samuel Taylor. *Biographia Literaria; or Biographical Sketches of My Literary Life and Opinions*. London: George Bell and Sons, 1889.

Creet, Julia, Sara R. Horowitz, and Amira Bojadzija-Dant, eds. *H. G. Adler: Life, Literature, Legacy*. Evanston, IL: Northwestern University Press, 2016.

Crowe, Catherine. *The Night Side of Nature, or Ghosts and Ghost-Seers*. London: T. C. Newby, 1848.

Dacqué, Edgar. *Urwelt, Sage, und Menschheit: Eine naturhistorisch-metaphysische Studie*. Munich: R. Oldenbourg, 1924.

Dauben, Joseph Warren. *Georg Cantor: His Mathematics and Philosophy of the Infinite*. Princeton, NJ: Princeton University Press, 1979.

Dedekind, Richard. *Stetigkeit und Irrationale Zahlen*. 2nd ed. Braunschweig: F. Vieweg und Sohn, 1892.

Diner, Dan. "'Grundbuch des Planeten': Zur Geopolitik Karl Haushofers." *Vierteljahrs-hefte für Zeitgeschichte* 1, no. 32 (1984): 1–28.

Dornseiff, Franz. *Das Alphabet in Mystik und Magie*. Leipzig: B. G. Teubner, 1922.

Drack, Manfred, Wilifried Apfalter, and David Pouveau. "On the Making of a System Theory of Life: Paul A. Weiss and Ludwig von Bertalanffy's Conceptual Connection." *Quarterly Review of Biology* 82, no. 4 (2007): 349–373.

Driesch, Hans. *Analytische Theorie der organischen Entwicklung*. Leipzig: Wilhelm Engelmann, 1894.

———. *Die Biologie als selbstständige Grundwissenschaft*. Leipzig: Wilhelm Engelmann, 1893.

———. *Die Logik als Aufgabe: Eine Studie über die Beziehung zwischen Phänomenologie und Logik. Zugleich eine Einleitung in die Ordnugslehre*. Tübingen: Mohr, 1913.

———. *Die "Seele" als elementarer Naturfaktor: Studien über die Bewegungen der Oganismen*. Leipzig: Wilhelm Engelmann, 1903.

———. "Entwicklungsmechanische Studien: I. Der Werthe der beiden ersten Furchungszellen in der Echinodermenentwicklung. Experimentelle Erzeugung von Theil- und Doppelbildungen. II. Über die Beziehungen des Lichtes zur ersten Etappe der thierischen Form-bildung." *Zeitschrift für wissenschaftliche Zoologie* 53 (1891): 160–184. English translation: "The Potency of the First Two Cleavage Cells in Echinoderm Development. Experimental Production of Partial and Double Formations." In *Foundations of Experimental Embryology*, edited by Benjamin H. Willier and Jane M. Oppenheimer, 38–50. New York: Hafner, 1964.

———. *The Science and Philosophy of the Organism*. 2 vols. London: Adam and Charles Black, 1908–1909.

———. *Wirklichkeitslehre: Ein metaphysischer Versuch*, 2nd ed. Leipzig: Emmanuel Reinike, 1922; 1st ed. 1917.

Ehrenfels, Christian von. *Kosmogonie*. Jena: Eugen Diederichs, 1916.

Ehrman, Esther. "Erich Unger's 'Der Universalismus des Hebraertums.'" *Journal of Jewish Thought and Philosophy* 4, no. 2 (1995): 271–314.

———. "Erich Unger's 'The Natural Order of Miracles': I. The Pentateuch and the Vitalist Myth." *Journal of Jewish Thought and Philosophy* 11, no. 2 (2002): 135–152.

———. "Erich Unger's 'The Natural Order of Miracles': II. The World of Nature and Miracles in the Pentateuch." *Journal of Jewish Thought and Philosophy* 11, no. 2 (2002): 153–189.

Einstein, Albert. "Die Relativitätstheorie." In *Die Kultur der Gegenwart: Ihre Entwicklung und ihre Ziele*, 3rd Abt., vol. 1. edited by Paul Hinneberg, 703–713. Leipzig: B. G. Teubner, 1915.

Eisler, Robert. *Weltenmantel und Himmelszelt: Religionsgeschichtliche Untersuchungen zur Urgeschichte des antiken Weltbildes.* 2 vols. Munich: C. B. Beck, 1910.

Fechner, Gustav Theodor (Dr. Mises). *Vier Paradoxa.* Leipzig: Leopold Voß, 1846.

———. *Zend-Avesta oder über die Dinge des Himmels und des Jenseits.* 3 vols. Leipzig: Leopold Voß, 1854.

Fenves, Peter. *The Messianic Reduction: Walter Benjamin and the Shape of Time.* Stanford, CA: Stanford University Press, 2011.

Ferreirós, José. *Labyrinth of Thought: A History of Set Theory and Its Role in Modern Mathematics.* Basel: Birkhäuser, 2007.

Fetz, Reto Luzius. "Forma formata—Forma formans: Zur historischen Stellung und systematischen Bedeutung von Cassirer's Metaphysik des Symbolischen." In *Lebendige Form: Zur Metaphysik des Symbolischen in Ernst Cassirers "Nachgelassen Manuskripten und Texten,"* edited by Reto Luzius Fetz, 15–34. Hamburg: Felix Meiner, 2008.

Fischer, Andreas. "'The Reciprocal Adaptation of Optics and Phenomena': The Photographic Recording of Materializations." In Chéroux et al., *The Perfect Medium,* 171–215.

Fischer, Manuela, Peter Bolz, and Susan Kamel, eds. *Adolf Bastian and His Universal Archive of Humanity.* Hildesheim: Georg Olms, 2007.

Flatscher, Markus, and Richard Hörmann, eds. *Ferdinand Ebner: Tagebuch 1918.* Vienna: LIT, 2014.

Fournier, Marcel. *Marcel Mauss: A Biography.* Translated by Jane Marie Todd. Princeton, NJ: Princeton University Press, 2006.

Frege, Gottlob. *Die Grundlagen der Arithmetik: Eine logisch mathematische Untersuchung über den Begriff der Zahl.* Breslau: Wilhelm Koebner, 1884.

Freud, Sigmund. *The Ego and the Id.* Translated by Joan Riviere. New York: Norton, 1960.

Freyhofer, Horst. *The Vitalism of Hans Driesch: The Success and Decline of a Scientific Theory.* Frankfurt am Main: Peter Lang, 1982.

Friedlander, Judith. "Religious Metaphysics and the Nation-State: The Case of Oskar Goldberg." *Social Research* 59, no. 1 (1992): 151–168.

Giovanelli, Marco. "Hermann Cohen's *Das Prinzip der Infinitesmal-Methode*: The History of an Unsuccessful Book." Available at http://philsciarchive.pitt.edu/id /eprint/11818.

Goldberg, Oskar. "The Development of Biology." *Science and Culture* (February 1944): 2–6.

———. *Die Fünf Bücher Mosis: Ein Zahlengebäude. Die Feststellung einer einheitlich durchgeführten Zahlenschrift.* Berlin: [Verlag David,] 1908. Reprinted in Goldberg, *Zahlengebäude, Ontologie, Maimonides, und Aufsätze,* 21–68.

———. "Die griechische Tragoedie." *Mass und Wert: Zweimonatschrift fuer Freie Deutsche Kultur* 1, no. 5 (1938): 728–752. Reprinted in Goldberg, *Zahlengebäude, Ontologie, Maimonides, und Aufsätze,* 227–248.

———. *Die Wirklichkeit der Hebräer.* Wissenschaftliche Neuausgabe. Edited by Manfred Voigts. Wiesbaden: Harrassowitz, 2005.

———. "Eine Geheimschrift in den fünf Büchern Moses: Das Zahlengebäude des Pentateuch." Reprinted in Goldberg, *Zahlengebäude, Ontologie, Maimonides, und Aufsätze,* 355–387.

———. *Maimonides: Kritik der jüdischen Glaubenslehre.* Vienna: Heinrich Glanz, 1935. Reprinted in Goldberg, *Zahlengebäude, Ontologie, Maimonides, und Aufsätze,* 123–217.

———. "Rasse und Ethik." Unpublished manuscript in the Deutsches Literaturarchiv Marbach Goldberg Nachlass.

———. *Zahlengebäude, Ontologie, Maimonides, und Aufsätze 1933 bis 1947.* Berlin: Königshausen & Neumann, 2013.

Goldstein, Kurt. *Der Aufbau des Organismus: Einführung in die Biologie unter besondere Berücksichtigung der Erfahrungen am kranken Menschen.* The Hague: Martinus Nijhoff, 1934.

———. *The Organism: A Holistic Approach to Biology Derived from Pathological Data in Man.* New York: Zone Books, 1996.

———. "The Smile of the Infant and the Problem of Understanding the 'Other.'" In Kurt Goldstein, *Selected Papers/Ausgewählte Schriften,* edited by Aron Gurwitsch, Else M. Goldstein Haudek, and William E. Haudek. The Hague: Martinus Nijhoff, 1971.

Gordon, Peter Eli. *Continental Divide: Heidegger, Cassirer, Davos.* Cambridge, MA: Harvard University Press, 2010.

Görs, Britta, Nikos Psarros, and Paul Ziche, eds. *Wilhelm Ostwald at the Crossroads between Chemistry, Philosophy, and Media Culture.* Leipzig: Leipziger Universitätsverlag, 2005.

Gould, Stephen Jay. *Ontogeny and Phylogeny.* Cambridge, MA: Harvard University Press, 1977. Available at www.sjgarchive.org/library/ontogeny.html.

Grey, Jeremy. *Worlds out of Nothing: A Course in the History of Geometry in the 19th Century.* London: Springer, 2007.

Gunning, Tom. "To Scan a Ghost: The Ontology of Mediated Vision." In *The Spectralities Reader: Ghosts and Hauntings in Contemporary Cultural Theory,* edited by María del Pilar Blanco and Esther Peerenn, 207–244. London: Bloomsbury, 2013.

Gurwitsch, Alexander. "On Practical Vitalism." *American Naturalist* 49, no. 588 (1915): 763–770.

———. *Versuch einer synthetischer Biologie.* Abhandlungen zur theoretischen Biologie 17. Berlin: Gebrüder Borntraeger, 1923.

Hallett, Michael. *Cantorian Set Theory and Limitation of Size.* Oxford: Clarendon, 1984.

Harpham, Geoffrey Galt. "Elaine Scarry and the Dream of Pain." *Salmagundi* 130/131 (Spring–Summer 2001): 202–234.

Harrington, Anne. "Kurt Goldstein's Neurology of Healing and Wholeness: A Weimar Story." In *Greater than the Parts: Holism in Biomedicine 1920–1950,* edited by Christopher Lawrence and George Weisz, 25–45. Oxford: Oxford University Press, 1998.

———. *Reenchanted Science: Holism in Science from Wilhelm II to Hitler*. Princeton, NJ: Princeton University Press, 1996.

Harris, Jay M. *Nachman Krochmal: Guiding the Perplexed of the Modern Age*. New York: New York University Press, 1993.

Harvey, Julien. "Is Biblical Man Still Alive?" *Biblical Theology Bulletin: A Journal of Bible and Theology* 3 (1973): 167–193.

Haushofer, Karl. *Geopolitik des Pazifischen Ozeans*. Berlin: K. Vowinckel, 1924.

Hedman, Bruce H. "Cantor's Concept of Infinity: Implications of Infinity for Contingence." *Perspectives on Science and Christian Faith* 45, no. 1 (1993): 8–16.

Hegel, Georg Wilhelm Friedrich. *Wissenschaft der Logik*. 2 vols. Frankfurt am Main: Suhrkamp, 1969.

Heidegger, Martin. *Contributions to Philosophy (of the Event)*. Translated by Richard Rojcewicz and Daniela Vallega-Neu. Bloomington: Indiana University Press, 2012.

———. *Ponderings II–VI: Black Notebooks 1931–1938*. Translated by Richard Rojcewicz. Bloomington: Indiana University Press, 2016.

Heidelberger, Michael. *Nature from Within: Gustav Theodor Fechner and His Psychophysical Worldview*. Pittsburgh: University of Pittsburgh Press, 2004.

Heman, F. "Immanuel Kants philosophisches Vermächtnis." In Vaihinger and Bauch, *Zu Kants Gedächtnis*, 155–195.

Henderson, Linda Dalrymple. *The Fourth Dimension and Non-Euclidean Geometry in Modern Art*. Princeton, NJ: Princeton University Press, 1983.

Herdenberg, Georg Philipp Friedrich Freiherr von. *Novalis' Werke in Vier Teilen*. Part 4. Edited by Hermann Friedemann. Berlin: Bong & Co., 1908.

Hilbert, David. "On the Infinite." In *Philosophy of Mathematics: Selected Readings*, edited by Paul Benaceraf and Hilary Putnam, 183–201. 2nd ed. Cambridge: Cambridge University Press, 1983.

Hitler, Adolf. *Mein Kampf*. Munich: Zentralverlag der N.S.D.A.P., 1936.

Horkheimer, Max, and Theodore Adorno. *Dialectic of Enlightenment: Philosophical Fragments*. Translated by Edmund Jephcott. Stanford, CA: Stanford University Press, 2002.

Hühlhörster, Christian. *Ein "jüdische Diener der faschistischen Epoche"? Oskar Goldberg und Thomas Mann*. Paris: Didier, 2004.

———. *Thomas Mann und Oskar Goldberg's "Wirklichkeit der Hebräer."* Frankfurt am Main: Vittorio Klostermann, 1999.

Humbolt, Alexander von. *Kosmos, Entwurf einer physischen Weltbeschreibung*. 5 vols. Stuttgart: Cott'sche, 1845–1858.

Husserl, Edmund. *Ideas: General Introduction to a Pure Phenomenology*. Translated by W. R. Boyce Gibson. London: Routledge, 2012.

Iber, Christian. "Hegels Konzeption des Begriffs." In *G. W. F. Hegel Wissenschaft der Logik*, edited by Anton Friedrich Koch and Fridrike Schick, 181–201. Berlin: Akademie, 2002.

Ifrah, Georges. *The Universal History of Numbers: From Prehistory to the Invention of the Computer*. Translated by David Bellos, E. F. Harding, Sophie Wood, and Ian Monk. New York: John Wiley & Sons, 2000.

Jacobs, Nicholas, and Diethart Kerbs. "Wilhelm Simon Guttmann, 1891–1990: A Documentary Portrait." *German Life and Letters* 62, no. 4 (October 2009): 401–414.

Jacquette, Dale, ed. *The Cambridge Companion to Brentano*. Cambridge: Cambridge University Press, 2004.

Jones, Donna V. *The Racial Discourses of Life Philosophy: Négritude, Vitalism, and Modernity*. New York: Columbia University Press, 2010.

Jünger, Ernst, Carl Schmitt, and Helmuth Kiesel. *Briefe 1930–1983*. Stuttgart: Klett-Cotta, 1999.

Kant, Immanuel. *Allgemeine Naturgeschichte und Theorie des Himmels, oder Versuch von der Verfassung und dem mechanischen Ursprunge des ganzen Weltgebäudes, nach Newtonischen Grundsätzen abgehandelt.* Königsberg: Johann Friederich Petersen, 1755. Republished in *Immanuel Kants Gesammelten Werke [Akademie-Ausgabe]*. 23 vols. Berlin: Walter de Gruyter, 1900–2006, 1:217–368.

———. *Gedanken von der wahren Schätzung der lebendigen Kräfte und Beurteilung der Beweise derer sich Herr von Leibniz und andere Mechaniker in dieser Streitsache bedienet haben, nebst einigen vorhergehenden Betrachtungen welche die Kraft der Körper überhaupt betreffen.* Königsberg: Martin Eberhard Dorn, 1746. Republished in *Akademie-Ausgabe* 1:3–181.

———. "Thoughts on the True Estimation of Living Forces" (1746–1749). Translated by Jeffrey B. Edwards and Martin Schönfeld. In *Immanuel Kant: Natural Science*, edited by Eric Watkins, translated by Lewis White Beck, Jeffrey B. Edwards, Olaf Reinhardt, Martin Schönfeld, and Eric Watkins, 1–155. Cambridge: Cambridge University Press, 2012.

———. "Universal Natural History and Theory of the Heavens or Essay on the Constitution and the Mechanical Origin of the Whole Universe According to Newtonian Principles" (1755). Translated by Olaf Reinhardt. In *Immanuel Kant: Natural Science*, edited by Eric Watkins, translated by Lewis White Beck, Jeffrey B. Edwards, Olaf Reinhardt, Martin Schönfeld, and Eric Watkins, 182–308. Cambridge: Cambridge University Press, 2012.

Kapp, Ernst. *Grundlinien einer Philosophie der Technik*. Braunschweig: George Westermann, 1877.

Kitano, Hiroaki. "Scientific Challenges in Systems Biology." In *Systems Biology for Signaling Networks*, edited by Sangdun Choi, 3–13. New York: Springer, 2010.

Kjellén, Rudolf. *Inledning till Sveriges geografi*. Göteborg: Wettergren & Kerber, 1900.

Knohl, Israel. "Sacred Architecture: The Numerical Dimensions of Biblical Poems." *Vetus Testamentum* 62 (2012): 189–197.

Koch, Katharina. *Franz Joseph Molitor und die jüdische Tradition*. Berlin: Walter de Gruyter, 2006.

Kontje, Todd Curtis. *Thomas Mann's World: Empire, Race, and the Jewish Question*. Ann Arbor: University of Michigan Press, 2011.

Köpping, Klaus-Peter. *Adolf Bastian and the Psychic Unity of Mankind*. St. Lucia: University of Queensland Press, 1983.

Krochmal, Nachman. *More Nebukhei ha'Zman*. Lemberg: Joseph Schnayder, 1851. [Hebrew, available at http://books.google.com/books?id=GtUFcSlkpKUC&pg=RA4-PT35&dq=inauthor:nachman+inauthor:krochmal#v=onepage&q&f=false].

German translation: *Führer der Verwirrten der Zeit*. Translated by Andreas Lehhardt. 2 vols. Hamburg: Felix Meiner, 2012.

Laugwitz, Detlef. *Bernhard Riemann 1826–1866: Turning Points in the Conceptions of Mathematics*. Translated by Abe Shenitzer. Boston: Birkhäuser, 1999.

Levin, Michael. "Morphogenetic Fields in Embryogenesis, Regeneration, and Cancer: Non-local Control of Complex Patterning." *Biosystems* 109, no. 3 (2012): 243–261.

Lindenfeld, David. *The Transformation of Positivism: Alexius Meinong and European Thought, 1880–1920*. Berkeley: University of California Press, 1980.

Mann, Thomas. *Doctor Faustus*. Translated by H. T. Lowe-Porter. New York: Random House, 1991.

———. *Joseph and His Brothers*. Translated by John E. Woods. New York: Alfred A. Knopf, 2005.

Martens, Bram. *Dark Images, Secret Hints: Benjamin, Scholem, Molitor and the Jewish Tradition*. Bern: Peter Lang, 2007.

Martens, Gunter. *Vitalismus und Expressionismus: Ein Beitrag zur Genese und Deutung expressionistischer Stilstrukturen und Motive*. Stuttgart: W. Kohlhammer, 1971.

Mendoza, Luis, Denis Thieffry, and Elena R. Alvarez-Buylla. "Genetic Control of Flower Morphogenesis in *Arabidopsis Thalliana*: A Logical Analysis." *Bioinformatics* 15, nos. 7/8 (1999): 593–606.

Merleau-Ponty, Maurice. *Nature: Course Notes from the Collège de France 1956–1960*. Translated by Robert Vallier. Evanston, IL: Northwestern University Press, 2003.

Milgrom, Jacob. *Leviticus: A Book of Ritual and Ethics*. Minneapolis: Fortress Press, 2004.

Möckel, Christian. *Das Urphänomen des Lebens: Ernst Cassirer's Lebensbegriff*. Hamburg: Felix Meiner, 2005.

Molitor, Franz Josef. *Philosophie der Geschichte, oder Über die Tradition*, part 1. Frankfurt am Main: Hermannschen Buchhandlung, 1827; part 1, 2nd ed. Münster: Teissing'sche Buchhandlund, 1857; part 2, Münster: Theissing'sche Buchhandlung, 1834; part 3, Münster: Theissing'sche Buchhandlung, 1839; part 4, vol. 1, Münster: Theissing'sche Buchhandlung, 1853.

Nicolai, Georg Friedrich. *Die Biologie des Krieges*. 2 vols. Zürich: Orell Füssli, 1919.

Oken, Lorenz. *Grundriß der Naturphilosophie, der Theorie der Sinne und der darauf gegründeten Classification der Tiere*. Frankfurt: Eichenberg, 1802.

———. *Lehrbuch der Naturphilosophie*, 3rd ed. Zürich: Friedrich Schulteß, 1843. English translation: *Elements of Physiophilosophy*. Translated by Alfred Tulk. London: Ray Society, 1847.

Ostwald, Wilhelm. *Grundriss der Naturphilosophie*. Leipzig: Philipp Reclam, 1908.

Overton, Jane. *Biographical Memoir for Paul Alfred Weiss 1898–1989*. Washington, DC: National Academies Press, 1997. Available at www.nasonline.org/publications /biographical-memoirs/memoir-pdfs/weiss-paul.pdf.

Penny, H. Glenn. "Bastian's Museum: On the Limits of Empiricism and the Transformation of German Ethnology." In *Worldly Provincialism: German Anthropology in the Age of Empire*, edited by H. Glenn Penny and Matti Bunzl, 86–126. Ann Arbor: University of Michigan Press, 2003.

Przibram, Hans. *Form und Formel in Tierreiche: Beiträge zu einer quantitativen Biologie I-XX*. Leipzig: Deuticke, 1922.

———. "Kristall-Analogien zur Entwicklungsmechanik der Organismen." *Archiv für Entwicklungsmechanik der Organismen* 26, nos. 1–2 (1906): 207–287.

Reinke, Johannes. *Einleitung in die theoretische Biologie*. Berlin: Gebrüder Paetel, 1901.

Richards, Robert J. *The Romantic Conception of Life: Science and Philosophy in the Age of Goethe*. Chicago: University of Chicago Press, 2002.

Rickert, Heinrich. *Die Philosophie des Lebens: Darstellung und Kritik der philosophischen Modeströmungen unserer Zeit*. Tübingen: J. C. B. Mohr, 1920.

Riehl, Alois. *Der philosophische Kritizismus: Geschichte und System*, 2nd ed. 2 vols. Leipzig: Wilhelm Engelmann, 1908.

Riemann, Bernhard. *Gesammelte mathematische Werke und wissenschaftlicher Nachlass*. Leipzig: B. G. Teubner, 1876.

Roelcke, Volker. "Jewish Mysticism in Romantic Medicine? Indirect Incorporation of Kabbalistic Elements in the Work of Gotthilf Heinrich Schubert." *History and Philosophy of the Life Sciences* 16 (1994): 117–140.

Rosen, Robert. *Anticipatory Systems: Philosophical, Mathematical, and Methodological Foundations*. New York: Springer, 2012.

Rosenstock, Bruce. "Abraham Miguel Cardoso's Messianic Theology: A Reappraisal." *Association of Jewish Studies Review* 23, no. 1 (1998): 63–104.

Rosenstock, Gershon George. *F. A. Trendelenburg: Forerunner to John Dewey*. Carbondale, IL: Southern Illinois University Press, 1964.

Rosslenbroich, Bernd. "Outline of a Concept for Organismic Systems Biology." *Seminars in Cancer Biology* 21, no. 3 (2011): 156–164.

Roux, Wilhelm. "Zur Orientierung über einige Probleme der embryonalen Entwicklung." *Zeitschrift für Biologie* 21 (1885).

Sasson, Jack M. "A Genealogical 'Convention' in Biblical Chronology?" *Zeitschrift für alttestamentische Wissenschaft* 90 (1978): 171–185.

Scarry, Elaine. *The Body in Pain: The Making and Unmaking of the World*. New York: Oxford University Press, 1985.

Schäfer, Peter. *Judeophobia: Attitudes towards the Jews in the Ancient World*. Cambridge, MA: Harvard University Press, 1998.

Schelling, Friedrich Wilhelm Joseph von. *Die Weltalter*. In *Friedrich Wilhelm Joseph von Schellings Sämtliche Werke*, Division 1, vol. 8. Stuttgart: J. G. Cotta'scher, 1861, 195–344.

———. *First Outline of a System of the Philosophy of Nature*. Translated by Keith R. Peterson. Albany: State University of New York Press, 2004.

———. *Historical-critical Introduction to the Philosophy of Mythology*. Translated by Mason Richey and Markus Zisselsberger. Albany: State University of New York Press, 2007.

———. *Philosophie der Kunst*. In *Friedrich Wilhelm Joseph von Schellings Sämtliche Werke*, Division 1, vol. 5. Stuttgart: J. G. Cotta'scher, 1859.

Schmidt, Ferdinand Jakob. *Grundzüge der konstitutiven Erfahrungsphilosophie als Theorie der immanenten Erfahrungsmonismus*. Berlin: B. Behr, 1901.

Schneider, Karl Camillo. "*Die Wirklichkeit der Hebräer* von Oskar Goldberg." *Zeitschrift für Parapsychologie* 2 (1928): 113–117.

———. *Euvitalistische Biologie: Zur Grundlegung der Kultur*. Munich: J. F. Bergmann, 1926.

Scholem, Gershom. *Briefe: Band I, 1914–1947*. Edited by Gershom Scholem and Theodor Adorno. Munich: C. H. Beck, 1994.

———. *Briefe: Band III, 1971–1982*. Edited by Itta Schedletzky. Munich: C. H. Beck, 1999.

———. "The Crisis of Tradition in Jewish Messianism." In Scholem, *The Messianic Idea*, 49–77.

———. "Franz Josef Molitor." In *Encyclopaedia Judaica*, vol. 14, 2nd ed., edited by Michael Berenbaum and Fred Skolnik, 426. Detroit: Macmillan Reference USA, 2007.

———. *From Berlin to Jerusalem: Memories of My Youth*. Translated by Harry Zohn. New York: Schocken Books, 1980.

———. *Major Trends in Jewish Mysticism*. New York: Schocken Books, 1947.

———. *The Messianic Idea in Judaism and Other Essays on Jewish Spirituality*. New York: Schocken Books, 1971.

———. *On Jews and Judaism in Crisis: Selected Essays*. New York: Shocken Books, 1976.

———. *On the Possibility of Jewish Mysticism*. Translated by Jonathan Chipman. Philadelphia: Jewish Publication Society, 1997.

———. *Origins of the Kabbalah*. Translated by Allan Arkush. New York: Jewish Publication Society, 1987.

———. "Redemption through Sin." In Scholem, *The Messianic Idea in Judaism*, 78–141.

———. "Toward an Understanding of the Messianic Idea in Judaism." In Scholem, *The Messianic Idea in Judaism*, 1–36.

———. "Über Die Theologie des Sabbatianismus im Lichte Abraham Cardosos." Originally published in *Der Jude* (1928): 123–139. Reprinted in Scholem, *Judaica*, 6 vols. Frankfurt am Main: Suhrkamp, 1968, 1:119–146. Available at http://samm lungen.ub.uni-frankfurt.de/cm/periodical/titleinfo/3110818.

———. "Walter Benjamin." In Scholem, *On Jews and Judaism*, 172–197.

———. *Walter Benjamin: The Story of a Friendship*. Translated by Henry Zohn. New York: Schocken Books, 1981.

———. "Walter Benjamin and His Angel." In Scholem, *On Jews and Judaism*, 198–236.

Scholem, Gershom, and Theodor W. Adorno, eds. *The Correspondence of Walter Benjamin*. Translated by Manfred R. Jacobson and Evelyn Jacobson. Chicago: University of Chicago Press, 1994.

Scholz, Erhard. "Weyls Infinitesmalgeometrie (1917–1925)." In *Hermann Weyl's Raum-Zeit-Materie and a General Introduction to His Scientific Work*, edited by Erhard Scholz, 48–104. Basel: Birkhäuser, 2001.

Schubert, Gotthilf Heinrich. *Ansichten von der Nachtseite der Naturwissenschaft*. Dresden: Arnoldische Buchhandlung, 1808.

Schulte, Christoph. "'Die Buchstaben haben ihre Wurzel oben': Scholem und Molitor." In *Kabbala und Romantik: Die jüdische Mystik in der romantischen Geistesgeschichte*, edited by Eveline Goodman Thau, Gert Mattenklott, and Christoph Schulte, 143–164. Tübingen: Niemeyer, 1994.

Schüring, Heinz-J. "Der Mythos als Seinsgrund der Erkenntnis (in memoriam Erich Unger, gestorben am 25. November 1950 in London)." *Zeitschrift für philosophische Forschung* 19, no. 3 (1965): 493–510.

Sheppard, Richard, ed. *Die Schriften des Neuen Clubs, 1908–1914*. 2 vols. Hildesheim: Gerstenberg, 1980.

Simmel, Georg. *Lebensanschauung: Vier metaphysische Kapitel,* 2nd ed. Munich: Duncker & Humblot, 1922.

Smith, Barry. *Austrian Philosophy: The Legacy of Franz Brentano.* Chicago: Open Court, 1994.

———. "Gestalt Theory: An Essay in Philosophy." In *Foundations of Gestalt Theory,* edited by Barry Smith, 11–81. Munich: Philosophia, 1988.

Smith, Barry, and Kevin Mulligan. "Pieces of a Theory." In *Parts and Moments: Studies in Logic and Formal Ontology,* edited by Barry Smith, 13–109. Munich: Philosophia, 1981.

Smith, William Robertson. *Lectures on the Religions of the Semites: First Series, the Fundamental Institutions.* New York: D. Appleton and Company, 1889.

Sommer, Benjamin D. *The Bodies of God and the World of Ancient Israel.* Cambridge: Cambridge University Press, 2009.

Spemann, Hans. "The Organizer-Effect in Embryonic Development." Nobel Lecture, December 12, 1935. Nobelprize.org, available at www.nobelprize.org/nobel_prizes /medicine/laureates/1935/spemann-lecture.html.

Stiegler, Bernard. *What Makes Life Worth Living.* Translated by Daniel Ross. Cambridge: Polity Press, 2013.

Stuckrad, Kocku von. *The Scientification of Religion: An Historical Study of Discursive Change, 1800–2000.* Boston: Walter de Gruyter, 2014.

Susman, Margarete. *Ich habe viele Leben gelebt: Erinnerungen.* Stuttgart: Deutsche Verlags-Anstalt, 1964.

Szymonowicz, Ladislaus. *Lehrbuch der Histologie und der microskopischen Anatomie.* Würzburg: A. Stuber, 1901.

Tapp, Christian. *Kardinalität und Kardinäle: Wissenschaftshistorische Aufarbeitung zwischen Georg Cantor und katholischen Theologen seiner Zeit.* Stuttgart: Franz Steiner, 2005.

Taubes, Jacob. "From Cult to Culture." In Jacob Taubes, *From Cult to Culture: Fragments towards a Critique of Historical Reason,* edited by Charlotte Fonrobert and Amir Engel, 235–247. Stanford, CA: Stanford University Press, 2010.

Thiele, Rüdiger. "Gregor Cantor (1845–1918)." In *Mathematics and the Divine: A Historical Survey,* edited by Teun Keutsier and Luc Bergmans, 523–548. Amsterdam: Elsevier, 2005.

Uexküll, Jakob von. *Theoretische Biologie.* Berlin: Gebrüder Paetel, 1920.

———. *Umwelt und Innenwelt der Tiere.* Berlin: Julius Springer, 1909.

Unger, Erich. *Das Lebendige und das Goettliche.* Jerusalem: Hatehiya, 1966. Available at www.torah-study-for-women.org/unger/index.htm.

———. "Das Psychophysiologische Probem und sein Arbeitsgebiet: Eine methologische Einleitung." Inaugural-Dissertation der Erlangung der Doktorwürde der philosophischen Fakultät der Friedrich-Alexanders Universität Erlangen, 1922.

———. "Der Universalismus des Hebräertums: Philosophie und Kabbalah, dargestellt aus dem Gesichtspunkt der Goldbergschen Schrift 'Die Wirklichkeit der Hebräer.' Eine Entgegnung auf G. Scholems 'Die Theologie des Sabbatianismus im Lichte Abraham Cardosos.'" In Unger, *Vom Expressionismus zum Mythos,* 97–143.

———. *Die staatlose Bildung eines jüdischen Volkes: Vorrede zu einer gesetzgebender Akademie.* Berlin: David, 1922.

———. *Gegen die Dichtung: Eine Begründung des Konstruktionsprinzips in der Erkenntnis*. Leipzig: F. Meiner, 1925.

———. *The Imagination of Reason: Two Philosophical Essays*. London: Routledge & Kegan Paul, 1952.

———. "Nachts." *Der Sturm* 2, no. 57 (1911): 452. Republished in Unger, *Von Expressionismus zum Mythos*, 26–27.

———. *Politik und Metaphysik*. Berlin: David, 1921. Republished in *Erich Unger: Politik und Metaphysik*, edited by Manfred Voigts. Würzburg: Königshausen & Neumann, 1989.

———. *Vom Expressionismus zum Mythos des Hebräertum: Schriften 1909 bis 1931*. Edited by Manfred Voigts. Würzburg: Königshausen & Neumann, 1992.

Vaihinger, H., and B. Bauch, eds. *Zu Kants Gedächtnis: Zwölf Festgaben zu seinem 100jährigen Todestage*. Berlin: von Reuter und Richard, 1904.

Voigts, Manfred. "Eine nicht ausgetragene Kontroverse: Die Beziehung Gershom Scholem zu Oskar Goldberg und Erich Unger." *Ashkenas* 25, no. 2 (2015): 313–364. Reprinted in Voigts, *Jüdische Geistesarbeit*, 329–379.

———. "H. G. Adler und Erich Unger: Versuch eines Zugangs zur 'Vorschule für eine Experimentaltheologie.'" In Voigts, *Jüdische Geistesarbeit*, 381–402.

———, ed. *Jacob Taubes und Oskar Goldberg: Aufsätze, Briefe, Dokumente*. Würzburg: Königshausen & Naumann, 2011.

———. "Jacob Taubes und Oskar Goldberg: Eine problematische Beziehung, dargestellt ahnend der erhaltenen Briefen." In *Abendländische Eschatologie: Ad Jacob Taubes*, edited by Richard Faber, Eveline Goodman-Thau, and Thomas Macho, 447–464. Würzburg: Königshausen & Neumann, 2001.

———. *Jüdische Geistesarbeit und andere Aufsätze über Jakob Frank bis H. G. Adler*. Würzburg: Königshausen & Neumann, 2016.

———. "Jüdisches Denken im Frühexpressionismus: Oskar Goldberg und Erich Unger im Zeichen Friedrich Nietzsches." In *Jüdischer Nietzscheanismus*, edited by Werner Stegmeier and Daniel Krochmalnik, 168–186. New York: de Gruyter, 1997.

———. *Oskar Goldberg: Ein Dossier*. Munich: Carl Hanser, 1989.

———. *Oskar Goldberg, der mythische Experimentalwissenschaftler: Ein verdrängtes Kaptiel jüdischer Geschichte*. Berlin: Agora, 1992.

———. "Oskar Goldberg und Thomas Mann: Die Revision eines Fehlurteils." In *Conditio Judaica: Judentum, Antisemitismus und deutschsprachige Literatur*, edited by Hans Otto Horch and Horst Denckler. Tübingen: Max Niemeyer, 1993.

Weidner, Daniel. *Gershom Scholem: Politisches, esoterisches und historiographisches Schreiben*. Munich: Wilhelm Fink, 2003.

Weiss, Paul. "Die Regeneration der Urodelenextremität als Selbstdifferenzierung des Organrestes." *Naturwissenschaft* 11, no. 31 (1923): 669–677.

———. *Dynamics of Development: Experiments and Inferences*. New York: Academic Press, 1968.

———. *Morphodynamik: Ein Einblick in die Gesetzung der organischen Gestaltung an Hand von experimentellen Ergebnissen*. Abhandlungen zur theoretischen Biologie 23. Berlin: Gebrüder Borntraeger, 1926.

———. "Morphodynamische Feldtheorie und Genetik." *Zeitschrift für Induktive Abstammungs- und Vererbungslehre*, Supp. 2 (1928): 1567–1574.

———. *Principles of Development: A Text in Experimental Embryology*. Chicago: University of Chicago Press, 1939.

Weiss, Tzahi. *Otiyot she-nivre'u ba-hen shamayim ya-arets: Ha-meḳorot yeha-mashma'uyot shel ha-'isuḳ be-otiyot ha-alefbet ke-yeḥidot 'atsma'iyot ba-sifrut ha-Yehudit ba-'et ha-'atiḳah ha-me'uḥeret* [Letters by which Heaven and the Earth were created: The origins and meanings of the perceptions of individual letters as alphabetic units in the Jewish literature of Late Antiquity]. [Hebrew]. Jerusalem: Mosad Bialik, 2015.

Weyl, Hermann. "Two Letters by Einstein and Weyl on a Metaphysical Question." In Hermann Weyl, *Mind and Nature: Selected Writings on Philosophy, Mathematics, and Physics*, edited by Peter Pesic, 25–28. Princeton, NJ: Princeton University Press, 2009.

Windelband, Wilhelm. "Nach hundert Jahren." In Vaihinger and Bauch, *Zu Kants Gedächtnis*, 5–20.

Worringer, Wilhelm. *Abstraktion und Einfühlung, ein Beitrag zur Stilpsychologie*. Neuwied: Heuser'sche Verlags-Druckerei, 1907.

Ziehen, Theodore. *Grundlagen der Naturphilosophie*. Leipzig: Quelle & Meyer, 1922.

Zillman, Paul. "Sri Mahatma Agamya Guru Parahamsa in Berlin." *Neue Metaphysische Rundschau* 11, no. 2 (1904): 67–74.

Zimmerman, Andrew. *Anthropology and Antihumanism in Imperial Germany*. Chicago: University of Chicago Press, 2001.

# Index

BRUCE ROSENSTOCK is professor of religion at the University of
Illinois at Urbana–Champaign. He is the author of *Philosophy and the
Jewish Question: Mendelssohn, Rosenzweig, and Beyond*. He is also
the creator and manager of the Folk Literature of the Sephardic Jews
multimedia digital library, sephardifolklit.illinois.edu.